THE POEMS OF
GERARD MANLEY HOPKINS

GERARD MANLEY HOPKINS
Born at Stratford, Essex, 28 July 1844
Died in Dublin, 8 June 1889

The Poems of
Gerard Manley Hopkins

✝ ✝ ✝ ✝ ✝ ✝

FOURTH EDITION

*based on the First Edition of 1918
and enlarged to incorporate all
known poems and fragments*

Edited by

W. H. GARDNER

and

N. H. MacKENZIE

Oxford   New York
OXFORD UNIVERSITY PRESS

Oxford University Press, Walton Street, Oxford OX2 6DP

Oxford New York Toronto
Delhi Bombay Calcutta Madras Karachi
Petaling Jaya Singapore Hong Kong Tokyo
Nairobi Dar es Salaam Cape Town
Melbourne Auckland
and associated companies in
Berlin Ibadan

Oxford is a trade mark of Oxford University Press

ISBN 0-19-281094-4

First edition, edited with notes by Robert Bridges, published
1918 by Oxford University Press
Second edition 1930, with additional poems and a critical introduction
by Charles Williams
Third edition 1948, enlarged and edited by W. H. Gardner and
N. H. Mackenzie
Reprinted 1970 with corrections

First issued as an Oxford University Press paperback 1970
Reprinted 1972, 1975, 1978, 1980, 1982, 1984, 1986, 1988

Printed in Hong Kong

ACKNOWLEDGEMENTS

As this Fourth Edition of the *Poems* is based on the Third Edition (as that was on the First), the editor of the Third Edition wishes to leave on record his gratitude to all those whose contributions to that work are still virtually incorporated in the present volume. Chief among these, of course, is Robert Bridges, the first editor: to him no adequate tribute can be paid. Charles Williams, the second editor, boldly enlarged the Hopkins canon and introduced a firmer note of editorial appreciation. The still larger Third Edition owed much to the late Humphry House, who had aroused a wider interest in the early poems and fragments by printing many of them in *The Notebooks and Papers of G. M. H.* (1937), and to the Rev. D. A. Bischoff, S.J., who, in 1947, had discovered the autographs of several more poems.

Access to original MSS. and permission to use copyright material were generously given by Mrs. Robert Bridges, Mrs. Elizabeth Daryush (*née* Bridges), the Very Rev. Martin C. D'Arcy, S.J., the Rev. T. C. Corbishley, S.J., and the late Gerard W. S. Hopkins, then custodian of the MSS. lodged at Amen House. The Welsh poems could not have been edited without the expert assistance of Sir Idris Bell and Dr. Thomas Parry, and in other matters valuable information or practical help was received from the Rev. Vincent Turner, S.J., the Rev. Geoffrey Bliss, S.J.; Professors C. C. Abbott, R. G. Howarth, and Alexander Petrie; also from Mr. E. L. Hillman, Mr. R. L. Brigden, Mr. G. M. Fahy, and the late Frederick Page.

In preparing the present edition we have been indebted to the Rev. F. Vavasour, S.J., and the Society of Jesus for permission to print copyright material; to Lord Bridges and the Rev. B. Fitz-Gibbon, S.J. (Librarian of Campion Hall, Oxford), not only for providing the readiest access to the original MSS. in their keeping, but for the scholarly precision with which they handled queries on points of detail. For similar facilities our thanks are due to Mr. L. Handley-Derry, the officials of the Bodleian Library, Mr. Michael Waterhouse, the Rev. R. Moffat, S.J., Lady Pooley (for permission to use two Hopkins autographs which she discovered in 1964), and once more to the Rev. D. A. Bischoff, S.J.—for checking the list of

'Contents' and certain texts, and for allowing us to use his decipherment of a smudged word in an early Oxford fragment.

Inestimable assistance in the establishing of texts has been afforded through their edition of *The Journals and Papers of G. M. H.* (1959), by Humphry House and Graham Storey. We also thank the Committee on the Use of Literary and Historical Manuscripts, University of Texas, for the loan of photostats of two unpublished letters of Hopkins to his brother Everard and for kindly allowing us to quote a passage from one of them (see p. 243), and the Librarian of the Fourier Library, College of Notre Dame of Maryland, Baltimore, Maryland, for a similar loan and for permission to publish the two versions of the Latin poem on St. Winefred (No. 175 and note). We acknowledge a special debt to Professor B. H. P. Farrer, who is mainly responsible for the translations of Hopkins's Latin poems and for the annotations on them; to Professor Harold Guite, who helped us to solve problems of Latin syntax; and to three benefactors in Natal—the Rt. Rev. Archbishop Denis Hurley, O.M.I., Fr. W. J. Vogt, O.M.I., and Mr. W. H. Hewitt—who by a joint effort elucidated the word *lamina* in the poem No. 173. For valuable eleventh-hour assistance we thank Fr. R. E. Ingram, S.J., who sent photo-copies of MS. poems in the archives of Lower Leeson Street, Dublin.

For a few glosses in the *Notes* we are beholden to the authors of critical works on Hopkins: W. A. M. Peters, S.J., R. V. Schoder, S.J., R. Boyle, S.J., A. Heuser, and J. E. Keating; and for other clarifications and suggestions we record our debt to sundry correspondents: Professors Elisabeth W. Schneider, R. G. Howarth, and J.-G. Ritz; Mrs. E. E. Duncan-Jones, Miss H. M. Wilson, Miss G. Rachel Levy, Mr. Bertram R. Davis, Mr. Cormac Rigby, and Mr. Emlyn Evans.

Finally, we are grateful to the Editors of the Oxford University Press, whose co-operation has always been both stimulating and encouraging.

N. H. MACKENZIE
W. H. GARDNER
1967

CONTENTS

UNFINISHED POEMS, FRAGMENTS, LIGHT VERSE, &c. (1862–89)

COVER ILLUSTRATION

Hopkins's drawing of himself, made on
a visit to North Wales in August 1864,
from a page cut out of his 1864 diary.

INTRODUCTION TO THE
FOURTH EDITION

I

THE steady growth and consolidation of the fame of Gerard
Manley Hopkins has now reached a point from which, it
would seem, there can be no permanent regression. His assured
position as one of the important poets of the nineteenth century—a poet 'major' in the unique quality of his best work if
'minor' in total output—has been indicated in the last thirty-
five years by the many editions of his verse and prose which
have been called for, as well as by the number and significance
of the critical studies which his writings have evoked.

Hopkins died in 1889, having seen none of his own verse in
print except a few early poems, three comic triolets, and Latin
versions of an epigram by Dryden and two songs by Shakespeare. Yet although his finest poetry was to remain almost
unknown until 1918, the light of his genius had not been
wholly extinguished. His influence on his friend Robert Bridges
had already enabled the latter to demonstrate (in such a poem
as *London Snow*) some of the fruitful innovations of the more
original master's Sprung Rhythm. Moreover, since 1893
Bridges had insinuated a number of Hopkins's mature poems
into anthologies, his purpose being to create, gradually and
tactfully, the taste by which this new and at first difficult poetry
could be sensitively judged. Interest thus aroused had eventually led to a widespread demand for a full collection.

The First Edition of 1918 was prepared by Bridges with a
devoted and scholarly care, yet the relatively small issue of 750
copies took ten years to exhaust. A few discerning critics in
both Britain and America put their fingers at once on the poet's
most striking and durable qualities; but many reviewers regarded the book as a gracious though rather costly monument
to the unfulfilled talent of the Poet Laureate's pious and ingenious friend. By 1930, however, the new poetic voice was

heard with sufficient clarity to justify a Second Edition. This was augmented by an Appendix containing sixteen more pieces (most of them early poems) and was graced by an appreciative Introduction from the pen of the new editor, Charles Williams, who had chosen the additional texts after consultation with Bridges.

Twenty years ago, when the present writer was invited to prepare a considerably enlarged Third Edition (1948), he gladly acceded to the publisher's request that the new collection should be firmly based on the historic First Edition and on the augmented text of 1930. Of the verse Hopkins had written before 1876, Bridges had withheld all save three poems and one fragment (viz. Nos. 9, 10, 22, and stanza 1 of No. 133 in the present edn.), on the grounds that Hopkins had not sent him copies of the other early verses, or because, in the case of certain occasional poems, 'G. M. H. would not have wished these "little presentation pieces" to be set among his more serious artistic work'.[1] By 1948, however, the position had changed. The intense general and critical interest in Hopkins manifested after 1930 had led to the publication of three volumes of his letters and a collection of his notebooks, journals and papers; it had also stirred in many scholars and students the desire to read everything he had ever written. I was therefore asked to include in the Third Edition as many of the unfinished poems and verse-fragments as seemed, at that stage, worthy of collective presentation. A selection of the early unfinished poems, or poems 'in progress', had already been printed by Humphry House in The Criterion and later in The Note-books and Papers of Gerard Manley Hopkins (1937), and although I was at first reluctant to see the comparatively few finished or unfinished poems of Hopkins's maturity submerged in a mass of less significant fragments, I decided that the intrinsic merit or biographical interest of much of the unrevised verse did in fact warrant our admitting a considerable portion of it (but by no means all) into the Poems.

<hr>

[1] First Edition (1918), pp. 104-5.

Preoccupied as I was from 1945 onwards with two urgent and exacting assignments—the critical elucidation of the poetry in the form of additional notes and glosses for the Third Edition and the completion, under a prior contract, of the second volume of a wide-ranging critical study of Hopkins—I could not in the time available check personally, or with an equally high degree of concentration, all the previously printed texts and new transcriptions against their manuscript sources. Such a thorough word-by-word collation has now been carried out; but at that time a mistrustful scrutiny of the work of earlier editors did not seem necessary, either to me or to House, whose advice and critical proof-reading I valued. For the much needed Third Edition I accepted, with a few emendations, the text of the poems and fragments of the poet's maturity (1876-89) as these works had been edited and printed by Bridges; and as the text of the already collected additional early poems I adopted, with one or two corrections, the versions which seemed to have been competently transcribed from the MSS. by Bridges or Williams. I regret now that I did not look more closely to find those errors of transcription which have since been detected.

Again, in taking over as authentic texts the further group of early poems and fragments printed in *Note-books and Papers*—versions which had been open to informed criticism for at least eleven years—I relied mainly upon the transcriptions from the pencilled drafts in the early diaries (C. I and C. II) which had been made by so fine a scholar as House. Not only had he been given greater facilities for making a long and close study of the diary-drafts; he was also the only scholar and prospective biographer who had been allowed full access to the Hopkins family papers. When House himself came later to publish a fuller edition of the *Journals and Papers* (admirably completed, after his premature death, by Graham Storey and published in 1959), he recognized that the wider reputation won for Hopkins by the earlier partial printings of his work both justified and demanded meticulous transcription and annotation. The result was one of the most learned and helpful editions accorded to any modern author. We have inserted throughout this Fourth Edition of the *Poems* cross-references to House's two publications, so that students may consult the context of the diaries in which the poems were originally written down.

Between 1948 and 1963, many scholars must have examined the autographs and authentic copies which constitute the original sources of the *Poems* (Third Edition); yet apart from two correspondents who expressed anxiety about a single comma, it was Professor N. H. MacKenzie alone who, after having made an exhaustive study of all the MSS., and a scrupulously careful comparison of these with the printed texts, made it clear to me that a number of textual errors had crept into, and remained undetected in, the various earlier printings and editions of the poems. Fortunately, most of the inaccuracies had occurred in the less important early poems and fragments. However, in order that this Fourth Edition might be as free from errors as possible, and that it might in other ways draw benefit in advance from the textual work already done by Professor MacKenzie towards the Oxford English Texts variorum edition of Hopkins, I was pleased to invite him to become co-editor of the present volume. His main responsibility has been the checking and establishing of the text and the rearrangement of the poems and fragments, where necessary, to ensure that they appear in the correct chronological order, as far as that can be ascertained.

I wish to pay tribute to my coadjutor's work in restoring many true readings, and in making good sense of certain passages, mainly in the early poems, which through faulty transcription had formerly been obscure. He convinced me of the desirability of printing, whenever possible, the latest of two or more variants, and the expediency, at this stage, of differentiating in the Notes between the scansions indicated in the poet's MSS. and those proffered by the editor as guides to the poet's probable rhythmical intentions. The important textual revisions in the present volume, all of which carry the approval of both editors, have been ably and amply described by Professor MacKenzie in the *Foreword* which follows this *Introduction*.

For the general plan of the book I myself am responsible. The same grouping as in the Third Edition has been adopted; but the *Author's Preface*, in which Hopkins explains his original prosody, has now been placed directly in front of the sequence of mature major poems (Nos. 28–76) to which it specifically applies. Classifying such light and occasional verse as Nos. 128 and 147 with such unfinished poems of serious import as Nos. 127 and 152 may appear arbitrary or discordant; but there is a drawback in any classification, and it seemed to me that there was too little of the light verse to justify a separate section.

As regards new material, we regret that we have no newly discovered poem of major importance to present. Every scrap of English verse which can be ascribed with certainty, or reasonable certainty, to Hopkins is now incorporated for the first time in the collected edition, either in the main text or in the Notes. We have included all the remaining Latin verse which offers a coherent text, and another special feature is the provision, in the relevant notes, of translations into English prose of *all* the Latin autographs which are in the strictest sense original compositions—that is to say, not merely Latin renderings of some of Hopkins's own verse or of well-known poems by other writers. Further information concerning the presentation and annotation of the text will be found in my revised *Preface to Notes* (p. 231): this retains all that is still editorially pertinent and of lasting historic and literary value in the original *Preface by* Robert Bridges.

II

Gerard Manley Hopkins, the eldest of nine children, was born at Stratford, Essex, on 28 July 1844, his parents being moderate High Church Anglicans. Accomplishment was in the family. In 1843 his father, Manley Hopkins, had published a volume of verse dedicated to Thomas Hood; later, as head of a firm of Average Adjusters, he wrote books on marine insurance. Two of the brothers became professional artists, and Gerard himself was as precocious in drawing as in his command of language. At Highgate School he won the Poetry Prize with 'The Escorial' (1860), and in 1863 an Exhibition took him to Balliol College, Oxford, where he read Classics.

His richly sensuous poem of 1862, 'A Vision of the Mermaids', had been headed by a vivid Blake-like illustration;[1] and his earliest ambition was to be a painter–poet, like D. G. Rossetti. Though influenced by the aesthetic doctrines of Ruskin and Walter Pater, Hopkins, as man and poet, was largely a child of the Oxford Movement. He decided that painting, as an art, would 'put a strain upon the passions which I should think it unsafe to encounter'; and in October 1866, after the period of spiritual stress reflected in such poems as 'The Halfway House' and 'Nondum', he left the ranks of the 'middle way' Puseyites and, against the wish of his parents, was received by Dr. (afterwards Cardinal) Newman into the Roman Catholic Church. His conversion, which he justified to his father with a firmness of will which almost resembled hardness of heart, caused a partial estrangement from his family. The wound was healed, but left a deep mark on him, as we know from a sonnet of 1885 (No. 66):

> Father and mother dear,
> Brothers and sisters are in Christ not near
> And he my peace / my parting, sword and strife.

A poem of 1866, 'The Habit of Perfection', indicates his desire to become a priest; but the surrender to asceticism is made in terms so delicately sensuous that the fusion of artist and neophyte is strangely tense and poignant.

The diaries, sketch-books, letters, and poems of the years 1862–66 all testify to his love of nature, his gift for friendship, the range of his interests, and above all the earnestness of his

[1] See the poem as published 'in complete facsimile', O.U.P., 1929, and below, p. 8.

character. His diaries contain notes on the inner connexions between the sounds and meanings of words—a musical etymology which anticipates the word-patterns of his mature poetry, e.g. *cling, clam, claudere, close, κλείς, clasp, cleave*. His drawings reveal a remarkable talent for minute Pre-Raphaelite draughtsmanship and a sure sense of organic design. Predominantly, his zest for poetic expression lured him on to ever new and almost always unfinished literary enterprises—monologues, lyrics, pastorals, plays. From sixteen to twenty-two he essayed with skill the styles of many poets, from Milton and George Herbert to Byron, Keats, Tennyson, Arnold, Swinburne, and Christina Rossetti: in poetry, as in religion, he was seeking 'the authentic cadence'. His inability to complete literary projects dogged him to the end; it was due partly to his versatility—a clash of impulses and interests which left him always unsatisfied—partly to a strictness of conscience which told him that first religion and then classical scholarship were his real duties in life, and partly to a constitutional lack of imaginative 'staying power'. Again, there was his theory of inspiration. Eschewing what he called 'Parnassian'—a true poet's competent second-best, a poeticizing without inspiration —he preferred to leave yet another fragment rather than carry through a piece of work about which he was not wholly 'in earnest'.

Some of the early poems are what Bridges termed 'sentimental aspects of death'; others are sensitive explorations in divine or secular love. A desire for the 'the wilderness' (No. 15)[1] contrasts with his affection for Oxford, and the tart satirical epigrams (No. 96) come oddly from the pen that wrote the tenderly elegiac 'Where art thou friend, whom I shall never see'. At twenty-one he feels 'the long success of sin'. The sonnet 'Myself unholy', and the moral misdemeanours recorded in his diaries (together with some mild acts of self-mortification), are early signs of that intense introspection and scrupulosity which gave more than a tinge of sombreness to his later years. Two poems of September 1865, 'My prayers must

[1] Cf. No. 5 and 'Inversnaid' (1881).

meet a brazen heaven' and 'Trees by their yield', express something like the frustration and despair which, in the so-called 'terrible sonnets' of 1885–89, were to force cries of anguish from a far deeper level of experience.[1] His concern about a personal moral issue—the struggle between self and duty—gives a symbolic force to the two dramatic monologues of 1864 (Nos. 5 and 80), which deal imaginatively with Biblical instances of backsliding, remorse, and retribution.

Having taken 'firsts' in Classical Moderations and Greats, Hopkins taught for a while under Newman at the Oratory School, Edgbaston; and in 1868, after a visit to Switzerland, he entered the Society of Jesus to begin his training for the priesthood. By 1875 he had written all that remains of his journal, in the prose of which a passionately keen observation of nature is combined with a poetic feeling for language. In his vivid descriptions of skies, cloud-formations, trees, waves breaking, flowers opening and withering, and other phenomena, Hopkins is mainly fascinated by those aspects of a thing, or *group* of things, which constitute its individual and 'especial' unity of being, its 'individually-distinctive beauty', or (if 'beauty' is not involved) the very essence of its nature. For this unified pattern of essential attributes (often made up of various sense-data) he coined the word 'inscape'; and to that energy or stress of being which holds the 'inscape' together he gave the name 'instress'. This 'instress' is often referred to as the force which also, as an impulse *from* the 'inscape', carries it whole into the mind of the perceiver. These original terms have been explained above only by deduction from many diverse contexts, of which the following are typical:

There is one notable dead tree . . . the inscape markedly holding its most simple and beautiful oneness up from the ground through a graceful swerve below (I think) the spring of the branches up to the tops of the timber.

I saw the inscape freshly, as if my mind were still growing, though with a companion the eye and the ear are for the most part shut and instress cannot come.

[1] See Nos. 65 and 74.

The remote origin of these concepts was probably the 'plastic stress' of Plato's 'One Spirit', which sweeps through the world of dull matter to impose upon it the predestined forms of the Prime Good.[1] For Hopkins, inscape was a glimpse or strain of a universal harmony, and as such revealed its divine origin. Writing in 1870 on the 'inscape [mixed of] strength and grace' of a single bluebell, he added: 'I know the beauty of our Lord by it.'

On becoming a Jesuit Hopkins had burnt (as he thought) all the verses he had written, resolving 'to write no more, as not belonging to my profession, unless it were by the wish of my superiors.' For seven years he wrote nothing but 'two or three little presentation pieces which occasion called for'. His genius lay fallow, but was abundantly fed by reading and meditation. In 1872 he discovered Duns Scotus, and in that subtle School-man's 'principle of individuation' and 'theory of knowledge' he found what seemed to be a corroboration of his own theory of inscape and instress. He was

... flush with a new stroke of enthusiasm. It may come to nothing or it may be a mercy from God. But just then when I took in any inscape of the sky or sea I thought of Scotus.

Contrary to St. Thomas Aquinas (the official theologian and philosopher of the Jesuits), Scotus asserts that 'individuality' or *haecceitas* (thisness) is the 'final perfection' of any creature; that the 'individual' is immediately knowable by the intellect in union with the senses; and that in man the Will, as the active principle of 'thisness', has primacy over the Intellect. Such ideas, based on intuitive experience rather than cold deduction, tallied so well with the ontological, aesthetic, and moral significance of inscape and instress (instress being ultimately the stress of God's Will in and through all things) that henceforth for Hopkins, as he wrote later, it was Scotus

... who of all men most sways my spirits to peace;
Of realty the rarest-veinèd unraveller; (No. 44—1879)

Henceforth Hopkins would insist that poetry, 'down to its least

[1] Cf. Hopkins in a letter to Patmore: 'Fineness, proportion, of feature comes from a moulding force which succeeds in asserting itself over the resistance of cumbersome or restraining matter.' (*Further Letters*, 2nd edn., p. 306.)

separable part, must have an individualizing touch': design, pattern, *inscape* is what he will above all aim at in poetry.[1] Although some matter or meaning is necessary to support the shape,

Poetry is in fact speech only employed to carry the inscape of speech for the inscape's sake—and therefore the inscape must be dwelt on.[2]

In 1874, when he wrote that, he seemed to place all the emphasis on significant form; yet he never underestimated the importance of meaning, and for him great poetry could never be entirely without moral significance.

In the same year he went to St. Beuno's College, North Wales, to read Theology. There he learnt Welsh, ostensibly to convert the inhabitants, but virtually, as it turned out, to study the beauty of 'consonant chime' and internal rhyme (*cynghanedd*) in the richly 'inscaped' texture of classical Welsh poetry. At the same time his character was being moulded by *The Spiritual Exercises* of St. Ignatius Loyola (founder of the Society of Jesus) and by the almost military discipline of his order. Hence in his subsequent poems we find the tension and fusion of seemingly opposite principles: the Ignatian ideal of self-abnegation, selfless heroic endeavour, is matched by an intense self-consciousness and a dwelling on selfhood as the 'final perfection'. Germane to both ideas is the Scotist concept of the individual form-and-activity ('selving' or the 'doing-be', as Hopkins called it) as the direct link between the finite thing and the Creator on Whom it depends. Selfhood as the key to the universal ('the very make and species of man') is stressed *aesthetically* in a poem of 1879, 'Henry Purcell':

it is the rehearsal
Of own, of abrúpt sélf there so thrusts on, so throngs the ear.

and *ethically* in the undated 'As kingfishers catch fire':

[1] See below, *Preface to Notes*, p. 240.

[2] He adds that '*once* of the inscape' may be enough for art and poetry, without repetition. 'If not/repetition, *oftening, over-and-overing, aftering* of the inscape must take place in order to detach it to the mind and in this light poetry is speech which afters and oftens its inscape, speech couched in a repeating figure . . .' ('Poetry and Verse' *Journals and Papers*, p. 289.)

Selves—goes itself; *myself* it speaks and spells,
Crying *What I do is me: for that I came.*

Í say more: the just man justices;
Keeps gráce: thát keeps all his goings graces;
Acts in God's eye what in God's eye he is—
Chríst. . . .

The great silence, broken only by such one-finger devotional exercises as 'Ad Mariam' and 'Rosa Mystica', was eventually terminated by 'The Wreck of the Deutschland', which peals out like a massive overture to this man's all-too-brief *opera*. As Bridges said, 'the labour spent on this great metrical experiment served to establish the poet's prosody and diction'. The 'new rhythm' which the poem embodies is not merely Sprung Rhythm as such, for that is simply a matter of timing the stressed and slack syllables; it is, in effect, a total complex of style, in which the natural strong beat of the freer kinds of accentual verse is reinforced by alliteration, assonance, internal rhyme, and half-rhyme. These devices, freely adapted from the more strict Welsh *cynghanedd*, are used not casually but with a deliberate sense of design (inscape), so that the whole pattern and texture of the poetry, while being 'dwelt on' for its own sake, echoes and fetches out the interior movement of thought and emotion. Far from being a mere 'metrical experiment', the ode is unique in showing the maximum of rhythmic flexibility within a fixed stanzaic form.

To the poet's disappointment, this his first really mature work was refused by the Jesuit magazine, *The Month*,[1] mainly because he would not tone down its metrical 'oddities'; but having been encouraged by his Rector, he felt free to write more poems. The 'charm and instress of Wales' fostered his muse, and in 1877 he produced ten superbly original sonnets in which a Wordsworthian feeling for nature and man was heightened by his view of the world as 'word, expression, news of God'.

After his ordination in 1877 Hopkins served for varying

[1] In 1878 'The Loss of the Eurydice' was also refused by *The Month*.

periods as select preacher, missioner, parish priest, and teacher of Classics in Jesuit establishments up and down the country—from London and Oxford to Liverpool, Glasgow, Chesterfield, and Stonyhurst. Though devout and conscientious, he achieved no marked distinction in his Society; yet he was probably more successful than he claimed to be. He was by nature contemplative rather than active. As an artist passionately devoted (with Christian reservations) to aesthetic ideals, and always eager (despite recurrent qualms of conscience) to write poetry or music, he could not easily maintain that degree of concentration on practical matters which is so necessary for the professional man. One cannot doubt that he was as earnest in carrying out his parish duties as he was in his detailed critiques on the poems of Bridges, R. W. Dixon, and Coventry Patmore; but one can guess which occupation was, for a man of his temperament, the more congenial. Suffering throughout his life from a certain nervous debility, he was dogged by a sense of failure; he was also extremely sensitive to environment, and was horrified when he saw the squalor of our great industrial towns and the social conditions which, in his view, oppressed the working classes.[1] In Liverpool and Chesterfield, he tells us, his muse turned 'sullen'.

Nevertheless his sermons of the period 1878–81 reveal his moral force, and most of the poems of the years 1879–82 were directly inspired by his experiences as a priest. Many of these poems elaborate his central themes: the value of Sacrifice (No. 49); the transience of 'mortal beauty' and the need to give beauty 'back to God' (Nos. 53, 55, 59); the spiritual well-being of the young (Nos. 47, 48), and his desire for the regeneration of 'dear and dogged man', on whom the ultimate redemption of all nature depends (No. 58). Lacking the stimulus of a wide audience, Hopkins was sustained in his poetic activity by his literary correspondence with Bridges (whom he had first met at Oxford) and his former schoolmaster,

---

[1] See his 'red' letter to Bridges, 2 August 1871, and his subsequent explanation, 22 January 1874; also poem No. 70.

Dixon. The latter gave the Jesuit's poems his 'deep and intense admiration', while Bridges aimed at preventing his friend from erring too far on the side of oddness.[1]

In 1884 Hopkins was made Professor of Greek Literature at University College, Dublin, in which had been incorporated the remains of Newman's Catholic University. Here, one would think, was an entirely suitable appointment; but no. One poem of 1879, 'Peace', had struck the keynote of an unquiet mind: 'pure peace', in this life, was not to be his. He never lost his sense of humour, and his letters show with what intellectual vigour he still maintained his interest in the arts. Yet in Ireland, where he was 'at a third remove' from home and kin,[2] many things worried him—Catholic support for Irish nationalism, heavy examination duties, doubts as to the usefulness or moral value of the work he was doing. Aggravated by bodily weakness, his constitutional melancholia began to show itself in an acute form which bordered, as he said, on madness, though his judgement was never impaired. These moods, and the deep spiritual unrest which underlies them, are reflected in 'Spelt from Sibyl's Leaves' and the six sonnets which begin with 'Carrion Comfort'.

Yet how easy it is to draw false conclusions from the 'terrible pathos' of these astringent poems! The 'desolations' they reveal are not unlike those accounted for, and carefully prescribed for, in *The Spiritual Exercises*—the temporary loss of joy and hope which marks the recoil from a rigorous discipline: at worst, the feeling of total separation from God. To some readers, the aridity and sense of deprivation expressed so poignantly in the sonnet 'I wake and feel the fell of dark' has suggested the 'purgative way' or the 'dark night of the soul', as experienced by certain mystics—and we know that one part of Hopkins desired 'to be busied only with God'. The partial inhibition of strong creative instincts was, no doubt, one of the immediate causes of his neurosis. Though he

---

[1] See below, *Preface to Notes*, pp. 238 ff.

[2] Separated by country, religion, political background? See No. 66.

declared that the want of fame as a poet was not one of the many mortifications to which the life he led was exposed, he admitted that fame was 'a spur very hard to find a substitute for or to do without'.[1] He was willing to allow his poems 'to be disposed of by obedience'—to be published, perhaps, by 'someone in authority' after his death; but he also complained, in 1879, that he had not the inducements which make others compose:

Feeling, love in particular, is the great moving power and spring of verse and the only person that I am in love with seldom, especially now, stirs my heart sensibly and when he does I cannot always 'make capital' of it, it would be a sacrilege to do so.[2]

Whatever the causes, whatever the ultimate gains, the effect was frustration: 'Unhappily I cannot produce anything at all,' he wrote in 1888, 'not only the luxuries like poetry, but the duties almost of my position. . . . I am a eunuch—but it is for the kingdom of heaven's sake.' As these words attest, he accepted his cross; he never lost his faith or consciously regretted his choice of profession: 'I have never wavered in my vocation, but I have not lived up to it.' This last admission has to be measured against the height of his standards. His vow of obedience may at times have proved irksome. The complaint he voiced as a struggling musical composer up against the strictures of the experts will strike some readers as carrying an overtone of truth about his general condition: 'a perfect organisation for crippling me exists and the one for "encouragemental purposes" (modern English) is not laid down yet.'[3] But as the humorous tone here suggests, he always remained loyal to his Society. When his poet-friends tried to persuade him to move, or let them move, in the direction of publishing some of his poems he would at first not hear of it: to 'steal

[1] Letter to Dixon, 13 June 1878. Cf. *Letters to R.B.*, p. 231.

[2] Letter to Bridges, 15 February 1879. For the identity of 'the only person', &c. cf. poem No. 67:

> 'cries like dead letters sent
> To dearest him that lives alas! away.'

[3] Letter to Bridges, 19 October 1888.

a march upon' his Jesuit superiors would be 'a great baseness'.

Because the Jesuit aim was to spread Christianity, Hopkins was grieved by what seemed to him a regression in the modern world. Like the supreme Captain he loved and served (*his* 'chevalier',[1] who 'was doomed to succeed by failure') he was an idealist afflicted with 'world-sorrow' (No. 65): the 'cynical' sonnet, No. 75, sounds his despair in the physical Waste Land, just as Nos. 65 to 69, while not divorced from the natural sphere, plumb the depths of his agony on the higher supernatural plane. These sonnets are certainly 'bass-viols' for Shakespearian 'tragic tones': as in *Hamlet* and *King Lear*, it is not the personal but the universal aspect of sorrow that gives his last poems their sublime and cathartic quality.

On 8 June 1889 Hopkins died of typhoid fever and was buried in the cemetery of Glasnevin, Dublin. For some years he had been too hard on himself:

> My own heart let me more have pity on; let
> Me live to my sad self hereafter kind, . . . (No. 69)

Often he could have rested but did not. He wished to write acceptable works on theology and Greek metres; but although his unfinished commentary on *The Spiritual Exercises* has great value for us, there was truth in his regret: 'All my world is scaffolding.' Again, he had made verse-writing so 'laborious' that he was loath to embark on it with a jaded mind. If as a poet he strove, as Bridges said, for an 'unattainable perfection of language', as a man he desired what was perhaps for him an unattainable perfection of sanctity. Both struggles gave his work that pure intensity ('the terrible crystal', as Dixon called it) which puts him, notwithstanding his limitations, in the class of Dante and Shakespeare. Yet we must not suppose that he was *always* melancholy. He could be playful and witty. After 1885 he studied musical composition with enormous zest, delighting in his bold anticipations of modern modal

[1] See 'The Windhover' and the notes on p. 268.

developments. In 1888 the joyous sacramental view of nature, and all the technical resourcefulness of the poems of 1877, were resurrected in 'That Nature is a Heraclitean Fire'; and only a year before he died he was writing 'Epithalamion', which was at once a new departure in form and a poem unsurpassed for its youthful delight in the inscape of trees, rocks, and tumbling water.

In spite of the 'terrible pathos', Hopkins's poetry as a whole gives the impression of strength—a strength which is often refined to delicacy. Even in the poems of desolation the note of heroic resistance, or stoic acceptance, or willing surrender to the higher necessity, is more marked than the tone of weak self-pity.[1] In spite of the poet's modest apology in No. 76, we seldom miss 'The roll, the rise, the carol, the creation', and even today there is no exaggeration in the finely turned compliment paid him by his first editor:

> Go forth: amidst our chaffinch flock display
> Thy plumage of far wonder and heavenward flight!

III

If we take 'plumage' to mean poetic qualities symbolized by the distinctively patterned wing-feathers of 'some great stormfowl' in flight[2]—remembering that wings are by function integral to the whole muscular body—the metaphor will serve to introduce a few more remarks on the particular stresses and splendours of Hopkins's style. His initial reaction against the tame conventionality of most of the verse of his age was violent and indeed revolutionary. He wanted a stronger 'rhetoric of verse', and saw the need for getting back to 'the naked thew and sinew of the English language'. Time has removed the fallacy that his mature poetry was mainly 'experimental', brilliant in patches but marred by numerous 'tricks' and 'errors of taste' which he virtually regretted and was rapidly discarding. True, there are many bold devices, but most of

[1] Cf. *Quique haec membra*, &c., note to No. 177. [2] See 'Henry Purcell' (No. 45).

them are successful; he confessed to the vice of erring 'on the side of oddness', but largely as a concession to the more finical taste of his friend Bridges.[1] New readers will always find Hopkins strange—at first; but the 'obscuring novelty of mode' (Patmore) is no serious obstacle if we keep our mind fixed on the *core* of thought and emotion: we shall recognize the phonal devices and grammatical liberties as the tone-colours and unifying ligaments of inscape, utilized not only to instress and call up the object or experience contemplated, but to give what Hopkins called 'more brilliancy, starriness, quain, margaretting' to the rhythm and texture, as for example in:

> As tumbled over rim in roundy wells
> Stones ring; like each tucked string tells, each hung bell's
> Bow swung finds tongue to fling out broad its name; (No. 57)

Sprung Rhythm is so called because of the syncopated 'spring' —the occasional 'abrupt' juxtaposing of stressed syllables, as in ordinary speech. This type of rhythm presents one difficulty which is not removed by the *Author's Preface*: when two strong syllables seem to compete for the metrical stress, the problem of scansion can be legitimately resolved by recourse to a half-stress (ˋ), so that 'though one [syllable] has and the other has not the metrical stress, in the recitation-stress they are to be about equal',[2] e.g.:

> 'Dó, deàl, lórd it with líving and déad;' (No. 28, st. 28)

Since Hopkins tends to subordinate grammatical and logical form to the melody or strongly marked pattern of his poetry, he sometimes matches his Counterpointed and Sprung Rhythms with a kind of 'sprung' syntax. This licence accounts for most of the 'faults' condemned by Bridges in his original *Preface to Notes*.[3] Even those who consider Hopkins a great poet will admit that his syntactical inversions, ellipses, far-stepping parentheses, and violent packing of words into unexpected

---

[1] Referring to 'The Wreck of the Deutschland', he wrote to Bridges: 'Besides you would have got more weathered to the style and its features—not really odd.' (13 May 1878).

[2] See below, note on No. 62, p. 285 and the note to No. 70 ('stresses of sense').

[3] See below, pp. 238–243.

places are devices which, however purposeful, do at times subject both the language and the reader to a strain all but disastrous. Yet what is crabbed or 'queer' to one critic is lucid and entirely acceptable to another. Charged by Bridges with obscurity, Hopkins replied that a subtle and recondite thought on a subtle and recondite matter sometimes demanded a subtle and recondite mode of expression. 'Obscurity,' he added, 'I do and will try to avoid so far as is consistent with excellences higher than clearness at a first reading.' His dark passages are never entirely opaque, and the meaning, when it is made out, will usually (as he said it should) 'explode'. Still, his striving after inscape, the subtle, the *tamquam exquisitius*, had its pitfalls; and occasionally he fell. But the compensations are great, and first among these may be reckoned what I have called 'syntactical magic'.

His skill in reducing a number of thoughts to what is almost one emotional point may be heard in the painful claustrophobic tension of the following:

> I cast for comfort I can no more get
> By groping round my comfortless, than blind
> Eyes in their dark can day or thirst can find
> Thirst's all-in-all in all a world of wet. (No. 69)

In No. 66 the most significant words are muscled into the most emphatic positions, while the colourless words like relative pronouns are either absorbed in the concise 'what' or elbowed out by the conversion of a verb into a noun ('began'):

> Only what word
> Wisest[1] my heart breeds dark heaven's baffling ban
> Bars or hell's spell thwarts. This to hoard unheard,
> Heard unheeded, leaves me a lonely began.

Again, how forcibly do those first three words in No. 28 emphasize the particular aspect of God with which the poet is immediately concerned! Subject, verb, and object are boldly inscaped in one compound attribute:

> Thou mastering me
> God!

[1] The reinforcement by position allows 'Wisest' to modify three words simultaneously—*word*, *heart*, and *breeds*.

Secondly there is the magic of diction, his superb refurbishing and regrouping of the diverse elements in a richly composite and flexible language so as to make all new, 'beautiful to individuation', as he put it. His power of 'forcibly and delicately giving the essence of things in nature' (Dixon) owed much to his intense feeling for words. He is surely the greatest master of the poetic compound word in English. In his coining and compounding he goes back to primordial word-making processes. Usually he prefers pure Anglo-Saxon roots, as in *fathers-forth, after-comers, sodden-with-its-sorrowing* heart, *brown-as-dawning-skinned*. The *Yore-flood* of No. 28, stanza 32, is understood more quickly by those who have met the Old English 'ȝēar-dagas' (days of yore), and many other compounds have the smack of Old English poetry: *bone-house* (the body), *man-wolf* (i.e. 'werewolf'), *hailropes, heavengravel, wanwood*. At the same time Hopkins does not neglect the rich accretions of Romance origin. Much of the beauty of 'The Windhover' is due to the panache given by terms of French extraction: *minion, dauphin, rein, chevalier, sillion*; and among the compound words in later poems we find *churlsgrace, downdolphinry*, and *million-fuelèd*.

Sometimes he adapts a well-known idiom or compound word to his immediate purpose, substituting a new element for an old one in such a way that the old lurks in the mind as an undertone, an extension of meaning. In No. 73 the expression 'world without event', by faintly recalling the liturgical 'world without end', underlines both the length *and* the monotony of the laybrother's outwardly unheroic service. Similarly the 'bloomfall' of youth in No. 48 invites a contrast with the maggoty 'windfall' of age, and 'treadmire toil' in No. 72 exploits the unpleasant associations of the 'treadmill'. In 'the heart, being *hard at bay*', two hackneyed phrases, 'hard pressed' and 'at bay' are effectively hammered into a new one which must remain ever fresh. Occasionally Hopkins forces a word into a new function: 'Deals out that being *indoors* each one dwells' (No. 57); but *indoors* as a preposition is so much richer in meaning than 'inside' that we accept the audacity. He always prefers the concrete to the abstract, the active to the static word, and with a Shakespearian boldness will increase the sense of dynamic reality by using the bare verb as a noun or the noun with verbal force: 'the *achieve* of, the mastery of the thing' (No. 36); 'with *dare* and with downdolphinry' (No. 159); and conversely: 'Let him *easter* in us' (No. 28); 'Patience . . . that *plumes* to Peace thereafter' (No. 51). With subtle expressiveness, moreover, he will use a verb once or perhaps twice in the same line to convey two slightly different meanings, one material and the other moral: 'Nor rescue, only rocket and lightship, *shone*' (No. 28); 'birds build—but not I build' (No. 74).

Hopkins's use of words with a vibrant overtone or poetic supersense I have illustrated elsewhere:[1] and he sometimes delighted in a delicate form of word-play, as in that description of the tall nun in No. 28, stanza 17:

A prophetess towered in the tumult, a virginal tongue told.

Here the literal meaning of *told* is precise and needs no reinforcement; but to some ears the alliterative link with *towered* suggests an exquisite bell-like overtone—'tolled'. In this context such a reading is admissible and convincing, but one may doubt the wisdom of searching for and finding too many puns and echoes of this sort in contexts where the evidence of deliberate intention on the poet's part is far from conspicuous: such a procedure tends to make Hopkins's poetry seem more self-consciously ingenious and 'difficult' than it actually is. There is, however, one example of 'ambiguity' which has proved a formidable crux and calls for some comment.

In that most famous of his sonnets, 'The Windhover', the word *Buckle!* in l. 10, although the key to the spiritual resolution in the sestet, has three main possible meanings, each of which has claimed ardent supporters among the commentators. The present writer confesses that the way these facets of meaning have been presented and interpreted in the relevant note[2]

[1] See below, *Preface to Notes*, Section 7, p. 237. [2] See below, p. 267 ff.

reveals his personal bias. Having contemplated this poem for over thirty years he still cannot read it without receiving the instress of a complex symbolism involving all three meanings. The sestet will usually be read first of all as a direct apostrophe to the Falcon. Then, in the light of the sub-title ('To Christ our Lord'), the reader will perceive the symbolic function of the bird as an analogue of Christ, and from that point he must decide for himself whether the apparent primary meaning of *Buckle!* ('buckle in', 'draw together'), and the complementary archaic meaning ('engage the enemy', cf. 'buckle to') can be legitimately supported by the undertone or underthought suggested by the third meaning ('buckle under pressure', 'collapse'), with its anticipation of the falling embers of the second tercet. Admittedly this third meaning cannot be convincingly applied to the swooping Falcon; but for me the images of falling, self-galling, and gashing into splendour (together with the emotional tone of 'ah my dear') seem to carry, like *Buckle!* in its third sense, a strong suggestion of the incarnate Christ as the Hero, Hunter of hearts, and Antagonist of Evil, who was, in Hopkins's own deeply-felt words, 'doomed to succeed by failure'.

Confirming his own practice with a precept, Hopkins held that the poetical language of an age should be 'the current language heightened, to any degree heightened, but not . . . normally . . . an obsolete one'. As occasional 'freaks and graces' he admitted into his poetry a number of expressive archaisms and dialect words. He revived with profit a few obsolete native forms, such as *hallows* (saints) and *housel* (communion wafer), but most of his archaisms are still kept in currency by Shakespeare (the verbs *fair fall* and *fettle*, the nouns *fetch* and *shives*, &c.); yet all these unfamiliar words, together with the few frank coinages (e.g. *twindles*, *sakes*, *instressed*) and provincialisms (e.g. *throng* = 'dense', *louchèd*, *all throughther*) are usually intelligible in their contexts and are easily assimilated in the variegated texture of his verse. In effect, his style, being by turns dramatic and contemplative, strenuous and graceful, is so malleable and yet so homogeneous in its total inscape that conversation and incantation can mingle and blend without dissonance, as for example in 'Felix Randal':

Felix Randal the farrier, O is he dead then? my duty all ended,
. . . .
When thou at the random grim forge, powerful amidst peers,
Didst fettle for the great grey drayhorse his bright and
                                  battering sandal!

Thirdly we must note the variety, originality, and organic function of his imagery, which is closely bound up with his diction and rhythm. Whether he is writing with controlled intensity, or in the urgency of feeling is emitting his sense-perceptions in a quick-fire of metaphor, his images may be simple or childlike ('Thrush's eggs look little low heavens'), or dynamic and tense ('Fínger . . . O of a féathery délicacy the bréast of the /Maiden could obey so, be a bell to, ring óf it and / Stártle the poor shéep back!'), or a vivid inscaping of natural forces ('Wiry and white-fiery and whirlwind-swivellèd snow'); now delicate and fanciful ('That dandled a sandalled /Shadow'), now cosmic and transcendental ('Dress his days to a dexterous and starlight order'), now profoundly metaphysical ('I am soft sift /In an hourglass').

Lastly, his unique command of rhythm, at once flexible and strictly disciplined, must be acknowledged in conjunction with his original handling of the Italian sonnet-form, an instrument from which he could evoke a music of constantly varying tone and harmonic range, according to the needs of mood, emotion, and theme. His later sonnets, especially those that 'came like inspirations unbidden and against my will', aim (as he said) 'at a more Miltonic plainness'. They certainly represent a natural, healthy development, and in some ways they are his crowning achievement; but any criticism that tends to rob the more exuberant earlier sonnets, and the more elaborate and studied later ones (like 'Spelt from Sibyl's Leaves' and 'Harry Ploughman'), of their title to an absolute beauty in their own kind and right is surely to be deprecated.

IV

To sum up, Hopkins's poetry was the outcome of a by no
means unfortunate tension between the free creative *personality*
of the artist and the acquired, dedicated *character* of the Jesuit
priest. As Professor J.-G. Ritz has pointed out,[1] Hopkins was
strongly influenced by the ascetic doctrines of St. Paul; but if
there was, deep down, some conflict between aesthetic and
ascetic ideals, there was also, at the conscious level, a remarkable
reconciliation and fusion, which gave depth and spiritual
power to everything he wrote. Hopkins's stature must be
gauged by 'the intensity of the artistic process', by the quality
rather than the quantity of his work. Like St. Francis and
Wordsworth, he combined a mystical insight into nature with
a profound humanity. The precarious beauty of youth, the
lilies and thorns of the virtuous life, the pathos of dissolution
and the hope of immortality—all these find the highest and
most memorable expression, because for this poet the loveliness
and worth of all things must be seen in and through the love
of God.

Hopkins is a religious, not merely a devotional, poet. Religion,
for him, was the total reaction of the whole man to the whole
of life. Man was created to serve and praise God. As Hopkins
did both with complete sincerity, so too his disappointments,
protests, and revulsions were stated with complete candour.
His attitude to God's mystery is summed up in the paradox which is central to his masterpiece, 'The Wreck of the
Deutschland':

> Thou art lightning and love, I found it, a winter and warm;
> Father and fondler of heart thou hast wrung:
> Hast thy dark descending and most art merciful then.

In his poetry it is often the dynamism of nature, the hurtling
and buffeting of things, that reveals the power and the glory:
'is the shipwreck then a harvest?' God's grandeur flames out
from a swooping hawk, a ploughshare, shaken gold-foil, oil

[1] *Le Poète Gérard Manley Hopkins, S.J.* (1963), p. 583.

from crushed olives or linseed, embers that gall and gash themselves. As violence and destruction are part of God's purpose in the physical world, so also in His dealings with the body and soul of man He shows rude mastery—

> But ah, but O thou terrible, why wouldst thou rude on me
> Thy wring-world right foot rock? (No. 64)

—as well as tender mercy. In this kind of religious realism Hopkins resembles Donne and Herbert, combining the passionate energy of the one with the gentle earnestness of the other; but his 'metaphysical' ingenuity was tempered by graces and insights acquired from Milton and the great Romantics.

Hopkins's classicism made him one of the last English poets to write original Latin verse.[1] His Latin poems and fragments are, as one would expect, scholarly, stimulating to the intellect, and in other ways characteristic of the man. In his 'Augustan' verses there are definite echoes of the classical poets, especially Virgil and Horace. Though real 'licences' are few, the style is at times involved and obscure; but what one takes to be the poet's preoccupation with inscape helps him to bring out the native strength of the Latin language in such terse repetition-with-variation as (my italics):

> It via per stellas sublimis et aureus ordo
> *Excipiens noctem nocte dieque diem:* (No. 164)

and accounts for the alliteration and word-play in

> At *vicibus vertisse* solum est, aegrosque calores
> Jam fugere: his non perpetui *versamur* in umbris. (No. 162)

He can draw a great deal of meaning from a single word in a context (e.g. *crescunt*, No. 162, l. 36), and very few words, if any, are otiose.

His poems in the medieval Christian mode (Nos. 178 and 179) have a delicate and typical *candorem* and are worthy of comparison with the best of their kind. Indeed, the Latin verses as a whole (like the two Welsh poems) are more than

[1] For some of the observations in this paragraph I am indebted to Professor B. H. P. Farrer.

curiosities: they are necessary to a full reading of Hopkins as poet and priest, whether we consider the subdued passion of No. 164, the reverent homage of No. 173, the wry humour of No. 174, the lyrical theology of No. 179, or the childlike piety and self-lacerating confession of No. 178, with its plangent rhymes:

> Nam tumeo et abundo
> Immundo adhuc mundo;
> Sum contristatus Sanctum
> Spiritum et planctum
> Custodi feci meo
> Cum exhiberem Deo
> Laesum atque caesum
> In mea carne Jesum.

[For I am puffed up and rank with the foul world; I have saddened the Holy Ghost and caused grief to my Guardian when to my God I showed Jesus wounded and battered in my flesh.]

The influence of Hopkins on later writers began in 1877—with the impact made on Robert Bridges by 'The Wreck of the Deutschland' and the early mature sonnets. That 'loosening of rhythm' which Yeats remarked on was generally admired after 1880 in R. B.'s description of London snow as

> Stealthily and perpetually settling and loosely lying

—and its importance was clearly acknowledged by the Georgians and their successors; but in 1918 the First Edition of Hopkins's poems diverted attention to Hopkins himself as the main liberating force. After the publication of the Second Edition the compelling verve and beauty of the new rhythm and style induced what can only be called a 'Hopkins cult'. Doing continuously what other poets had succeeded in doing, or had been content to do, only by rare moments, Hopkins made the texture of Georgian verse look thin and prosaic; hence his phonal effects and compound words were widely imitated—until at last it was realized that such imitation led, with a fatal certainty, to pastiche. Some critics declared that Hopkins had carried verbal and grammatical subtleties to their utmost limits: to advance beyond 'Tom's Garland' ('I must go no farther on this road'—G. M. H.) would lead to the total break-down of meaning. A few later writers have taken the risk, and it is likely that James Joyce, E. E. Cummings, and Dylan Thomas were decisively affected by a reading of Hopkins.

Perhaps the most salutary influence has been registered by those on whom 'the effect of studying masterpieces' has been to make them (in Hopkins's words) 'admire and do otherwise'. Even T. S. Eliot, whose religious affinity with Hopkins is deep and significant, could have strong reservations about him and yet speak of 'Glow-worm glowlight on a grassblade'; but the internal rhymes in *Ash-Wednesday* and elsewhere do not toll reminiscent bells too obtrusively. The main impact was on younger men. By their own admission, Hopkins acted like a new leaven in the gifted group, headed by W. H. Auden, which gave English poetry a new actuality and intellectual toughness after 1930. Indeed we may still say with Stephen Spender that Hopkins, though inimitable, 'ferments in other poets'; and with Charles Williams (Second Edition, p.xvi):

poets will return to him as to a source not a channel of poetry; he is one who revivifies, not merely delights, equivalent genius.

Here the word 'equivalent' seems unduly restrictive; but whatever their natural endowment, genuine poets may well learn from Hopkins, as he himself did from Shakespeare, how to utilize the full resources of the English language; and they will not easily be satisfied with themselves if they fall too far below the high standards of integrity, concentration, musicality, and formal beauty which he, unmistakably, has established.

University of Natal,   W. H. GARDNER
Pietermaritzburg.

FOREWORD ON THE REVISED TEXT AND CHRONOLOGICAL REARRANGEMENT OF THE POEMS

BY NORMAN H. MACKENZIE

1. *New Features of this Edition*

When, in 1950, Maurice Charney surveyed the previous thirty years of Hopkins criticism,[1] examining in turn the attention which had been paid to Hopkins's sources, to his themes and their exposition, his prosody and style, his several gifts as literary critic, composer, and artist, he felt compelled in practically every section to state that the most thorough and illuminating work had been done by Professor W. H. Gardner. His two-volume *Study* and the annotations in his Third Edition of the *Poems* have made a fundamental contribution to the understanding of the verse. It has therefore been a particular pleasure to find myself associated with him in preparing the Fourth Edition of the *Poems*. To Professor Gardner belongs the major credit: he has enlarged the edition and provided the helpful and learned glosses, now brought up to date and greatly extended beyond those in the Third Edition. My own special contribution has lain in checking and establishing the text, and in seeking to achieve a strict chronological arrangement of the poems within their various divisions; but we have discussed all points of doubt, and benefited from mutual criticism.

This volume differs from previous editions of Hopkins's verse in one significant respect: it has aimed at including the latest known versions of all his extant poems and verse fragments. I have thoroughly revised the text from a scrutiny of virtually all the surviving autographs and contemporary transcripts, a process which has resulted in about a hundred interesting changes, and several times as many minor corrections to

[1] *Thought*, Vol. XXV, June 1950, pp. 297–326.

punctuation, &c. The latter have been amended without comment, but in view of the considerable volume of close textual analysis which the poetry of Hopkins continues to attract, some of the more significant restorations have been explained in Sections 7 to 11 below, and others tabulated in Section 12.

2. *Metrical Marks and Punctuation*

All three previous editions of the *Poems* have tried to assist readers by adding metrical accents in places where the rhythm might be in doubt. The great majority of these are indicated in the MSS., either by the poet's various stress marks or through his practice of signposting an instance of sprung rhythm by inserting a 'great colon' between two adjacent accents (otherwise unmarked); but some stresses had been added in places where they seemed to an editor to represent the poet's rhythmical intention.

In the actual printed text of the thirty poems and fragments in which Hopkins used stress marks (about 240 in all) there were, in the previous editions, no more than six deviations from MS. authority, and these all occurred in one sonnet, 'As kingfishers catch fire' (No. 57). In the more extensive *Notes* to the Third Edition, the Editor introduced many more metrical signs from the MSS. (including outrides, ties, slurs, &c.). These have been much help to students, and are amplified in the present edition. They were, however, sometimes accompanied by detailed editorial scansions of which only the broad outlines were provided in the MSS. The finer points of sprung rhythm are still a subject on which no finality has been reached: in the Fourth Edition, therefore, it seemed to us important that any stresses which were added in the notes for the benefit of the general reader should be clearly differentiated from those which the poet had himself inserted. This we have done, also eliminating from the text of No. 57 all stresses save the four indicated by Hopkins in his autograph.

We have, however, not attempted to record all Hopkins's metrical marks. The poet himself was doubtful about the wisdom of confronting readers with such an array (see *L. I.*,[1] p. 189), and every subsequent editor has limited himself to those cases where the intended rhythm might otherwise be misinterpreted. Moreover, the various MSS. of a poem may differ among themselves in the precise distribution of outrides, slurs, and accents, so that all the various readings would have to be supplied to create a full picture. Such detail seemed to us beyond the proper scope of the Fourth Edition.

Although the punctuation of the Edition has been brought into line with the best MSS. in a large number of places, it would be unwise to claim finality. Many of the poems have had to be printed from rough drafts, and in numerous other instances a punctuation mark in the MS. might be construed equally well as a comma or a stop, while a semi-colon might have possibly been meant for a colon. In doubtful cases we have pursued a conservative policy, letting the old text stand.

3. *The Chronological Rearrangement of the Poems*

The inclusion, within their relevant sections, of many pieces which have not hitherto appeared among the collected *Poems* has necessitated an entire resetting of the book. Some readers who have become accustomed to finding their way around Professor Gardner's very successful Third Edition may regret that the poems have not been left in the same sequence. But where many other alterations were being made, it seemed to us very desirable that we should take the opportunity, wherever necessary, of rearranging the poems within each section to ensure that they were in the essential order of their composition, in so far as this could be ascertained.

The marshalling of the poems in chronological order has been no mere mechanical process. It is true that Hopkins often assigned a definite date to a poem—even to the very day—whenever its birth had appeared to be an event rather than a slowly maturing process. In such cases he cited this natal date on each new copy, no matter how thoroughly he might sub-

[1] For an explanation of the abbreviations, see p. 244.

sequently have modified and improved it. With other poems, however, even the year itself is arguable—as with his unfinished 'Floris in Italy', fragments of which lie scattered here and there in his two tiny diaries through a hundred successive pages, representing a time-span from about August 1864 until September 1865. In still other instances we have no certain means of dating the poems precisely: 'As kingfishers catch fire' may have been written at Oxford in 1879, or during his Tertianship in 1882, or during his Liverpool ministry in between. We cannot therefore claim in this edition to have arranged the poems in an indisputable order of composition: indeed, the phrase blurs in definition as one examines it more closely.

During his harassèd labours in Ireland Hopkins could often compose only in short jets of activity. Thus with 'Spelt from Sibyl's Leaves' (No. 61), the first half is to be found drafted out in the rough Dublin Notebook on a page which we can date October 1884; another page, worked upon two months later, carries the sonnet through successive revisions up to the middle of l. 10: 'O this is our tale too!'. Here he seems to have stuck, as though his work of art had itself fallen victim to the crushing blackness which he had so powerfully described. Not until two years later did he finish the poem. Yet the whole sonnet issues out of that soul-dark winter of 1884–85 revealed in his in-timate meditation notes, which show the continual action of his elective will seeking to rise above his own misery. (See S., pp. 152, 257–9 and L. I, pp. 245–6.) We have deemed this good warrant for placing 'Spelt from Sibyl's Leaves' before 'To what serves mortal beauty' (which Hopkins himself dated 23 August, 1885), and in this edition we have therefore reversed the accustomed order.

4. The Sequence of his Undergraduate Poems

We have thought it worth while to attempt a careful re-arrangement of his undergraduate poems into the order of their composition. Hopkins's growth in literary originality and spiritual conviction may be obscured, e.g. by intruding

at its point of delayed publication a poem which was funda-
mentally the product of an earlier period. Although 'Barnfloor
and Winepress' was published by the *Union Review* in the
autumn of 1865, we can find it in substantially its printed form
among the diary entries of July 1864. We have therefore moved
it back from its old position as No. 18 to No. 6.[1]

'Heaven-Haven' in the Third Edition immediately preceded
a poem of January 1866. But we reasoned that the first draft
of July 1864 was so similar to the final version that on the whole
it was better to move it back from its old place as No. 20 to No.
9, among the other poems written that summer. Along with
it we have shifted 'For a Picture of St. Dorothea' (now No. 10),
and have thus emphasized the gap in time between its composition (October/November 1864) and that of its metrically
revolutionized revision (No. 25), which even contains anticipations of sprung rhythm.

The rearrangements bring together some curious neighbours: for instance, 'The Habit of Perfection' now occurs along-
side 'The Nightingale'. Indeed, in the autographs Hopkins has
given them identical composition dates, 'Jan. 18, 19, 1866',
though it is hard to imagine two such dissimilar poems being
born together. 'The Nightingale' is a traditional romantic
narrative, achingly alive to sensory detail. It laments the loss of
an earthly love, whereas 'The Habit of Perfection' is a marriage
hymn to chastity and austerity, its own sensory vividness being
dedicated to the sublimation of the senses. But taken together
as they are dated, these two poems offer a contrast which appears as deliberate as that between 'Heaven-Haven' and 'I must
hunt down the prize' (Nos. 9 and 88).

5. *Changed Order of the Poems written in Wales*

We have transposed 'Penmaen Pool' and 'The Silver Jubilee'
(Nos. 30 and 29). The second of these was clearly the earlier

[1] For a chronological arrangement of all the main poems and fragments in one
sequence, see p. 617 seq. Professor J.-G. Ritz: *Le Poète Gérard Manley Hopkins*. Our
order has been reached independently and differs materially in many cases discussed
here.

xliii

in composition, since it was ready for the Bishop's visit to St. Beuno's in July 1876—and indeed had before then been 'set effectively by a very musical and very noisy member of the community', so that the Bishop could hear it over dessert 'sung as a glee by the choir' (*L. III*, p. 140). Its last stanza picks up a theme with which the 'Wreck of the Deutschland' had ended. 'Penmaen Pool' belongs to August, while Hopkins was spending the traditional holiday fortnight in the Jesuit villa at Barmouth.

The ten sonnets written in Wales during 1877 (Nos. 31 to 40), form a well-defined group of their own, and contain some of the best-known and most widely enjoyed poems which he ever wrote. During 1964, Lady Christabel Pooley, a niece of the poet's, discovered in a table-desk which had belonged to the poet's sister, Grace Hopkins, new autograph MSS. of two of these poems—a most heartening find which suggests that further autographs may yet come to light. These fair copies appear to have been made by the poet so that Grace, an unusually musical girl, might compose airs to which they could be sung. In addition to variant readings, the new MSS. provide 'In the Valley of the Elwy' (which has hitherto had to be relegated to the end of the year) with the poet's exact dating, 23 May 1877. It has seemed to us appropriate to interchange this sonnet with 'The Lantern out of Doors'. The poems of 1877 vary in imagery or subject with the varying seasons, enriching themselves with unusual directness from the inscapes of the countryside through eight fascinating months. 'Spring' (written in May) now introduces 'In the Valley of the Elwy', a sonnet which draws comforting imagery from the nesting of birds and the mild nights of May. We round off this group of sonnets with 'The Lantern out of Doors'. Although the month of its composition is unknown, the wistful regret of the first eleven lines mirrors the mood against which he had to wrestle that autumn after learning that he would have to leave Wales in October. The imagery of the poem too blends with the autumn fogs that gathered in the river valleys below the seminary—'our much-thick and marsh air'. A valedictory in some sort to the friends with whom he had spent three happy sessions in Wales, it is an appropriate sonnet with which to end his poetic description of a remarkably fruitful year. (See *L. III*, p. 142 and *J.*, pp. 260–1.)

Two other undated poems seem to me also to belong to 1877, or possibly the year preceding it. Bridges used the first of these (First Edition, pp. 92, 95: Third Edition, p. 168, Fourth Edition, No. 140) as the coda to the First Edition:

> To him who ever thought with love of me
> Or ever did for my sake some good deed
> I will appear . . .

Bridges did not attempt to arrange the fragmentary and un-completed poems in sequence of composition, preferring a 'fanciful grouping': his placing of this piece therefore carries no implications as to date. In the Third Edition it was tenta-tively put among work belonging to 1885–86. Professor Ritz guesses at 1887. My arguments for assigning it to a point ten years earlier than this are fourfold. Firstly, the MS. draft (which is our only authority for the poem) uses as a sign for counter-point or reversed rhythm a virtually closed figure-of-eight on its side, ∞. This was the earliest form of that metrical mark, and was always placed over the first syllable of the inverted foot. A study of all the extant autographs reveals that every other occurrence of this symbol can be assigned to 1877. Apart from its appearance in the sonnets of that year, it is also found in a letter to Bridges dated 8 August 1877; but by the time Hopkins came to write 'The Candle Indoors' at Oxford in 1879, he had decided to substitute the musical turn, ⌣⌣, straddling the whole foot. This evidence in itself might be thought conclu-sive, but we may add that in the letter just referred to (*L. I.*, p. 43), Hopkins warns Bridges not to confuse '∞' which means a counterpoint', with 'a circumflex, over words like *hēre*, *hēar*, *thēre*, *bēar* . . . No, it should be ⌣, not ⌣'. Now the poem we are discussing contains an instance where the poet himself had slipped: 'I will appear lõoking such charity . . .' Clearly counterpoint is intended, though he has used the sign for 'a quiver or circumflexion, making one syllable nearly two', as explained in his notes to 'Harry Ploughman' (No. 71). I conclude that the poem we are seeking to date belongs to the earliest period of his innovations in sprung rhythm and metrical marks, for after 1877 he used the circumflex scores of times without any such confusion. The third argument lies in the handwriting. A chronological study of the autographs reveals a progressive change in certain letters, so that doubtful MSS. can generally be assigned to particular broad periods. In this case we can affirm that the hand closely resembles that in the draft of 'Moonrise' (No. 137, 19 June 1876), that both are on similar cream laid paper, and that the capital *W* (in a variant of the last line) is of a shape characteristic of his Welsh days, and quite distinct from that of the Dublin period. Finally, we may point to the kinship in thought between this poem—a versified paraphrase of *The Life and Revelations of St. Gertrude* (see p. 311 below)—and stanza 8 of 'The Wreck of the Deutschland,' which he completed in 1876. Hopkins had apparently been reading this *Life* about the time he composed the 'Wreck', for that great poem picks up from the *Life* the fact that St. Gertrude and Luther were both born in the same town (see stanza 20) as well as the metaphor which Hopkins uses for St. Gertrude, 'Christ's lily'. The evidence for the early dating of *To him who ever thought with love of me* therefore seems to us conclusive.

The second poem offers no such concatenation of proofs. It consists of three rhyming couplets, 'On St. Winefred' (No. 139), written out large under the heading A. M. D. G., and ending with L. D. S.—almost certainly meant to be fastened to a statue on a Saint's Day. The existence of a Latin version with the same dedicatory initials strengthens this theory. We can only add that the handwriting bears closest affinity with the autographs of his Welsh theological days: even the MSS. of his Oxford poems of 1879 show the trend away from this script in certain letters, e.g. a tendency towards the printed *W* which characterized his later hand. And St. Beuno's, only a few miles from St. Winefred's Well, would seem the most natural seminary in which to expect poems to be exhibited in the Welsh saint's honour.

Some slight alterations in sequence have been required among the poems written while Hopkins was a priest at Oxford. 'The Candle Indoors' and 'The Handsome Heart', bearing in MS. only a general dating, 'Oxford 1879', have hitherto been remitted to the end of his Oxford period. But as they were sent to Bridges in a letter dated 22 June 1879 (*L. I*, pp. 84–6), they should transpose places with 'Peace', so as to follow immediately the sonnet 'Henry Purcell'. The last poem which he attempted at Oxford must surely have been 'Peace', hitherto inserted too soon. Its early draft is dated 2 October 1879, probably the very day before he left the university city to minister among the dark mills and stenching foundries of Bedford Leigh. Yet there he was to find in great measure the peace which Oxford had brought him only in occasional lulls.

6. *Modifications in the Arrangement of the Irish poems*

We have already reasoned the case for interchanging 'Spelt from Sibyl's Leaves' and 'To what serves mortal beauty' (see sect. 3 above). The six sonnets, Nos. 64 to 69, often referred to as 'The sonnets of desolation' (though this convenient title is not equally appropriate to each member of the group), all appear to belong to 1885, and have now been brought together. In arranging the First Edition, Bridges inserted after the second of these six sonnets two contrasting poems, 'Tom's Garland' and 'Harry Ploughman' (Nos. 70, 71). This had the artistic advantage of breaking up the mood of the introspective and troubled sonnets. But the first two of these, in their only known autograph drafts, follow on the same sheet of paper an unfinished version of 'Tom's Garland', while the completed poem belongs to a time two years later than all six sonnets. Hopkins himself assigned both to it and to its companion-piece, 'Harry Ploughman', the date 'Dromore Sept. 1887'. In the Fourth Edition we have accepted the poet's own dating of those two robustly descriptive pieces, transferring them to the end of the 'sonnets of desolation', as had already been done in Professor Gardner's Penguin Poets edition (1953).

But although the sonnets rightly come together among his 'finished' poems, we must not forget that even during the difficulties of 1885 out of which they emerged there were many periods when the clouds lifted. The very sheet of paper which contained the last four of his 'desolations' began with cheerful working drafts of his fragmentary 'Ashboughs':

Not of all my eyes see, wandering on the world,
Is anything a milk to the mind so, so sighs deep
Poetry tó it, as a tree whose boughs break in the sky.

References to 'dark heaven's baffling ban', and to the combs of ash which 'new-nestle at heaven most high', counterpoise each other upon the same page. If he turned from 'Tom Heart-at-ease' to his own pitiful storm-drenched, cliff-clinging soul, he could also turn back again to complete the verbal subtleties of that sonnet on the unemployed. And in September 1887 he was able to write within a few days the whole of his 'direct picture of a ploughman' (L. I, p. 262)—the sturdy figure who could guide the plough-horse, not with sheer plod, but with an exhilarating co-ordination of muscle.

Another contrast in mood is emphasized by the transfer of 'The shepherd's brow, fronting forked lightning' to the main section of finished poems (from its old place among the fragments) as in the Penguin selection (1963). Although a complete sonnet, it had been relegated to the back of the book in the First Edition because Bridges felt that it reflected a temporary cynicism for which Hopkins himself would not have wanted a permanent home among his last completed works. But for reasons set out in the Notes it has now been given its correct position (No. 75).

Among the unfinished poems written in Ireland is a tragedy called 'St. Winefred's Well'. He had already made some progress with it before he left Oxford in October 1879 (L. I, p. 92), and in the Third Edition it was therefore placed after the other fragments begun in that parish. But his inexperience of life proved a severe handicap to his dramatic writing, and though he completed a fine maidens' choral song for it—'The Leaden Echo and the Golden Echo' (No. 59)—pages of successive drafts in the Dublin Notebook of 1884–85 (along with 'Spelt from Sibyl's Leaves') show that five years from the outset scarcely a line of Act II had even then reached a shape which satisfied him. He sent Bridges samples of it on 1 April 1885, from which we can see that he had made further progress in the intervening months. The imagery brings continual reminders of the 'sonnets of desolation', written that same year:

'to storm and strive and
Be at every assault fresh foiled, worse flung, deeper disappointed,
The turmoil and the torment, it has, I swear, a sweetness,
Keeps a kind of joy in it, a zest, an edge, an ecstasy,
Next after sweet success.'

('Carrion Comfort') and 'No worst, there is none' spring to mind as we read. In short, the dramatic portions of the poem seem to belong to 1884–85 rather than to his Oxford ministry. The appropriate position has seemed to be after 'The times are nightfall, look, their light grows less' (No. 150, which is close to 'Sibyl's Leaves' in thought and probably in date) and 'Hope holds to Christ the mind's own mirror out' (No. 151), written on a scrap of paper which I have identified as having been torn from the Dublin Notebook. He was still at work on the play in October 1886 while on holiday in Wales (L. I, p. 227), but of his additions nothing is now known. Yet remembering other remarkable literary finds among MSS. hidden for two and three centuries, we may continue to hope that more Hopkins autographs may come to light, that fragmentary poems may be found in completer form, and our knowledge of his inimitable work may become less imperfect.

7. The Text of the First Edition (edited by Robert Bridges)

All students and editors of Hopkins owe an immense debt to Robert Bridges. Without his personal encouragement,

Hopkins might even have abandoned the effort to compose. Moreover, if Bridges had not systematically preserved in his album the autograph poems which he received from the busy Jesuit priest, and transcribed into this album (now known as MS. A) every subsequent piece which came his way, meticulously recording later emendations, our text might now be seriously defective. It was Bridges, too, who in 1883 carefully copied into another album (MS. B) for Hopkins's benefit all the poems which he himself had been sent: the poet himself had often not even preserved fair copies of his own work. It will be remembered that Keats showed a similar disregard for some of his own offspring: one remembers the way in which Charles Brown had to rescue the scraps of paper on which some of the now famous odes and sonnets had been jotted down.

The long-delayed First Edition of 1918 was of tastefully selected items only: Bridges was anxious to attract the admiration of the public, and to avoid encumbering the book with examples of the poet's undergraduate verses, or too many of his unfinished poems. This policy, though somewhat over-cautious, was successful; step by step there has been a gradual expansion of interest in his productions, until there is now a demand for everything which Hopkins wrote to be made accessible in print.

Robert Bridges had a familiarity with Hopkins's handwriting which gave him a basic advantage as editor, enabling him to cope with the numerous erasures and substitutions in the MSS. It was not often that Bridges was baffled by a problem of decipherment. A rare instance is in 'No worst, there is none' (No. 65), where he notes under l. 5: 'at end are some marks which look like a hyphen and a comma.' The 'comma' is actually a stress mark upon *sing* in the line below, and the hyphen (which we insert) makes *chief-/woe* parallel *world-sorrow* in its structure. But Bridges had pioneer responsibility in trying to decide which version to adopt. Thus with 'The Handsome Heart' (No. 47), he made three quite different

1

attempts to blend into a satisfactory sonnet the first draft and three subsequent revisions which the poet (partly in response to his own and Dixon's suggestions) had produced. In the Fourth Edition of Hopkins's poems we have followed the conservative policy of accepting Bridges's latest compromise: the Oxford English Texts Edition will provide the reader with the opportunity of exercising his own judgement. Bridges was, on the whole, a scrupulously accurate editor, drawing attention in his notes to any deviations between a poem as he printed it and the particular MS. whose authority he had accepted as representing probably the best indication of the poet's final wishes for that piece. How complex the problems sometimes are can only be realized by a comparison between all the alternative readings of the various MSS. One of Bridges's few errors of transcription (or proof-reading) occurs in the opening line of 'Felix Randal', where instead of 'O *he is* dead then?' both the extant MSS. read: 'Felix Randal the farrier, O is he dead then? my duty all ended.' This correction hardly affects the sense, but there is certainly some benefit from two changes in 'The Loss of the Eurydice' (No. 41) where we have replaced the commas formerly printed after *capsize* (l. 37) and *thousands more* (l. 85) with the full stops found in the autograph.

Other corrections to the text of poems printed by Bridges will be found in this edition for the first time. The MS. of 'Epithalamion' (No. 159) is in a ferment: the unfinished draft covers some eight sides of paper, some in ink, some pencil, scribbled and crossed out again, the text as Bridges has miraculously pieced it together jumping from one page to another. The poem begins on a sheet from an examination answer book headed: 'Royal University of Ireland'. Bridges has underlined in red ink by way of amusement two of the instructions to candidates which struck him as piquantly relevant: 'Fill up the following blanks', and 'The rough work and calculations, as well as the final results, should be shown in this Book.' The poem is an ode on the marriage of G. M. H.s brother Everard, and

Bridges conjectured that the poet, hard pressed for time, but feeling that the occasion called for the best wedding gift within his power, was attempting to compose it while invigilating an examination.

In view of the general dishevelment within the MS., with false beginnings and much re-working of material, it is not to be wondered at that two words have dropped out from the revised version which Bridges printed. In l. 37 *hoar-huskèd* has been missed: 'Built of chancequarrièd, selfquainèd, hoar-huskèd rocks'. The final lines of the poem, 'Father, mother, brothers . . .', are introduced by a hitherto overlooked *turns*, which rhymes with *ferns*, and provides the verb which has been missing. In l. 19 the poet wrote, not *gambols*, but:

> This garland of their gambol flashes in his breast
> Into such a sudden zest
> Of summertime joys

avoiding the extra sibilant. In l. 47, 'What is water?' should run 'What the water?'.

Another example to which we might call attention is in his patriotic song: 'What shall I do for the land that bred me,' (No. 156) where the Chorus for the first verse should read 'Under her banner *we* live for her honour', the previously omitted *we* matching this refrain with all the others.

In 'Moonrise' (No. 137), l. 1, we restore, as inscaping a phrase typical of Hopkins, some omitted hyphens:

> I awoke in the Midsummer not-to-call night . . .

These changes are for the most part refinements, deserving note in the verse of a man now generally recognized as a major poet, but certainly no serious reflection upon an editor. But Robert Bridges laid himself open to a charge of editorial presumption when he altered a word which he did not like in the sonnet addressed to himself (No. 76).

> Nine months she then, nay years, nine years she long
> Within her wears, bears, cares and *combs* the same.

Since *combs* seemed to Bridges not to make good sense, he borrowed from 'The Blessed Virgin compared to the Air we Breathe' (No. 60), l. 104, the verb *mould*, used of the incarnation of Christ: 'A mother came to mould/Those limbs . . .' In his note Bridges drew attention to the change: 'In line 6 the word *moulds* was substituted by me for *combs* of original, when the sonnet was published by Miles, and I leave it, having no doubt that G. M. H. would have made some such alteration.' Hopkins frequently did change his lines in response to his friends' criticisms, and would quite probably have made some alteration here if Bridges had asked him to do so, especially as the sonnet was addressed to Bridges himself. The fact remains that Hopkins died before any interchange of letters could take place: the sonnet did not reach his friend until Hopkins lay dying (*L. I*, p. 304, *L. III*, p. 195). From the autograph draft Bridges might with some more warrant have substituted the earlier reading:

> nine years long
> She wears within, she bears and cares the same.

This would have been in keeping with a practice followed on occasion in all three Hopkins editions, of preferring an earlier reading to G. M. H.'s last correction. Nevertheless this is a practice which is always liable to lay an editor open to the criticism of those whose taste differs from his own, and Professor Gardner took the most logical course when he restored *combs* from the original autograph. A parallel editorial replacement was made in ('The Soldier'), No. 63, where Bridges substituted in l. 10 his own *handle* for G. M. H.'s *reave*—though in this instance the MS. draft proffers no alternative reading.

8. *The Text of the Second Edition* (1930)

Shortly before the death of Bridges, Charles Williams took over from him the preparation of a Second Edition. Dr. Bridges had charged him with the task of re-collating the MSS. of the poems which he himself had printed, and of adding sixteen further pieces. Few more appreciative fellow-poets could have been selected for this privilege, judging from his discriminating and sympathetic *Introduction* to the Second Edition; but if he was more outspoken in his commendation of Hopkins than Bridges had been, he was also far less aware of the hidden snares which beset an editor's path. Among the poems added in his Appendix, some had been quoted, in part, only a few months earlier in Father Lahey's pioneer book, *Gerard Manley Hopkins*. Who had been responsible for their transcription is not clear, but the number of errors which were common to the Second Edition and Father Lahey's book certainly points to a single origin. (In the case of three poems, Williams printed 'From a MS. sent by Rev. G. F. Lahey, S. J.', which would appear to refer to an original MS. The text is relatively accurate in these three pieces.)

A particularly unfortunate victim was 'The Escorial' (No. 1), from which Fr. Lahey had published inaccurate excerpts. It has been left to us in this Fourth Edition to restore the text. Stanza 10 alone contained seven mistakes. '*The* rang'd long corridors' had puzzled me for years until I saw that the MS. read: '*He* rang'd long corridors ...', i.e. 'stretched out'. The identity of *He* was explained by the poet in a note: '*He* refers to Philip'. Philip's building and decorating of the Palace was no doubt the subject of the omitted ninth stanza, which (I conjecture) the boy had to sacrifice to keep the poem within a prescribed limit of 125 lines. One further line would still need to be cut, and it may be significant that the third Spenserian stanza has only eight lines. In l. 2 of stanza 10, *piled* is a verb followed in the MS. by a full stop and a dash: i.e. '(He) piled (up) damasqu'd arms and foliag'd carving'. The next line also ends with a full stop. Williams's *There* in l. 4 represented *Here* in the MS., whereas the same word in l. 8 was a careless decoding of *Thus*. Stanza 14, which in our revised text will be seen to run on into the final stanza, appeared too complex in syntax to be understood: it was therefore silently altered to end with *rude!*, the exclamation mark being a misinterpretation of the closing bracket begun with (*fearing*. The editor, having failed to discover where the parenthesis ended, inserted another bracket quite mistakenly after *flight*. To cap some thirty errors in the 'Escorial' text, the transcriber turned the last phrase of the poem into '*in age* more wonderful', where the MS. reads:

> For grandeur barren left and dull
> Than changeful pomp of courts *is aye* more wonderful.

On top of all this, the Second Edition unintentionally omitted four of the marginal notes which the poet himself had supplied to the poem. These now appear in print for the first time.

Only one serious error marks 'A Vision of the Mermaids'. In the Second Edition, ll. 72-3 formed an anacoluthon, verbless:

> Which, lightening o'er the body rosy-pale,
> Like shiver'd rubies' dance or sheen of sapphire frail.

This poem had been published in facsimile the previous year, but neither Williams nor subsequent scholars saw how the syntax in fact runs. The last word is not *frail* but *hail*, and the apostrophe after *rubies* was an editorial attempt to lend the line sense.

Another Second Edition mistake has gone undetected for thirty-four years, as anthologists, past and future, should note: it is the inadvertent corruption of the First Edition text of 'Hurrahing in Harvest': the first line became '*arise* around'. We have restored the correct word, in which all three extant MSS. accord:

> Summer ends now; now, barbarous in beauty, the stooks *rise*
> Around;

Again in 'The Wreck of the Deutschland', stanza 12, the Second Edition changed Bridges's 'the million of rounds of thy mercy', with which MSS. A and B agree, into '*millions* of rounds'.

The sixth stanza of the hymn of St. Thomas Aquinas (No. 168) of which Hopkins made four translations, has suffered from dittography. The current version (first published by

Williams), prints *world to win* for the MS. reading *worth to win* in l. 3, obscuring the sense:

> Blood that but one drop of has the *world* [worth] to win
> All the world forgiveness of its world of sin.

9. The Text of Poems in the Notebooks (1937) and Journals (1959)

In 1937 Humphry House published his careful edition of the *Note-books and Papers of Gerard Manley Hopkins*. In the *Preface* he discussed the editorial problems which confronted him when he set out to print examples of Hopkins's undergraduate verse preserved in the early Diaries. The drafts are all in minute pencilled writing, frequently smudged, and at times almost illegible. Hopkins often does not appear to have made final copies of his poems: in the last letter which he ever wrote to Bridges he confessed that he found the task 'repulsive', and that he let his verses 'lie months and years in rough copy untransferred to my book'. (*L. I*, p. 304. 29 April 1889). House found it necessary to bring scattered entries together to form more or less consecutive poems. He drew attention in particular pieces to the way in which 'the drafts represent different stages in them, and how precarious the printed texts are. What in the MSS. is changing and fluid is here artificially stabilized.' (*N.*, Preface, p. xvi.) The poems could not have been appreciated in their disarray, and House's fine contribution to the canon of Hopkins's verse was to rearrange the uncompleted fragments into some artistic order. In doing so he showed the insight of a true poet himself. In 1937 the reputation of Hopkins had not yet reached the point where any attempt to achieve absolute accuracy in reproducing these drafts would have been either sensible or welcome. By 1959 the situation was different, and when the greatly extended *Journals and Papers of Gerard Manley Hopkins* was edited with its magnificent exactitude of annotation by House, and completed after his death by Graham Storey, a number of new fragments of verse were carefully reproduced, along with a high proportion of the variants in the drafts—though by no means all of them. These skilfully edited versions have been accepted as the basis for this edition, though I have thoroughly examined the MSS. and corrected any deviations where this seemed justified by the resulting improvement in the sense.

The enlarged and revised *Journals* of 1959 contains very few departures from the MSS., but unfortunately House did not have space, in a closely packed volume of over 600 pages, to re-edit with equal exactness the full texts of the poems which had already appeared in *Note-books*. With these poems he had room only to quote the first line, and to give the page reference to the Third Edition of the *Poems* where his old text had, with his authority, been reproduced from these versions. The changes in the Fourth Edition have frequently been due to the principle of following the last known reading unless there was good cause in sense or sound for preferring an earlier one. Thus in the 'Soliloquy of One of the Spies' (No. 5), l. 43, the poet began 'Strike cymbals . . .,' but broke off, and began again:

Strike timbrels, sing, eat, drink, be full of mirth.

With Exodus xv. 20 to support the appropriateness of timbrels in this context, and the apparent intention of the MS., we have substituted G.M.H.'s second thought for the *cymbals* hitherto printed. In such instances, where passages have been rewritten, or phrases deleted and replaced, we have felt impelled to print the last surviving version. But the matter is not always as clear-cut. In l. 50 of the 'Soliloquy' the MS. progresses unsatisfied from one verb to another:

To tread with cool ⎫
   „   knead   „   „ ⎬ feet the clay juicy soil
   „   plash   „   „ ⎭

Since no fair copy of the poem has survived, and none of the three verbs was cancelled, House picked the one he liked best, *to knead*. Our judgement has favoured the last alternative: *plash* seems to fit into the speaker's thirst-maddened nostalgia for Egypt, in which all the oppressions of Israel's past slavery are viewed through a transforming liquid haze. Even the making of bricks is remembered by the sand-blistered spy as a luxurious plashing of cool clay. Another example where the last alternative in the MS. has now replaced an earlier one is in l. 10, where the frankly physical 'And have your fill of meat' has been substituted for the more delicate 'And break your pleasant meat'.

Other alterations have been made to the text because the minute pencilled MS. was understandably enough misread. A close inspection of 'The Alchemist in the City' (No. 15) reveals that in stanza 7 Hopkins wrote 'tower swallows' not 'lower swallows'. The faint cross-bar of the 't' is only just visible, but its identity can be checked against 'tower-top' in the following line. The anaphora is echoed in stanza 10: 'Or *rocks* where *rock*doves do repair'. In 'Pilate' (No. 80) the lacuna in stanza 3 before *wharves* was due to the difficulty of reading the MS., but I am satisfied that the passage reads:

> as between *icy* wharves
> A freezing runnel sobs and dwarfs.

Here we would like to pay tribute to the Rev. Professor Anthony Bischoff, S.J., for his convincing decipherment of a badly smudged word (*J.*, p. 61—No. 117 in Fourth Edition). This has deteriorated in the years since Fr. Bischoff inspected it, and only the vaguest outlines of letters can now be seen at the turn of the page—not two words, as was conjectured, but the single word *expressionless*.

> Who lies on grass and pores upon the sky
> Shall see the azure turn expressionless.

If finished copies of many of Hopkins's early poems existed, they must have been mostly burned just before he entered the Society of Jesus. We are therefore faced with numerous passages which were hurriedly committed in pencil to the pages of a diary which measured less than $5'' \times 3''$ in size, creating almost palaeographic problems. An instance occurs in 'Pilate' (No. 80), where my own transcript differs from that in the *Note-books* in half-a-dozen details within two stanzas. Thus in stanza 6 I read *Folds off*, not *Holds off*: the sudden lifting of the imprisoning clouds would provide the *signal* of l. 3, and be in keeping with the speaker's *eager shift* to see the houses far away. But even the displacement of a punctuation mark from its MS. position can modify or mist the sense of a passage. In stanza 5 the phrase 'I desire' was in the *Note-books* marooned by a full stop from the last two lines, which need it to complete their syntax. We print:

> The fretful fire
> Breathe o'er my bare nerve rather. I desire
> They swathe and lace the shroud-plaits o'er my face,
> But to be ransom'd from this place.

Throughout his early poetry, unlike that written after he became a priest, Hopkins tended to use capitals in his references to God. One anomaly has been 'The Half-way House' (No. 20). But a scrutiny of the diary itself shows that with the first *thou* (in l. 3) he altered the thin lower-case theta (which he used as shorthand for *th*) to the rounder Greek capital letter, and thereafter the intention seems to me to be clearly *Thou* and *Thy*, as we now print the poem. But G.M.H.s capitalization can on occasion be anything but reverent. We have pleasure in restoring the emphatic capital R used for the Victorian Head of the Family in No. 97, 'By Mrs. Hopley, On seeing her children say Goodnight to their father':

> Bid your Papa Goodnight. Sweet exhibition!
> They kiss the *Rod* with filial submission.

10. *The Text of the Third Edition*

We have taken the opportunity in this edition of correcting a number of small misprints which crept into the Third Edition. These amendments include an insistence upon the original punctuation, to which however we have drawn no attention except where the sense was affected. A few more important changes may be briefly cited. There is the improvement in the meaning of 'Myself unholy' (No. 16), l. 3, through the insertion from the MS. of the hyphen after *eye*. 'Eye-greeting doves' is now recognizable as a description of the poet's attractive friends, contrasting with himself—a dull rook. In the sestet of this sonnet, l. 10, we have substituted the fourth revision of a line which gave its composer special difficulty:

> He has a sin of mine, he its near brother,
> Knowing them well I can but see the fall.

Here *them* refers both to his friends and to their sins, imperceptible except to a man striving for perfection with intense inner scrutiny. In 'Il Mystico' (now No. 77), l. 13, *pointed cithern* was due to a confusion with *pointed wing* in the line above and should read *heavenly cithern*. To the spirited and unflattering portrait of Miss Story (No. 94) we can now add one more cutting stroke: in l. 12, *only* should read *inly*:

> And, hide it though she does, one may divine
> She inly nourishes a wish to shine.

11. The Classical Texts and Translations

This section has been greatly strengthened in the Fourth Edition through our inclusion of many hitherto unprinted fragments of G.M.H.'s Latin verse, which Professor Gardner has gathered together. The translations, for which Professor Farrer is largely responsible, will make it easier for general readers to trace the links between the poet's Latin and his English verse. The previously published pieces had gone through the fingers of various classical scholars, and in checking the text for this volume I found that G.M.H.'s eccentricities in metre or vocabulary had been tactfully corrected in some instances, usually without any betraying note.

The classical poems range from undergraduate exercises to the product of his Dublin years as a harassed Professor of Greek and Latin Literature, but they all tend at moments towards the fastidiously individual word or the rare construction. Thus in 'Ad Episcopum Salopiensem' (No. 173), Hopkins referred in l. 8 to the twenty-five years since the Bishop had first been crowned with the sacred *lamina*. This term, being considered inexplicable by the Latin scholars who looked at it, was altered to the unexceptionable *laurea*; but as our note now explains (see p. 329), thin plates of gold or silver formerly adorned the 'Precious Mitre', a distinctive feature which Hopkins selected as a reference to the whole head-dress. One of G.M.H.'s earlier Latin poems, dating probably from his final year's study at Oxford, is his description of the flooded river meadows: 'Inundatio Oxoniana' (No. 162). In l. 34, the poet apparently thought to improve upon his straightforward 'limum . . . sequacem' ('pursuing mud'). Photographs of the MS. would fail to show that this has been faintly corrected in pencil, I would say in G.M.H.'s own hand, to read 'limos . . . sequaces.' We have rendered this stylized phrase 'mud deposited in a succession of streaks and patches' (cf. Arnobius I : 3). The desire to strike upon the least common diction was active in the poet from his earliest days, and we have ventured to insert in the printed text his bold emendation to this line.

The individual touch of genius in these classical renderings must not be obscured by their occasional oversights. The two Greek translations of Shakespeare's songs contain at least one word which is hard to construe and which has been with some justification replaced. Where Shakespeare asks if Fancy is bred 'Or in the heart or in the head', the MS. has an illogical καρδίαν (No. 182, v, l. 3). This seems to have survived from a different grammatical context in an earlier draft of the line (preserved in A), where it was quite defensible. If he had been checking his MS. for the press Hopkins would no doubt have changed the case ending in his second version of the line to καρδίας—as was done in the Third Edition. But there seems no necessity in l. 9 to have changed προσώπου into πρόσωπον.

In 'Orpheus with his lute', which Hopkins rendered into both Latin and Greek (vii), Shakespeare sang:

> Orpheus with his lute made trees,
> And the mountain tops that freeze,
> Bow themselves when he did sing.

I conjecture that Hopkins rationalized this hyperbole into the unleashing of an Alpine avalanche by the vibrations of sound, as in stanza 4 of his 'Pilate' (No. 80), for in the Greek version the tops of his snowy mountains are described as νιφοκτύπων ὄρεων κορυφαῖσιν. The unusual first word, 'roaring with snow', has been a trifle obscured because of the ligature in the MS. which links its last two letters, making it appear as νιφοκτύπαν. This reading has now been corrected; we have also restored G.M.H.'s original complicated metrical σχῆμα (which had been simplified and altered).

Every aspect of G.M.H.'s remarkable achievement is worthy of scrutiny, and since comparatively few have hitherto made acquaintance with his Greek and Latin translations, it is our hope that this Fourth Edition may stimulate greater attention to this barely prospected demesne.

12. *Some other textual changes.*

A number of lesser changes, mostly of a more technical nature, may be conveniently tabulated here. Others again may be found in the *Editors' Notes*.

SOLILOQUY (No. 5) l. 12: 'And fear no law nor rod', now 'And fear no iron rod'; —l. 46: 'Not manna bring, but straw', now 'Bring in the glistery straw'. (Both these were later alternatives.)

EASTER COMMUNION (No. 11), l. 5: 'Jesus'. MS. reading 'Jesu's'.

THE WRECK OF THE DEUTSCHLAND (No. 28), st. 21, l. 3: the swifter comma in MSS. A & B after 'refused them' now replaces the stop;—st. 34, ll. 2, 5: for consistency, we have now brought 'name' and 'he' into line with MS. B in its avoidance of capitals. This is closer to the poet's own usage at this period than is the transcript in MS. A.

PENMAEN POOL (No. 30), st. 3, l. 2: 'Stool', the logical place-name capital in the autograph had been overlooked because the poet's uppercase S was only medium in size. So too with

SPRING (No. 33), l. 1: where the Pooley MS. is unambiguous in reading 'so beautiful as Spring'.

WINDHOVER (No. 36), l. 9: comma after 'plume' (justified by the autographs) now restored.

THE LOSS OF THE EURYDICE (No. 41), l. 55: 'No or Yes', in place of '. . . yes'.

MORNING, MIDDAY, AND EVENING SACRIFICE (No. 49), later versions preferred in ll. 2, 19, 20: l. 2: 'and wimpled lip', now 'and the wimpled lip'; —l. 19: 'What life half lifts', now 'What death half lifts'; —l. 20: 'What hell stalks towards', now 'What hell hopes soon'.

ANDROMEDA (No. 50), l. 4: 'dragon's food', now 'dragon food'; l. 14: comma after 'barebill', now virgule.

AT THE WEDDING MARCH (No. 52), st. 3, l. 1: 'Then let the March' in the autograph has a capital M, which the poet later reinforced by including 'March' in the title.

FELIX RANDAL (No. 53), l. 5: The original comma after 'impatient', which R. B. omitted in his transcript and 1st. Edn. (although it occurs at a natural pause), is now restored.

BROTHERS (No. 54), revisions have been accepted in l. 10: 'Their night was come now', changed to 'Now the night come'; —l. 21: 'Clutched hands down through clasped knees', now 'Clutched hands through claspèd knees'; —l. 22: 'Truth's tokens tricks', now 'And many a mark'; —l. 23: 'Old telltales, with what stress', now 'Told tales with what heart's stress'; —l. 33: 'Eh, how áll rúng!' now 'Thére! the háll rúng'; —l. 34: 'Young dog', now 'Dog'; —l. 43: 'I'll cry', now 'Dearly'.

SPRING AND FALL (No. 55), l. 9: in the autograph in A, 'will' is underlined, a more forceful form of emphasis than the accent formerly printed from a transcript. The poet placed metrical accents over no fewer than 24 stressed syllables elsewhere in this poem (e.g. on 'are', l. 1. and 'as', l. 5).

GOLDEN ECHO (No. 59), l. 8: 'prizèd' marked as two syllables in the autograph; —l. 14: 'maiden gear' now taken as one word.

SPELT FROM SIBYL'S LEAVES (No. 61), l. 4, 'earl-stars' now 'earlstars', l. 9, 'beak-leaved' now 'beakleaved'.

'To SEEM THE STRANGER' (No. 66), l. 4: after 'peace' we restore the thin oblique stroke or virgule of the autograph, meant to indicate a very slight pause (as in No. 50, l. 14).

THAT NATURE IS A HERACLITEAN FIRE (No. 72), l. 6: 'rut peel' now accepted as being inscaped into one word.

PILATE (No. 80), st. 1, ll. 3, 4: phrasing improved by transferring comma to its MS. position after 'man' instead of 'old'; —st. 3, l. 1: 'the shadow of stones' instead of '. . . and stones'; —st. 7: formerly 'The clouds come like ill-balanced crags,/ Shouldering, Down valleys smokes the gloom. The thunder brags. In joints of sparkling jags . . ./I cry "O rocks and mountains make me room".' For six changes in this st., compare the new text, p. 118, below.

A VOICE FROM THE WORLD (No. 81), l. 15: the poet's unintelligible phrase 'used the thrill', due to a slip in his shorthand, is amended from an earlier draft into 'used to thrill'. After l. 17 I add from the MS. a lost line: 'Tho[ugh] far or sick or heavy or still'. The sense of l. 116, now illegible, has been inserted from a deleted passage: ('To her the gift').

SEVEN EPIGRAMS (No. 96-i), in ll. 1, 2: formerly 'Of virtues I most warmly bless,/Most rarely seen, Unselfishness'/. Here 'seen' was a mistake for 'see'.

'—I AM LIKE A SLIP OF COMET' (No. 103), l. 16: 'And then she goes out into the cavernous dark'—a crowded line— should not have had 'she' in it.

'Now I AM MINDED' (No. 105), l. 16: 'Too', the poet's capital T was particularly hard to distinguish from his small letter. This, and a metrical irregularity, led to the assumption of a lacuna before 'too', now removed.

CASTARA VICTRIX (No. 125), l. 4: 'A wander in the country', now 'wonder. . .'.

A COMPLAINT (No. 128), st. 2, l. 1: the two autographs vary in text, but both read 'were', not 'are'.

'MOONLESS DARKNESS' (No. 129), l. 2: 'the Past'. The poet's shorthand sign for 'the', a Greek theta, was read as 'O', the cross-bar being indistinct.

CHEERY BEGGAR (No. 142), l.4: 'fineflour' (pollen), was wrongly transcribed by R. B.'s wife as 'fineflower', and so printed. See note to the poem.

(MARGARET CLITHEROE) (No. 145). G.M.H. began to re-arrange the stanzas of this unfinished poem, but did not carry the renumbering beyond st. 3. Formerly printed in MS. order, the rest of the verses have now been re-edited to follow the sequence of thought and event.

(ON A PIECE OF MUSIC) (No. 148): The title, now given in brackets, has no MS. authority, but was supplied by R. B.

'HOPE HOLDS TO CHRIST' (No. 151), l. 4: a later alternative, 'A growing burnish brighter than before', replaces 'An ever brighter burnish than before.'

ST. WINEFRED'S WELL (No. 152), Act II, l. 7: 'Warned her! well she knew I warned her of this work.' Stop formerly supplied after 'knew' is now omitted.

PROMETHEUS DESMOTES (No. 160), l. 23: 'Or half-human', not 'Of. . .'.

INUNDATIO OXONIANA (No. 162), l. 4: now 'ferentibus' instead of 'furentibus'.

ELEGIACS: after THE CONVENT THRESHOLD (No. 164), l. 10: 'Purpurei infecta' replaces 'Purpurea infecti'.

HORACE: PERSICOS ODI (No. 165) l. 1: a hyphen, making 'Persian-perfect' a compound adjective, now replaces the dash which separated these two words.

HORACE: ODI PROFANUM VOLGUS (No. 166). For later variants now substituted, see *Notes*, p. 322 below.

JESU DULCIS MEMORIA (No. 167), st. 5, l. 4: 'That men have wished for or have had', a revision of 'That can be wished or can be had'.

(MAY LINES) (No. 179), l. 2: 'Quae', formerly printed 'Quo'.

Songs from Shakespeare (No. 182), iii, l. 5: 'Qui', for
former 'Tui'.—
   iv, l. 9: 'cunas' (cradle) instead of 'curas' (cares).—
   viii, l. 5: 'Marcipor', a personal name, now given a capital M

Queen's University,
Kingston,
Ontario.

NOTE TO THE SECOND IMPRESSION
(1970)

SINCE this edition was first published, Hopkins scholarship has been made the poorer by the death of Professor W. H. Gardner in January 1969. During the past twenty-five years no name has been more closely associated with Hopkins than his. We can only be grateful that he lived to see our work on the Fourth Edition of the *Poems* completed.

It has been gratifying to note the increased interest in the text which has followed the publication of this edition. The need for a new impression, as well as its issue as a paperback, has made possible the correction of a few misprints and slips. (See p. 343.) My editing of the Oxford English Texts, which will reproduce the successive readings of the different MSS., has progressed well. When this has been finished, some further changes (e.g. in placing or punctuation) may result. But a comparison of the various autographs indicates how flexible was Hopkins's use of such devices as capitals, hyphens, punctuation marks and outrides: three different fair-copies of a poem, e.g., may interchange a comma, an exclamation mark, and a semi-colon. An important emendation in our text, however, has been made in 'The Lantern out of Doors' (No. 40), where the first line in the final version (Bridges's transcript 'checked' and revised by Hopkins) seemed to end with a comma. But I am now convinced that the comma is actually a smudged full stop, and as the original autograph has a full stop (made with a rather broad pen, but quite distinct from the commas on the same sheet) the poem now opens graphically:

> Sometimes a lantern moves along the night.
> That interests our eyes. And who goes there?
> I think;

During my reassessment of the relative dependability of various MSS. and transcripts, other emendations have seemed desirable. Some have been introduced into this impression, but where explanations would have been required in the notes, with complicated resetting, it has been thought better to postpone such revisions until a new edition is needed (following upon the publication of the Oxford English Texts *Hopkins*).

The rector of Stonyhurst College has kindly given permission for the use of their autograph of No. 25 in place of the Campion Hall transcript.

Several Hopkins scholars have sent me useful comments upon the dating of the poems or their reading of the MSS.: my particular thanks go to Dr. H.-W. Ludwig, Mrs. E. E. Duncan-Jones (see note to No. 97), and Mrs. M. C. Patterson (see especially notes added to the commentaries on Nos. 39 and 70). Two others call for particular mention, since some readers may wonder why their suggestions have not been incorporated.

Mr. Eugene August (*PMLA* 82:5 (October 1967) pp. 465–8) offers a fascinating account of 'The Growth of "The Windhover"', but since he had to rely upon photocopies of the MSS., minor confusions arose between Hopkins's own hand and the several different styles used by Bridges. Moreover, he omitted the commas after 'swing' and 'plume', present in both autographs, through following Bridges's punctuation (which Bridges himself avoided doing in his edition, even when Hopkins was thought to have checked a transcript). His article nevertheless holds much of interest.

Mr. Norman White (*TLS*, 22 August, 19 December 1968, etc.) has strenuously contended that in l.3 of 'To his Watch' (No. 153) 'force' should read 'forge'. The emendation has its attractions. But after re-examining the MS. I feel that the evidence has been misread. Confusion arises because Hopkins inserted 'at our force' interlinearily below 'company' (l.2), in such a way that the tail of the 'y' closed off the 'c' of 'force', making it resemble 'forde'. He therefore prolonged the tail of the 'y' downwards, though his pen began the downstroke one-hundredth of an inch to the left. Only when considerably magnified does the word look as 'forge' might do *in someone else's hand*. But how many places can be found in his mature writing where Hopkins has formed a 'g' out of a 'c' closed off with a tail slightly curving to the left? If he had wished to write 'forge', his usual figure-of-eight 'g' would have avoided all ambiguity. After careful discussion with experts in Oxford, I concluded that the weight of argument was against a change. However I am indebted to Mr. White for pointing out that the comma after 'force' should be omitted.

I shall much appreciate receiving further corrections or queries from other scholars, so as to ensure the best possible text.

NORMAN H. MACKENZIE

Queen's University,
Kingston,
Ontario.

EARLY POEMS
(1860–75?)

I

The Escorial

Βάτραχος δὲ ποτ᾽ ἀκρίδας ὥς τις ἐρίσδω

I

THERE is a massy pile above the waste
Amongst Castilian barrens mountain-bound;
A sombre length of grey; four towers placed
At corners flank the stretching compass round;
A pious work with threefold purpose crown'd—
A cloister'd convent first, the proudest home
Of those who strove God's gospel to confound
With barren rigour and a frigid gloom—
Hard by a royal palace and a royal tomb.

2

They tell its story thus; amidst the heat
Of battle once upon St. Lawrence' day
Philip took oath, while glory or defeat
Hung in the swaying of the fierce melée,
'So I am victor now, I swear to pay
The richest gift St. Lawrence ever bore,
When chiefs and monarchs came their gifts to lay
Upon his altar, and with rarest store
To deck and make most lordly evermore.'

3

For that staunch saint still prais'd his Master's name
While his crack'd flesh lay hissing on the grate;
Then fail'd the tongue; the poor collapsing frame,
Hung like a wreck that flames not billows beat—
So, grown fantastic in his piety,
Philip, supposing that the gift most meet,
The sculptur'd image of such faith would be,
Uprais'd an emblem of that fiery constancy.

3

He rais'd the convent as a monstrous grate;
The cloisters cross'd with equal courts betwixt
Formed bars of stone; Beyond in stiffen'd state
The stretching palace lay as handle fix'd.
Then laver'd founts and postur'd stone he mix'd.
—Before the sepulchre there stood a gate,
A faithful guard of inner darkness fix'd—
But open'd twice, in life and death, to state,
To newborn prince, and royal corse inanimate.

5

While from the pulpit in a heretic land
Ranters scream'd rank rebellion, this should be
A fortress of true faith, and central stand
Whence with the scourge of ready piety
Legates might rush, zeal-rampant, fiery,
*Upon the stubborn Fleming; and the rod
Of forc'd persuasion issue o'er the free.—
For, where the martyr's bones were thickest trod,
They shrive themselves and cry, 'Good service to our God.'

6

No finish'd proof was this of Gothic grace
With flowing tracery engemming rays
Of colour in high casements face to face;
And foliag'd crownals (pointing how the ways
Of art best follow nature) in a maze
Of finish'd diapers, that fills the eye
And scarcely traces where one beauty strays
And melts amidst another; ciel'd on high
With blazoned groins, and crowned with hues of majesty.

7

This was no classic temple order'd round
With massy pillars of the Doric mood
Broad-fluted, nor with shafts acanthus-crown'd,
Pourtray'd along the frieze with Titan's brood
That battled Gods for heaven; brilliant-hued,*
With golden fillets and rich blazonry,
Wherein beneath the cornice, horsemen rode†
With form divine, a fiery chivalry—
Triumph of airy grace and perfect harmony.

8

*Fair relics too the changeful Moor had left
Splendid with phantasies aerial,
Of mazy shape and hue, but now bereft
By conqu'rors rude of honor; and not all
Unmindful of their grace, the Escorial
Arose in gloom, a solemn mockery
Of those gilt webs that languish'd in a fall.
This to remotest ages was to be
The pride of faith, and home of sternest piety.

9

.   .   .   .

10

He rang'd long corridors and cornic'd halls,
And damasqu'd arms and foliag'd carving piled.—
With painting gleam'd the rich pilaster'd walls—.
*Here play'd the virgin mother with her Child
In some broad palmy mead, and saintly smiled,
And held a cross of flowers, in purple bloom;
†He, where the crownals droop'd, himself reviled
And bleeding saw.—Thus hung from room to room
The skill of dreamy Claude, and Titian's mellow gloom.

5

11

Here in some‡ darken'd landscape Paris fair
Stretches the envied fruit with fatal smile
To golden-girdled Cypris;—Ceres there
Raves through Sicilian pastures many a mile;
¶But, hapless youth, Antinous the while
Gazes aslant his shoulder, viewing nigh
Where Phoebus weeps for him whom Zephyr's guile
‖Chang'd to a flower; and there, with placid eye
§Apollo views the smitten Python writhe and die.

.   .   .   .

12

Then through the afternoon the summer beam
Slop'd on the galleries; upon the wall
Rich Titians faded; in the straying gleam
The motes in ceaseless eddy shine and fall
Into the cooling gloom; till slowly all
Dimm'd in the long accumulated dust;
Pendant in formal line from cornice tall
*Blades of Milan in circles rang'd, grew rust
And silver damasqu'd plates obscur'd in age's crust.

13

†But from the mountain glens in autumn late
Adown the clattering gullies swept the rain;
The driving storm at hour of vespers beat
Upon the mould'ring terraces amain;
The Altar-tapers flar'd in gusts; in vain
Louder the monks dron'd out Gregorians slow;
Afar in corridors with painèd strain
Doors slamm'd to the blasts continually; more low,
Then pass'd the wind, and sobb'd with mountain-echo'd
woe.

6

14

Next morn a peasant from the mountain side
Came midst the drizzle telling how last night
Two mazèd shepherds perish'd in the tide;
But further down the valley, left and right,
Down-splinter'd rocks crush'd cottages.—Drear sight,
An endless round of dead'ning solitude:
×Till, (fearing ravage worse than in his flight,
What time the baffled Frank swept back pursu'd
Fell on the palace, and the lust of rabble rude,)

15

*Since trampled Spain by royal discord torn
Lay bleeding, to Madrid the last they bore,
The choicest remnants thence;—such home forlorn
The monks left long ago: Since which no more
†Eighth wonder of the earth, in size, in store
And art and beauty: Title now too full—
More wondrous to have borne such hope before
It seems; for grandeur barren left and dull
Than changeful pomp of courts is aye more wonderful.

A Vision of the Mermaids

ROWING, I reach'd a rock—the sea was low—
Which the tides cover in their overflow,
Marking the spot, when they have gurgled o'er,
With a thin floating veil of water hoar.
A mile astern lay the blue shores away;
And it was at the setting of the day.
    Plum-purple was the west; but spikes of light
Spear'd open lustrous gashes, crimson-white;
(Where the eye fix'd, fled the encrimsoning spot,
And gathering, floated where the gaze was not;)   10
And thro' their parting lids there came and went
Keen glimpses of the inner firmament:
Fair beds they seem'd of water-lily flakes
Clustering entrancingly in beryl lakes:
Anon, across their swimming splendour strook,
An intense line of throbbing blood-light shook
A quivering pennon; then, for eye too keen,
Ebb'd back beneath its snowy lids, unseen.
    Now all things rosy turn'd: the west had grown
To an orb'd rose, which, by hot pantings blown   20
Apart, betwixt ten thousand petall'd lips
By interchange gasp'd splendour and eclipse.
The zenith melted to a rose of air;
The waves were rosy-lipp'd; the crimson glare
Shower'd the cliffs and every fret and spire
With garnet wreaths and blooms of rosy-budded fire.
    Then, looking on the waters, I was ware
Of something drifting thro' delighted air,
—An isle of roses,—and another near;—
And more, on each hand, thicken, and appear   30
In shoals of bloom; as in unpeopled skies,
Save by two stars, more crowding lights arise,
And planets bud where'er we turn our mazèd eyes.

I gazed unhinder'd: Mermaids six or seven,
Ris'n from the deeps to gaze on sun and heaven,
Cluster'd in troops and halo'd by the light,
Those Cyclads made that thicken'd on my sight.
   This was their manner: one translucent crest
Of tremulous film, more subtle than the vest
Of dewy gorse blurr'd with the gossamer fine,   40
From crown to tail-fin floating, fringed the spine,
Droop'd o'er the brows like Hector's casque, and sway'd
In silken undulation, spurr'd and ray'd
With spikèd quills all of intensest hue;
And was as tho' some sapphire molten-blue
Were vein'd and streak'd with dusk-deep lazuli,
Or tender pinks with bloody Tyrian dye.
From their white waists a silver skirt was spread
To mantle-o'er the tail, such as is shed
Around the Water-Nymphs in fretted falls,   50
At red Pompeii on medallion'd walls.
A tinted fin on either shoulder hung;
Their pansy-dark or bronzen locks were strung
With coral, shells, thick-pearlèd cords, whate'er
The abysmal Ocean hoards of strange and rare.
Some trail'd the Nautilus; or on the swell
Tugg'd the boss'd, smooth-lipp'd, giant Strombus-shell.
Some carried the sea-fan; some round the head
With lace of rosy weed were chapleted;
One bound o'er dripping gold a turquoise-gemm'd   60
Circlet of astral flowerets—diadem'd
Like an Assyrian prince, with buds unsheath'd
From flesh-flowers of the rock; but more were wreath'd
With the dainty-delicate fretted fringe of fingers
Of that jacinthine thing, that, where it lingers,
Broiders the nets with fans of amethyst
And silver films, beneath with pearly mist,
The Glaucus cleped; others small braids encluster'd
Of glassy-clear Aeolis, metal-lustred
With growths of myriad feelers, crystalline   70

9

To shew the crimson streams that inward shine,
Which, lightening o'er the body rosy-pale,
Like shiver'd rubies dance or sheen of sapphire hail.

Then saw I sudden from the waters break
Far off a Nereid company, and shake
From wings swan-fledged a wheel of watery light
Flickering with sunny spokes, and left and right
Plunge orb'd in rainbow arcs, and trample and tread
The satin-purfled smooth to foam, and spread
Slim-pointed sea-gull plumes, and droop behind   80
One scarlet feather trailing to the wind;
Then, like a flock of sea-fowl mounting higher,
Thro' crimson-golden floods pass swallow'd into fire.

Soon—as when Summer of his sister Spring
Crushes and tears the rare enjewelling,
And boasting 'I have fairer things than these'
Plashes amidst the billowy apple-trees
His lusty hands, in gusts of scented wind
Swirling out bloom till all the air is blind
With rosy foam and pelting blossom and mists   90
Of driving vermeil-rain; and, as he lists,
The dainty onyx-coronals deflowers,
A glorious wanton;—all the wrecks in showers
Crowd down upon a stream, and, jostling thick
With bubbles bugle-eyed, struggle and stick
On tangled shoals that bar the brook—a crowd
Of filmy globes and rosy floating cloud:—
So those Mermaidens crowded to my rock,
And thicken'd, like that drifted bloom, the flock
Sun-flush'd, until it seem'd their father Sea   100
Had gotten him a wreath of sweet Spring-broidery.

Careless of me they sported: some would plash
The languent smooth with dimpling drops, and flash
Their filmy tails adown whose length there show'd
An azure ridge; or clouds of violet glow'd
On prankèd scale; or threads of carmine, shot
Thro' silver, gloom'd to a blood-vivid clot.

Some, diving merrily, downward drove, and gleam'd
With arm and fin; the argent bubbles stream'd
Airwards, disturb'd; and the scarce troubled sea   110
Gurgled, where they had sunk, melodiously.
Others with fingers white would comb among
The drenchèd hair of slabby weeds that swung
Swimming, and languish'd green upon the deep
Down that dank rock o'er which their lush long tresses weep.
    But most in a half-circle watch'd the sun;
And a sweet sadness dwelt on everyone;
I knew not why,—but know that sadness dwells
On Mermaids—whether that they ring the knells
Of seamen whelm'd in chasms of the mid-main,   120
As poets sing; or that it is a pain
To know the dusk depths of the ponderous sea,
The miles profound of solid green, and be
With loath'd cold fishes, far from man—or what;—
I know the sadness but the cause know not.
Then they, thus ranged, 'gan make full plaintively
A piteous Siren sweetness on the sea,
Withouten instrument, or conch, or bell,
Or stretch'd chords tuneable on turtle's shell;
Only with utterance of sweet breath they sung   130
An antique chaunt and in an unknown tongue.
Now melting upward thro' the sloping scale
Swell'd the sweet strain to a melodious wail;
Now ringing clarion-clear to whence it rose
Slumber'd at last in one sweet, deep, heart-broken close.
    But when the sun had lapsed to Ocean, lo
A stealthy wind crept round seeking to blow,
Linger'd, then raised the washing waves and drench'd
The floating blooms and with tide flowing quench'd
The rosy isles: so that I stole away   140
And gain'd thro' growing dusk the stirless bay;
White loom'd my rock, the water gurgling o'er,
Whence oft I watch but see those Mermaids now no more.

                        The End.

3

Winter with the Gulf Stream

THE boughs, the boughs are bare enough
But earth has never felt the snow.
Frost-furred our ivies are and rough

With bills of rime the brambles shew.
The hoarse leaves crawl on hissing ground
Because the sighing wind is low.

But if the rain-blasts be unbound
And from dank feathers wring the drops
The clogged brook runs with choking sound

Kneading the mounded mire that stops
His channel under clammy coats
Of foliage fallen in the copse.

A simple passage of weak notes
Is all the winter bird dare try.
The bugle moon by daylight floats

So glassy white about the sky,
So like a berg of hyaline,
And pencilled blue so daintily,

I never saw her so divine.
But through black branches, rarely drest
In scarves of silky shot and shine,

The webbed and the watery west
Where yonder crimson fireball sets
Looks laid for feasting and for rest.

I see long reefs of violets
In beryl-covered fens so dim,
A gold-water Pactolus frets

Its brindled wharves and yellow brim,
The waxen colours weep and run,
And slendering to his burning rim

Into the flat blue mist the sun
Drops out and all our day is done.

4

Spring and Death

I HAD a dream. A wondrous thing:
It seem'd an evening in the Spring;
—A little sickness in the air
From too much fragrance everywhere:—
As I walk'd a stilly wood,
Sudden, Death before me stood:
In a hollow lush and damp,
He seem'd a dismal mirky stamp
On the flowers that were seen
His charnelhouse-grate ribs between,
And with coffin-black he barr'd the green.
'Death,' said I, 'what do you here
At this Spring season of the year?'
'I mark the flowers ere the prime
Which I may tell at Autumn-time.'
Ere I had further question made
Death was vanish'd from the glade.
Then I saw that he had bound
Many trees and flowers round
With a subtle web of black,
And that such a sable track

Lay along the grasses green
From the spot where he had been.
  But the Spring-tide pass'd the same;
Summer was as full of flame;
Autumn-time no earlier came.
And the flowers that he had tied,
As I mark'd, not always died
Sooner than their mates; and yet
Their fall was fuller of regret:
It seem'd so hard and dismal thing,
Death, to mark them in the Spring.

5

*A Soliloquy of One of the Spies
left in the Wilderness*

WHO is this Moses? who made him, we say,
To be a judge and ruler over us?
He slew the Egyptian yesterday. To-day
    In hot sands perilous
He hides our corpses dropping by the way
    Wherein he makes us stray.   6

Your hands have borne the tent-poles: on you plod:
The trumpet waxes loud: tired are your feet.
Come by the flesh-pots: you shall sit unshod
    And have your fill of meat;
And bring your offerings to a grateful god,
    And fear no iron rod.   12

He feeds me with His manna every day:
My soul does loathe it and my spirit fails.
A press of wingèd things comes down this way:
    The gross flock call them quails.
Into my hand he gives a host for prey,
    Come up, Arise and slay.   18

Sicken'd and thicken'd by the glare and sand
Who would drink water from a stony rock?
Are all the manna-bushes in the land
    A shelter for this flock?
Behold at Elim wells on every hand
    And seventy palms there stand.   24

Egypt, the valley of our pleasance, there!
Most wide ye are who call this gust Simoom.
Your parchèd nostrils snuff Egyptian air,
    The comfortable gloom
After the sandfield and the unreinèd glare!
    Goshen is green and fair.   30

Not Goshen. Wasteful wide huge-girthèd Nile
Unbakes my pores, and streams, and makes all fresh.
I gather points of lote-flower from an isle
    Of leaves of greenest flesh.
Ye sandblind! Slabs of water many a mile
    Blaze for him all this while.   36

In beds, in gardens, in thick plots I stand,
Handle the fig, suck the full-sapp'd vine-shoot.
From easy runnels the rich-piecèd land
    I water with my foot.
Must you be gorged with proof? Did ever sand
    So trickle from your hand?   42

Strike timbrels, sing, eat, drink, be full of mirth.
Forget the waking trumpet, the long law.
Spread o'er the swart face of this prodigal earth.
    Bring in the glistery straw.
Here are sweet messes without price or worth,
    And never thirst or dearth.   48

Give us the tale of bricks as heretofore;
To plash with cool feet the clay juicy soil.
Who tread the grapes are splay'd with stripes of gore,
    And they who crush the oil
Are spatter'd. We desire the yoke we bore,
    The easy burden of yore.   54

•   •   •   •

Go then: I am contented here to lie.
Take Canaan with your sword and with your bow.
Rise: match your strength with monstrous Talmai
    At Kirjath-Arba: go.—
Sure, this is Nile: I sicken, I know not why,
    And faint as though to die.   60

6

Barnfloor and Winepress

And he said, If the Lord do not help thee, whence shall I help thee?
Out of the barnfloor, or out of the winepress?
                            2 KINGS vi. 27.

    THOU that on sin's wages starvest,
    Behold we have the joy in harvest:
    For us was gather'd the first-fruits,
    For us was lifted from the roots,

Sheaved in cruel bands, bruised sore,
Scourged upon the threshing-floor;
Where the upper mill-stone roof'd His head,
At morn we found the heavenly Bread,
And, on a thousand altars laid,
Christ our Sacrifice is made!

Thou whose dry plot for moisture gapes,
We shout with them that tread the grapes:
For us the Vine was fenced with thorn,
Five ways the precious branches torn;
Terrible fruit was on the tree
In the acre of Gethsemane;
For us by Calvary's distress
The wine was rackèd from the press;
Now in our altar-vessels stored
Is the sweet Vintage of our Lord.

In Joseph's garden they threw by
The riv'n Vine, leafless, lifeless, dry:
On Easter morn the Tree was forth,
In forty days reach'd Heaven from earth;
Soon the whole world is overspread;
Ye weary, come into the shade.

The field where He has planted us
Shall shake her fruit as Libanus,
When He has sheaved us in His sheaf,
When He has made us bear His leaf.—
We scarcely call that banquet food,
But even our Saviour's and our blood,
We are so grafted on His wood.

7
New Readings

ALTHOUGH the letter said
On thistles that men look not grapes to gather,
   I read the story rather
How soldiers platting thorns around CHRIST'S Head
   Grapes grew and drops of wine were shed.

Though when the sower sowed,
The wingèd fowls took part, part fell in thorn
   And never turned to corn,
Part found no root upon the flinty road,—
   CHRIST at all hazards fruit hath shewed.

From wastes of rock He brings
Food for five thousand: on the thorns He shed
   Grains from His drooping Head;
And would not have that legion of winged things
   Bear Him to heaven on easeful wings.

8

HE hath abolished the old drouth,
And rivers run where all was dry,
The field is sopp'd with merciful dew.
He hath put a new song in my mouth,
The words are old, the purport new,
And taught my lips to quote this word
That I shall live, I shall not die,
But I shall when the shocks are stored
See the salvation of the Lord.

We meet together, you and I,
Meet in one acre of one land,
And I will turn my looks to you,
And you shall meet me with reply,
We shall be sheavèd with one band
In harvest and in garnering,
When heavenly vales so thick shall stand
With corn that they shall laugh and sing.

9

Heaven-Haven

A nun takes the veil

I HAVE desired to go
    Where springs not fail,
To fields where flies no sharp and sided hail
    And a few lilies blow.

And I have asked to be
    Where no storms come,
Where the green swell is in the havens dumb,
    And out of the swing of the sea.

10

For a Picture of St. Dorothea

I BEAR a basket lined with grass;
I am so light, I am so fair,
That men must wonder as I pass
And at the basket that I bear,

Where in a newly-drawn green litter
Sweet flowers I carry,—sweets for bitter.

Lilies I shew you, lilies none,
None in Caesar's gardens blow,—
And a quince in hand,—not one
Is set upon your boughs below;
Not set, because their buds not spring;
Spring not, 'cause world is wintering.

But these were found in the East and South
Where Winter is the clime forgot.—
The dewdrop on the larkspur's mouth
O should it then be quenchèd not?
In starry water-meads they drew
These drops: which be they? stars or dew?

Had she a quince in hand? Yet gaze:
Rather it is the sizing moon.
Lo, linkèd heavens with milky ways!
That was her larkspur row.—So soon?
Sphered so fast, sweet soul?—We see
Nor fruit, nor flowers, nor Dorothy.

11

Easter Communion

Pure fasted faces draw unto this feast:
God comes all sweetness to your Lenten lips.
You striped in secret with breath-taking whips,
Those crookèd rough-scored chequers may be pieced

20

To crosses meant for Jesu's; you whom the East
With draught of thin and pursuant cold so nips
Breathe Easter now; you sergèd fellowships,
You vigil-keepers with low flames decreased,
God shall o'er-brim the measures you have spent
With oil of gladness; for sackcloth and frieze
And the ever-fretting shirt of punishment
Give myrrhy-threaded golden folds of ease.
Your scarce-sheathed bones are weary of being bent:
Lo, God shall strengthen all the feeble knees.

12

To Oxford

(i)

NEW-DATED from the terms that reappear,
More sweet-familiar grows my love to thee,
And still thou bind'st me to fresh fealty
With long-superfluous ties, for nothing here
Nor elsewhere can thy sweetness unendear.
This is my park, my pleasaunce; this to me
As public is my greater privacy,
All mine, yet common to my every peer.
Those charms accepted of my inmost thought,
The towers musical, quiet-wallèd grove,
The window-circles, these may all be sought
By other eyes, and other suitors move,
And all like me may boast, impeachèd not,
Their special-general title to thy love.

Thus, I come underneath this chapel-side,
So that the mason's levels, courses, all
The vigorous horizontals, each way fall
In bows above my head, as falsified
By visual compulsion, till I hide
The steep-up roof at last behind the small
Eclipsing parapet; yet above the wall
The sumptuous ridge-crest leave to poise and ride.
None besides me this bye-ways beauty try.
Or if they try it, I am happier then:
The shapen flags and drillèd holes of sky,
Just seen, may be to many unknown men
The one peculiar of their pleasured eye,
And I have only set the same to pen.

13

WHERE art thou friend, whom I shall never see,
Conceiving whom I must conceive amiss?
Or sunder'd from my sight in the age that is
Or far-off promise of a time to be;
Thou who canst best accept the certainty
That thou hadst borne proportion in my bliss,
That likest in me either that or this,—
Oh! even for the weakness of the plea
That I have taken to plead with,—if the sound
Of God's dear pleadings have as yet not moved thee,—
And for those virtues I in thee have found,
Who say that had I known I had approved thee,—
For these, make all the virtues to abound,—
No, but for Christ who hath foreknown and loved thee.

14

The Beginning of the End

(i)

MY love is lessened and must soon be past.
　　I never promised such persistency
　　In its condition. No, the tropic tree
Has not a charter that its sap shall last

Into all seasons, though no Winter cast
　　The happy leafing. It is so with me:
　　My love is less, my love is less for thee.
I cease the mourning and the abject fast,

And rise and go about my works again
　　And, save by darting accidents, forget.
　　But ah! if you could understand how then

That *less* is heavens higher even yet
　　Than treble-fervent *more* of other men,
　　Even your unpassion'd eyelids might be wet.

(ii)

I must feed Fancy. Show me any one
　　That reads or holds the astrologic lore,
　　And I'll pretend the credit given of yore;
And let him prove my passion was begun

In the worst hour that's measured by the sun,
　　With such malign conjunctions as before
　　No influential heaven ever wore;
That no recorded devilish thing was done

With such a seconding, nor Saturn took
　　Such opposition to the Lady-star
　　In the most murderous passage of his book;

And I'll love my distinction: Near or far
　　He says his science helps him not to look
　　At hopes so evil-heaven'd as mine are.

(iii)

You see that I have come to passion's end;
   This means you need not fear the storms, the cries,
   That gave you vantage when you would despise:
My bankrupt heart has no more tears to spend.

Else I am well assured I should offend
   With fiercer weepings of these desperate eyes
   For poor love's failure than his hopeless rise.
But now I am so tired I soon shall send

Barely a sigh to thought of hopes forgone.
   Is this made plain? What have I come across
   That here will serve me for comparison?

The sceptic disappointment and the loss
   A boy feels when the poet he pores upon
   Grows less and less sweet to him, and knows no cause.

15

The Alchemist in the City

My window shews the travelling clouds,
Leaves spent, new seasons, alter'd sky,
The making and the melting crowds:
The whole world passes; I stand by.

They do not waste their meted hours,
But men and masters plan and build:
I see the crowning of their towers,
And happy promises fulfill'd.

And I—perhaps if my intent
Could count on prediluvian age,
The labours I should then have spent
Might so attain their heritage,

24

But now before the pot can glow
With not to be discover'd gold,
At length the bellows shall not blow,
The furnace shall at last be cold.

Yet it is now too late to heal
The incapable and cumbrous shame
Which makes me when with men I deal
More powerless than the blind or lame.

No, I should love the city less
Even than this my thankless lore;
But I desire the wilderness
Or weeded landslips of the shore.

I walk my breezy belvedere
To watch the low or levant sun,
I see the city pigeons veer,
I mark the tower swallows run

Between the tower-top and the ground
Below me in the bearing air;
Then find in the horizon-round
One spot and hunger to be there.

And then I hate the most that lore
That holds no promise of success;
Then sweetest seems the houseless shore,
Then free and kind the wilderness,

Or ancient mounds that cover bones,
Or rocks where rockdoves do repair
And trees of terebinth and stones
And silence and a gulf of air.

There on a long and squarèd height
After the sunset I would lie,
And pierce the yellow waxen light
With free long looking, ere I die.

16

MYSELF unholy, from myself unholy
To the sweet living of my friends I look—
Eye-greeting doves bright-counter to the rook,
Fresh brooks to salt sand-teasing waters shoaly:—
And they are purer, but alas! not solely
The unquestion'd readings of a blotless book.
And so my trust, confusèd, struck, and shook
Yields to the sultry siege of melancholy.
He has a sin of mine, he its near brother;
Knowing them well I can but see the fall.
This fault in one I found, that in another:
And so, though each have one while I have all,
No *better* serves me now, save *best*; no other
Save Christ: to Christ I look, on Christ I call.

17

SEE how Spring opens with disabling cold,
And hunting winds and the long-lying snow.
Is it a wonder if the buds are slow?
Or where is strength to make the leaf unfold?

Chilling remembrance of my days of old
Afflicts no less, what yet I hope may blow,
That seed which the good sower once did sow,
So loading with obstruction that threshold
Which should ere now have led my feet to the field.
It is the waste done in unreticent youth
Which makes so small the promise of that yield
That I may win with late-learnt skill uncouth
From furrows of the poor and stinting weald.
Therefore how bitter, and learnt how late, the truth!

18

My prayers must meet a brazen heaven
And fail and scatter all away.
Unclean and seeming unforgiven
My prayers I scarcely call to pray.
I cannot buoy my heart above;
Above I cannot entrance win.
I reckon precedents of love,
But feel the long success of sin.

My heaven is brass and iron my earth:
Yea iron is mingled with my clay,
So harden'd is it in this dearth
Which praying fails to do away.
Nor tears, nor tears this clay uncouth
Could mould, if any tears there were.
A warfare of my lips in truth,
Battling with God, is now my prayer.

19

Let me be to Thee as the circling bird,
Or bat with tender and air-crisping wings
That shapes in half-light his departing rings,
From both of whom a changeless note is heard.
I have found my music in a common word,
Trying each pleasurable throat that sings
And every praisèd sequence of sweet strings,
And know infallibly which I preferred.
The authentic cadence was discovered late
Which ends those only strains that I approve,
And other science all gone out of date
And minor sweetness scarce made mention of:
I have found the dominant of my range and state—
Love, O my God, to call Thee Love and Love.

20

The Half-way House

Love I was shewn upon the mountain-side
And bid to catch Him ere the drop of day.
See, Love, I creep and Thou on wings dost ride:
Love, it is evening now and Thou away;
Love, it grows darker here and Thou art above;
Love, come down to me if Thy name be Love.

My national old Egyptian reed gave way;
I took of vine a cross-barred rod or rood.
Then next I hungered: Love when here, they say,
Or once or never took Love's proper food;
But I must yield the chase, or rest and eat.—
Peace and food cheered me where four rough ways meet.

28

Hear yet my paradox: Love, when all is given,
To see Thee I must see Thee, to love, love;
I must o'ertake Thee at once and under heaven
If I shall overtake Thee at last above.
You have your wish; enter these walls, one said:
He is with you in the breaking of the bread.

21

The Nightingale

'FROM nine o'clock till morning light
The copse was never more than grey.
The darkness did not close that night
    But day passed into day.
And soon I saw it shewing new
Beyond the hurst with such a hue
As silky garden-poppies do.

'A crimson East, that bids for rain.
So from the dawn was ill begun
The day that brought my lasting pain
    And put away my sun.
But watching while the colour grew
I only feared the wet for you
Bound for the Harbour and your crew.

'I did not mean to sleep, but found
I had slept a little and was chill.
And I could hear the tiniest sound,
    The morning was so still—

The bats' wings lisping as they flew
And water draining through and through
The wood: but not a dove would coo.

'You know you said the nightingale
In all our western shires was rare,
That more he shuns our special dale
    Or never lodges there:
And I had thought so hitherto—
Up till that morning's fall of dew,
And now I wish that it were true.

'For he began at once and shook
My head to hear. He might have strung
A row of ripples in the brook,
    So forcibly he sung,
The mist upon the leaves have strewed,
And danced the balls of dew that stood
In acres all above the wood.

'I thought the air must cut and strain
The windpipe when he sucked his breath
And when he turned it back again
    The music must be death.
With not a thing to make me fear,
A singing bird in morning clear
To me was terrible to hear.

'Yet as he changed his mighty stops
Betweens I heard the water still
All down the stair-way of the copse
    And churning in the mill.
But that sweet sound which I preferred,
Your passing steps, I never heard
For warbling of the warbling bird.'

Thus Frances sighed at home, while Luke
Made headway in the frothy deep.
She listened how the sea-gust shook
And then lay back to sleep.
While he was washing from on deck
She pillowing low her lily neck
Timed her sad visions with his wreck.

22

The Habit of Perfection

ELECTED Silence, sing to me
And beat upon my whorlèd ear,
Pipe me to pastures still and be
The music that I care to hear.

Shape nothing, lips; be lovely-dumb:
It is the shut, the curfew sent
From there where all surrenders come
Which only makes you eloquent.

Be shellèd, eyes, with double dark
And find the uncreated light:
This ruck and reel which you remark
Coils, keeps, and teases simple sight.

Palate, the hutch of tasty lust,
Desire not to be rinsed with wine:
The can must be so sweet, the crust
So fresh that come in fasts divine!

Nostrils, your careless breath that spend
Upon the stir and keep of pride,
What relish shall the censers send
Along the sanctuary side!

O feel-of-primrose hands, O feet
That want the yield of plushy sward,
But you shall walk the golden street
And you unhouse and house the Lord.

And, Poverty, be thou the bride
And now the marriage feast begun,
And lily-coloured clothes provide
Your spouse not laboured-at nor spun.

23

Nondum

'Verily Thou art a God that hidest Thyself.'
ISAIAH xlv. 15.

GOD, though to Thee our psalm we raise
No answering voice comes from the skies;
To Thee the trembling sinner prays
But no forgiving voice replies;
Our prayer seems lost in desert ways,
Our hymn in the vast silence dies.

We see the glories of the earth
But not the hand that wrought them all:
Night to a myriad worlds gives birth,
Yet like a lighted empty hall
Where stands no host at door or hearth
Vacant creation's lamps appal.

We guess; we clothe Thee, unseen King,
With attributes we deem are meet;
Each in his own imagining
Sets up a shadow in Thy seat;
Yet know not how our gifts to bring,
Where seek Thee with unsandalled feet.

And still th'unbroken silence broods
While ages and while aeons run,
As erst upon chaotic floods
The Spirit hovered ere the sun
Had called the seasons' changeful moods
And life's first germs from death had won.

And still th'abysses infinite
Surround the peak from which we gaze.
Deep calls to deep, and blackest night
Giddies the soul with blinding daze
That dares to cast its searching sight
On being's dread and vacant maze.

And Thou art silent, whilst Thy world
Contends about its many creeds
And hosts confront with flags unfurled
And zeal is flushed and pity bleeds
And truth is heard, with tears impearled,
A moaning voice among the reeds.

My hand upon my lips I lay;
The breast's desponding sob I quell;
I move along life's tomb-decked way
And listen to the passing bell
Summoning men from speechless day
To death's more silent, darker spell.

Oh! till Thou givest that sense beyond,
To shew Thee that Thou art, and near,
Let patience with her chastening wand
Dispel the doubt and dry the tear;
And lead me child-like by the hand
If still in darkness not in fear.

Speak! whisper to my watching heart
One word—as when a mother speaks
Soft, when she sees her infant start,
Till dimpled joy steals o'er its cheeks.
Then, to behold Thee as Thou art,
I'll wait till morn eternal breaks.

24

Easter

BREAK the box and shed the nard;
Stop not now to count the cost;
Hither bring pearl, opal, sard;
Reck not what the poor have lost;
Upon Christ throw all away:
Know ye, this is Easter Day.

Build His church and deck His shrine,
Empty though it be on earth;
Ye have kept your choicest wine—
Let it flow for heavenly mirth;
Pluck the harp and breathe the horn:
Know ye not 'tis Easter morn?

Gather gladness from the skies;
Take a lesson from the ground;
Flowers do ope their heavenward eyes
And a Spring-time joy have found;
Earth throws Winter's robes away,
Decks herself for Easter Day.

Beauty now for ashes wear,
Perfumes for the garb of woe,
Chaplets for dishevelled hair,
Dances for sad footsteps slow;
Open wide your hearts that they
Let in joy this Easter Day.

Seek God's house in happy throng;
Crowded let His table be;
Mingle praises, prayer, and song,
Singing to the Trinity.
Henceforth let your souls alway
Make each morn an Easter Day.

25

Lines for a Picture of St. Dorothea
Dorothea and Theophilus

I BEAR a basket lined with grass.
I' am so' light' and fair'
Men are amazed to watch me pass
With' the básket I bear',
Which in newly drawn green litter
Carries treats of sweet for bitter.

See my lilies: lilies none,
None in Caesar's garden blow.
Quínces, look', when' not onc'
Is set in any orchard; no,
Not set because their buds not spring;
Spring not for world is wintering.

But' they came' from' the South',
Where winter-while is all forgot.—
The dew-bell in the mallow's mouth
Is' it quénchèd or not'?
In starry, starry shire it grew:
Which' is it', star' or dew'?—

That a quince I pore upon?
O no it is the sizing moon.
Now her mallow-row is gone
In tufts of evening sky.—So soon?
Sphered so fast, sweet soul?—We see
Fruit nor flower nor Dorothy.

How to name it, blessed it!
Suiting its grace with *him* or *her*?
Dorothea—or was your writ
Sérvèd bý méssenger'?
Your parley was not done and there!
You went into the partless air.

It waned into the world of light,
Yet made its market here as well:
My eyes hold yet the rinds and bright
Remainder of a miracle.
O this is bringing! Tears may swarm
Indeed while such a wonder's warm.

Ah dip in blood the palmtree pen
And wordy warrants are flawed through.
More will wear this wand and then
The warpèd world we shall undo.
Proconsul!—Is Sapricius near?—
I find another Christian here.

26

Ad Mariam

WHEN a sister, born for each strong month-brother,
   Spring's one daughter, the sweet child May,
Lies in the breast of the young year-mother
   With light on her face like the waves at play,
Man from the lips of him speaketh and saith,
At the touch of her wandering wondering breath
Warm on his brow: lo! where is another
   Fairer than this one to brighten our day?

We have suffered the sons of Winter in sorrow
   And been in their ruinous reigns oppressed,
And fain in the springtime surcease would borrow
   From all the pain of the past's unrest;
And May has come, hair-bound in flowers,
With eyes that smile thro' the tears of the hours,
With joy for to-day and hope for to-morrow
   And the promise of Summer within her breast!

And we that joy in this month joy-laden,
   The gladdest thing that our eyes have seen,
Oh thou, proud mother and much proud maiden—
   Maid yet mother as May hath been—

To thee we tender the beauties all
Of the month by men called virginal
And, where thou dwellest in deep-groved Aidenn,
　　Salute thee, mother, the maid-month's Queen!

For thou, as she, wert the one fair daughter
　　That came when a line of kings did cease,
Princes strong for the sword and slaughter,
　　That, warring, wasted the land's increase,
And like the storm-months smote the earth
Till a maid in David's house had birth,
That was unto Judah as May, and brought her
　　A son for King, whose name was peace.

Wherefore we love thee, wherefore we sing to thee,
　　We, all we, thro' the length of our days,
The praise of the lips and the hearts of us bring to thee,
　　Thee, oh maiden, most worthy of praise;
For lips and hearts they belong to thee
Who to us are as dew unto grass and tree,
For the fallen rise and the stricken spring to thee,
　　Thee, May-hope of our darkened ways!

27
Rosa Mystica

THE rose in a mystery—where is it found?
Is it anything true? Does it grow upon ground?
It was made of earth's mould but it went from men's eyes
And its place is a secret and shut in the skies.
Refrain—
　　In the gardens of God, in the daylight divine
　　Find me a place by thee, mother of mine.

But where was it formerly? which is the spot
That was blest in it once, though now it is not?—
It is Galilee's growth: it grew at God's will
And broke into bloom upon Nazareth hill.
  In the gardens of God, in the daylight divine
  I shall look on thy loveliness, mother of mine.

What was its season then? how long ago?
When was the summer that saw the bud blow?—
Two thousands of years are near upon past
Since its birth, and its bloom, and its breathing its last.
  In the gardens of God, in the daylight divine
  I shall keep time with thee, mother of mine.

Tell me the name now, tell me its name.
The heart guesses easily: is it the same?—
Mary the Virgin, well the heart knows,
She is the mystery, she is that rose.
  In the gardens of God, in the daylight divine
  I shall come home to thee, mother of mine.

Is Mary the rose then? Mary the tree?
But the blossom, the blossom there, who can it be?—
Who can her rose be? It could be but one:
Christ Jesus our Lord, her God and her son.
  In the gardens of God, in the daylight divine
  Shew me thy son, mother, mother of mine.

What was the colour of that blossom bright?—
White to begin with, immaculate white.
But what a wild flush on the flakes of it stood
When the rose ran in crimsonings down the cross-wood!
  In the gardens of God, in the daylight divine
  I shall worship His wounds with thee, mother of mine.

39

How many leaves had it?—Five they were then,
Five like the senses and members of men;
Five is their number by nature, but now
They multiply, multiply who can tell how?
  In the gardens of God, in the daylight divine
  Make me a leaf in thee, mother of mine.

Does it smell sweet too in that holy place?—
Sweet unto God, and the sweetness is grace:
O breath of it bathes great heaven above
In grace that is charity, grace that is love.
  To thy breast, to thy rest, to thy glory divine
  Draw me by charity, mother of mine.

POEMS
(1876–89)

POEMS
(1876-89)

CATHARINAE

HVNC LIBRVM
QVI FILII EIVS CARISSIMI
POETAE DEBITAM INGENIO LAVDEM EXPECTANTIS
SERVM TAMEN MONVMENTVM ESSET
ANNVM AETATIS XCVIII AGENTI
VETERIS AMICITIAE PIGNVS

D D D

R B

OUR generation already is overpast,
And thy lov'd legacy, Gerard, hath lain
Coy in my home; as once thy heart was fain
Of shelter, when God's terror held thee fast
In life's wild wood at Beauty and Sorrow aghast;
Thy sainted sense trammel'd in ghostly pain,
Thy rare ill-broker'd talent in disdain:
Yet love of Christ will win man's love at last.

  Hell wars without; but, dear, the while my hands
Gather'd thy book, I heard, this wintry day,
Thy spirit thank me, in his young delight
Stepping again upon the yellow sands.
  Go forth: amidst our chaffinch flock display
Thy plumage of far wonder and heavenward flight!

Chilswell, Jan. 1918   ROBERT BRIDGES

44

AUTHOR'S PREFACE

THE poems in this book[1] are written some in Running
Rhythm, the common rhythm in English use, some in
Sprung Rhythm, and some in a mixture of the two. And those
in the common rhythm are some counterpointed, some not.

Common English rhythm, called Running Rhythm[2] above,
is measured by feet of either two or three syllables and (putting
aside the imperfect feet at the beginning and end of lines and also
some unusual measures in which feet seem to be paired together and double or composite feet to arise) never more nor less.

Every foot has one principal stress or accent, and this or the
syllable it falls on may be called the Stress of the foot and the
other part, the one or two unaccented syllables, the Slack.[3]
Feet (and the rhythms made out of them) in which the Stress
comes first are called Falling Feet and Falling Rhythms, feet
and rhythm in which the Slack comes first are called Rising
Feet and Rhythms, and if the Stress is between two Slacks there
will be Rocking Feet and Rhythms. These distinctions are real
and true to nature; but for purposes of scanning it is a great
convenience to follow the example of music and take the stress
always first, as the accent or the chief accent always comes first
in a musical bar. If this is done there will be in common English verse only two possible feet—the so-called accentual
Trochee and Dactyl, and correspondingly only two possible
uniform rhythms, the so-called Trochaic and Dactylic. But
they may be mixed and then what the Greeks called a Logaoedic Rhythm arises.[4] These are the facts and according to these
the scanning of ordinary regularly-written English verse is

---

[1] That is, the MS. described in the first Editor's preface as B. The Author's Preface
does not apply to the Early Poems.

[2] G. M. H. used also the term 'Standard Rhythm': see notes to Nos. 31, 32, &c.

[3] In the following footnotes (and *Notes* to the poems) the Stress = (′) and the Slack
= (×) or (×× &c.)

[4] E.g. in Swinburne's famous *Atalanta* chorus and G. M. H.'s imitation of it in No.
26:
    × ×: ′ × ′ × ′ × × × ′ × ′ × ′ ×
'When a sister, born for each strong month-brother,' (l. 1).

45

very simple indeed and to bring in other principles is here unnecessary.

But because verse written strictly in these feet and by these principles will become same and tame the poets have brought in licences and departures from rule to give variety, and especially when the natural rhythm is rising, as in the common ten-syllable or five-foot verse, rhymed or blank. These irregularities are chiefly Reversed Feet and Reversed or Counterpoint Rhythm, which two things are two steps or degrees of licence in the same kind. By a reversed foot I mean the putting the stress where, to judge by the rest of the measure, the slack should be and the slack where the stress, and this is done freely at the beginning of a line and, in the course of a line, after a pause; only scarcely ever in the second foot or place and never in the last, unless when the poet designs some extraordinary effect; for these places are characteristic and sensitive and cannot well be touched. But the reversal of the first foot and of some middle foot after a strong pause is a thing so natural that our poets have generally done it, from Chaucer down, without remark and it commonly passes unnoticed and cannot be said to amount to a formal change of rhythm, but rather is that irregularity which all natural growth and motion shews. If however the reversal is repeated in two feet running, especially so as to include the sensitive second foot, it must be due either to great want of ear or else is a calculated effect, the superinducing or *mounting* of a new rhythm upon the old; and since the new or mounted rhythm is actually heard and at the same time the mind naturally supplies the natural or standard foregoing rhythm, for we do not forget what the rhythm is that by rights we should be hearing, two rhythms are in some manner running at once and we have something answerable to counterpoint in music, which is two or more strains of tune going on together, and this is Counterpoint Rhythm.[1] Of this

[1] First heard in *God's Grandeur:*

'Generations have trod, have trod, have trod,' (l. 5). See note to No. 31, and below, p. 48.

46

kind of verse Milton is the great master[1] and the choruses of *Samson Agonistes* are written throughout in it—but with the disadvantage that he does not let the reader clearly know what the ground-rhythm is meant to be and so they have struck most readers as merely irregular. And in fact if you counterpoint throughout, since one only of the counter rhythms is actually heard, the other is really destroyed or cannot come to exist and what is written is one rhythm only and probably Sprung Rhythm, of which I now speak.

Sprung Rhythm, as used in this book, is measured by feet of from one to four syllables, regularly, and for particular effects any number of weak or slack syllables may be used. It has one stress, which falls on the only syllable, if there is only one, or, if there are more, then scanning as above, on the first, and so gives rise to four sorts of feet, a monosyllable and the so-called accentual Trochee, Dactyl, and the First Paeon.[2] And there will be four corresponding natural rhythms; but nominally the feet are mixed and any one may follow any other. And hence Sprung Rhythm differs from Running Rhythm in having or being only one nominal rhythm, a mixed or 'logaoedic' one, instead of three, but on the other hand in having twice the flexibility of foot, so that any two stresses may either follow one another running or be divided by one, two, or three slack syllables. But strict Sprung Rhythm cannot be counterpointed. In Sprung Rhythm, as in logaoedic rhythm generally, the feet

---

[1] For G. M. H.'s examples of Counterpoint Rhythm in *Paradise Lost* and *Paradise Regained* see *Letters to R. B.*, p. 38, and *Correspondence of G. M. H. and R. W. Dixon*, p. 15.

[2] E.g. in 'The Wreck of the Deutschland' (only the stressed syllables are marked in MSS.):

(*a*) Monosyllabic feet:

×│ / │ / │ / ‖ ×   × / │ / │ /
'The sour scythe cringe, and the blear share come,' (xi. 8).

(*b*) Paeons:

/ × × × │ / × × × × │ / × ‖ × ×│ / × × │ / × × ×
'Startle the poor sheep back! is the shipwrack then a harvest, does tempest carry

×│ / × × ×
the grain for thee?' (xxxi. 8).

In both lines the caesura really breaks the third foot. Note the extended fifth foot in (*b*) and cf. line 6 of the same stanza. See notes to No. 28.

47

are assumed to be equally long or strong and their seeming inequality is made up by pause or stressing.

Remark also that it is natural in Sprung Rhythm for the lines to be *rove over*,[1] that is for the scanning of each line immediately to take up that of the one before, so that if the first has one or more syllables at its end the other must have so many the less at its beginning; and in fact the scanning runs on without break from the beginning, say, of a stanza to the end and all the stanza is one long strain, though written in lines asunder.

Two licences are natural to Sprung Rhythm. The one is rests, as in music; but of this an example is scarcely to be found in this book, unless in the *Echos*, second line.[2] The other is *hangers* or *outrides*, that is one, two, or three slack syllables added to a foot and not counting in the nominal scanning. They are so called because they seem to hang below the line or ride forward or backward from it in another dimension than the line itself, according to a principle needless to explain here.[3] These outriding half feet or hangers are marked by a loop underneath them, and plenty of them will be found.

The other marks are easily understood, namely accents, where the reader might be in doubt which syllable should have the stress; slurs, that is loops *over* syllables, to tie them together into the time of one; little loops at the end of a line to shew that the rhyme goes on to the first letter of the next line; what in music are called pauses ⌒, to shew that the syllable should be dwelt on; and twirls ∿ , to mark reversed or counterpointed rhythm.[4]

Note on the nature and history of Sprung Rhythm— Sprung Rhythm is the most natural of things. For (1) it is the

[1] See R. B.'s note on p. 254; also *Letters to R. B.*, p. 86.

[2] No. 59; but see also the first line of No. 61.

[3] Further explained in G. M. H.'s note to No. 38 (below, p. 269). For examples of outrides see notes to Nos. 36, 38, 39, &c. An historical exposition is given in my *Gerard Manley Hopkins*, vol. i, pp. 84–90. (W. H. G.)

[4] Illustrations of these marks and others are given below in notes to Nos. 59, 62, 65, 67, and 71. For the 'little loops' to indicate linked rhyme, see note to No. 28, st. 14, ll. 3–4. G. M. H. used the smaller twirl ∿ (sometimes ⌣) as 'a circumflex,

over words like *here*, . . . *there* . . ., to express that they are to be made to approach two syllables—he-ar, etc.' He also used the larger twirl ∾, as well as ∿ and a variant ∞ , to mark 'reversed or counterpointed rhythm'. (Cf. *Letters to R. B.*, p. 43.)

rhythm of common speech and of written prose, when rhythm is perceived in them. (2) It is the rhythm of all but the most monotonously regular music, so that in the words of choruses and refrains and in songs written closely to music it arises. (3) It is found in nursery rhymes,[1] weather saws,[2] and so on; because, however these may have been once made in running rhythm, the terminations having dropped off by the change of language, the stresses come together and so the rhythm is sprung. (4) It arises in common verse when reversed or counterpointed, for the same reason.

But nevertheless in spite of all this and though Greek and Latin lyric verse, which is well known, and the old English verse seen in *Pierce Ploughman* are in sprung rhythm, it has in fact ceased to be used since the Elizabethan age, Greene being the last writer who can be said to have recognized it. For perhaps there was not, down to our days, a single, even short, poem in English in which sprung rhythm is employed—not for single effects or in fixed places—but as the governing principle of the scansion. I say this because the contrary has been asserted: if it is otherwise the poem should be cited.

Some of the sonnets in this book[3] are in five-foot, some in six-foot or Alexandrine lines.

Nos. 13 and 22[4] are Curtal-Sonnets, that is they are constructed in proportions resembling those of the sonnet proper, namely 6+4 instead of 8+6, with however a halfline tailpiece (so that the equation is rather $\frac{12}{2}+\frac{9}{2} = \frac{21}{2} = 10\frac{1}{2}$).

[1] Cf. letter to R. W. Dixon (Oct. 5, 1878): 'Here are instances—Ding, dong, bell, Pussy's in the well: Who put her in? Little Johnny Thin...'

[2] E.g.: 'Red at night, shepherd's delight.'—[W.H.G.]

[3] See above, p. 45, note 1.

[4] I.e. in the First Edition; Nos. 37 and 51 in the present edition.

POEMS
(1876–89)

28

The Wreck of the
Deutschland

*To the
happy memory of five Franciscan nuns
exiles by the Falck Laws
drowned between midnight and morning of
Dec. 7th, 1875*

PART THE FIRST

I

THOU mastering me
God! giver of breath and bread;
World's strand, sway of the sea;
Lord of living and dead;
Thou hast bound bones and veins in me, fastened me flesh,
And after it almost unmade, what with dread,
Thy doing: and dost thou touch me afresh?
Over again I feel thy finger and find thee.

2

I did say yes
O at lightning and lashed rod;
Thou heardst me truer than tongue confess
Thy terror, O Christ, O God;
Thou knowest the walls, altar and hour and night:
The swoon of a heart that the sweep and the hurl of thee
trod
Hard down with a horror of height:
And the midriff astrain with leaning of, laced with fire of stress.

3

The frown of his face
Before me, the hurtle of hell
Behind, where, where was a, where was a place?
I whirled out wings that spell
And fled with a fling of the heart to the heart of the Host.
My heart, but you were dovewinged, I can tell,
Carrier-witted, I am bold to boast,
To flash from the flame to the flame then, tower from the grace
to the grace.

4

I am soft sift
In an hourglass—at the wall
Fast, but mined with a motion, a drift,
And it crowds and it combs to the fall;
I steady as a water in a well, to a poise, to a pane,
But roped with, always, all the way down from the tall
Fells or flanks of the voel, a vein
Of the gospel proffer, a pressure, a principle, Christ's gift.

5

I kiss my hand
To the stars, lovely-asunder
Starlight, wafting him out of it; and
Glow, glory in thunder;
Kiss my hand to the dappled-with-damson west:
Since, tho' he is under the world's splendour and wonder,
His mystery must be instressed, stressed;
For I greet him the days I meet him, and bless when I under-
stand.

6

Not out of his bliss
Springs the stress felt
Nor first from heaven (and few know this)
Swings the stroke dealt—
Stroke and a stress that stars and storms deliver,
That guilt is hushed by, hearts are flushed by and melt—
But it rides time like riding a river
(And here the faithful waver, the faithless fable and miss).

7

It dates from day
Of his going in Galilee;
Warm-laid grave of a womb-life grey;
Manger, maiden's knee;
The dense and the driven Passion, and frightful sweat:
Thence the discharge of it, there its swelling to be,
Though felt before, though in high flood yet—
What none would have known of it, only the heart, being hard
at bay,

8

Is out with it! Oh,
We lash with the best or worst
Word last! How a lush-kept plush-capped sloe
Will, mouthed to flesh-burst,
Gush!—flush the man, the being with it, sour or sweet,
Brim, in a flash, full!—Hither then, last or first,
To hero of Calvary, Christ,'s feet—
Never ask if meaning it, wanting it, warned of it—men go.

9

Be adored among men,
God, three-numberèd form;
Wring thy rebel, dogged in den,
Man's malice, with wrecking and storm.
Beyond saying sweet, past telling of tongue,
Thou art lightning and love, I found it, a winter and warm;
Father and fondler of heart thou hast wrung:
Hast thy dark descending and most art merciful then.

10

With an anvil-ding
And with fire in him forge thy will
Or rather, rather then, stealing as Spring
Through him, melt him but master him still:
Whether at once, as once at a crash Paul,
Or as Austin, a lingering-out swéet skíll,
Make mercy in all of us, out of us all
Mastery, but be adored, but be adored King.

11

'Some find me a sword; some
The flange and the rail; flame,
Fang, or flood' goes Death on drum,
And storms bugle his fame.
But wé dream we are rooted in earth—Dust!
Flesh falls within sight of us, we, though our flower the
same,
Wave with the meadow, forget that there must
The sour scythe cringe, and the blear share come.

12

On Saturday sailed from Bremen,
American-outward-bound,
Take settler and seamen, tell men with women,
Two hundred souls in the round—
O Father, not under thy feathers nor ever as guessing
The goal was a shoal, of a fourth the doom to be drowned;
Yet did the dark side of the bay of thy blessing
Not vault them, the million of rounds of thy mercy not reeve
even them in?

13

Into the snows she sweeps,
Hurling the haven behind,
The Deutschland, on Sunday; and so the sky keeps,
For the infinite air is unkind,
And the sea flint-flake, black-backed in the regular blow,
Sitting Eastnortheast, in cursed quarter, the wind;
Wiry and white-fiery and whirlwind-swivellèd snow
Spins to the widow-making unchilding unfathering deeps.

She drove in the dark to leeward,
    She struck—not a reef or a rock
But the combs of a smother of sand: night drew her
    Dead to the Kentish Knock;
And she beat the bank down with her bows and the ride
    of her keel;
The breakers rolled on her beam with ruinous shock;
    And canvas and compass, the whorl and the wheel
Idle for ever to waft her or wind her with, these she endured.

15

Hope had grown grey hairs,
    Hope had mourning on,
Trenched with tears, carved with cares,
    Hope was twelve hours gone;
And frightful a nightfall folded rueful a day
Nor rescue, only rocket and lightship, shone,
    And lives at last were washing away:
To the shrouds they took,—they shook in the hurling and
    horrible airs.

16

One stirred from the rigging to save
    The wild woman-kind below,
With a rope's end round the man, handy and brave—
    He was pitched to his death at a blow,
For all his dreadnought breast and braids of thew:
They could tell him for hours, dandled the to and fro
    Through the cobbled foam-fleece. What could he do
With the burl of the fountains of air, buck and the flood of the
    wave?

17

They fought with God's cold—
And they could not and fell to the deck
(Crushed them) or water (and drowned them) or
rolled
With the sea-romp over the wreck.
Night roared, with the heart-break hearing a heart-broke
rabble,
The woman's wailing, the crying of child without check—
Till a lioness arose breasting the babble,
A prophetess towered in the tumult, a virginal tongue told.

18

Ah, touched in your bower of bone,
Are you! turned for an exquisite smart,
Have you! make words break from me here all alone,
Do you!—mother of being in me, heart.
O unteachably after evil, but uttering truth,
Why, tears! is it? tears; such a melting, a madrigal start!
Never-eldering revel and river of youth,
What can it be, this glee? the good you have there of your own?

19

Sister, a sister calling
A master, her master and mine!—
And the inboard seas run swirling and hawling;
The rash smart sloggering brine
Blinds her; but she that weather sees one thing, one;
Has one fetch in her: she rears herself to divine
Ears, and the call of the tall nun
To the men in the tops and the tackle rode over the storm's
brawling.

20

She was first of a five and came
　　Of a coifèd sisterhood.
　　(O Deutschland, double a desperate name!
　　O world wide of its good!
But Gertrude, lily, and Luther, are two of a town,
　　Christ's lily and beast of the waste wood:
　　From life's dawn it is drawn down,
Abel is Cain's brother and breasts they have sucked the same.)

Loathed for a love men knew in them,
　　Banned by the land of their birth,
　　Rhine refused them, Thames would ruin them;
　　Surf, snow, river and earth
Gnashed: but thou art above, thou Orion of light;
　　Thy unchancelling poising palms were weighing the worth,
　　Thou martyr-master: in thy sight
Storm flakes were scroll-leaved flowers, lily showers—sweet
　　heaven was astrew in them.

Five! the finding and sake
　　And cipher of suffering Christ.
　　Mark, the mark is of man's make
　　And the word of it Sacrificed.
But he scores it in scarlet himself on his own bespoken,
　　Before-time-taken, dearest prizèd and priced—
　　Stigma, signal, cinquefoil token
For lettering of the lamb's fleece, ruddying of the rose-flake.

Joy fall to thee, father Francis,
Drawn to the Life that died;
With the gnarls of the nails in thee, niche of the lance,
his
Lovescape crucified
And seal of his seraph-arrival! and these thy daughters
And five-livèd and leavèd favour and pride,
Are sisterly sealed in wild waters,
To bathe in his fall-gold mercies, to breathe in his all-fire
glances.

24

Away in the loveable west,
On a pastoral forehead of Wales,
I was under a roof here, I was at rest,
And they the prey of the gales;
She to the black-about air, to the breaker, the thickly
Falling flakes, to the throng that catches and quails
Was calling 'O Christ, Christ, come quickly':
The cross to her she calls Christ to her, christens her wild-worst
Best.

25

The majesty! what did she mean?
Breathe, arch and original Breath.
Is it love in her of the being as her lover had been?
Breathe, body of lovely Death.
They were else-minded then, altogether, the men
Woke thee with a *We are perishing* in the weather of Gen-
nesareth.
Or is it that she cried for the crown then,
The keener to come at the comfort for feeling the combating
keen?

26

For how to the heart's cheering
The down-dugged ground-hugged grey
Hovers off, the jay-blue heavens appearing
Of pied and peeled May!
Blue-beating and hoary-glow height; or night, still higher,
With belled fire and the moth-soft Milky Way,
What by your measure is the heaven of desire,
The treasure never eyesight got, nor was ever guessed what for
the hearing?

No, but it was not these.
The jading and jar of the cart,
Time's tasking, it is fathers that asking for ease
Of the sodden-with-its-sorrowing heart,
Not danger, electrical horror; then further it finds
The appealing of the Passion is tenderer in prayer apart:
Other, I gather, in measure her mind's
Burden, in wind's burly and beat of endragonèd seas.

But how shall I . . . make me room there:
Reach me a . . . Fancy, come faster—
Strike you the sight of it? look at it loom there,
Thing that she . . . There then! the Master,
Ipse, the only one, Christ, King, Head:
He was to cure the extremity where he had cast her;
Do, deal, lord it with living and dead;
Let him ride, her pride, in his triumph, despatch and have done
with his doom there.

Ah! there was a heart right!
There was single eye!
Read the unshapeable shock night
And knew the who and the why;
Wording it how but by him that present and past,
Heaven and earth are word of, worded by?—
The Simon Peter of a soul! to the blast
Tarpeïan-fast, but a blown beacon of light.

Jesu, heart's light,
Jesu, maid's son,
What was the feast followed the night
Thou hadst glory of this nun?—
Feast of the one woman without stain.
For so conceivèd, so to conceive thee is done;
But here was heart-throe, birth of a brain,
Word, that heard and kept thee and uttered thee outright.

Well, she has thee for the pain, for the
Patience; but pity of the rest of them!
Heart, go and bleed at a bitterer vein for the
Comfortless unconfessed of them—
No not uncomforted: lovely-felicitous Providence
Finger of a tender of, O of a feathery delicacy, the breast of the
Maiden could obey so, be a bell to, ring of it, and
Startle the poor sheep back! is the shipwrack then a harvest,
does tempest carry the grain for thee?

I admire thee, master of the tides,
      Of the Yore-flood, of the year's fall;
The recurb and the recovery of the gulf's sides,
      The girth of it and the wharf of it and the wall;
Stanching, quenching ocean of a motionable mind;
      Ground of being, and granite of it: past all
            Grasp God, throned behind
Death with a sovereignty that heeds but hides, bodes but abides;

      With a mercy that outrides
      The all of water, an ark
For the listener; for the lingerer with a love glides
      Lower than death and the dark;
A vein for the visiting of the past-prayer, pent in prison,
      The-last-breath penitent spirits—the uttermost mark
            Our passion-plungèd giant risen,
The Christ of the Father compassionate, fetched in the storm
      of his strides.

      Now burn, new born to the world,
      Double-naturèd name,
The heaven-flung, heart-fleshed, maiden-furled
      Miracle-in-Mary-of-flame,
Mid-numberèd he in three of the thunder-throne!
Not a dooms-day dazzle in his coming nor dark as he
      came;
      Kind, but royally reclaiming his own;
A released shower, let flash to the shire, not a lightning of fire
      hard-hurled.

Dame, at our door
Drowned, and among our shoals,
Remember us in the roads, the heaven-haven of the
reward:
Our King back, Oh, upon English souls!
Let him easter in us, be a dayspring to the dimness of us,
be a crimson-cresseted east,
More brightening her, rare-dear Britain, as his reign rolls,
Pride, rose, prince, hero of us, high-priest,
Our hearts' charity's hearth's fire, our thoughts' chivalry's
throng's Lord.

29

The Silver Jubilee:

*To James First Bishop of Shrewsbury on the
25th Year of his Episcopate July 28, 1876.*

THOUGH no high-hung bells or din
Of braggart bugles cry it in—
    What is sound? Nature's round
Makes the Silver Jubilee.

Five and twenty years have run
Since sacred fountains to the sun
    Sprang, that but now were shut,
Showering Silver Jubilee.

Feasts, when we shall fall asleep,
Shrewsbury may see others keep;
    None but you this her true,
This her Silver Jubilee.

Not today we need lament
Your wealth of life is some way spent:
    Toil has shed round your head
Silver but for Jubilee.

Then for her whose velvet vales
Should have pealed with welcome, Wales,
    Let the chime of a rhyme
Utter Silver Jubilee.

30

Penmaen Pool

For the Visitors' Book at the Inn

Who long for rest, who look for pleasure
Away from counter, court, or school
O where live well your lease of leisure
But here at, here at Penmaen Pool?

You'll dare the Alp? you'll dart the skiff?
Each sport has here its tackle and tool:
Come, plant the staff by Cadair cliff;
Come, swing the sculls on Penmaen Pool.

What's yonder? Grizzled Dyphwys dim:
The triple-hummocked Giant's Stool,
Hoar messmate, hobs and nobs with him
To halve the bowl of Penmaen Pool.

And all the landscape under survey,
At tranquil turns, by nature's rule,
Rides repeated topsyturvy
In frank, in fairy Penmaen Pool.

And Charles's Wain, the wondrous seven,
And sheep-flock clouds like worlds of wool,
For all they shine so, high in heaven,
Shew brighter shaken in Penmaen Pool.

The Mawddach, how she trips! though throttled
If floodtide teeming thrills her full,
And mazy sands all water-wattled
Waylay her at ebb, past Penmaen Pool.

But what's to see in stormy weather,
When grey showers gather and gusts are cool?—
Why, raindrop-roundels looped together
That lace the face of Penmaen Pool.

Then even in weariest wintry hour
Of New Year's month or surly Yule
Furred snows, charged tuft above tuft, tower
From darksome darksome Penmaen Pool.

And ever, if bound here hardest home,
You've parlour-pastime left and (who'll
Not honour it?) ale like goldy foam
That frocks an oar in Penmaen Pool.

Then come who pine for peace or pleasure
Away from counter, court, or school,
Spend here your measure of time and treasure
And taste the treats of Penmaen Pool.

31

God's Grandeur

THE world is charged with the grandeur of God.
  It will flame out, like shining from shook foil;
  It gathers to a greatness, like the ooze of oil
Crushed. Why do men then now not reck his rod?
Generations have trod, have trod, have trod;
  And all is seared with trade; bleared, smeared with toil;
  And wears man's smudge and shares man's smell: the soil
Is bare now, nor can foot feel, being shod.

And, for all this, nature is never spent;
  There lives the dearest freshness deep down things;
And though the last lights off the black West went
  Oh, morning, at the brown brink eastward, springs—
Because the Holy Ghost over the bent
  World broods with warm breast and with ah! bright wings.

32

The Starlight Night

LOOK at the stars! look, look up at the skies!
  O look at all the fire-folk sitting in the air!
  The bright boroughs, the circle-citadels there!
Down in dim woods the diamond delves! the elves'-eyes!
The grey lawns cold where gold, where quickgold lies!
  Wind-beat whitebeam! airy abeles set on a flare!
  Flake-doves sent floating forth at a farmyard scare!—
Ah well! it is all a purchase, all is a prize.

Buy then! bid then!—What?—Prayer, patience, alms, vows.
Look, look: a May-mess, like on orchard boughs!
   Look! March-bloom, like on mealed-with-yellow sallows!
These are indeed the barn; withindoors house
The shocks. This piece-bright paling shuts the spouse
   Christ home, Christ and his mother and all his hallows.

33

Spring

NOTHING is so beautiful as Spring—
   When weeds, in wheels, shoot long and lovely and lush;
   Thrush's eggs look little low heavens, and thrush
Through the echoing timber does so rinse and wring
The ear, it strikes like lightnings to hear him sing;
   The glassy peartree leaves and blooms, they brush
   The descending blue; that blue is all in a rush
With richness; the racing lambs too have fair their fling.

What is all this juice and all this joy?
   A strain of the earth's sweet being in the beginning
In Eden garden.—Have, get, before it cloy,

   Before it cloud, Christ, lord, and sour with sinning,
Innocent mind and Mayday in girl and boy,
   Most, O maid's child, thy choice and worthy the winning.

34

In the Valley of the Elwy

I REMEMBER a house where all were good
   To me, God knows, deserving no such thing:
   Comforting smell breathed at very entering,
Fetched fresh, as I suppose, off some sweet wood.

That cordial air made those kind people a hood
    All over, as a bevy of eggs the mothering wing
    Will, or mild nights the new morsels of Spring:
Why, it seemed of course; seemed of right it should.

Lovely the woods, waters, meadows, combes, vales,
All the air things wear that build this world of Wales;
    Only the inmate does not correspond:

God, lover of souls, swaying considerate scales,
Complete thy creature dear O where it fails,
    Being mighty a master, being a father and fond.

35
The Sea and the Skylark

ON ear and ear two noises too old to end
    Trench—right, the tide that ramps against the shore;
    With a flood or a fall, low lull-off or all roar,
Frequenting there while moon shall wear and wend.

Left hand, off land, I hear the lark ascend,
    His rash-fresh re-winded new-skeinèd score
    In crisps of curl off wild winch whirl, and pour
And pelt music, till none's to spill nor spend.

How these two shame this shallow and frail town!
    How ring right out our sordid turbid time,
Being pure! We, life's pride and cared-for crown,

    Have lost that cheer and charm of earth's past prime:
Our make and making break, are breaking, down
    To man's last dust, drain fast towards man's first slime.

36

The Windhover:

To Christ our Lord

I CAUGHT this morning morning's minion, king-
   dom of daylight's dauphin, dapple-dawn-drawn Falcon, in
     his riding
Of the rolling level underneath him steady air, and striding
High there, how he rung upon the rein of a wimpling wing
In his ecstasy! then off, off forth on swing,
   As a skate's heel sweeps smooth on a bow-bend: the hurl and
     gliding
Rebuffed the big wind. My heart in hiding
Stirred for a bird,—the achieve of, the mastery of the thing!

Brute beauty and valour and act, oh, air, pride, plume, here
   Buckle! AND the fire that breaks from thee then, a billion
Times told lovelier, more dangerous, O my chevalier!

   No wonder of it: shéer plód makes plough down sillion
Shine, and blue-bleak embers, ah my dear,
   Fall, gall themselves, and gash gold-vermilion.

37

Pied Beauty

GLORY be to God for dappled things—
   For skies of couple-colour as a brinded cow;
     For rose-moles all in stipple upon trout that swim;
Fresh-firecoal chestnut-falls; finches' wings;
   Landscape plotted and pieced—fold, fallow, and plough;
     And áll trádes, their gear and tackle and trim.

All things counter, original, spare, strange;
   Whatever is fickle, freckled (who knows how?)
      With swift, slow; sweet, sour; adazzle, dim;
He fathers-forth whose beauty is past change:
                        Praise him.

38

Hurrahing in Harvest

SUMMER ends now; now, barbarous in beauty, the stooks rise
Around; up above, what wind-walks! what lovely
         behaviour
Of silk-sack clouds! has wilder, wilful-wavier
Meal-drift moulded ever and melted across skies?

I walk, I lift up, I lift up heart, eyes,
Down all that glory in the heavens to glean our Saviour;
And, éyes, heárt, what looks, what lips yet gave you a
Rapturous love's greeting of realer, of rounder replies?

And the azurous hung hills are his world-wielding shoulder
Majestic—as a stallion stalwart, very-violet-sweet!—
These things, these things were here and but the beholder
Wanting; which two when they once meet,
The heart rears wings bold and bolder
And hurls for him, O half hurls earth for him off under his
      feet.

39

The Caged Skylark

As a dare-gale skylark scanted in a dull cage
   Man's mounting spirit in his bone-house, mean house,
         dwells—
   That bird beyond the remembering his free fells,
This in drudgery, day-labouring-out life's age.

Though aloft on turf or perch or poor low stage,
    Both sing sometímes the sweetest, sweetest spells,
    Yet both droop deadly sómetimes in their cells
Or wring their barriers in bursts of fear or rage.

Not that the sweet-fowl, song-fowl, needs no rest—
Why, hear him, hear him babble and drop down to his nest,
    But his own nest, wild nest, no prison.

Man's spirit will be flesh-bound when found at best,
But uncumberèd: meadow-down is not distressed
    For a rainbow footing it nor he for his bónes rísen.

40

The Lantern out of Doors

SOMETIMES a lantern moves along the night.
    That interests our eyes. And who goes there?
    I think; where from and bound, I wonder, where,
With, all down darkness wide, his wading light?

Men go by me whom either beauty bright
    In mould or mind or what not else makes rare:
    They rain against our much-thick and marsh air
Rich beams, till death or distance buys them quite.

Death or distance soon consumes them: wind,
    What most I may eye after, be in at the end
I cannot, and out of sight is out of mind.

Christ minds: Christ's interest, what to avow or amend
    There, éyes them, heart wánts, care haúnts, foot fóllows kínd,
Their ránsom, théir rescue, ánd first, fást, last friénd.

41

The Loss of the Eurydice

Foundered March 24, 1878

THE Eurydice—it concerned thee, O Lord:
Three hundred souls, O alas! on board,
  Some asleep unawakened, all un-
warned, eleven fathoms fallen   4

Where she foundered! One stroke
Felled and furled them, the hearts of oak!
  And flockbells off the aerial
Downs' forefalls beat to the burial.   8

For did she pride her, freighted fully, on
Bounden bales or a hoard of bullion?—
  Precious passing measure,
Lads and men her lade and treasure.   12

She had come from a cruise, training seamen—
Men, boldboys soon to be men:
  Must it, worst weather,
Blast bole and bloom together?   16

No Atlantic squall overwrought her
Or rearing billow of the Biscay water:
  Home was hard at hand
And the blow bore from land.   20

And you were a liar, O blue March day.
Bright sun lanced fire in the heavenly bay;
  But what black Boreas wrecked her? he
Came equipped, deadly-electric,   24

A beetling baldbright cloud thorough England
Riding: there did storms not mingle? and
    Hailropes hustle and grind their
Heavengravel? wolfsnow, worlds of it, wind there?   28

Now Carisbrook keep goes under in gloom;
Now it overvaults Appledurcombe;
    Now near by Ventnor town
It hurls, hurls off Boniface Down.   32

Too proud, too proud, what a press she bore!
Royal, and all her royals wore.
    Sharp with her, shorten sail!
Too late; lost; gone with the gale.   36

This was that fell capsize.
As half she had righted and hoped to rise
    Death teeming in by her portholes
Raced down decks, round messes of mortals.   40

Then a lurch forward, frigate and men;
'All hands for themselves' the cry ran then;
    But she who had housed them thither
Was around them, bound them or wound them with her.   44

Marcus Hare, high her captain,
Kept to her—care-drowned and wrapped in
    Cheer's death, would follow
His charge through the champ-white water-in-a-wallow,   48

All under Channel to bury in a beach her
Cheeks: Right, rude of feature,
    He thought he heard say
'Her commander! and thou too, and thou this way.'   52

It is even seen, time's something server,
In mankind's medley a duty-swerver,
    At downright 'No or Yes?'
Doffs all, drives full for righteousness.   56

Sydney Fletcher, Bristol-bred,
(Low lie his mates now on watery bed)
    Takes to the seas and snows
As sheer down the ship goes.   60

Now her afterdraught gullies him too down;
Now he wrings for breath with the deathgush brown;
    Till a lifebelt and God's will
Lend him a lift from the sea-swill.   64

Now he shoots short up to the round air;
Now he gasps, now he gazes everywhere;
    But his eye no cliff, no coast or
Mark makes in the rivelling snowstorm.   68

Him, after an hour of wintry waves,
A schooner sights, with another, and saves,
    And he boards her in Oh! such joy
He has lost count what came next, poor boy.—   72

They say who saw one sea-corpse cold
He was all of lovely manly mould,
    Every inch a tar,
Of the best we boast our sailors are.   76

Look, foot to forelock, how all things suit! he
Is strung by duty, is strained to beauty,
    And brown-as-dawning-skinned
With brine and shine and whirling wind.   80

O his nimble finger, his gnarled grip!
Leagues, leagues of seamanship
    Slumber in these forsaken
Bones, this sinew, and will not waken.   84

He was but one like thousands more.
Day and night I deplore
    My people and born own nation,
Fast foundering own generation.   88

I might let bygones be—our curse
Of ruinous shrine no hand or, worse,
    Robbery's hand is busy to
Dress, hoar-hallowèd shrines unvisited;   92

Only the breathing temple and fleet
Life, this wildworth blown so sweet,
    These daredeaths, ay this crew, in
Unchrist, all rolled in ruin—   96

Deeply surely I need to deplore it,
Wondering why my master bore it,
    The riving off that race
So at home, time was, to his truth and grace   100

That a starlight-wender of ours would say
The marvellous Milk was Walsingham Way
    And one—but let be, let be:
More, more than was will yet be.—   104

O well wept, mother have lost son;
Wept, wife; wept, sweetheart would be one:
    Though grief yield them no good
Yet shed what tears sad truelove should.   108

But to Christ lord of thunder
Crouch; lay knee by earth low under:
   'Holiest, loveliest, bravest,
Save my hero, O Hero savest.   112

And the prayer thou hearst me making
Have, at the awful overtaking,
   Heard; have heard and granted
Grace that day grace was wanted.'   116

Not that hell knows redeeming,
But for souls sunk in seeming
   Fresh, till doomfire burn all,
Prayer shall fetch pity eternal.   120

42

The May Magnificat

MAY is Mary's month, and I
Muse at that and wonder why:
   Her feasts follow reason,
   Dated due to season—

Candlemas, Lady Day;
But the Lady Month, May,
   Why fasten that upon her,
   With a feasting in her honour?

Is it only its being brighter
Than the most are must delight her?
   Is it opportunest
   And flowers finds soonest?

Ask of her, the mighty mother:
Her reply puts this other
    Question: What is Spring?—
    Growth in everything—

Flesh and fleece, fur and feather,
Grass and greenworld all together;
    Star-eyed strawberry-breasted
    Throstle above her nested

Cluster of bugle blue eggs thin
Forms and warms the life within;
    And bird and blossom swell
    In sod or sheath or shell.

All things rising, all things sizing
Mary sees, sympathising
    With that world of good,
    Nature's motherhood.

Their magnifying of each its kind
With delight calls to mind
    How she did in her stored
    Magnify the Lord.

Well but there was more than this:
Spring's universal bliss
    Much, had much to say
    To offering Mary May.

When drop-of-blood-and-foam-dapple
Bloom lights the orchard-apple
    And thicket and thorp are merry
    With silver-surfèd cherry

And azuring-over greybell makes
Wood banks and brakes wash wet like lakes
    And magic cuckoocall
    Caps, clears, and clinches all—

This ecstasy all through mothering earth
Tells Mary her mirth till Christ's birth
    To remember and exultation
    In God who was her salvation.

43

Binsey Poplars
felled 1879

My aspens dear, whose airy cages quelled,
Quelled or quenched in leaves the leaping sun,
All felled, felled, are all felled;
    Of a fresh and following folded rank
        Not spared, not one
        That dandled a sandalled
      Shadow that swam or sank
On meadow and river and wind-wandering
    weed-winding bank.

O if we but knew what we do
      When we delve or hew—
    Hack and rack the growing green!
      Since country is so tender
    To touch, her being só slender,
    That, like this sleek and seeing ball
    But a prick will make no eye at all,

Where we, even where we mean
    To mend her we end her,
    When we hew or delve:
After-comers cannot guess the beauty been.
Ten or twelve, only ten or twelve
    Strokes of havoc únselve
    The sweet especial scene,
    Rural scene, a rural scene,
    Sweet especial rural scene.

44

Duns Scotus's Oxford

TOWERY city and branchy between towers;
Cuckoo-echoing, bell-swarmèd, lark-charmèd, rook-racked,
    river-rounded;
The dapple-eared lily below thee; that country and town did
Once encounter in, here coped and poisèd powers;

Thou hast a base and brickish skirt there, sours
That neighbour-nature thy grey beauty is grounded
Best in; graceless growth, thou hast confounded
Rural rural keeping—folk, flocks, and flowers.

Yet ah! this air I gather and I release
He lived on; these weeds and waters, these walls are what
He haunted who of all men most sways my spirits to peace;

Of realty the rarest-veinèd unraveller; a not
Rivalled insight, be rival Italy or Greece;
Who fired France for Mary without spot.

45

Henry Purcell

The poet wishes well to the divine genius of Purcell and praises him that, whereas other musicians have given utterance to the moods of man's mind, he has, beyond that, uttered in notes the very make and species of man as created both in him and in all men generally.

HAVE fair fallen, O fair, fair have fallen, so dear
To me, so arch-especial a spirit as heaves in Henry Purcell,
An age is now since passed, since parted; with the reversal
Of the outward sentence low lays him, listed to a heresy, here.

Not mood in him nor meaning, proud fire or sacred fear,
Or love, or pity, or all that sweet notes not his might nursle:
It is the forgèd feature finds me; it is the rehearsal
Of own, of abrúpt sélf there so thrusts on, so throngs the ear.

Let him oh! with his air of angels then lift me, lay me! only I'll
Have an eye to the sakes of him, quaint moonmarks, to his
    pelted plumage under
Wings: so some great stormfowl, whenever he has walked his
    while

The thunder-purple seabeach, plumèd purple-of-thunder,
If a wuthering of his palmy snow-pinions scatter a colossal
    smile
Off him, but meaning motion fans fresh our wits with wonder.

46

The Candle Indoors

SOME candle clear burns somewhere I come by.
I muse at how its being puts blissful back
With yellowy moisture mild night's blear-all black
Or to-fro tender trambeams truckle at the eye.

By that window what task what fingers ply,
I plod wondering, a-wanting, just for lack
Of answer the eagerer a-wanting Jessy or Jack
There / God to aggrándise, God to glorify.—

Come you indoors, come home; your fading fire
Mend first and vital candle in close heart's vault:
You there are master, do your own desire;

What hinders? Are you beam-blind, yet to a fault
In a neighbour deft-handed? Are you that liar
And, cast by conscience out, spendsavour salt?

47

The Handsome Heart:

at a Gracious Answer

'BUT tell me, child, your choice; what shall I buy
You?'—'Father, what you buy me I like best.'
With the sweetest air that said, still plied and pressed,
He swung to his first poised purport of reply.

What the heart is! which, like carriers let fly—
Doff darkness, homing nature knows the rest—
To its own fine function, wild and self-instressed,
Falls light as ten years long taught how to and why.

81

Mannerly-hearted! more than handsome face—
Beauty's bearing or muse of mounting vein,
All, in this case, bathed in high hallowing grace . . .

Of heaven what boon to buy you, boy, or gain
Not granted?—Only . . . O on that path you pace
Run all your race, O brace sterner that strain!

48

The Bugler's First Communion

A BUGLER boy from barrack (it is over the hill
There)—boy bugler, born, he tells me, of Irish
        Mother to an English sire (he
Shares their best gifts surely, fall how things will),

This very very day came down to us after a boon he on
My late being there begged of me, overflowing
        Boon in my bestowing,
Came, I say, this day to it—to a First Communion.

Here he knelt then ín regimental red.
Forth Christ from cupboard fetched, how fain I of feet
        To his youngster take his treat!
Low-latched in leaf-light housel his too huge godhead.

There! and your sweetest sendings, ah divine,
By it, heavens, befall him! as a heart Christ's darling, dauntless;
        Tongue true, vaunt- and tauntless;
Breathing bloom of a chastity in mansex fine.

Frowning and forefending angel-warder
Squander the hell-rook ranks sally to molest him;
        March, kind comrade, abreast him;
Dress his days to a dexterous and starlight order.

How it dóes my heart good, visiting at that bleak hill,
When limber liquid youth, that to all I teach
　　　Yields tender as a pushed peach,
Hies headstrong to its wellbeing of a self-wise self-will!

Then though I should tread tufts of consolation
Dáys áfter, só I in a sort deserve to
　　　And do serve God to serve to
Just such slips of soldiery Christ's royal ration.

Nothing élse is like it, no, not all so strains
Us: freshyouth fretted in a bloomfall all portending
　　　That sweet's sweeter ending;
Realm both Christ is heir to and thére réigns.

O now well work that sealing sacred ointment!
O for now charms, arms, what bans off bad
　　　And locks love ever in a lad!
Let mé though see no more of him, and not disappointment

Those sweet hopes quell whose least me quickenings lift,
In scarlet or somewhere of some day seeing
　　　That brow and bead of being,
An our day's God's own Galahad. Though this child's drift

Seems by a divíne doom chánnelled, nor do I cry
Disaster there; but may he not rankle and roam
　　　In backwheels though bound home?—
That left to the Lord of the Eucharist, I here lie by;

Recorded only, I have put my lips on pleas
Would brandle adamantine heaven with ride and jar, did
　　　Prayer go disregarded:
Forward-like, but however, and like favourable heaven heard
　　these.

49

Morning, Midday, and Evening Sacrifice

THE dappled die-away
Cheek and the wimpled lip,
The gold-wisp, the airy-grey
Eye, all in fellowship—
This, all this beauty blooming,
This, all this freshness fuming,
Give God while worth consuming.

Both thought and thew now bolder
And told by Nature: Tower;
Head, heart, hand, heel, and shoulder
That beat and breathe in power—
This pride of prime's enjoyment
Take as for tool, not toy meant
And hold at Christ's employment.

The vault and scope and schooling
And mastery in the mind,
In silk-ash kept from cooling,
And ripest under rind—
What death half lifts the latch of,
What hell hopes soon the snatch of,
Your offering, with despatch, of!

50

Andromeda

Now Time's Andromeda on this rock rude,
With not her either beauty's equal or
Her injury's, looks off by both horns of shore,
Her flower, her piece of being, doomed dragon food.

Time past she has been attempted and pursued
By many blows and banes; but now hears roar
A wilder beast from West than all were, more
Rife in her wrongs, more lawless, and more lewd.

Her Perseus linger and leave her tó her extremes?—
Pillowy air he treads a time and hangs
His thoughts on her, forsaken that she seems,

All while her patience, morselled into pangs,
Mounts; then to alight disarming, no one dreams,
With Gorgon's gear and barebill / thongs and fangs.

51

Peace

WHEN will you ever, Peace, wild wooddove, shy wings shut,
Your round me roaming end, and under be my boughs?
When, when, Peace, will you, Peace?—I'll not play hypocrite

To own my heart: I yield you do come sometimes; but
That piecemeal peace is poor peace. What pure peace allows
Alarms of wars, the daunting wars, the death of it?

O surely, reaving Peace, my Lord should leave in lieu
Some good! And so he does leave Patience exquisite,
That plumes to Peace thereafter. And when Peace here does
    house
He comes with work to do, he does not come to coo,
            He comes to brood and sit.

52

At the Wedding March

God with honour hang your head,
Groom, and grace you, bride, your bed
With lissome scions, sweet scions,
Out of hallowed bodies bred.

Each be other's comfort kind:
Déep, déeper than divined,
Divine charity, dear charity,
Fast you ever, fast bind.

Then let the March tread our ears:
I to him turn with tears
Who to wedlock, his wonder wedlock,
Déals tríumph and immortal years.

53

Felix Randal

Felix Randal the farrier, O is he dead then? my duty all
    ended,
Who have watched his mould of man, big-boned and hardy-
    handsome
Pining, pining, till time when reason rambled in it and some
Fatal four disorders, fleshed there, all contended?

Sickness broke him. Impatient, he cursed at first, but mended
Being anointed and all; though a heavenlier heart began some
Months earlier, since I had our sweet reprieve and ransom
Tendered to him. Ah well, God rest him all road ever he
    offended!

This seeing the sick endears them to us, us too it endears.
My tongue had taught thee comfort, touch had quenched thy
tears,
Thy tears that touched my heart, child, Felix, poor Felix
Randal;

How far from then forethought of, all thy more boisterous
years,
When thou at the random grim forge, powerful amidst peers,
Didst fettle for the great grey drayhorse his bright and battering
sandal!

54

Brothers

How lovely the elder brother's
Life all laced in the other's,
Lóve-laced!—what once I well
Witnessed; so fortune fell.
When Shrovetide, two years gone,   5
Our boys' plays brought on
Part was picked for John,
Young Jóhn; then fear, then joy
Ran revel in the elder boy.
Now the night come, all   10
Our company thronged the hall;
Henry, by the wall,
Beckoned me beside him:
I came where called, and eyed him
By meanwhiles; making mý play   15
Turn most on tender byplay.
For, wrung all on love's rack,
My lad, and lost in Jack,
Smiled, blushed, and bit his lip;
Or drove, with a diver's dip,   20

Clutched hands through claspèd knees;
And many a mark like these,
Told tales with what heart's stress
He hung on the imp's success.
Now the other was bráss-bóld: 25
Hé had no work to hold
His heart up at the strain;
Nay, roguish ran the vein.
Two tedious acts were past;
Jack's call and cue at last; 30
When Henry, heart-forsook,
Dropped eyes and dared not look.
Thére! the háll rúng!
Dog, he did give tongue!
But Harry—in his hands he has flung 35
His tear-tricked cheeks of flame
For fond love and for shame.

    Ah Nature, framed in fault,
There's comfort then, there's salt;
Nature, bad, base, and blind, 40
Dearly thou canst be kind;
There dearly thén, deárly,
Dearly thou canst be kind.

55

Spring and Fall:
to a young child

MÁRGARÉT, áre you gríeving
Over Goldengrove unleaving?
Leáves, líke the things of man, you
With your fresh thoughts care for, can you?

Áh! ás the heart grows older
It will come to such sights colder
By and by, nor spare a sigh
Though worlds of wanwood leafmeal lie;
And yet you *will* weep and know why.
Now no matter, child, the name:
Sórrow's spríngs áre the same.
Nor mouth had, no nor mind, expressed
What heart heard of, ghost guessed:
It ís the blight man was born for,
It is Margaret you mourn for.

56

Inversnaid

THIS darksome burn, horseback brown,
His rollrock highroad roaring down,
In coop and in comb the fleece of his foam
Flutes and low to the lake falls home.

A windpuff-bonnet of fáwn-fróth
Turns and twindles over the broth
Of a pool so pitchblack, féll-frówning,
It rounds and rounds Despair to drowning.

Degged with dew, dappled with dew
Are the groins of the braes that the brook treads through,
Wiry heathpacks, flitches of fern,
And the beadbonny ash that sits over the burn.

What would the world be, once bereft
Of wet and of wildness? Let them be left,
O let them be left, wildness and wet;
Long live the weeds and the wilderness yet.

57

As kingfishers catch fire, dragonflies draw flame;
　　As tumbled over rim in roundy wells
　　Stones ring; like each tucked string tells, each hung bell's
Bow swung finds tongue to fling out broad its name;
Each mortal thing does one thing and the same:
　　Deals out that being indoors each one dwells;
　　Selves—goes itself; *myself* it speaks and spells,
Crying *What I do is me: for that I came.*

Í say more: the just man justices;
　　Keeps gráce: thát keeps all his goings graces;
Acts in God's eye what in God's eye he is—
　　Chríst. For Christ plays in ten thousand places,
Lovely in limbs, and lovely in eyes not his
　　To the Father through the features of men's faces.

58

Ribblesdale

EARTH, sweet Earth, sweet landscape, with leavès throng
And louchèd low grass, heaven that dost appeal
To, with no tongue to plead, no heart to feel;
That canst but only be, but dost that long—

Thou canst but be, but that thou well dost; strong
Thy plea with him who dealt, nay does now deal,
Thy lovely dale down thus and thus bids reel
Thy river, and o'er gives all to rack or wrong.

And what is Earth's eye, tongue, or heart else, where
Else, but in dear and dogged man?—Ah, the heir
To his own selfbent so bound, so tied to his turn,

To thriftless reave both our rich round world bare
And none reck of world after, this bids wear
Earth brows of such care, care and dear concern.

<h1 style="text-align:center">59</h1>

The Leaden Echo and the Golden Echo

(Maidens' song from St. Winefred's Well)

THE LEADEN ECHO

How to kéep—is there ány any, is there none such, nowhere
    known some, bow or brooch or braid or brace, láce,
    latch or catch or key to keep
Back beauty, keep it, beauty, beauty, beauty, . . . from vanish-
    ing away?
Ó is there no frowning of these wrinkles, rankèd wrinkles
    deep,
Dówn? no waving off of these most mournful messengers,
    still messengers, sad and stealing messengers of grey?—
No there 's none, there 's none, O no there 's none,
Nor can you long be, what you now are, called fair,
Do what you may do, what, do what you may,
And wisdom is early to despair:
Be beginning; since, no, nothing can be done
To keep at bay   10
Age and age's evils, hoar hair,
Ruck and wrinkle, drooping, dying, death's worst, winding
    sheets, tombs and worms and tumbling to decay;
So be beginning, be beginning to despair.
O there 's none; no no no there 's none:
Be beginning to despair, to despair,
Despair, despair, despair, despair.

Spare!

There ís one, yes I have one (Hush there!),
Only not within seeing of the sun.
Not within the singeing of the strong sun,
Tall sun's tingeing, or treacherous the tainting of the earth's
    air,
Somewhere elsewhere there is ah well where! one,
Óne. Yes I cán tell such a key, I dó know such a place,
Where whatever's prizèd and passes of us, everything that's
    fresh and fast flying of us, seems to us sweet of us and
    swiftly away with, done away with, undone,
Undone, done with, soon done with, and yet dearly and
    dangerously sweet
Of us, the wimpled water-dimpled, not-by-morning-matchèd
    face,   10
The flower of beauty, fleece of beauty, too too apt to, ah! to
    fleet,
Never fleets móre, fastened with the tenderest truth
To its own best being and its loveliness of youth: it is an ever-
    lastingness of, O it is an all youth!
Come then, your ways and airs and looks, locks, maidengear,
    gallantry and gaiety and grace,
Winning ways, airs innocent, maiden manners, sweet looks,
    loose locks, long locks, lovelocks, gaygear, going gallant,
    girlgrace—
Resign them, sign them, seal them, send them, motion them
    with breath,
And with sighs soaring, soaring síghs, deliver
Them; beauty-in-the-ghost, deliver it, early now, long before
    death
Give beauty back, beauty, beauty, beauty, back to God,
    beauty's self and beauty's giver.
See; not a hair is, not an eyelash, not the least lash lost; every
    hair   20
Is, hair of the head, numbered.

Nay, what we had lighthanded left in surly the mere mould
Will have waked and have waxed and have walked with the
     wind what while we slept,
This side, that side hurling a heavyheaded hundredfold
What while we, while we slumbered.
O then, weary then whý should we tread? O why are we so
     haggard at the heart, so care-coiled, care-killed, so fagged,
     so fashed, so cogged, so cumbered,
When the thing we freely fórfeit is kept with fonder a care,
Fonder a care kept than we could have kept it, kept
Far with fonder a care (and we, we should have lost it) finer,
     fonder
A care kept.—Where kept? do but tell us where kept, where.—
Yonder.—What high as that! We follow, now we follow.—
     Yonder, yes yonder, yonder,   31
Yonder.

60

The Blessed Virgin compared to the Air
we Breathe

    WILD air, world-mothering air,
    Nestling me everywhere,
    That each eyelash or hair
    Girdles; goes home betwixt
    The fleeciest, frailest-flixed
    Snowflake; that's fairly mixed
    With, riddles, and is rife
    In every least thing's life;

This needful, never spent,
And nursing element;   10
My more than meat and drink,
My meal at every wink;
This air, which, by life's law,
My lung must draw and draw
Now but to breathe its praise,
Minds me in many ways
Of her who not only
Gave God's infinity
Dwindled to infancy
Welcome in womb and breast,   20
Birth, milk, and all the rest
But mothers each new grace
That does now reach our race—
Mary Immaculate,
Merely a woman, yet
Whose presence, power is
Great as no goddess's
Was deemèd, dreamèd; who
This one work has to do—
Let all God's glory through,   30
God's glory which would go
Through her and from her flow
Off, and no way but so.
    I say that we are wound
With mercy round and round
As if with air: the same
Is Mary, more by name.
She, wild web, wondrous robe,
Mantles the guilty globe,
Since God has let dispense   40
Her prayers his providence:
Nay, more than almoner,
The sweet alms' self is her

94

And men are meant to share
Her life as life does air.
　　If I have understood,
She holds high motherhood
Towards all our ghostly good
And plays in grace her part
About man's beating heart,　　　　50
Laying, like air's fine flood,
The deathdance in his blood;
Yet no part but what will
Be Christ our Saviour still.
Of her flesh he took flesh:
He does take fresh and fresh,
Though much the mystery how,
Not flesh but spirit now
And makes, O marvellous!
New Nazareths in us,　　　　60
Where she shall yet conceive
Him, morning, noon, and eve;
New Bethlems, and he born
There, evening, noon, and morn—
Bethlem or Nazareth,
Men here may draw like breath
More Christ and baffle death;
Who, born so, comes to be
New self and nobler me
In each one and each one　　　　70
More makes, when all is done,
Both God's and Mary's Son.
　　Again, look overhead
How air is azurèd;
O how! Nay do but stand
Where you can lift your hand
Skywards: rich, rich it laps
Round the four fingergaps.
Yet such a sapphire-shot,

Charged, steepèd sky will not   80
Stain light. Yea, mark you this:
It does no prejudice.
The glass-blue days are those
When every colour glows,
Each shape and shadow shows.
Blue be it: this blue heaven
The seven or seven times seven
Hued sunbeam will transmit
Perfect, not alter it.
Or if there does some soft,   90
On things aloof, aloft,
Bloom breathe, that one breath more
Earth is the fairer for.
Whereas did air not make
This bath of blue and slake
His fire, the sun would shake,
A blear and blinding ball
With blackness bound, and all
The thick stars round him roll
Flashing like flecks of coal,   100
Quartz-fret, or sparks of salt,
In grimy vasty vault.
     So God was god of old:
A mother came to mould
Those limbs like ours which are
What must make our daystar
Much dearer to mankind;
Whose glory bare would blind
Or less would win man's mind.
Through her we may see him   110
Made sweeter, not made dim,
And her hand leaves his light
Sifted to suit our sight.
     Be thou then, O thou dear
Mother, my atmosphere;

My happier world, wherein
To wend and meet no sin;
Above me, round me lie
Fronting my froward eye
With sweet and scarless sky;   120
Stir in my ears, speak there
Of God's love, O live air,
Of patience, penance, prayer:
Worldmothering air, air wild,
Wound with thee, in thee isled,
Fold home, fast fold thy child.

61

Spelt from Sibyl's Leaves

EARNEST, earthless, equal, attuneable, ' vaulty, voluminous,
 . . . stupendous
Evening strains to be tíme's vást, ' womb-of-all, home-of-all,
 hearse-of-all night.
Her fond yellow hornlight wound to the west, ' her wild
 hollow hoarlight hung to the height
Waste; her earliest stars, earlstars, ' stárs principal, overbend
 us,
Fíre-féaturing heaven. For earth ' her being has unbound; her
 dapple is at end, as-
tray or aswarm, all throughther, in throngs; ' self ín self
 steepèd and páshed—qúite
Disremembering, dísmémbering ' áll now. Heart, you round
 me right
With: Óur évening is over us; óur night ' whélms, whélms,
 ánd will end us.

97

Only the beakleaved boughs dragonish ǀ damask the tool-
smooth bleak light; black,
Ever so black on it. Óur tale, O óur oracle! ǀ Lét life, wáned,
ah lét life wind
Off hér once skéined stained véined varíety ǀ upon, áll on twó
spools; párt, pen, páck
Now her áll in twó flocks, twó folds—black, white; ǀ right,
wrong; reckon but, reck but, mind
But thése two; wáre of a wórld where bút these ǀ twó tell, each
off the óther; of a rack
Where, selfwrung, selfstrung, sheathe- and shelterless,ǀ thóughts
agaínst thoughts ín groans grínd.

62

To what serves Mortal Beauty?

To what serves mortal beauty ǀ —dangerous; does set danc-
ing blood—the O-seal-that-so ǀ feature, flung prouder form
Than Purcell tune lets tread to? ǀ See: it does this: keeps warm
Men's wits to the things that are; ǀ what good means—where a
glance
Master more may than gaze, ǀ gaze out of countenance.
Those lovely lads once, wet-fresh ǀ windfalls of war's storm,
How then should Gregory, a father, ǀ have gleanèd else from
swarm-
èd Rome? But God to a nation ǀ dealt that day's dear chance.
To man, that needs would worship ǀ block or barren stone,
Our law says: Love what are ǀ love's worthiest, were all known;
World's loveliest—men's selves. Self ǀ flashes off frame and
face.
What do then? how meet beauty? ǀ Merely meet it; own,
Home at heart, heaven's sweet gift; ǀ then leave, let that alone.
Yea, wish that though, wish all, ǀ God's better beauty, grace.

63

(The Soldier)

Yes. Whý do we áll, seeing of a soldier, bless him? bless
Our redcoats, our tars? Both these being, the greater part,
But frail clay, nay but foul clay. Here it is: the heart,
Since, proud, it calls the calling manly, gives a guess
That, hopes that, makesbelieve, the men must be no less;
It fancies, feigns, deems, dears the artist after his art;
And fain will find as sterling all as all is smart,
And scarlet wear the spirit of wár thére express.
Mark Christ our King. He knows war, served this soldiering
     through;
He of all can reeve a rope best. There he bides in bliss
Now, and séeing somewhére some mán do all that man can do,
For love he leans forth, needs his neck must fall on, kiss,
And cry 'O Christ-done deed! So God-made-flesh does too:
Were I come o'er again' cries Christ 'it should be this'.

64

(Carrion Comfort)

Nót, I'll not, carrion comfort, Despair, not feast on thee;
Not untwist—slack they may be—these last strands of man
In me ór, most weary, cry I can no more. I can;
Can something, hope, wish day come, not choose not to be.

But ah, but O thou terrible, why wouldst thou rude on me
Thy wring-world right foot rock? lay a lionlimb against me?
     scan
With darksome devouring eyes my bruisèd bones? and fan,
O in turns of tempest, me heaped there; me frantic to avoid
     thee and flee?

Why? That my chaff might fly; my grain lie, sheer and clear.
Nay in all that toil, that coil, since (seems) I kissed the rod,
Hand rather, my heart lo! lapped strength, stole joy, would
    laugh, chéer.
Cheer whom though? The hero whose heaven-handling flung
    me, fóot tród
Me? or me that fought him? O which one? is it each one?
    That night, that year
Of now done darkness I wretch lay wrestling with (my God!)
    my God.

65

No worst, there is none. Pitched past pitch of grief,
More pangs will, schooled at forepangs, wilder wring.
Comforter, where, where is your comforting?
Mary, mother of us, where is your relief?
My cries heave, herds-long; huddle in a main, a chief-
woe, world-sorrow; on an age-old anvil wince and sing—
Then lull, then leave off. Fury had shrieked 'No ling-
ering! Let me be fell: force I must be brief'.
O the mind, mind has mountains; cliffs of fall
Frightful, sheer, no-man-fathomed. Hold them cheap
May who ne'er hung there. Nor does long our small
Durance deal with that steep or deep. Here! creep,
Wretch, under a comfort serves in a whirlwind: all
Life death does end and each day dies with sleep.

66

To seem the stranger lies my lot, my life
Among strangers. Father and mother dear,
Brothers and sisters are in Christ not near
And he my peace/my parting, sword and strife.

England, whose honour O all my heart woos, wife
To my creating thought, would neither hear
Me, were I pleading, plead nor do I: I wear-
y of idle a being but by where wars are rife.

I am in Ireland now; now I am at a thírd
Remove. Not but in all removes I can
Kind love both give and get. Only what word

Wisest my heart breeds dark heaven's baffling ban
Bars or hell's spell thwarts. This to hoard unheard,
Heard unheeded, leaves me a lonely began.

67

I WAKE and feel the fell of dark, not day.
What hours, O what black hoürs we have spent
This night! what sights you, heart, saw; ways you went!
And more must, in yet longer light's delay.

With witness I speak this. But where I say
Hours I mean years, mean life. And my lament
Is cries countless, cries like dead letters sent
To dearest him that lives alas! away.

I am gall, I am heartburn. God's most deep decree
Bitter would have me taste: my taste was me;
Bones built in me, flesh filled, blood brimmed the curse.

Selfyeast of spirit a dull dough sours. I see
The lost are like this, and their scourge to be
As I am mine, their sweating selves; but worse.

68

PATIENCE, hard thing! the hard thing but to pray,
But bid for, Patience is! Patience who asks
Wants war, wants wounds; weary his times, his tasks;
To do without, take tosses, and obey.

Rare patience roots in these, and, these away,
Nowhere. Natural heart's-ivy Patience masks
Our ruins of wrecked past purpose. There she basks
Purple eyes and seas of liquid leaves all day.

We hear our hearts grate on themselves: it kills
To bruise them dearer. Yet the rebellious wills
Of us we do bid God bend to him even so.

And where is he who more and more distills
Delicious kindness?—He is patient. Patience fills
His crisp combs, and that comes those ways we know.

69

MY own heart let me more have pity on; let
Me live to my sad self hereafter kind,
Charitable; not live this tormented mind
With this tormented mind tormenting yet.

I cast for comfort I can no more get
By groping round my comfortless, than blind
Eyes in their dark can day or thirst can find
Thirst's all-in-all in all a world of wet.

Soul, self; come, poor Jackself, I do advise
You, jaded, let be; call off thoughts awhile
Elsewhere; leave comfort root-room; let joy size

At God knows when to God knows what; whose smile
's not wrung, see you; unforeseen times rather—as skies
Betweenpie mountains—lights a lovely mile.

70

Tom's Garland:

upon the Unemployed

TOM—garlanded with squat and surly steel
Tom; then Tom's fallowbootfellow piles pick
By him and rips out rockfire homeforth—sturdy Dick;
Tom Heart-at-ease, Tom Navvy: he is all for his meal
Sure, 's bed now. Low be it: lustily he his low lot (feel
That ne'er need hunger, Tom; Tom seldom sick,
Seldomer heartsore; that treads through, prickproof, thick
Thousands of thorns, thoughts) swings though. Commonweal
Little I reck ho! lacklevel in, if all had bread:
What! Country is honour enough in all us—lordly head,
With heaven's lights high hung round, or, mother-ground
That mammocks, mighty foot. But nó way sped,
Nor mind nor mainstrength; gold go garlanded
With, perilous, O nó; nor yet plod safe shod sound;
　　　　　　Undenizened, beyond bound
Of earth's glory, earth's ease, all; no one, nowhere,
In wide the world's weal; rare gold, bold steel, bare
　　　　　　In both; care, but share care—
This, by Despair, bred Hangdog dull; by Rage,
Manwolf, worse; and their packs infest the age.

Harry Ploughman

HARD as hurdle arms, with a broth of goldish flue
Breathed round; the rack of ribs; the scooped flank; lank
Rope-over thigh; knee-nave; and barrelled shank—
      Head and foot, shoulder and shank—
By a grey eye's heed steered well, one crew, fall to;
Stand at stress. Each limb's barrowy brawn, his thew
That onewhere curded, onewhere sucked or sank—
      Soared ór sánk—,
Though as a beechbole firm, finds his, as at a rollcall, rank
And features, in flesh, what deed he each must do—
      His sinew-service where do.

He leans to it, Harry bends, look. Back, elbow, and liquid
      waist
In him, all quail to the wallowing o' the plough. 'S check
      crimsons; curls
Wag or crossbridle, in a wind lifted, windlaced—
      See his wind- lilylocks -laced;
Churlsgrace too, child of Amansstrength, how it hangs or
      hurls
Them—broad in bluff hide his frowning feet lashed! raced
With, along them, cragiron under and cold furls—
      With-a-fountain's shining-shot furls.

That Nature is a Heraclitean Fire and of the comfort of the Resurrection

CLOUD-PUFFBALL, torn tufts, tossed pillows ˈ flaunt forth, then chevy on an air-
built thoroughfare: heaven-roysterers, in gay-gangs ˈ they throng; they glitter in marches.
Down roughcast, down dazzling whitewash, ˈ wherever an elm arches,
Shivelights and shadowtackle in long ˈ lashes lace, lance, and pair.
Delightfully the bright wind boisterous ˈ ropes, wrestles, beats earth bare
Of yestertempest's creases; ˈ in pool and rutpeel parches
Squandering ooze to squeezed ˈ dough, crust, dust; stanches, starches
Squadroned masks and manmarks ˈ treadmire toil there
Footfretted in it. Million-fuelèd, ˈ nature's bonfire burns on.
But quench her bonniest, dearest ˈ to her, her clearest-selvèd spark
Man, how fast his firedint, ˈ his mark on mind, is gone!
Both are in an unfathomable, all is in an enormous dark
Drowned. O pity and indig ˈ nation! Manshape, that shone
Sheer off, disseveral, a star, ˈ death blots black out; nor mark
       Is any of him at all so stark
But vastness blurs and time ˈ beats level. Enough! the Resur-rection,
A heart's-clarion! Away grief's gasping, ˈ joyless days, dejection.
          Across my foundering deck shone
A beacon, an eternal beam. ˈ Flesh fade, and mortal trash
Fall to the residuary worm; ˈ world's wildfire, leave but ash:

In a flash, at a trumpet crash,
I am all at once what Christ is, ¦ since he was what I am, and
This Jack, joke, poor potsherd, ¦ patch, matchwood, immortal
    diamond,
                    Is immortal diamond.

73

In honour of

St. Alphonsus Rodriguez

Laybrother of the Society of Jesus

HONOUR is flashed off exploit, so we say;
And those strokes once that gashed flesh or galled shield
Should tongue that time now, trumpet now that field,
And, on the fighter, forge his glorious day.
On Christ they do and on the martyr may;
But be the war within, the brand we wield
Unseen, the heroic breast not outward-steeled,
Earth hears no hurtle then from fiercest fray.
Yet God (that hews mountain and continent,
Earth, all, out; who, with trickling increment,
Veins violets and tall trees makes more and more)
Could crowd career with conquest while there went
Those years and years by of world without event
That in Majorca Alfonso watched the door.

74

Justus quidem tu es, Domine, si disputem tecum; verumtamen
justa loquar ad te: Quare via impiorum prosperatur? &c.

  THOU art indeed just, Lord, if I contend
  With thee; but, sir, so what I plead is just.
  Why do sinners' ways prosper? and why must
  Disappointment all I endeavour end?

Wert thou my enemy, O thou my friend,
How wouldst thou worse, I wonder, than thou dost
Defeat, thwart me? Oh, the sots and thralls of lust
Do in spare hours more thrive than I that spend,

Sir, life upon thy cause. See, banks and brakes
Now, leavèd how thick! lacèd they are again
With fretty chervil, look, and fresh wind shakes

Them; birds build—but not I build; no, but strain,
Time's eunuch, and not breed one work that wakes.
Mine, O thou lord of life, send my roots rain.

75

THE shepherd's brow, fronting forked lightning, owns
The horror and the havoc and the glory
Of it. Angels fall, they are towers, from heaven—a story
Of just, majestical, and giant groans.
But man—we, scaffold of score brittle bones;
Who breathe, from groundlong babyhood to hoary
Age gasp; whose breath is our *memento mori*—
What bass is *our* viol for tragic tones?
He! Hand to mouth he lives, and voids with shame;
And, blazoned in however bold the name,
Man Jack the man is, just; his mate a hussy.
And I that die these deaths, that feed this flame,
That...in smooth spoons spy life's masque mirrored: tame
My tempests there, my fire and fever fussy.

7

76

To R. B.

THE fine delight that fathers thought; the strong
Spur, live and lancing like the blowpipe flame,
Breathes once and, quenchèd faster than it came,
Leaves yet the mind a mother of immortal song.

Nine months she then, nay years, nine years she long
Within her wears, bears, cares and combs the same:
The widow of an insight lost she lives, with aim
Now known and hand at work now never wrong.

Sweet fire the sire of muse, my soul needs this;
I want the one rapture of an inspiration.
O then if in my lagging lines you miss

The roll, the rise, the carol, the creation,
My winter world, that scarcely breathes that bliss
Now, yields you, with some sighs, our explanation.

UNFINISHED POEMS
FRAGMENTS
LIGHT VERSE
&c.

(1862–89)

A. Poems written 1862–68

77

Il Mystico

HENCE sensual gross desires,
Right offspring of your grimy mother Earth!
　My Spirit hath a birth
Alien from yours as heaven from Nadir-fires:
　You rank and reeking things,
Scoop you from teeming filth some sickly hovel,
　And there for ever grovel
'Mid fever'd fumes and slime and cakèd clot:
　But foul and cumber not
The shaken plumage of my Spirit's wings.　　　　10
　But come, thou balm to aching soul,
　Of pointed wing and silver stole,
　With heavenly cithern from high choir,
　Tresses dipp'd in rainbow fire,
　An olive-branch whence richly reek
　Earthless dews on ancles sleek;
　Be discover'd to my sight
　From a haze of sapphire light,
　Let incense hang across the room
　And sober lustres take the gloom;　　　　20
　Come when night clings to what is hers
　Closer because faint morning stirs;
　When chill woods wake and think of morn,
　But sleep again ere day be born;
　When sick men turn, and lights are low,
　And death falls gently as the snow;

When wholesome spirits rustle about,
And the tide of ill is out;
When waking hearts can pardon much
And hard men feel a softening touch;   30
When strangely loom all shapes that be,
And watches change upon the sea;
Silence holds breath upon her throne,
And the waked stars are all alone.

   Come because then most thinly lies
The veil that covers mysteries;
And soul is subtle and flesh weak
And pride is nerveless and hearts meek.

     .   .   .   .   .

Touch me and purify, and shew
Some of the secrets I would know.   40

     .   .   .   .   .

Grant that close-folded peace that clad
The seraph brows of Galahad,
Who knew the inner spirit that fills
Questioning winds around the hills;
Who made conjecture nearest far
To what the chords of angels are;
And to the mystery of those Things

     .   .   .   .   .

Shewn to Ezekiel's open'd sight
On Chebar's banks, and why they went
Unswerving through the firmament;   50
Whose ken through amber of dark eyes
Went forth to compass mysteries;
Who knowing all the sins and sores
That nest within close-barrèd doors,
And that grief masters joy on earth,
Yet found unstinted place for mirth;

112

Who could forgive without grudge after
Gross mind discharging foulèd laughter;
To whom the common earth and air
Were limn'd about with radiance rare   60
Most like those hues that in the prism
Melt as from a heavenly chrism;
Who could keep silence, tho' the smart
Yawn'd like long furrow in the heart;

.   .   .

Or, like a lark to glide aloof
Under the cloud-festoonèd roof,
That with a turning of the wings
Light and darkness from him flings;
To drift in air, the circled earth
Spreading still its sunnèd girth;   70
To hear the sheep-bells dimly die
Till the lifted clouds were nigh;
In breezy belts of upper air
Melting into aether rare;
And when the silent height were won,
And all in lone air stood the sun,
To sing scarce heard, and singing fill
The airy empire at his will;
To hear his strain descend less loud
On to ledges of grey cloud;   80
And fainter, finer, trickle far
To where the listening uplands are;
To pause—then from his gurgling bill
Let the warbled sweetness rill,
And down the welkin, gushing free,
Hark the molten melody;
In fits of music till sunset
Starting the silver rivulet;
Sweetly then and of free act
To quench the fine-drawn cataract;   90

113

And in the dews beside his nest
To cool his plumy throbbing breast.
　Or, if a sudden silver shower
Has drench'd the molten sunset hour,
And with weeping cloud is spread
All the welkin overhead,
Save where the unvexèd west
Lies divinely still, at rest,
Where liquid heaven sapphire-pale
Does into amber splendours fail,　　　　　　100
And fretted clouds with burnish'd rim,
Phoebus' loosen'd tresses, swim;
While the sun streams forth amain
On the tumblings of the rain,
When his mellow smile he sees
Caught on the dank-ytressèd trees,
When the rainbow arching high
Looks from the zenith round the sky,
Lit with exquisite tints seven
Caught from angels' wings in heaven,　　　　110
Double, and higher than his wont,
The wrought rim of heaven's font,—
Then may I upwards gaze and see
The deepening intensity
Of the air-blended diadem,
All a sevenfold-single gem,
Each hue so rarely wrought that where
It melts, new lights arise as fair,
Sapphire, jacinth, chrysolite,
The rim with ruby fringes dight,　　　　　　120
Ending in sweet uncertainty
'Twixt real hue and phantasy.
Then while the rain-born arc glows higher
Westward on his sinking sire;
While the upgazing country seems
Touch'd from heaven in sweet dreams;

While a subtle spirit and rare
Breathes in the mysterious air;
While sheeny tears and sunlit mirth
Mix o'er the not unmovèd earth,—   130
Then would I fling me up to sip
Sweetness from the hour, and dip
Deeply in the archèd lustres,
And look abroad on sunny clusters
Of wringing tree-tops, chalky lanes,
Wheatfields tumbled with the rains,
Streaks of shadow, thistled leas,
Whence spring the jewell'd harmonies
That meet in mid-air; and be so
Melted in the dizzy bow   140
That I may drink that ecstacy
Which to pure souls alone may be . . . .

78

A Windy Day in Summer

THE vex'd elm-heads are pale with the view
Of a mastering heaven utterly blue;
Swoll'n is the wind that in argent billows
Rolls across the labouring willows;
The chestnut-fans are loosely flirting,
And bared is the aspen's silky skirting;
The sapphire pools are smit with white
And silver-shot with gusty light;
While the breeze by rank and measure
Paves the clouds on the swept azure.

79

A Fragment of Anything You Like

FAIR, but of fairness as a vision dream'd;
Dry were her sad eyes that would fain have stream'd;
She stood before a light not hers, and seem'd

The lorn Moon, pale with piteous dismay,
Who rising late had miss'd her painful way
In wandering until broad light of day;

Then was discover'd in the pathless sky
White-faced, as one in sad assay to fly
Who asks not life but only place to die.

80

Fragments of

Pilate

THE pang of Tartarus, Christians hold,
    Is this, from Christ to be shut out.
This outer cold, my exile from of old
    From God and man, is hell no doubt.
Would I could hear the other Pilates shout.
But yet they say Christ comes at the last day.
    Then will he keep in this stay?

2

Unchill'd I handle stinging snow;
   The sun whose vast afflictive heat
Does lay men low with one blade's sudden blow
   Cleaves not my brain, burns not my feet,
When the fierce skies are blue to black, albeit
The shearing rays contract me with their blaze
    Most dead-alive upon those days.

3

Then I seek out the shadow of stones
   And to those stones become akin
My several moans come distant in their tones
   As though they were not from within
And for that fearful hour life is more thin
And numbs and starves, as between icy wharves
    A freezing runnel sobs and dwarfs.

4

Sometimes I see the summit stake
   High up the balanced stony air
In whose dead lake even a voice may make
   The hanging snows rush down and bare
Their rocky lodges. Then the weather rare
Allows the sound of bells in hamlets round
    To come to me from the underground.

5

Often when winds impenitent
   Beat, heave and the strong mountain tire
I can stand pent in the monstrous element
   And feel no blast.—O fretful fire
Breathe o'er my bare nerve rather. I desire
They swathe and lace the shroud-plaits o'er my face,
    But to be ransom'd from this place.

6

Whatever time this vapourous roof,
    The screen of my captivity,
Folds off aloof, that signal is and proof
    Not of clear skies, but storm to be.
But then I make an eager shift to see
Houses that make abode beside the lake,
    And then my heart goes near to break.

7

Then clouds come, like ill-balanced crags,
    Shouldering. Down valleys smokes the gloom.
The thunder brags. In joints and sparkling jags
    The lightnings leap. The day of doom!
I cry 'O rocks and mountain make me room'
And yet I know it would be better so,
    Ay, sweet to taste beside this woe.

•   •   •   •

There is a day of all the year
    When life revisits me, nerve and vein.
They all come here and stand before me clear
    I try the Christus o'er again.
Sir! Christ! against this multitude I strain.—
Lord, but they cry so loud. And what am I?
    And all in one say 'Crucify!'

Before that rock, my seat, He stands;
    And then—I choke to tell this out—
I give commands for water for my hands;
    And some of those who stand about,—
Vespillo my centurion hacks out
Some ice that locks the glacier to the rocks
    And in a bason brings the blocks.

I choose one; but when I desire
    To wash before the multitude
The vital fire does suddenly retire
    From hands now clammy with strange blood.
My frenzied working is not understood.
Now I grow numb. My tongue strikes on the gum
    And cleaves, I struggle and am dumb.

    I hear the multitude tramp by.
    O here is the most piteous part,
For He whom I send forth to crucify,
    Whispers 'If thou have warmth at heart
Take courage; this shall need no further art.'

                    . . .

    I have a hope if so it be,
        A hope of an approved device;
I will break free from the Jews' company,
    And find a flint, a fang of ice,
Or fray a granite from the precipice:
When this is sought trees will be wanting not,
    And I shall shape one to my thought.

    Thus I shall make a cross, and in't
        Will add a footrest there to stand,
And with sharp flint will part my feet and dint
        The point fast in, and my left hand
Lock with my right; then knot a barken band
To hold me quite fix'd in the selfsame plight;
    And thus I will thrust in my right:—

    I'll take in hand the blady stone
        And to my palm the point apply,
And press it down, on either side a bone,
        With hope, with shut eyes, fixedly;
Thus crucified as I did crucify.

                    . . .

81

A Voice from the World

Fragments of 'An answer to Miss Rossetti's
Convent Threshold'[1]

At last I hear the voice well known;
Doubtless the voice: now fall'n, now spent,
Now coming from the alien eaves,—
You would not house beneath my own;
To alien eaves you fled and went,—
Now like the bird that shapes alone
A turn of seven notes or five,
When skies are hard as any stone,
The fall is o'er, told off the leaves,
'Tis marvel she is yet alive.   10
Once it was scarce perceivèd Lent
For orience of the daffodil;
Once, jostling thick, the bluebell sheaves
The peacock'd copse were known to fill;
Through other bars it used to thrill,
And carried me with ravishment,
Your signal, when apart we stood,
Tho' far or sick or heavy or still
Or thorn-engaged, impalèd and pent
With just such sweet-potential skill,   20
Late in the green weeks of April
Cuckoo calls cuckoo up the wood.
Five notes or seven, late and few.
From parts unlook'd-for, alter'd, spent
At last I hear the voice I knew.

. . . . .

[1] The text of *The Convent Threshold* is given in Appendix B, p. 346.

I plead: familiarness endears
My evil words thorny with pain:
I plead: and you will give your tears:
I plead: and ah! how much in vain!

. . . . . .

I know I mar my cause with words: 30
So be it; I must maim and mar.
Your comfort is as sharp as swords;
And I cry out for wounded love.
And you are gone so heavenly far
You hear nor care of love and pain.
My tears are but a cloud of rain;
My passion like a foolish wind
Lifts them a little way above.
But you, so spherèd, see no more—
You see but with a holier mind—   40
You hear and, alter'd, do not hear
Being a stoled apparel'd star.
You should have been with me as near
As halves of sweet-pea-blossom are;
But now are fled, and hard to find
As the last Pleiad, yea behind
Exilèd most remote El Khor.

. . . . . .

The love of women is not so strong,—
'Tis falsely given—as love in men;
A thing that weeps, enduring long: 50

But mine is dreadful leaping pain,
Phrenzy, but edged and clear of brain
Ruinous heart-beat, wandering, death.
I walk towards eve our walks again;
When lily-yellow is the west.
Say, o'er it hangs a water-cloud
And ravell'd into strings of rain.
At once I struggle with my breath.
'The light was so, the wind so loud
No louder, when I was with you.   60
Always the time remembereth
His very looks in other years,
Only with us is old and new.'
I fall, I tear and shower the weed,
I bite my hands, my looks I shroud;
My cry is like a bleat; a few
Intolerable tears I bleed.
Then is my misery full indeed:
I die, I die, I do not live.—
Alas! I rave, where calm is due;   70
I would remember. Love, forgive.
I cannot calm, I cannot heed.

I storm and shock you. So I fail.
And like a self-outwitted blast
Fling to the convent wicket fast.
Who would not shelter from the hail?
But is there a place for tenderness,
There was a charm would countervail
The spell of woe if any could.
Once in a drawer of Indian wood   80
You folded (did you not?) your dress.
The essence ne'er forgot the fold;
And I esteem'd the sandal good
And now I get some precious slips.

* . . . . upon you dreamed:
I [dream'd] my counterpart. It seem'd
[A bell] at midnight woke the town
[And all] into the Duomo ran:
You met me, I had hasten'd down:
That night the judgment day began: 90
'Twas said of none but all men knew:
Nocturns I thought were hurried through.
Some knelt, some stood: I seem'd to feel
Who knelt were for the Lord's right hand;
They are the goats who stand, said I.
I stood; but does she stand or kneel?
I strove to look; I lost the trick
Of nerve; the clammy ball was dry.
Then came the benediction.
His lips moved fast in sense too thick!   100
The others heard; I could not hear
Him . . . .†
Save me: and you were standing near.

An angel came: 'The judgment done,
Mercy is left enough for one:
Choose, one for hell and one for heaven!'
You cried 'But I have served thee well,
O Lord; but I have wrought and striven;
Duly, dear Lord, my prize is won.
I did repent; I am forgiven.   110
Give him the gift.' I cannot tell
But all the while it seem'd to me
I reason'd the futility.
—
Or this, or else I do not love,
I inly said; but could not move

* Two pages of the MS. at this place are badly smudged: words in brackets are conjectural—[H. H.].

† This line is at the bottom of the page, and quite illegible—[H. H.].

123

My fast-lodged tongue. '[To her the gift]★
I yield' I would have cried. At last
Something I said; I swooned and fell.
The angel lifted us above.
The bitterness of death was past,   120
My love; and all was sweet and well.

.   .   .   .   .

.   .   .   .

Who say that angels, in your ear
Are heard, that cry 'She does repent',
Let charity thus begin at home,—
Teach me the paces that you went
I can send up an Esau's cry;
Tune it to words of good intent.
This ice, this lead, this steel, this stone,
This heart is warm to you alone;
Make it to God. I am not spent   130
So far but I have yet within
The penetrative element
That shall unglue the crust of sin.
Steel may be melted and rock rent.
Penance shall clothe me to the bone.
Teach me the way: I will repent.

.   .   .   .

But grant my penitence begun:
I need not, love, I need not break
Remember'd sweetness. For my thought
No house of Rimmon may I take,   140
To bow but little, and worship not?
Is not some little Bela set
Before the mountain?—No, not one,

★ Apparently not completed in MS., though space is left for the missing words—
[H. H.]. The sense is revealed by cancelled variants. [N. H. M.].

124

The heaven-enforcèd answer comes,
Yea, to myself I answer make:
Who can but barter slender sums
By slender losses are undone;
They breathe not who are late to run.—
O hideous vice to haggle yet
For more with Him who gives thee all,   150
Freely forgives the monstrous debt!
Having the infinitely great
Therewith to hanker for the small!

Knowledge is strong but love is sweet.—
I found the ways were sown with salt
Where you and I were wont to tread;
Not further'd far my travell'd feet
For all the miles that they were sped;
No flowers to find, no place to halt,
No colour in the overhead,   160
No running in the river-bed;
And passages where we used to meet,—
Fruit-cloistering hyacinth-warding woods,
I call'd them and I thought them then—
When you were learner and I read,
Are waste, and had no wholesome foods,
Unpalateable fruits to eat.
What have I more than other men,
For learning stored and garnerèd?
And barely to escape the curse,   170
I who was wise would be untaught,
And fain would follow I who led.
How shall I search, who never sought?
How turn my passion-pastured thought
To gentle manna and simple bread?

82

She schools the flighty pupils of her eyes,
    With levell'd lashes stilling their disquiet;
And puts in leash her pair'd lips lest surprise
    Bare the condition of a realm at riot.
If he suspect that she has ought to sigh at
    His injury she'll avenge with raging shame.
She kept her love-thoughts on most lenten diet,
    And learnt her not to startle at his name.

83
The Lover's Stars

The destined lover, whom his stars
    More golden than the world of lights,
O'er passes bleak, o'er perilous bars
    Of rivers, lead, thro' storms and nights,

Or if he leave the West behind,
    Or father'd by the sunder'd South,
Shall, when his star is zenith'd, find
    Acceptance round his mistress' mouth:

Altho' unchallenged, where she sits,
    Three rivals throng her garden chair,
And tho' the silver seed that flits
    Above them, down the draught of air,

And keeps the breeze and clears the seas
    And tangles on a down of France,
Yet leaves him in ungirdled ease
    8000 furlongs in advance.

126

But in the other's horoscope
   Bad Saturn with a swart aspect
Fronts Venus.—His ill-launchèd hope
   In unimperill'd haven is wreck'd.

He meets her, stintless of her smile;
   Her choice in roses knows by heart;
Has danced with her: and all the while
   They are Antipodes apart.

His sick stars falter. More he may
   Not win, if this be not enough.
He meets upon Midsummer day
   The stabbing coldness of rebuff.

84

DURING the eastering of untainted morns,
In the ascendancy of rainbow's horns,
In the first signals of the several drops
That lick the shelly leaves which floor the copse,
In the quick fragrance of tall rolling pines,
Under the cloister-light of greenhouse vines,

· · · ·

85

         —Hill,
Heaven and every field, are still
  { As a self-embraced sweet thought:
  { — - —-caress'd   ——— :
  { And the thin stars tremble not.
  { —— — lessen'd stars ray —.

86

The Peacock's Eye

MARK you how the peacock's eye
Winks away its ring of green,
Barter'd for an azure dye,
And the piece that's like a bean,
The pupil, plays its liquid jet
To win a look of violet.

87

Love preparing to fly

HE play'd his wings as though for flight;
They webb'd the sky with glassy light.
His body sway'd upon tiptoes,
Like a wind-perplexèd rose;
In eddies of the wind he went
At last up the blue element.

88

I MUST hunt down the prize
Where my heart lists.
Must see the eagle's bulk, render'd in mists,
Hang of a treble size.

Must see the waters roll
Where the seas set
Towards wastes where round the ice-blocks tilt and fret
Not so far from the pole.

>   Must see the green seas roll
>   Where waters set
>   Towards those wastes where the ice-blocks tilt and fret,
>   Not so far from the pole.

89

WHY should their foolish bands, their hopeless hearses
Blot the perpetual festival of day?
Ravens, for prosperously-boded curses
Returning thanks, might offer such array.
Heaven comfort sends, but harry it away,
Gather the sooty plumage from Death's wings
And the poor corse impale with it and fray
Far from its head an angel's hoverings.
And count the rosy cross with bann'd disastrous things.

90

WHY if it be so, for the dismal morn
Into his hollow'd palm should moan the blast;
And in grey bands the sun should lie still born;
And straight showers parallel should follow fast;
And, swarter still, the rolling pines should cast
Their heads together in a stormy blot.

Bala.

91

IT was a hard thing to undo this knot.
The rainbow shines, but only in the thought
Of him that looks. Yet not in that alone,
For who makes rainbows by invention?

And many standing round a waterfall
See one bow each, yet not the same to all,
But each a hand's breadth further than the next.
The sun on falling waters writes the text
Which yet is in the eye or in the thought.
It was a hard thing to undo this knot.

Maentwrog.

92

GLIMMER'D along the square-cut steep.
They chew'd the cud in hollows deep.
Their cheeks moved and the bones therein.
The lawless honey eaten of old
Has lost its savour and is roll'd
Into the bitterness of sin.

What would befal* the godless flock
Appear'd not for the present, till
A thread of light betray'd the hill
Which with its lined and creased flank
The outgoings of the vale does block.
Death's bones fell in with sudden clank
As wrecks of minèd embers will.

93

(a)

LATE I fell in the ecstacy*
And saw the men before the flood
Which once were disobedient

* Thus in MS.

Think of an opening page illuminèd
With the ready azure and high carmine:—think
Her face was such, as being diaperèd
With loops of veins; not of an even pink,
Maentwrog.

94

MISS STORY's character! too much you ask,
When 'tis the confidante that sets the task.
How dare I paint Miss Story to Miss May?
And what if she my confidence betray!
What if my Subject, seeing this, resent
What were worth nothing if all compliment!
No: shewn to her it cannot but offend;
But candour never hurt the dearest *friend*.

  Miss Story has a moderate power of will,
But, having that, believes it greater still: 10
And, hide it though she does, one may divine
She inly nourishes a wish to shine;
Is very capable of strong affection
Tho' apt to throw it in a strange direction;
Is fond of flattery, as any she,
But has not learnt to take it gracefully;
Things that she likes seems often to despise,
And loves—a fatal fault—to patronize;
Has wit enough, but less than female tact,
Sees the right thing to do, and does not act;   20
About herself she is most sensitive,
Talks of self-sacrifice, yet can't forgive;
She's framed to triumph in adversity;
Prudence she has, but wise she'll never be;
Her character she does not realize,
And cannot see at all with others' eyes;

(And, well supplied with virtues on the whole,
Is slightly selfish in her inmost soul)
Believes herself religious, and is not;
And, thinking that she thinks, has never thought;   30
Married, will make a sweet and matchless wife,
But single, lead a misdirected life.

95

Did Helen steal my love from me?
    She never had the wit.
Or was it Jane? She is too plain,
    And could not compass it.

A bad verse in the middle, then—

It might be Helen, Jane, or Kate,
    It might be none of the three:
But I'm alone, for my love's gone
    That should have been true to me.

96

Seven Epigrams

(i)

Of virtues I most warmly bless,
Most rarely see, Unselfishness.
And to put graver sins aside
I own a preference for Pride.

(In the van between Ffestiniog and Bala.)

(ii)

Modern Poets

Our swans are now of such remorseless quill,
Themselves live singing and their hearers kill.

On a Poetess

Miss M.'s a nightingale. 'Tis well
    Your simile I keep.
It is the way with Philomel
    To sing while others sleep.

(iv)

You ask why can't Clarissa hold her tongue.
Because she fears her fingers will be stung.

(v)

On one who borrowed his sermons

Herclots's preachings I'll no longer hear:
They're out of date—lent sermons all the year.

(vi)

*By one of the old school who was bid to follow Mr. Browning's
flights*

To rise you bid me with the lark:
With me 'tis rising in the dark.

(vii)

'Boughs being pruned, birds preenèd, show more fair;
    To grace them spires are shaped with corner squinches;
Enrichèd posts are chamfer'd; everywhere
    He heightens worth who guardedly diminishes;
Diamonds are better cut; who pare, repair;
    Is statuary rated by its inches?
Thus we shall profit, while gold coinage still
Is worth and current with a lessen'd mill.'

By Mrs. Hopley

He's wedded to his theory, they say.
If that were true, it could not live a day.
And did the children of his brains enjoy
But half the pains he spends upon his boy,
You may depend that ere a week was fled,
There would not be a whole place in his head.

On seeing her children say Goodnight to their father.

Bid your Papa Goodnight. Sweet exhibition!
They kiss the Rod with filial submission.

98

(Sundry Fragments and Images)

(a)   (*Wind and rain*, &c.)

(i)

The wind, that passes by so fleet,
Runs his fingers through the wheat,
And leaves the blades, where'er he will veer,
Tingling between dusk and silver.

(ii)

Or else their cooings came from bays of trees,
Like a contented wind, or gentle shocks
Of falling water. This and all of these
We tunèd to one key and made their harmonies.

Maentwrog.

(iii)

Like shuttles fleet the clouds, and after
A drop of shade rolls over field and flock;
The wind comes breaking here and there with laughter:
The violet moves and copses rock.

. . . .

When the wind drops you hear the skylarks sing;
From Oxford comes the throng and hum of bells
Breaking the . . . . air of spring.

(iv)

There is an island, wester'd in the main,
Around it balances the level sea.

(v)

The time was late and the wet yellow woods
Told off their leaves along the piercing gale,

(vi)

—now the rain,
A brittle sheen, runs upward like a cliff,
Flying a bow.

(b) (*Flowers, leaves, trees, &c.*)

(vii)

—and on their brittle green quils*
Shake the balanced daffodils.

(viii)

Distance
Dappled with diminish'd trees
Spann'd with shadow every one.

* Thus in MS.

135

(ix)

—the shallow folds of the wood
We found were dabbled with a colouring growth,
In lakes of bluebells, pieced with primroses.

(x)

In the green spots of that wood
Were eyes of central primrose: bluebells ran
In skeins about the brakes.

(xi)

{ Thick-fleeced
{ Out-fleeced   bushes like a   { heifer's
{   { spaniel's   ear

(xii)

They came
Next to meadows abundant, pierced with flowers,
With sulphur-colour'd lilies, brittle in stalk,
{ And seals of red carnation which had each
{ —— —— — live ————— ——— —— ——
{ —— —— — vive ———— ——— —— ——
Two tongues like butterflies.

(xiii)

Dewy fields in the morning under the sun
Stand shock and silver-coated.

(xiv)

The ends of the crisp buds she chips
And the flower strips,
The breaking leaves of gold are curl'd upon her lips.

136

(xv)

A pure gold lily, but by the pure gold lily
We will charge our flocks that they not feed.
        Leave it with its grove hard by
'Some are pretty enough, and some are poor indeed.'
Give us our green lots in another mead
Fit for flowers, water-pierced and rilly.
Lead shepherd, now we follow, shepherd lead.

(xvi)

        bringing heads of daffodillies,
Gold gallant, flowers much looked at in April-weather

(xvii)

A silver scarce-call-silver gloss
⎧ Lighted the watery-plated leaves.
⎩ The watery-plated plane-leaves lit.

(xviii)

From any hedgerow, any copse,
Bring me palm with pearlèd knops,
And primrose bring, and make a sheaf
With his pull'd and plotted leaf.

(xix)

A. A basket broad of woven white rods
        I have fill'd, that hard to fill is,
    With the multitude of the lily-buds
        Of the brakes of lilies.

B. And I come laden from such floods
        Of flowers that counting closes,
    With the warm'd and the water'd buds
        Of the press of roses.

137

(c) (*Stars*)

(xx)

[Stars] float from the borders of the main.

(xxi)

Above
The vast of heaven stung with brilliant stars.

(xxii)

How looks the night? There does not miss a star.
The million sorts of unaccounted motes
Now quicken, sheathed in the yellow galaxy.
There is no parting or bare interstice
Where the stint compass of a skylark's wings
Would not put out some tiny golden centre.

(xxiii)

Stars waving their indivisible rays.
Sky fleeced with the milky way.

(xxiv)

Night's lantern
Pointed with piercèd lights, and breaks of rays
Discover'd everywhere.

(xxv)

The sky minted into golden sequins.
 Stars like gold tufts.
Stars like golden bees.
Stars like golden rowels.
Sky peak'd with tiny flames.

(xxvi)

His gilded rowels
Now stars of blood.

(xxvii)

A star most spiritual, principal, preeminent
Of all the golden press.

(xxviii)

Or ever the early stirrings of skylark
Might cover the neighbour downs with a span of singing,
　While Phosphor, risen upon the shallowing dark,
　　In the ruddied county of the day's upbringing
Stood capital, eminent, . . . gonfalon bearer
　　　To all the starry press.—

(xxix)

The stars were packed so close that night
　They seemed to press and stare
And gather in like hurdles bright
　The liberties of air.

(d) (*Dawn, clouds*)

(xxx)

In more precision now of light and dark
The heightening dawn with milky orience
Rounds its still-purpling centreings of cloud.

—

Now more precisely touched in light and gloom,
The place of the east with earliest milky morn
Rounds its still-purpling centre-darks of cloud.

Dawn that the pebbly low-down East
Covers with shallow silver, that unsets
The lock of clouds betimes and hangs the day.

—

Dawn that the low-down pebbly East
Covers with shallow silver, the lock of clouds
That early 'sperses, and high hangs the day.

(e)   (*Sun, &c.*)
(xxxii)

Whose braggart 'scutcheon, whose complaisant crest
Catch sunlight and one strain of stupid praise.

(xxxiii)

The sparky air
Leaps up before my vision,—thou art gone.

(xxxiv)

The sun just risen
Flares his wet brilliance in the dintless heaven.

(f)   (*Miscellaneous*)
(xxxv)

We live to see
How Shakespeare's England weds with Dante's Italy.

(xxxvi)

The moonlight-mated glowless glowworms shine.

(xxxvii)

When cuckoo calls and I may hear,
And thrice and four times and again.

(xxxviii)

He shook with racing notes the standing air.

(xxxix)

Glazed water vaulted o'er a drowsy stone.

(xl)

They are not dead who die, they are but lost who live.

99

Io

FORWARD she leans, with hollowing back, stock-still,
Her white weed-bathèd knees are shut together,
Her silky coat is sheeny, like a hill
Gem-fleeced at morn, so brilliant is the weather.
Her nostril glistens; and her wet black eye
Her lids half-meshing shelter from the sky.

Her finger-long new horns are capp'd with black;
In hollows of her form the shadow clings;
Her milk-white throat and folded dew-lap slack
Are still; her neck is creased in close-ply rings;
Her hue's a various brown with creamy lakes,
Like a cupp'd chestnut damask'd with dark breaks.

Backward are laid her pretty black-fleeced ears;
The knot of feathery locks upon her head
Plays to the breeze; where now are fled her fears,
Her jailor with his vigil-organ dead?
Morn does not now new-basilisk his stare,
Nor night is blown with flame-rings everywhere.

141

100

The rainbow

SEE on one hand
He drops his bright roots in the water'd sward,
And rosing part, on part dispenses green;
But with his other foot three miles beyond
He rises from the flocks of villages
That bead the plain; did ever Havering church-tower
Breathe in such ether? or the Quickly elms
{ With such a violet slight their distanced green?
{ Slight with such violet their bright-mask'd green?

or

Mask'd with such violet disallow their green?

101

A. —YES for a time they held as well
Together, as the criss-cross'd shelly cup
Sucks close the acorn; as the hand and glove;
As water moulded to the duct it runs in;
As keel locks close to kelson—

B.   Let me now
{ Jolt
{ Shake and unset your morticed metaphors.
The hand draws off the glove; the acorn-cup
Drops the fruit out; the duct runs dry or breaks;
The stranded keel and kelson warp apart;
And your two etc.

102

Fragments of *Floris in Italy*

(i)

It does amaze me, when the clicking hour
Clings on the stroke of death, that I can smile.
Yet when my unset tresses hung loose-traced
Round this unsexing doublet,—while I set
This downy counterfeit upon my lip,

. . . .

       —Lately I fear'd
My signalling tears might ring up Floris; now
{ Methinks my laughter is more perilous
{ ————there is more peril from my laughter.
Well, I know not. But all things seem to-night   10
Double as sharp, meaning and forcible,
With twice as fine a sense to apprehend them,
As ever I remember in my life.
Laughing or tears. I think I could do either—
So strangely elemented is my mind's weather,
That tears and laughter are hung close together.
(*Comes to the bed.*)
Sleep Floris while I rob you. Tighten, O sleep,
Thy impalpable oppression. Pin him down,
Ply fold on fold across his dangerous eyes,
Lodge his eyes fast; but yet as easy and light   20
As the laid gossamers of Michaelmas
Whose silver skins lie level and thick in field.
Hold him.—
I must not turn the lantern on his face.—
No I'll not hazard it. Only his hand,
(*Turns the lantern on Floris' hand.*)

(*Trying on the ring.*)
It is too large for me. What does that mean?
No time to think. I'll knot it on this ribbon,
And wear it thus, a pectoral, by my heart.

—

Did I say but lately
That I was so near laughter? Alas now   30
I find I am as ready with my tears
As the fine morsels of a dwindling cloud
That piece themselves into a race of drops
To spill o'er fields of lilies. So could I
So waste in tears over this bed of sweetness,
This flower, this Floris, this dear majesty,
This royal manhood.—'Tis in me rebellion
To speak so, yet I'll speak it for this once;
Deep shame it were to be discover'd so,
Worse than when Floris found me in the garden   40
Weeping,—Even now I curse myself remembering;—
No, let that go; I have said Goodnight to shame.
Now let me see you, you large princely hand,
Since on the face it is unsafe to look;
Yet this could be no other's hand than his,
'Tis so conceivèd in his lineament.
[*or* 'Tis so conceived in his true lineament.]
I have wrong'd it of its coronet, and now
I outrage it with treasonable kissing.
Ah Floris, Floris, let me speak this little   50

—

What I do now is but the least least thing.
But since I have no scope for benefits
Though ill-contented, precious precious Floris,
Most ill-content, this least least thing I do.
Now one word more and then I am gone indeed,
Warn'd by the bright procession of the stars.

My cousin will not love you as I love,
Floris; she will not hit thy sum of worth,
Thou jacinth; nor have skill of all thy virtues,
Floris, thou late-found All-heal;   60
—

        With what bold grace
This sweet Deserter lists herself anew
⎧ Sexing and ranking with our ruder files
⎨ Enroll'd and sexing⎫
⎩   sexèd ⎭ with —— —— ——
And marching to false colours! those few strokes
That forge her title of inheritance
To Manhood, on the upper lip,—they look'd
⎧ Most like the tuft of plighted silver round
⎨ —— —— — plighted tuft of —— ——
⎩ —— —— — silver plighted tuft about   70
The mouthèd centre of a violet.

              (ii)
       —O Guinevere
I read that the recital of thy sin,
Like knocking thunder all round Britain's welkin,
Jarr'd down the balanced storm; the bleeding heavens
Left not a rood with curses unimpregnate;
There was no crease or gather in the clouds
But dropp'd its coil of woes: and Arthur's Britain,
The mint of current courtesies, the forge
Where all the virtues were illustrated
In blazon, gilt   and images of bronze, ⎫
— gilt and blazon — bronze statuary,   ⎬ 10
—— —— —— —— — mail'd shapes of bronze, ⎭
Abandoned by her saints, turn'd black and blasted,
Like scalded banks topp'd once with principal flowers:
Such heathenish misadventure ⎧ dogg'd one sin.
                        ⎩ dogs

145

Floris in Italy. Floris, having found by chance that Giulia loves him, reasons with himself (or perhaps with Henry) in defence of his not returning her love. Her beauty is urged.

> BEAUTY it may be is the meet of lines,
> Or careful-spacèd sequences of sound,
> These rather are the arc where beauty shines,
> The temper'd soil where only her flower is found.
> Allow at least it has one term and part
> Beyond, and one within the looker's eye;
> And I must have the centre in my heart
> To spread the compass on the all-starr'd sky:
> For only try by gazing to divide
> One star by daylight from the strong blue air,   10
> And find it will not therefore be descried
> Because its place is known and charted there.
> No, love prescriptive, love with place assign'd,
> Love by monition, heritage, or lot,
> Love by prenatal serfdom still confined
> Even to the tillage of the sweetest spot,—
> It is a regimen on the imperfect wind,
> Piecing the elements out by plan and plot.
> Though self-made bands at last may true love bind,
> New love is free love, or true love 'tis not.   20

or Say beauty lies but in the meet of lines,
> In careful-spacèd sequences of sound

. . . . .

> To turn the compass on the all-starr'd sky

. . . . .

> Is to give regimen to the imperfect wind,

{ And slender element to piece and plot.
{ The ——— elements ——— ——— ———

.   .   .

New love is free love, or true love 'tis not.   [*exit*

Henry. Thus he ties spider's web across his sight
       And gives for tropes his judgment all away,
       Gilds with some sparky fancies his black night
       And stumbling swears he walks by light of day.
       Blindness! A learnèd fool and well-bred churl
       That swinishly refuses such a pearl!

   or Such spider's web he ties across his sight,
       And gives for tropes his judgment all away,
       Gilds with some sparky fancies blinding night,
       And stumbling swears he walks by light of day.
       A learnèd fool indeed and well-bred churl
       That swinishly refuses such a pearl!

103

               —I AM like a slip of comet,
       Scarce worth discovery, in some corner seen
       Bridging the slender difference of two stars,
       Come out of space, or suddenly engender'd
       By heady elements, for no man knows:
       But when she sights the sun she grows and sizes
       And spins her skirts out, while her central star
       Shakes its cocooning mists; and so she comes
       To fields of light; millions of travelling rays
       Pierce her; she hangs upon the flame-cased sun,
       And sucks the light as full as Gideon's fleece:
       But then her tether calls her; she falls off,
       And as she dwindles shreds her smock of gold

Amidst the sistering planets, till she comes
To single Saturn, last and solitary;
And then goes out into the cavernous dark.
So I go out: my little sweet is done:
I have drawn heat from this contagious sun:
To not ungentle death now forth I run.

104

No, they are come; their horn is lifted up;
They stand, they shine in the sun; Fame has foregone
All quests save the recital of their greatness;
Their clarions from all corners of the field
With potent lips call down cemented towers;
Their harness beams like scythes in morning grass;
Like flame they gather on our cliffs at evening,
At morn they come upon our lands like rains;
They plough our vales; you see the unsteady flare
Flush thro' their heaving columns; when they halt
They seem to fold the hills with golden capes;
They draw all coverts, cut the fields, and suck
The treasure from all cities. . . .

105

Now I am minded to take pipe in hand
And yield a song to the decaying year;
Now while the full-leaved hursts unalter'd stand,
    And scarcely does appear
The Autumn yellow feather in the boughs;
    While there is neither sun nor rain;
And a grey heaven does the hush'd earth house,
And bluer grey the flocks of trees look in the plain.

So late the hoar green chestnut breaks a bud,
And feeds new leaves upon the winds of Fall;
So late there is no force in sap or blood;
    The fruit against the wall
Loose on the stem has done its summering;
These should have starv'd with the green broods of spring,
    Or never been at all;
Too late or else much, much too soon,
Who first knew moonlight by the hunters' moon.

106

THE cold whip-adder unespied
With wavèd passes there shall glide
Too near thee, and thou must abide
The ringèd blindworm hard beside.

107

Fragments of *Richard*

(i)

As void as clouds that house and harbour none,
Whose gaps and hollows are not browzed upon,
As void as those the gentle downs appear
On such a season of the day and year.
There was no bleat of ewe, no chime of wether,
Only the bellèd foxgloves lisp'd together.
Yet there came one who sent his flock before him,
Alone upon the hill-top, heaven o'er him,
And where the brow in first descending bow'd
He sat and wrought his outline on a cloud.   10
His sheep seem'd to come from it as they stept,
One and then one, along their walks, and kept

Their changing feet in flicker all the time
And to their feet the narrow bells gave rhyme.
Affinèd well to that sweet solitude,   15
He was a shepherd of the Arcadian mood
That not Arcadia knew nor Haemony.
His tale and telling has been given to me.

.   .   .   .

(ii)

But what drew shepherd Richard from his downs,
And bred acquaintance of unusèd towns?
What put taught graces on his country lip,
And brought the sense of gentle fellowship,
That many centres found in many hearts?   5
What taught the humanities and the round of arts?
And for the tinklings on the falls and swells
Gave the much music of our Oxford bells?

.   .   .   .

(iii)

'Sylvester, come, Sylvester; you may trust
Your footing now to the much-dreaded dust,
Crisp'd up and starchy from a short half-hour
Of standing to the blossom-hitting shower
That still makes counter-roundels in the pond.
A rainbow also shapes itself beyond
The shining slates and houses. Come and see.
You may quote Wordsworth, if you like, to me.'
Sylvester came: they went by Cumnor hill,
Met a new shower, and saw the rainbow fill   10
From one frail horn that crumbled to the plain
His steady wheel quite to the full again.
They watched the brush of the swift stringy drops,
Help'd by the darkness of a block of copse
Close-rooted in the downward-hollowing fields;
Then sought such leafy shelter as it yields,

And each drew bluebells up, and for relief
Took primroses, their pull'd and plotted leaf
Being not forgotten, for primroses note
The blue with brighter places not remote.   20

(iv)

There was a meadow level almost: you traced
The river wound about it as a waist.
Beyond, the banks were steep; a brush of trees
Rounded it, thinning skywards by degrees,
With parallel shafts,—as upward-parted ashes,—
Their highest sprays were drawn as fine as lashes,
With centres duly touch'd and nestlike spots,—
And oaks,—but these were leaved in sharper knots.
Great butter-burr leaves floor'd the slope corpse ground
Beyond the river, all the meadow's round,   10
And each a dinted circle. The grass was red
And long, the trees were colour'd, but the o'er-head,
Milky and dark, with an attuning stress
Controll'd them to a grey-green temperateness,
Making the shadow sweeter. A spiritual grace
Which Wordsworth would have dwelt on, about the place
Led Richard with a sweet undoing pain
To trace some traceless loss of thought again.
Here at the very furthest reach away
(The furthest reach this side, on that the bay   20
Most dented) lay Sylvester, reading Keats'
Epistles, while the running pastoral bleats
Of sheep from the high fields and other wild
Sounds reach'd him. Richard came. Sylvester smiled
And said 'I like this: it is almost isled,
The river spans it with so deep a hip.
I hope that all the places on our trip
Will please us so.'

.   .   .   .

151

108

ALL as that moth call'd Underwing, alighted,
Pacing, and turning so by slips discloses
Her sober simple coverlid underplighted
To colour as smooth and fresh as cheeks of roses,
{ Her showy leaves staid watchet counterfoiling
{ Her showy leaves with gentle watchet foiling
Even so my thought the rose and grey disposes

109

The Queen's Crowning

1. THEY were wedded at midnight
   By shine of candles three,
   And they were bedded till daylight
   Before he went to sea.

2. 'When are you home, my love,' she said,
   'When are you home from sea?'
   'You may look for me home, my love,' he said,
   'In two years or in three.'

3. 'Heaven make the time be short,' she said,
   'Although it were years three.
   Heaven make it sweet to you,' she said,
   'And make it short to me.

4. And what is your true name?' she said,
   'Your name and your degree?
   How shall I call my love,' she said,
   'When he is over the sea?'

5. 'O I am the king's son,' he said,
   'Lord William they call me.
   I give you my love and I give you my land,
   When I come home from sea.'

6. He yearn'd, he yearn'd to have his love,
   For two years and for three.
   Then he set sail in a golden ship
   With a golden company.

7. Or ever he set his foot to the land
   He saw his brothers three.
   'O have you here a foreign lady
   Come with you from over the sea?'

8. 'O I have here no foreign lady
   Come with me from over the sea.'
   'Then will you wed with an English lady,
   As wedded you must be?'

9. Says 'Get you, get you a lady to wed
   That has both gold and fee.
   Ere you set sail the king was dead.
   The crown has come to thee.'

10. 'And if I chose a love to wed
    That was of low degree?
    The crown should be unto her head
    And what were that to thee?'

11. One has gone to the king's steward,
    Shewn him both gold and fee:
    Said 'Who then is this lowly woman,
    And truly tell to me.'

12. The king's friend told the thing that was hid
    Because of gold and fee.
    Said, it was not meet the king should wed
    With one of low degree.

13. They have held his eyes with blindfold bands
    Because he should not see.
    They have bound his feet, they have bound his hands:
    It was but one to three.

14. They have taken out their long brands,
    They made him kneel on knee.
    'It is for the shame of the lowly woman
    That this has come to thee.'

15. They have happ'd him with the sand and stone
    That was beside the sea.
    In his heart said everyone
    The crown shall be for me.

16. Lowly Alice sat in her bower
    With a two years child at her knee.
    'I think it is seven days,' she said,
    'Thy father thou shalt see.'

17. Lowly Alice look'd abroad
    Over field and tree,
    And she was ware of a servingman
    Came running over the lea.

18. 'O what will you now, good servingman,
    O what will you now with me?'
    Says 'Are you not Lord William's love
    That is of low degree?'

19. 'I am Lord William's love,' she said,
      'And Alice they call me.'
    'Lord William comes hunting tomorrow morning,
      And he will come to thee.

20. But how will you Lord William know
      Beside his brothers three?'
    'Because he is my love,' she said,
      'And is so fair to see.'

21. 'Yet how will you Lord William know
      Beside his brothers three?
    His three brothers are each as tall
      And each as fair as he.

22. If it be a white rose in his hand,
      A lily if it should be,
    In this wise you may know your lord
      Beside his brothers three:

23. If he wear the crown upon his head
      Among his brothers three,
    If he wear a crown upon his head
      And bring a crown for thee.'

24. She heard the hunt the morrow morning
      And she came out to see.
    And there she never saw the king,
      But saw his brothers three.

25. She stood before them in the glen,
      She kneeled upon her knee.
    'O where is Lord William, my lords,' she said,
      'I pray you tell to me.'

26. Two made answer in one breath
    And each said 'I am he.'
    'Fie, you are not Lord William,' she said;
    'O fie that this should be.'

27. Then up and spake the third brother,
    Said 'Listen now to me.
    Lord William is king of all this land
    And thou of low degree.'

28. 'Fie,' she said unto them all,
    'No truth between you three.
    If he were king of all this land
    He would have come for me.'

29. As she lay weeping at the night
    She heard but knockings three.
    'It is as cold as death without:
    Open the door to me.'

30. Said 'Who is this that stands without?'
    Said 'Open, open to me.'
    When she had made the door wide
    Her true love she might see.

31. 'O why art thou so wan,' she said,
    'And why so short with me?
    And art thou come from English land,
    Or come from over the sea?'

32. 'I am not come from English land,
    Nor yet from over the sea.
    If I were come from Paradise,
    It were more like to be.'

33. 'Is it a lily in your hand,
       Is it a rose I see?
    Did you pull it in the king's garden
       When you came forth for me?'

34. 'I did not pull it in king's garden
       When I came forth for thee.
    If it were a flower of Paradise,
       It were more like to be.'

35. 'Is that the King's crown on your head,
       And have you a crown for me?'
    'If it were a crown of Paradise,
       It were more like to be.'

36. The more she ask'd, the more he spoke,
       The fairer waxèd he.
    The more he told, the less she spoke,
       The wanner wanèd she.

37. 'Wilt thou follow me, my true love,
       If I give thee kisses three?
    Wilt thou follow me, my true love?
       I have a crown for thee.'

38. 'O I will follow thee, my true love.
       Give me thy kisses three.
    Sweeter thy kisses, my own love,
       Than all the crowns to me.'

39. He gave her kisses cold as ice;
       Down upon ground fell she.
    She has gone with him to Paradise.
       There shall her crowning be.

157

110

TOMORROW meet you? O not tomorrow.
   I would not make the trial.
   Fear hindrance and espial
   ×   And after that sad sorrow.
But with a sweet persistency
He dallies yet and yet with me
   And will not take denial.

× [*or* Then severance and sorrow.]

111

Fragment of
Stephen and Barberie

—SHE by a sycamore,
Whose all-belated leaves yield up themselves
To the often takings of desirous winds,
Sits without consolation, marking not
The time save when her tears which still [descend]★
Her barrèd fingers clasp'd upon her eyes,
Shape on the under side and size and drop.
Meanwhile a litter of the jaggèd leaves
Lies in her lap, which she anon sweeps off.
'This weary Martinmas, would it were summer'
I heard her say, poor poor afflictèd soul,—
'Would it were summer-time.' Anon she sang
The country song of *Willow*. 'The poor soul—
(Like me)—*sat sighing by a sycamore-tree.*'
Perhaps it was for this she chose the place.

★ *Conjectural: the MS. is badly smudged here, but de . . . is visible.*

112

I HEAR a noise of waters drawn away,
And, headed always downwards, with less sounding
Work through a cover'd copse whose hollow rounding
Rather to ear than eye shews where they stray,
Making them double-musical. And they
Low-covered pass, and brace the woodland clods
With shining-hilted curves, that they may stay
The bluebells up whose crystal-ending rods
. . . . . in their natural sods.

     a standing fell
Of hyacinths . . . . . .
And pledgèd purply in a half-lit dell.

113

WHEN eyes that cast about the heights of heaven
To canvass the retirement of the lark
(Because the music from his bill forth-driven
So takes the sister sense) can find no mark,
But many a silver visionary spark
Springs in the floating air and the skies swim,—
Then often the ears in a new fashion hark,
Beside them, about the hedges, hearing him:
At last the bird is found a flickering shape and slim.

At once the senses give the music back,
 ⎧ The proper sweet re-attributing above.
 ⎩ That sweetness re-attributing above.—

114

The Summer Malison

MAIDENS shall weep at merry morn,
And hedges break, and lose the kine,
And field-flowers make the fields forlorn,
And noonday have a shallow shine,
And barley turn to weed and wild,
And seven ears crown the lodgèd corn,
And mother have no milk for child,
    And father be overworn.

And John shall lie, where winds are dead,
And hate the ill-visaged cursing tars,
And James shall hate his faded red,
Grown wicked in the wicked wars.
No rains shall fresh the flats of sea,
Nor close the clayfield's sharded sores,
And every heart think loathingly
    Its dearest changed to bores.

115

O DEATH, Death, He is come.
O grounds of Hell make room.
Who came from further than the stars
    Now comes as low beneath.
    Thy ribbèd ports, O Death
Make wide; and Thou, O Lord of Sin,
    Lay open thine estates.
    Lift up your heads, O Gates;
Be ye lift up, ye everlasting doors
    The King of Glory will come in.

116

BELLISLE! that is a fabling name, but we
Have here a true one, echoing the sound;
And one to each of us is holy ground;
But let me sing that which is known to me.

117

CONFIRMED beauty will not bear a stress;—
Bright hues long look'd at thin, dissolve and fly:
Who lies on grass and pores upon the sky
Shall see the azure turn expressionless
And Tantalean slaty ashiness
Like Pharaoh's ears of windy harvest dry
Dry up the blue and be not slaked thereby.
Ah! surely all who have written will profess
The sweetest sonnet five or six times read
Is tasteless nothing: and in my degree
I prove it. What then when these lines are dead
And coldly do belie the thought of thee?
I'll lay them by, and freshly turn instead
To thy not-staled uncharted memory.

118

BUT what indeed is ask'd of me?
Not this. Some spirits, it is told,
Have will'd to be disparadised
For love and greater glory of Christ.

But I was ignorantly bold
To dream I dared so much for thee.
This was not ask'd, but what instead?
Waking I thought; and it sufficed:
My hopes and my unworthiness,
At once perceivèd, with excess
Of burden came and bow'd my head.

　　　　·　　·　　·　　·

Yea, crush'd my heart, and made me dumb.
I thought: Before I gather strength . . . .

119

To Oxford

As Devonshire letters, earlier in the year
Than we in the East dare look for buds, disclose
Smells that are sweeter-memoried than the rose,
And pressèd violets in the folds appear,
So is it with my friends, I note, to hear
News from Belleisle, even such a sweetness blows
(I know it, knowing not) across from those
Meadows to them inexplicably dear.
'As when a soul laments, which hath been blest'—
I'll cite no further what the initiate know.
I never saw those fields whereon their best
And undivulgèd love does overflow.

120

Continuation of R. Garnett's *Nix*

SHE mark'd where I and Fabian met;
She loves his face, she knows the spot;
And there she waits with locks unwet
For Fabian that suspects her not.

I see her riving fingers tear
A branch of walnut leaves, and that
More sweetly shades her stolen hair
Than fan or hood or strawy plait.

He sees her, O but he must miss
A something in her face of guile,
And relish not her loveless kiss
And wonder at her shallow smile.

[*or* And half mislike her loveless kiss.]

Ah no! and she who sits beside
Bids him this way his gazes fix.
Then she seems sweet who seems his bride,
She sour who seems the slighted Nix.

[*or* Then sweetest seems the seeming bride
When maddest looks the slighted Nix.]

I know of the bored and bitten rocks
Not so far outward in the sea:
There lives the witch shall win my locks
And my blue eyes again for me.

Alas! but I am all at fault,
Nor locks nor eyes shall win again.
I dare not taste the thickening salt,
I cannot meet the swallowing main.

Or if I go, she stays meanwhile,
Who means to wed or means to kill,
And speeds uncheck'd her murderous guile
Or wholly winds him to her will.

121

A NOISE of falls I am possessèd by
⎧ Of streams; and clouds like mesh'd and parted moss
⎩ Of water. Clouds like parted moss
Attain the windy levels of the sky
Which between ash-tops suffers loss
Of its concavity.

122

O WHAT a silence is this wilderness!
Might we not think the sweet (?) and daring rises
Of the flown skylark, and his traverse flight
At highest when he seems to brush the clouds,
† Had been more fertile and had sown with notes   5

The unenduring fallows of the heaven?
Or take it thus—that the concording stars
Had let such music down, without impediment
Falling along the breakless pool of air,
* As struck with rings of sound the close-shut palms   10
Of the wood-sorrel and all things sensitive?

† [or Had been effectual to have sown with notes]

* [As might have struck and shook the close-shut palms]

164

A. As the wood-sorrel and all things sensitive
   That thrive in the loamy greenness of this place?   15
B. What spirit is that makes stillness obsolete
   With ear-caressing speech? Where is the tongue
   Which drives this stony air to utterance?—
   Who is it? how come to this forgotten land?

123

MOTHERS are doubtless happier for their babes
And risen sons: yet are the childless free
From tears shed over children's graves.
So those who [born in] Thee
Take their peculiar thorns and natural pain
Among the lilies and thy good domain.

124

Daphne

WHO loves me here and has my love,
I think he will not tire of me,
But sing contented as the dove
That comes again to the woodland tree.

He shall have summer sweets and dress
His pleasure to the changing clime,
And I can teach him happiness
That shall not fail in winter-time.

[or He shall have summer goods and trim
His pleasure to the changing clime,
And I shall know of sweets for him
That are not less in winter-time.]

His cap shall be shining fur,
And stained, and knots of golden thread,
He shall be warm with miniver
Lined all with silk of juicy red.

In spring our river-banks are topt
With yellow flags will suit his brow,
In summer are our orchards knopt
With green-white apples on the bough.

But if I cannot tempt his thought
With wealth that mocks his high degree,
The shepherds, whom I value not,
Have told me I am fair to see.

125

Fragments of *Castara Victrix*

Scene: a bare hollow between hills. Enter Castara and her Esquire

C. WHAT was it we should strike the road again?
E. There was a wood of dwarf and sourèd oaks
    Crept all along a hill upon our left,
    A wonder in the country, and a landmark
    They said we could not miss. A pushing brook
    Ran through it, following which we should have sight
    Of mile-long reaches of our road below us.
    My thought was, there to rest against the trees
    And watch until our horses and the men
    Circled the safe flanks of the bulky hills.
C. And how long was the way?
E.   This shorter way?
    Two miles indeed.

C.   We have come four, do you think?
    Somewhere we slipt astray, you cannot doubt.
E. True, madam. I am sorry now to see
    I better'd all our path with sanguine eyes.

         ·   ·   ·   ·

At the picnic or whatever we call it. Daphnis, Castara.
D.   —Can I do any harm?
C. If you are silent, that I know of, none.
D. Ill meant, yet true. I best should flatter then,
    In copying well what you have best begun.
C. In copying? how?
D.   Must I give tongue again?
    In copying your sweet silence.
C.   Am I so
    Guilty of silence?
D.   Quite, as ladies go.
    Yet what you are, the world would say, remain:
    It never yet so sweetly was put on
    By any lauded statue, nor again
    By speech so sweetly broken up and gone.
C. What if I hated flattery?
D.   Say you do:
    The hatred comes with a good grace from you:
    Flattery's all out of place where praise is true.

         ·   ·   ·   ·

Valerian, Daphnis.
V. Come, Daphnis.
D.   Good Valerian, I will come. (*exit V.*
    Why should I go because Castara goes?
    I do not, but to please Valerian.
    But why then should Castara weigh with me?
    Why, there's an interest and sweet soul in beauty
    Which makes us eye-attentive to the eye
    That has it; and she is fairer than Colomb,
    Selvaggia, Orinda, and Adela, and the rest.

Fairer? These are the flaring shows unlovely
That make my eyes sore and cross-colour things
With fickle spots of sadness; accessories
{ Familiar and so hated by the sick;
{ Hated and too familiar to — —;
These are my very text of discontent;
These names, these faces? They are customary
And kindred to my lamentable days,
Of which I say there is no joy in them.
To these Castara is rain or breeze or spring,
— — — — dew, is dawn, is day,
Sheet lightning to the stifling lid of night
Bright-lifting with a little-lasting smile
And breath upon it. That is, her face is this.
And if it is why there is cause enough
To say I go because Castara goes.
Yet I'd not say it is her face alone
That this is true of: 'tis Castara's self;
But this distemper'd court will change it all:—
Which says at least then go while all is fresh,—
Much cause to go because Castara goes.

126

Shakspere

IN the lodges of the perishable souls
He has his portion. God, who stretch'd apart
Doomsday and death—whose dateless thought must chart
All time at once and span the distanced goals,
Sees what his place is; but for us the rolls
Are shut against the canvassing of art.
Something we guess or know: some spirits start
Upwards at once and win their aureoles.

·   ·   ·   ·   ·   ·

168

127

TREES by their yield
Are known; but I—
My sap is sealed,
My root is dry.
If life within
I none can shew
(Except for sin),
Nor fruit above,—
It must be so—
I do not love.

Will no one show
I argued ill?
Because, although
Self-sentenced, still
I keep my trust.
If He would prove
And search me through
Would He not find
(What yet there must
Be hid behind

·   ·   ·   ·

128

A Complaint

I THOUGHT that you would have written: my birthday came
    and went,
And with the last post over I knew no letter was sent.
And if you write at last, it never can be the same:
What *would* be a birthday letter that after the birthday came?

I know what you will tell me—neglectful that you were not.
But is not that my grievance—you promised and you forgot?
It's the day that makes the charm; no after-words could suc-
ceed
Though they took till the seventeenth of next October to read.

Think this, my birthday falls in saddening time of year;
Only the dahlias blow, and all is Autumn here.
Hampstead was never bright; and whatever Miss Cully's
charms
It is hardly a proper treat for a birthday to rest in her arms.

Our sex should be born in April perhaps or the lily-time;
But the lily is past, as I say, and the rose is not in its prime:
What I did ask then was a circle of rose-red sealing-wax
And a few leaves not lily-white but charactered over with
blacks.

But late is better than never: you see you have managed so,
You have made me quote almost the dismalest proverb I know:
For a letter comes at last: (shall I say before Christmas is come?)
And I must take your amends, cry Pardon, and then be dumb.

129

MOONLESS darkness stands between.
Past, the Past, no more be seen!
But the Bethlehem star may lead me
To the sight of Him Who freed me
From the self that I have been.
Make me pure, Lord: Thou art holy;
Make me meek, Lord: Thou wert lowly;
Now beginning, and alway:
Now begin, on Christmas day.

130

THE earth and heaven, so little known,
Are measured outwards from my breast.
I am the midst of every zone
And justify the East and West;

The unchanging register of change
My all-accepting fixèd eye,
While all things else may stir and range,
All else may whirl or dive or fly.

The swallow, favourite of the gale,
Will on the moulding strike and cling,
Unvalve or shut his vanèd tail
And sheathe at once his leger wing.

He drops upon the wind again;
His little pennon is unfurled.
In motion is no weight or pain,
Nor permanence in the solid world.

There is a vapour stands in the wind;
It shapes itself in taper skeins:
You look again and cannot find,
Save in the body of the rains.

And these are spent and ended quite;
The sky is blue, and the winds pull
Their clouds with breathing edges white
Beyond the world; the streams are full

And millbrook-slips with pretty pace
Gallop along the meadow grass.—
O lovely ease in change of place!
I have desired, desired to pass . . . .

131

As it fell upon a day
There was a lady very gay,
She was dressed in silk attire
For all to see and to admire.

. . . . .

But the boatman on the green
Told of the wonders he had seen.

132

In the staring darkness
I can hear the harshness
Of the cold wind blowing.
I am warmly clad,
And I'm very glad
That I've got a home.

133

Summa

The best ideal is the true
    And other truth is none,
All glory be ascribèd to
    The holy Three in One.

Man is most low, God is most high.
    As sure as heaven it is
There must be something to supply
    All insufficiencies.

For souls that might have blessed the time
    And breathed delightful breath
In sordidness of care and crime
    The city tires to death,
And faces fit for leisure gaze
    And daylight and sweet air,
Missing prosperity and praise,
    Are never known for fair.

134

Not kind! to freeze me with forecast,
Dear grace and girder of mine and me.
You to be gone and I lag last—
Nor I nor heaven would have it be.

135

The Elopement

All slumbered whom our rud red tiles
Do cover from the starry spread,
When I with never-needed wiles
    Crept trembling out of bed.
Then at the door what work there was, good lack,
To keep the loaded bolt from plunging back.

When this was done and I could look
I saw the stars like flash of fire.
My heart irregularly shook,
    I cried with my desire.
I put the door to with the bolts unpinned,
Upon my forehead hit the burly wind.

No tumbler woke and shook the cot,
The rookery never stirred a wing,
At roost and rest they shifted not,
　　Blessed be everything.
And all within the house were sound as posts,
Or listening thought of linen-winded ghosts.

The stars are packed so thick to-night
They seem to press and droop and stare,
And gather in like hurdles bright
　　The liberties of air.
I spy the nearest daisies through the dark,
The air smells strong of sweetbriar in the park.

I knew the brook that parts in two
The cart road with a shallowy bed
Of small and sugar flints, I knew
　　The footway, Stephen said,
And where cold daffodils in April are
Think you want daffodils and follow as far

As where the little hurling sound
To the point of silence in the air
Dies off in hyacinthed ground,
　　And I should find him there.
O heart, have done, you beat you beat so high,
You spoil the plot I find my true love by.

136

St. Thecla

THAT his fast-flowing hours with sandy silt
Should choke sweet virtue's glory is Time's great guilt.
Who thinks of Thecla? Yet her name was known,
Time was, next whitest after Mary's own.
To that first golden age of Gospel times
And bright Iconium eastwards reach my rhymes.
Near by is Paul's free Tarsus, fabled where
Spent Pegasus down the stark-precipitous air
Flung rider and wings away; though these were none,
And Paul is Tarsus' true Bellerophon.   10
They are neighbours; but (what nearness could not do)
Christ's only charity charmed and chained these two.
   She, high at the housetop sitting, as they say,
Young Thecla, scanned the dazzling streets one day;
Twice lovely, tinted eastern, turnèd Greek—
Crisp lips, straight nose, and tender-slanted cheek.
Her weeds all mark her maiden, though to wed,
And bridegroom waits and ready are bower and bed.
Withal her mien is modest, ways are wise,
And grave past girlhood earnest in her eyes.   20
   Firm accents strike her fine and scrollèd ear,
A man's voice and a new voice speaking near.
The words came from a court across the way.
She looked, she listened: Paul taught long that day.
He spoke of God the Father and His Son,
Of world made, marred, and mended, lost and won;
Of virtue and vice; but most (it seemed his sense)
He praised the lovely lot of continence:
All over, some such words as these, though dark,
The world was saved by virgins, made the mark.   30
   He taught another time there and a third.
The earnest-hearted maiden sat and heard,
And called to come at mealtime she would not:
They rose at last and forced her from the spot.

B. Poems written 1876–89

137

Moonrise June 19
1876

I AWOKE in the Midsummer not-to-call night, ǀ in the white
and the walk of the morning:
The moon, dwindled and thinned to the fringe ǀ of a fingernail
held to the candle,
Or paring of paradisaïcal fruit, ǀ lovely in waning but lustre-
less,
Stepped from the stool, drew back from the barrow, ǀ of dark
Maenefa the mountain;
A cusp still clasped him, a fluke yet fanged him, ǀ entangled
him, not quit utterly.
This was the prized, the desirable sight, ǀ unsought, presented
so easily,
Parted me leaf and leaf, divided me, ǀ eyelid and eyelid of
slumber.

138

The Woodlark

Teevo cheevo cheevio chee:
O where, what can thát be?
Weedio-weedio: there again!
So tiny a trickle of sóng-strain;

And all round not to be found
For brier, bough, furrow, or gréen ground
Before or behind or far or at hand
Either left either right
Anywhere in the súnlight.

Well, after all! Ah but hark—   10
'I am the little wóodlark.
The skylark is my cousin and he
Is known to men more than me.
Round a ring, around a ring
And while I sail (must listen) I sing.

To-day the sky is two and two
With white strokes and strains of the blue.
The blue wheat-acre is underneath
And the corn is corded and shoulders its sheaf,
The ear in milk, lush the sash,   20
And crush-silk poppies aflash,
The blood-gush blade-gash
Flame-rash rudred
Bud shelling or broad-shed
Tatter-tangled and dingle-a-danglèd
Dandy-hung dainty head.

And down ... the furrow dry
Sunspurge and oxeye
And lace-leaved lovely
Foam-tuft fumitory.   30

I ám so véry, O só very glád
That I dó thínk there is not to be had
[Anywhere any more joy to be in.
Cheevio:] when the cry within
Says Go on then I go on
Till the longing is less and the good gone,

But down drop, if it says Stop,
To the all-a-leaf of the tréetop.
And after that off the bough
[Hover-float to the hedge brow.]   40

Through the velvety wind V-winged
[Where shake shadow is sun's-eye-ringed]
To the nest's nook I balance and buoy
With a sweet joy of a sweet joy,
Sweet, of a sweet, of a sweet joy
Of a sweet—a sweet—sweet—joy.'

139

On St. Winefred

besides her miraculous cures
filling a bath and turning a mill

As wishing all about us sweet,
She brims her bath in cold or heat;
She lends, in aid of work and will,
Her hand from heaven to turn a mill—
Sweet soul! not scorning honest sweat
And favouring virgin freshness yet.

140

To him who ever thought with love of me
Or ever did for my sake some good deed
I will appear, looking such charity
And kind compassion, at his life's last need
That he will out of hand and heartily
Repent he sinned and all his sins be freed.

178

141

WHAT being in rank-old nature should earlier have that breath
  been
That hére pérsonal tells off these heart-song powerful peals?—
• A bush-browed, beetle-brówed bíllow is it?
With a soúth-wésterly wínd blústering, with a tide rolls reels
Of crumbling, fore-foundering, thundering all-surfy seas in;
  seen
Únderneath, their glassy barrel, of a fairy green.

· · · · · · · · · ·

Or a jaunting vaunting vaulting assaulting trumpet telling.

142

Cheery Beggar

BEYOND Mágdalen and by the Bridge, on a place called there
  the Plain,
  In Summer, in a burst of summertime
  Following falls and falls of rain,
When the air was sweet-and-sour of the flown fineflour of
Those goldnails and their gaylinks that hang along a lime;

· · · · · · · · ·

  The motion of that man's heart is fine
  Whom want could not make píne, píne
That struggling should not sear him, a gift should cheer him
Like that poor pocket of pence, poor pence of mine.

· · · · · · · · ·

143

DENIS, whose motionable, alert, most vaulting wit
Caps occasion with an intellectual fit.
Yet Arthur is a Bowman: his three-heeled timber'll hit
The bald and bóld blínking gold when áll's dóne
Right rooting in the bare butt's wincing navel in the sight of
    the sun.

. . . .

144

THE furl of fresh-leaved dogrose down
His cheeks the forth-and-flaunting sun
Had swarthed about with lion-brown
    Before the Spring was done.

His locks like all a ravel-rope's-end,
    With hempen strands in spray—
Fallow, foam-fallow, hanks—fall'n off their ranks,
    Swung down at a disarray.

Or like a juicy and jostling shock
    Of bluebells sheaved in May
Or wind-long fleeces on the flock
    A day off shearing day.

Then over his turnèd temples—here—
    Was a rose, or, failing that,
Rough-Robin or five-lipped campion clear
    For a beauty-bow to his hat,
And the sunlight sidled, like dewdrops, like dandled
    diamonds
    Through the sieve of the straw of the plait.

. . . .

145

(Margaret Clitheroe)

GOD'S counsel cólumnar-severe
But chaptered in the chief of bliss
Had always doomed her down to this—
Pressed to death. He plants the year;
The weighty weeks without hands grow,
Heaved drum on drum; but hands álso
Must deal with Margaret Clitheroe.

The very victim would prepare.
Like water soon to be sucked in
Will crisp itself or settle and spin   10
So she: one sees that here and there
She mends the way she means to go.
The last thing Margaret's fingers sew
Is a shroud for Margaret Clitheroe.

The Christ-ed beauty of her mind
Her mould of features mated well.
She was admired. The spirit of hell
Being to her virtue clinching-blind
No wonder therefore was not slow
To the bargain of its hate to throw   20
The body of Margaret Clitheroe.

Fawning fawning crocodiles
Days and days came round about
With tears to put her candle out;
They wound their winch of wicked smiles
To take her; while their tongues would go
God lighten your dark heart—but no,
Christ lived in Margaret Clitheroe.

She caught the crying of those Three,
The Immortals of the eternal ring,
The Utterer, Utterèd, Uttering,
And witness in her place would she.
She not considered whether or no
She pleased the Queen and Council. So
To the death with Margaret Clitheroe!

She was a woman, upright, outright;
Her will was bent at God. For that
Word went she should be crushed out flat

    .   .   .   .   .   .

Within her womb the child was quick.
Small matter of that then! Let him smother
And wreck in ruins of his mother

    .   .   .   .   .

Great Thecla, the plumed passionflower,
Next Mary mother of maid and nun,

    .   .   .   .   .

And every saint of bloody hour
And breath immortal thronged that show;
Heaven turned its starlight eyes below
To the murder of Margaret Clitheroe.

She held her hands to, like in prayer;
They had them out and laid them wide
(Just like Jesus crucified);
They brought their hundredweights to bear.
Jews killed Jesus long ago
God's son; these (they did not know)
God's daughter Margaret Clitheroe.

When she felt the kill-weights crush
She told His name times-over three;
I suffer this she said *for Thee.*
After that in perfect hush
For a quarter of an hour or so
She was with the choke of woe.—
It is over, Margaret Clitheroe.

60

. . . . .

146

REPEAT that, repeat,
Cuckoo, bird, and open ear wells, heart-springs, delightfully
    sweet,
With a ballad, with a ballad, a rebound
Off trundled timber and scoops of the hillside ground, hollow
    hollow hollow ground:
The whole landscape flushes on a sudden at a sound.

147

'The Child is Father to the Man'
(*Wordsworth*)

'THE child is father to the man.'
How can he be? The words are wild.
Suck any sense from that who can:
'The child is father to the man.'
No; what the poet did write ran,
'The man is father to the child.'
'The child is father to the man!'
How *can* he be? The words are wild.

148

(On a Piece of Music)

How all's to one thing wrought!
The members, how they sit!
O what a tune the thought
Must be that fancied it.

Nor angel insight can
Learn how the heart is hence:
Since all the make of man
Is law's indifference.

[Who shaped these walls has shewn
The music of his mind,
Made known, though thick through stone
What beauty beat behind.]

Not free in this because
His powers seemed free to play:
He swept what scope he was
To sweep and must obey.

Though down his being's bent
Like air he changed in choice,
That was an instrument
Which overvaulted voice.

What makes the man and what
The man within that makes:
Ask whom he serves or not
Serves and what side he takes.

For good grows wild and wide,
Has shades, is nowhere none;
But right must seek a side
And choose for chieftain one.

Therefore this masterhood,
This piece of perfect song,
This fault-not-found-with good
Is neither right nor wrong,

No more than red and blue,
No more than Re and Mi,
Or sweet the golden glue
That's built for by the bee.

[Who built these walls made known
The music of his mind,
Yet here he has but shewn
His ruder-rounded rind.
His brightest blooms lie there unblown,
His sweetest nectar hides behind.]

149

(Ashboughs)

a.

NOT of all my eyes see, wandering on the world,
Is anything a milk to the mind so, so sighs deep
Poetry tó it, as a tree whose boughs break in the sky.
Say it is áshboughs: whether on a December day and furled
Fast ór they in clammyish lashtender combs creep
Apart wide and new-nestle at heaven most high.

They touch heaven, tabour on it; how their talons sweep
The smouldering enormous winter welkin! May
Mells blue and snowwhite through them, a fringe and fray
Of greenery: it is old earth's groping towards the steep
        Heaven whom she childs us by.

They touch, they tabour on it, hover on it[; here, there
   hurled],
                              With talons sweep
The smouldering enormous winter welkin. [Eye,
                     But more cheer is when] May
Mells blue with snowwhite through their fringe and fray
Of greenery and old earth gropes for, grasps at steep
      Heaven with it whom she childs things by.

150

THE times are nightfall, look, their light grows less;
The times are winter, watch, a world undone:
They waste, they wither worse; they as they run
Or bring more or more blazon man's distress.
And I not help. Nor word now of success:
All is from wreck, here, there, to rescue one—
Work which to see scarce so much as begun
Makes welcome death, does dear forgetfulness.

Or what is else? There is your world within.
There rid the dragons, root out there the sin.
Your will is law in that small commonweal . . . .

151

HOPE holds to Christ the mind's own mirror out
To take His lovely likeness more and more.
It will not well, so she would bring about
A growing burnish brighter than before

And turns to wash it from her welling eyes
And breathes the blots off all with sighs on sighs.

Her glass is blest but she as good as blind
Holds till hand aches and wonders what is there;
Her glass drinks light, she darkles down behind,
All of her glorious gainings unaware.

I told you that she turned her mirror dim
Betweenwhiles, but she sees herself not Him.

152

St. Winefred's Well

ACT I. SC. 1

Enter Teryth from riding, Winefred following.

T. WHAT is it, Gwen, my girl? ¹ why do you hover and
    haunt me?

W. You came by Caerwys, sir? ¹

T.   I came by Caerwys.

W.   There
    Some messenger there might have ¹ met you from my
    uncle.

T. Your uncle met the messenger— ¹ met me; and this the
    message:
    Lord Beuno comes tonight. ¹

W.   Tonight, sir!

T.   Soon, now: therefore
    Have all things ready in his room. ¹

W.   There needs but little doing.

T.   Let what there needs be done. ˈ Stay! with him one companion,

His deacon, Dirvan. Warm ˈ twice over must the welcome be,

But both will share one cell.— ˈ This was good news, Gwenvrewi.

W. Ah yes!

T.   Why, get thee gone then; ˈ tell thy mother I want her.   *Exit Winefred.*   10

No man has such a daughter. ˈ The fathers of the world

Call no such maiden 'mine'. ˈ The deeper grows her dearness

And more and more times laces ˈ round and round my heart,

The more some monstrous hand ˈ gropes with clammy fingers there,

Tampering with those sweet bines, ˈ draws them out, strains them, strains them;

Meantime some tongue cries 'What, Teryth! ˈ what, thou poor fond father!

How when this bloom, this honeysuckle, ˈ that rides the air so rich about thee,

Is all, all sheared away, ˈ thus!' Then I sweat for fear.

Or else a funeral, ˈ and yet 'tis not a funeral,

Some pageant which takes tears ˈ and I must foot with feeling that   20

Alive or dead my girl ˈ is carried in it, endlessly

Goes marching thro' my mind. ˈ What sense is this? It has none.

This is too much the father; ˈ nay the mother. Fanciful!

I here forbid my thoughts ˈ to fool themselves with fears.

                   Enter Gwenlo.

.   .   .   .

Act II.—*Scene, a wood ending in a steep bank over a dry dean. Winefred having been murdered within, re-enter Caradoc with a bloody sword.*

C. My héart, where have we been? ˥ What have we séen, my
        mind?
     What stroke has Carádoc's right arm dealt? ˥ what done?
        Head of a rebel
     Struck óff it has; written ˥ upon lovely limbs,
     In bloody letters, lessons ˥ of earnest, of revenge;
     Monuments of my earnest, ˥ records of my revenge,
     On one that went against me ˥ whéreas I had warned her—
     Warned her! well she knew ˥ I warned her of this work.
     What work? what harm's done? There is ˥ no harm done,
        none yet;
     Perhaps we struck no blow, ˥ Gwenvrewi lives perhaps;
     To make believe my mood was— ˥ mock. O I might think
        so   10
     But here, here is a workman ˥ from his day's task sweats.
     Wiped I am sure this was; ˥ it seems, not well; for still,
     Still the scarlet swings ˥ and dances on the blade.
     So be it. Thou steel, thou butcher,
     I cán scour thee, fresh burnish thee, ˥ sheathe thee in thy
        dark lair; these drops
     Never, never, never ˥ in their blue banks again.
     The woeful, Cradock, O ˥ the woeful word! Then what,
     What have we seen? Her head, ˥ sheared from her shoul-
        ders, fall,
     And lapped in shining hair, ˥ roll to the bank's edge; then
     Down the beetling banks, ˥ like water in waterfalls,   20
     It stooped and flashed and fell ˥ and ran like water away.
     Her eyes, oh and her eyes!
     In all her beauty, and sunlight ˥ tó it is a pit, den, darkness,
     Foamfalling is not fresh to it, ˥ rainbow by it not beam-
        ing,
     In all her body, I say, ˥ no place was like her eyes,

189

No piece matched those eyes ' kept most part much cast
    down
But, being lifted, ímmortal, ' of immórtal brightness.
Several times I saw them, ' thrice or four times turning;
Round and round they came ' and flashed towards heaven:
    O there,
There they did appeal. ' Therefore airy vengeances   30
Are afoot; heaven-vault fast purpling ' portends, and what
    first lightning
Any instant falls means me. ' And I do not repent;
I do not and I will not ' repent, not repent.
The blame bear who aroused me. ' What I have done
    violent
I have líke a líon dóne, ' líonlíke dóne,
Honouring an uncontrolled ' royal wrathful nature,
Mantling passion in a grandeur, ' crimson grandeur.
Now be my pride then perfect, ' all one piece. Henceforth
In a wide world of defiance ' Caradoc lives alone,
Loyal to his own soul, laying his ' ówn law down, no law
    nor   40
Lord now curb him for ever. ' O daring! O deep insight!
What is virtue? Valour; ' only the heart valiant.
And right? Only resolution; ' will, his will unwavering
Who, like me, knowing his nature ' to the heart home,
    nature's business,
Despatches with no flinching. ' But wíll flesh, O can flésh
Second this fiery strain? ' Not always; O no no!
We cannot live this life out; ' sometimes we must weary
And in this darksome world ' what comfort can I find?
Down this darksome world ' cómfort whére can I find
When 'ts light I quenched; its rose, ' time's one rich rose,
    my hand,   50
By her bloom, fast by ' her fresh, her fleecèd bloom,
Hideous dáshed dówn, leaving ' earth a winter withering
With no now, no Gwenvrewi. ' I must miss her most
That might have spared her were it ' but for passion-sake.

Yes,
To hunger and not have, yét ' hope ón for, to storm and
    strive and
Be at every assault fresh foiled, ' worse flung, deeper dis-
    appointed,
The turmoil and the torment, ' it has, I swear, a sweetness,
Keeps a kind of joy in it, ' a zest, an edge, an ecstasy,
Next after sweet success. ' I am not left even this;
I all my being have hacked ' in half with hér neck: one
    part,   60
Reason, selfdisposal, ' choice of better or worse way,
Is corpse now, cannot change; ' my other self, this soul,
Life's quick, this kínd, this kéen self-feeling,
With dreadful distillation ' of thoughts sour as blood,
Must all day long taste murder. ' What do nów then? Do?
    Nay,
Déed-bound I am; óne deed tréads all dówn here ' cramps
    all doing. What do? Not yield,
Not hope, not pray; despair; ' ay, that: brazen despair out,
Brave all, and take what comes— ' as here this rabble is
    come,
Whose bloods I reck no more of, ' no more rank with hers
Than sewers with sacred oils. ' Mankind, that mob, comes.
    Come!   70

Enter a crowd, among them Teryth, Gwenlo, Beuno.

.   .   .   .

(C.) *After Winefred's raising from the dead and the breaking
    out of the fountain.*

BEUNO. O now while skies are blue, ' now while seas are salt,
    While rushy rains shall fall ' or brooks shall fleet from
        fountains,
    While sick men shall cast sighs, ' of sweet health all des-
        pairing,

While blind men's eyes shall thírst after ˡ daylight, draughts
    of daylight,
Or deaf ears shall desire that ˡ lípmusic that's lóst upon
    them,
While cripples are, while lepers, ˡ dancers in dismal limb-
    dance,
Fallers in dreadful frothpits, ˡ waterfearers wild,
Stone, palsy, cancer, cough, ˡ lung-wasting, womb-not-
    bearing,
Rupture, running sores, ˡ what more? in brief, in burden,
As long as men are mortal ˡ and God merciful,   10
So long to this sweet spot, ˡ this leafy lean-over,
This Dry Dean, nów no longer dry ˡ nor dumb, but moist
    and musical
With the uproll and the downcarol ˡ of day and night
    delivering
Water, which keeps thy name, ˡ (for not in róck wrítten,
But in pale water, fráil water, ˡ wild rash and reeling
    water,
That will not wear a print, ˡ that will not stain a pen,
Thy venerable record, ˡ virgin, is recorded)
Here to this holy well ˡ shall pilgrimages be,
And not from purple Wales only ˡ nor from elmy England,
But from beyond seas, Erin, ˡ France and Flanders, every-
    where,   20
Pilgrims, still pilgrims, móre ˡ pilgrims, still more poor
    pilgrims.

   .   .   .   .

What sights shall be when some ˡ that swung, wretches, on
    crutches
Their crutches shall cast from them, ˡ on heels of air de-
    parting,
Or they go rich as roseleaves ˡ hence that loathsome cáme
    hither!
Not now to náme even

Those dearer, more divine ǀ boons whose haven the heart
   is.

.   .   .   .

As sure as what is most sure, ǀ sure as that spring primroses
Shall new-dapple next year, ǀ sure as to-morrow morning,
Amongst come-back-again things, ǀ things with a revival,
   things with a recovery,
Thy name . . .   30

.   .   .   .

153
To his Watch

MORTAL my mate, bearing my rock-a-heart
Warm beat with cold beat company, shall I
Earlier or you fail at our force and lie
The ruins of, rifled, once a world of art?
The telling time our task is; time's some part,
Not all, but we were framed to fail and die—
One spell and well that one. There, ah thereby
Is comfort's carol of all or woe's worst smart.

Field-flown, the departed day no morning brings
Saying 'This was yours' with her, but new one, worse,
And then that last and shortest . . .

154

STRIKE, churl; hurl, cheerless wind, then; heltering hail
May's beauty massacre and wispèd wild clouds grow
Out on the giant air; tell Summer No,
Bid joy back, have at the harvest, keep Hope pale.

THEE, God, I come from, to thee go,
All dáy long I like fountain flow
From thy hand out, swayed about
Mote-like in thy mighty glow.

What I know of thee I bless,
As acknowledging thy stress
On my being and as seeing
Something of thy holiness.

Once I turned from thee and hid,
Bound on what thou hadst forbid;
Sow the wind I would; I sinned:
I repent of what I did.

Bad I am, but yet thy child.
Father, be thou reconciled.
Spare thou me, since I see
With thy might that thou art mild.

I have life left with me still
And thy purpose to fulfil;
Yea a debt to pay thee yet:
Help me, sir, and so I will.

But thou bidst, and just thou art,
Me shew mercy from my heart
Towards my brother, every other
Man my mate and counterpart.

.   .   .   .   .   .

WHAT shall I do for the land that bred me,
Her homes and fields that folded and fed me?
Be under her banner and live for her honour:
Under her banner I'll live for her honour.
    CHORUS. Under her banner we live for her honour.

Not the pleasure, the pay, the plunder,
But country and flag, the flag I am under—
There is the shilling that finds me willing
To follow a banner and fight for honour.
    CH. We follow her banner, we fight for her honour.

Call me England's fame's fond lover,
Her fame to keep, her fame to recover.
Spend me or end me what God shall send me,
But under her banner I live for her honour.
    CH. Under her banner we march for her honour.

Where is the field I must play the man on?
O welcome there their steel or cannon.
Immortal beauty is death with duty,
If under her banner I fall for her honour.
    CH. Under her banner we fall for her honour.

157

On the Portrait of Two Beautiful Young People

A Brother and Sister

O I ADMIRE and sorrow! The heart's eye grieves
Discovering you, dark tramplers, tyrant years.
A juice rides rich through bluebells, in vine leaves,
And beauty's dearest veriest vein is tears.

Happy the father, mother of these! Too fast:
Not that, but thus far, all with frailty, blest
In one fair fall; but, for time's aftercast,
Creatures all heft, hope, hazard, interest.

And are they thus? The fine, the fingering beams
Their young delightful hour do feature down
That fleeted else like day-dissolvèd dreams
Or ringlet-race on burling Barrow brown.

She leans on him with such contentment fond
As well the sister sits, would well the wife;
His looks, the soul's own letters, see beyond,
Gaze on, and fall directly forth on life.

But ah, bright forelock, cluster that you are
Of favoured make and mind and health and youth,
Where lies your landmark, seamark, or soul's star?
There's none but truth can stead you. Christ is truth.

There's none but good can bé good, both for you
And what sways with you, maybe this sweet maid;
None good but God—a warning wavèd to
One once that was found wanting when Good weighed.

Man lives that list, that leaning in the will
No wisdom can forecast by gauge or guess,
The selfless self of self, most strange, most still,
Fast furled and all foredrawn to No or Yes.

Your feast of; that most in you earnest eye
May but call on your banes to more carouse.
Worst will the best. What worm was here, we cry,
To have havoc-pocked so, see, the hung-heavenward
        boughs?

Enough: corruption was the world's first woe.
What need I strain my heart beyond my ken?
O but I bear my burning witness though
Against the wild and wanton work of men.

. . . .

158

THE sea took pity: it interposed with doom:
'I have tall daughters dear that heed my hand:
Let Winter wed one, sow them in her womb,
And she shall child them on the New-world strand.'

. . . .

159

Epithalamion

HARK, hearer, hear what I do; lend a thought now, make be-
        lieve
We are leafwhelmed somewhere with the hood
Of some branchy bunchy bushybowered wood,
Southern dean or Lancashire clough or Devon cleave,

That leans along the loins of hills, where a candycoloured,
    where a gluegold-brown 5
Marbled river, boisterously beautiful, between
Roots and rocks is danced and dandled, all in froth and water-
    blowballs, down.
We are there, when we hear a shout
That the hanging honeysuck, the dogeared hazels in the cover
Makes dither, makes hover 10
And the riot of a rout
Of, it must be, boys from the town
Bathing: it is summer's sovereign good.

By there comes a listless stranger: beckoned by the noise
He drops towards the river: unseen 15
Sees the bevy of them, how the boys
With dare and with downdolfinry and bellbright bodies
    huddling out,
Are earthworld, airworld, waterworld thorough hurled, all by
    turn and turn about.

This garland of their gambol flashes in his breast
Into such a sudden zest 20
Of summertime joys
That he hies to a pool neighbouring; sees it is the best
There; sweetest, freshest, shadowiest;
Fairyland; silk-beech, scrolled ash, packed sycamore, wild
    wychelm, hornbeam fretty overstood
By. Rafts and rafts of flake leaves light, dealt so, painted on the
    air, 25
Hang as still as hawk or hawkmoth, as the stars or as the
    angels there,
Like the thing that never knew the earth, never off roots
Rose. Here he feasts: lovely all is! No more: off with—down
    he dings
His bleachèd both and woolwoven wear:

Careless these in coloured wisp   30
All lie tumbled-to; then with loop-locks
Forward falling, forehead frowning, lips crisp
Over finger-teasing task, his twiny boots
Fast he opens, last he off wrings
Till walk the world he can with bare his feet   35
And come where lies a coffer, burly all of blocks
Built of chancequarrièd, selfquainèd, hoar-huskèd rocks
And the water warbles over into, filleted ¹ with glassy grassy
    quicksilvery shivès and shoots
And with heavenfallen freshness down from moorland still
    brims,
Dark or daylight on and on. Here he will then, here he will
    the fleet   40
Flinty kindcold element let break across his limbs
Long. Where we leave him, froliclavish, while he looks about
    him, laughs, swims.

Enough now; since the sacred matter that I mean
I should be wronging longer leaving it to float
Upon this only gambolling and echoing-of-earth note—   45

What is . . . . the delightful dean?
Wedlock. What the water? Spousal love.

   .   .   .   .

    .   .   .   .

                     turns
Father, mother, brothers, sisters, friends
Into fairy trees, wildflowers, woodferns   50
Rankèd round the bower

   .   .   .   .

TRANSLATIONS
LATIN AND
WELSH POEMS
&c.

160

Aeschylus: Prometheus Desmotes

Lines 88–127

PROMETHEUS

DIVINITY of air, fleet-feather'd gales,
Ye river-heads, thou billowy deep that laugh'st
A countless laughter, Earth mother of all,
Thou sun, allseeing eyeball of the day,
Witness to me! Look you, I am a god,
And these are from the gods my penalties.
  Look with what unseemliness
  I a thousand thousand years
  Must watch down with weariness
    Fallen from my peers.   10
  The young chief of the bless'd of heaven
  Hath devis'd new pains for me
    And hath given
  This indignity of chains.
  What is, and what is to be,
  All alike is grief to me;
  I look all ways but only see
The drear dull burthen of unending pains.

     .   .   .   .   .

    Ah well a day!—
  What was that echo caught anigh me,   20
  That scent from breezes breathing by me,

Sped of gods, or mortal sign,
Or half-human, half-divine?
To the world's end, to the last hill
Comes one to gaze upon my ill;
Be this thy quest or other, see
A god enchain'd of destiny,
Foe of Zeus and hate of all
That wont to throng Zeus' banquet-hall,
Sith I lov'd and lov'd too well   30
The race of man; and hence I fell.
Woe is me, what do I hear?
Fledgèd things do rustle near;
Whispers of the mid-air stirring
With light pulse of pinions skirring,
And all that comes is fraught to me with fear.

161

(From the Greek)

LOVE me as I love thee. O double sweet!
But if thou hate me who love thee, albeit
    Even thus I have the better of thee:
Thou canst not hate so much as I do love thee.

162

Inundatio Oxoniana

VERNA diu saevas senserunt pascua nubes
Imbribus assiduis, et aquosi copia caeli
Ingruit et spretae direpto limine ripae
Fit mare per patulos ventisque ferentibus agros.

Interrupta locis candenti gramina surgunt
Laetius in pelago, pars lenibus edita dorsis
Quae viret: at vacuus jam caetera condidit humor.
Vix indiscretas proprio deducitur alveo
Isis aquas; liquidos exercent libera tractus
Flabra, vadisque novis Austro juvat ire secundo;   10
Invia velificant nemorum et penetratur opacas
In salices; inter discussae culmina silvae
Populus insolitis dat currere mersa carinis.
   At quinto tandem si sol equitaverit orbi
Per purum, toties si riserit igneus aether,
Deficient reduces undae. Tum saepe marinus
Fertur odor campo et madidas levis occupat auras,
Urbem qui subeat mediam lustretque domorum
Intima; tristem adeo non usquam averteris algam.
Hinc quota vis morbi, quoties adiisse querentur,   20
Tecta petis nostri vicinam obnoxia febrem.
At vicibus vertisse solum est, aegrosque calores
Jam fugere: his non perpetui versamur in umbris.
Pars ascripta solo sedes servabit avitas
Tutior, indigenae plebes assueta periclo:
Hinc almo certe submotae numine pestes,
Namque licet tepidos in nostra Favonius imbres
Arva iteret pernox, resupina impune fatigat
Ipse loca et campis obducitur aequor inerme.
Vix rubeant immo siccis sua lilia pratis,   30
Quot capita ad notos agitari videris amnes,
Debita ni paullum fecundo luserit unda
Diluvio interea, dubii se pandere fluctus
Ni poterint prius et limos posuisse sequaces.
Dulcia sic fluviis praetendit fortior arbos
Vimina; sic crescunt salices; eques avia quaerit
Aequora sic, tumidasque libentius itur in herbas.

163

ELEGIACS: *Tristi tu, memini*

TRISTI tu, memini, virgo cum sorte fuisti,
    Illo nec steterat tempore primus amor.
Jamque abeo: rursus tu sola relinqueris: ergo
    Tristior haec aetas; tristis et illa fuit.
Adsum gratus ego necopini apparitor ignis,
    Inter ego vacuas stella serena nives.

164

ELEGIACS: after *The Convent Threshold*

(Paragraphs 1 and 9)

FRATERNO nobis interluit unda cruore
    Et novus exstincti stat patris, Aule, cruor.
O mihi tu summe et semper suavissime rerum,
    Divisam longe jam cruor ille tenet.
It via per stellas sublimis et aureus ordo
    Excipiens noctem nocte dieque diem:
Hanc ingressa poli seras elabar ad arces
    Sub vitreasque domos ad vitreumque mare.
Candida quos perhibes praecellere lilia forma
    Purpurei infecta sunt male labe pedes.   10
Purpurea sunt labe pedes et tristibus exsto
    Indicio guttis criminis ipsa mei,
Gaudia quae fuerint et qui post gaudia fletus
    Et qui conciderit nec recidivus amor.
At neque habent illi tantum nec sanguis inhaeret
    Scilicet admotis ille abolendus aquis:

206

Si penitus caecum possim recludere pectus
    Haec penitus caeco pectore culpa latet.
Sed mare quod mixta rutilat flammaque vitroque—
    Illud molle vitrum, limpidus ignis erat—   20
Afferat ah captis oro medicamina plantis
    Infectaeque notae suppositique doli.
Quumque sit exstructo monstratum limite caelum
    O adeas mecum quae subit astra viam.

. . . .

Hesternae referam quot vidi insomnia noctis
    Ambiguaeque umbrae noxve diesve foret.
Plurima tum nobis gelido coma rore madebat:
    Creverat ex gelida ros liquefactus humo.
Huc ades atque tua num tangar imagine quaeris,
    An memor et requies hactenus illa tui.   30
Ista quod quondam saliebat imagine pectus
    Urgenti dictis stat tibi pulvis iners.
Percipio quaesita tamen, nec reddere vocem
    Non erat, et tardo pauca sopore dabam:
Sunt tristes thalami, funesta toralia nobis;
    Impositoque rigent frigida saxa toro.
Tu dulces thalamos, tu quaere novos hymenaeos,
    Adde, licet, grato mollia membra toro.
Est tibi quae melius te foverit altera conjunx,
    Suavior exstat amor qui sit amore meo.   40
Perculeras valide trepidas ad talia palmas
    Visaque sunt subitis membra labare modis.
Extrema haec sensi; crassae simul intima terrae
    Volvor et in vacuos praecipitata locos.
Ah neque te festis plausu dare signa choreis
    Nec rata sum nimio membra labare mero.

165

HORACE: *Persicos odi, puer, apparatus*

(ODES I. XXXVIII)

AH child, no Persian-perfect art!
Crowns composite and braided bast
They tease me. Never know the part
　　Where roses linger last.

Bring natural myrtle, and have done:
Myrtle will suit your place and mine:
And set the glasses from the sun
　　Beneath the tackled vine.

166

HORACE: *Odi profanum volgus et arceo*

(ODES III. i)

TREAD back—and back, the lewd and lay!—
Grace love your lips!—what never ear
Heard yet, the Muses' man, today
I bid the boys and maidens hear.

Kings herd it on their subject droves
But Jove's the herd that keeps the kings—
Jove of the Giants: simple Jove's
Mere eyebrow rocks this round of things.

Say man than man may rank his rows
Wider, more wholesale; one with claim
Of blood to our green hustings goes;
One with more conscience, cleaner fame;

One better backed comes crowding by:—
That level power whose word is Must
Dances the balls for low or high:
Her urn takes all, her deal is just.

Sinner who saw the blade that hung
Vertical home, could Sicily fare
Be managed tasty to that tongue?
Or bird with pipe, viol with air

Bring sleep round then?—sleep not afraid
Of country bidder's calls or low
Entries or banks all over shade
Or Tempe with the west to blow.

Who stops his asking mood at par
The burly sea may quite forget
Nor fear the violent calendar
At Haedus-rise, Arcturus-set,

For hail upon the vine nor break
His heart at farming, what between
The dog-star with the fields abake
And spiting snows to choke the green.

Fish feel their waters drawing to
With our abutments: there we see
The lades discharged and laded new,
And Italy flies from Italy.

But fears, fore-motions of the mind,
Climb quits: one boards the master there
On brazèd barge and hard behind
Sits to the beast that seats him—Care.

O if there's that which Phrygian stone
And crimson wear of starry shot
Not sleek away; Falernian-grown
And oils of Shushan comfort not,

Why . . . .
. . . .
Why should I change a Sabine dale
For wealth as wide as weariness?

167

Jesu Dulcis Memoria

JESUS to cast one thought upon
Makes gladness after He is gone,
But more than honey and honeycomb
Is to come near and take Him home.

Song never was so sweet in ear,
Word never was such news to hear,
Thought half so sweet there is not one
As Jesus God the Father's Son.

Jesu, their hope who go astray,
So kind to those who ask the way,
So good to those who look for Thee,
To those who find what must Thou be?

To speak of that no tongue will do
Nor letters suit to spell it true:
But they can guess who have tasted of
What Jesus is and what is love.

Jesu, a springing well Thou art,
Daylight to head and treat to heart,
And matched with Thee there's nothing glad
That men have wished for or have had.

Wish us Good morning when we wake
And light us, Lord, with Thy day-break.
Beat from our brains the thicky night
And fill the world up with delight.

Be our delight, O Jesu, now
As by and by our prize art Thou,
And grant our glorying may be
World without end alone in Thee.

168

S. Thomae Aquinatis

Rhythmus ad SS. Sacramentum
'*Adoro te supplex, latens deitas*'

GODHEAD here in hiding, whom I do adore
Masked by these bare shadows, shape and nothing more,
See, Lord, at thy service low lies here a heart
Lost, all lost in wonder at the God thou art.

Seeing, touching, tasting are in thee deceived;
How says trusty hearing? that shall be believed:
What God's Son has told me, take for truth I do;
Truth himself speaks truly or there's nothing true.

On the cross thy godhead made no sign to men;
Here thy very manhood steals from human ken:
Both are my confession, both are my belief,
And I pray the prayer of the dying thief.

I am not like Thomas, wounds I cannot see,
But can plainly call thee Lord and God as he:
This faith each day deeper be my holding of,
Daily make me harder hope and dearer love.

O thou our reminder of Christ crucified,
Living Bread the life of us for whom he died,
Lend this life to me then: feed and feast my mind,
There be thou the sweetness man was meant to find.

Bring the tender tale true of the Pelican;
Bathe me, Jesu Lord, in what thy bosom ran—
Blood that but one drop of has the worth to win
All the world forgiveness of its world of sin.

Jesu whom I look at shrouded here below,
I beseech thee send me what I thirst for so,
Some day to gaze on thee face to face in light
And be blest for ever with thy glory's sight.

169
Oratio Patris Condren: O Jesu vivens in Maria

Jesu that dost in Mary dwell,
Be in thy servants' hearts as well,
In the spirit of thy holiness,
In the fullness of thy force and stress,
In the very ways that thy life goes
And virtues that thy pattern shows,

In the sharing of thy mysteries;
And every power in us that is
Against thy power put under feet
In the Holy Ghost the Paraclete
    To the glory of the Father. Amen.

170

O Deus, ego amo te

O GOD, I love thee, I love thee—
Not out of hope of heaven for me
Nor fearing not to love and be
    In the everlasting burning.
Thou, thou, my Jesus, after me
    Didst reach thine arms out dying,
For my sake sufferedst nails and lance,
Mocked and marrèd countenance,
    Sorrows passing number,
    Sweat and care and cumber,
Yea and death, and this for me,
    And thou couldst see me sinning:
Then I, why should not I love thee,
Jesu so much in love with me?
Not for heaven's sake; not to be
Out of hell by loving thee;
Not for any gains I see;
But just the way that thou didst me
I do love and I will love thee:
What must I love thee, Lord, for then?—
For being my king and God. Amen.

171

The Same

(*Welsh Version*)

*Ochenaid Sant Francis Xavier,
Apostol yr Indiaid.*

NID, am i Ti fy ngwared i,
    Y'th garaf, Duw, yn lân,
Nac, am mai'r rhai na'th garant Di,
    Y berni am fyth i dân.

Ti, ti a'm hymgofleidiaist oll,
    Fy Jesu, ar y Groes;
Gan wayw, hoelion, enllib mawr,
    Goddefaist ddirfawr loes;

Aneirif ddolur darfu it',
    A phoen, a chwŷs eu dwyn,
Hyn erofi pechadur oll,
    Hyd farw er fy mwyn.

Gan hyny, 'r hygar Jesu, pam
    Na'th garwn yn ddilyth?
Nid er cael gennyt nef na phwyth,
    Na rhag fy mhoeni byth;

Ond megis Ti a'm ceraist i,
    A'th garaf, garu'r wyf,
Yn unig am Dy fod yn Dduw,
    A'th fod i mi yn Rhwyf.

Cywydd

Annerch i'r tra pharcedig Dr. Th. Brown esgob yr Amwy-
thig, wedi cyrhaedd o hono ei bummed flwyddyn ar hugain,
yr hon a elwir y Jubil; a chwyno y mae'r bardd fôd daiar a
dŵr yn tystiolaethu yn fwy i hên grefydd Gwynedd nag y
bydd dŷn, a dywed hefyd mai gobeithia fod hyny i gael ei
gyfnewid o waith yr esgob.

Y MAE'N llewyn yma'n llon
Â ffrydan llawer ffynon,
Gweddill gwyn gadwyd i ni
Gan Feuno a Gwenfrewi.
Wlaw neu wlith, ni chei wlâd braidd   5
Tan rôd sydd fal hon iraidd.
Gwan ddwfr a ddwg, nis dwg dŷn,
Dyst ffyddlon am ein dyffryn;
Hên ddaiar ddengys â'i gwêdd
Ran drag'wyddawl o rinwedd;   10
Ni ddiffyg ond naws ddyniol,
Dŷn sydd yn unig yn ôl.
Dâd, o dy law di ela
Tardd a lîf â'r hardd brîf dda;
Tydi a ddygi trwy ffŷdd   15
Croyw feddygiaeth, maeth crefydd;
A gwela Gwalia'r awr hon
Gwîr saint, glân îr gwyryfon.

Brân Maenefa a'i cant
Ebrill y pedwerydd ar hugain
1876

173

Ad Episcopum Salopiensem

QUÒD festas luces juvat instaurare Beatis
    Natalesque suis mos cumulare rosis,
His, pater, indiciis et consuetudine laeti
    Hac, colimus lecto te, pia turba, die;
Quique tuam quamcumque alias foret aptus in horam
    Serus in hanc nobis est revolutus honor.
Venit enim quintus vegeto et vigesimus annus
    Ex quo sacra tuumst lamina nacta caput.
Ut reor, is numerus mortalia saecula quadrat:
    Saecla quadras, eadem dimidiare queas.   10
Si Pius ille Petri pertingit et amplius annos
    Est cui longaevi nempe Joannis erunt.
Haud tamen ista animis in tempora vertor aruspex:
    Unum ego qui nunc est auguror esse diem;
Qui felix—at enim est felix patriaeque tibique:
    Tu quod es, hoc ut sis, id putat illa suum.
Te pastore, Deo quod visumst, integer Angli
    Grex in divinum coepimus ire gregem.
Quin etiam alma tuis sic secum agit Anglia lustris:
    'Scilicet ex illo tempore sancta feror.   20
His mihi post tantas, immania saecula, clades,
    His mihi, prisca, viris tu recidiva, fides.
Ergo optatarum salvete exordia rerum,
    Vos in fortunis O elementa meis.
Hinc ego jam numeror; fastis ego candida vestris;
    Quae potui per vos sponsa placere Deo.'

174
AD REVERENDUM PATREM FRATREM THOMAM BURKE O.P. COLLEGIUM S. BEUNONIS INVISENTEM

IGNOTUM spatiari horto, discumbere mensis,
    Et nova mirabar sacra litare virum.
Simplicibus propior quam nos candore columbis
    Ille erat et qualis veste referret ovem.
Mox ut quaesivi: Monacho quod nomen et ordo
    Qui velit ad nostros unicus esse lares;
Pura caput tonsum cui velat lana cucullo
    Et cadit ad medium cui toga pura pedem,
Nescio quod duplex a tergo, a pectore peplum est,
    Atque terit laevum magna corona latus?   10
Respondent: Haec vox toto clamantis in orbe
    Perque hominum Domino corda parantis iter.
Huic fuit Oceanus submissis utilis undis;
    Audiit occidua hunc, hunc oriente plaga.
Sed monachus non est verum est ex Fratribus unus,
    Quem pater agnoscit stelliger ille suum;
Doctus Aquinatis reserare oracula Thomae,
    Si tamen est illo nunc quod in ore latet,
Quem tam Gudinus, Godatus, tamque Gonetus,
    Tam Cajetanus perspicuum esse jubent,   20
Jamdudum innumeri patientem interpretis et quem
    Torqueat in sensus, nec mora, quisque suos.
Praeterea teneris fuit hic tironibus olim
    Ductor et insuetae candida norma viae.
At non omnis in his, vel, si placet, omnis in his est,
    Sic tamen in magnis ut levis esse queat,
Intermiscet enim cum sacris ludicra curis,
    Nec vox nec facies constet ut una viro.
Haec et plura monent atque addunt nomen, at illud
    Non tulit aut aegre nostra Camoena tulit.   30
Talem ego nunc hominem multum salvere juberem
    Ancipitem sed me scrupulus unus habet;

Num sese velit ille a me laudarier Anglo,
    Toto qui cives sternit in orbe meos.
Quidquid erit, passim mea dat Guenefrida salutem:
    Huic det et aversum solvat amore sinum.
Quodque etiam possit plebi prodesse fideli,
    Muneris id nostro debeat ille solo.

175

In S. Winefridam

praeter miraculorum gratiam
operam dantem
et balneis et molae

TEMPERAT aestiva fessis sua balnea membris,
    Hiberna rigidis temperat alma manu;
Quin etiam nostros dextra dignata labores
    Utilis assiduae, nec pudet esse, molaest;
Scilicet alta polo sordes non temnit honestas
    Virgineum quamvis suadeat ipsa decus.

176

HAEC te jubent salvere, quod possunt, loca
    Diluta nimiis imbribus,
Multum, Pater, salvere deserens jubet
    Infecta prata foenisex.
Sed candidatus quem vides nostrum chorus
    Ipso colore prospera
Videtur augurari et ore optat meo
    Et gratias et gaudia.
Intonsus ergo hic cum suis pastoribus
    Bene vertat oro grex tuus
Et quae tuae novella cura dexterae
    Remittitur provincia.

218

MIROR surgentem per puram Oriona noctem,
    Candida luna licet
Adstet et exiguis incumbat durior astris
    Nec simul esse sinat.
Verum hic Orion miror quam crescat in altum et
    Quam micet igne suo,
Non suus aetherium quem purpurat impetus, itque
    Molle reditque decus:
Quin versare aliquos septena cacumina ventos
    Turbine posse putes.
Miror item suaves adeo spirarier auras
    Egelidumque Notum
Atque hiemem tantum primasque tepere Kalendas
    Quas novus annus agit,
Namque ab eo qui jam pulcerrimus occidit anni
    Dicimus ire dies.
O Jesu qui nos homines caelestis et alta haec
    Contrahis astra manu,
Omnia sunt a te: precor a te currat et annus:
    Is bonus annus erit.
Omnia sunt in te: nostrum vivat genus in te,
    Quod tua membra sumus,
Omnes concessas inquam quot carpimus auras
    Suspicimusque polum.
Gratia deest sed enim multis: ut gratia desit,
    Omnibus alma tamen,
Alma etiam natura subest, cui tenditur ista
    Provida cunque manus.

178

A.M.D.G.

In Festo Nativitatis

Ad Matrem Virginem

Hymnus Eucharisticus

MATER Jesu mei,
Mater magni Dei,
Doce me de Eo,
De parvo dulci Deo.
  Quantum amavisti
Quem tu concepisti,
Non concipiendum,
Dominum tremendum,
Sed in te contractum,
Verbum carnem factum?
Et contemnit idem
Ne cor meum quidem:
Meum cor indignum
Quod capiat tantum signum,
Indignum O quod gerat
Qui mane mecum erat,
Subit, O Maria,
In eücharistia.
Ipse vult intrare:
Nolo me negare.
Candens exemplare,
Doce me amare.
  Dic, ut plus ametur,
Qualis videretur
Vulva dum lateret,
Necdum appareret,
Cum tua fecit laetam
Vox Elisabetham,

Laetam matre matrem,
Laetum fratre fratrem.
Doce me gaudere,
Rosa, tuo vere,
Virga, tuo flore,
Vellus, tuo rore,
Arca, tua lege,
Thronus, tuo rege,
Acies, tuo duce,
Luna, tua luce,
Stella, tuo sole,
Parens, tua prole.
Nam tumeo et abundo
Immundo adhuc mundo;
Sum contristatus Sanctum
Spiritum et planctum
Custodi feci meo
Cum exhiberem Deo
Laesum atque caesum
In mea carne Jesum.
  Demum quid sensisti
Ipsum cum vidisti
Tandem visu pleno
Parvulum in foeno,
Ecce tremebundum
Qui fixum firmat mundum
Et involutum pannos
Qui aeternos annos

Nondum natus de te
Volvebat in quiete?
Quae tu tum dicebas
Et quae audiebas?
Etsi fuit mutus
Tamen est locutus.
Da complecti Illum,
Mihi da pauxillum

Tuo ex amore
Et oscula ab ore.
Qui pro me vult dari,
Infans mihi fari,
Mecum conversari,
Tu da contemplari,
Mater magni Dei,
Mater Jesu mei.

L. D. S.

179

(May Lines)

*Ab initio et ante saecula creata sum et usque
ad futurum saeculum non desinam*

O PRAEDESTINATA bis
Quae fuisti
A saeculorum saeculis
Mater Christi,
Post praevisa merita
Innocentis,
Iterum post scelera
Nostrae gentis,
Quamvis illa purior
Sit corona
Magis haec commendat cor-
di Dei dona.
Utique deiparam
Te mirarer,
At non partu tuo tam
Delectarer;

Confiterer virginem
     Matrem factam
At non inter omnes sem-
     per te intactam.,
Sed bifronti gloriae
     Tibi erunt
Haec quae stant et illa quae
     Conciderunt—
Et redempta scelera
     Nostrae gentis
Et praevisa merita
     Innocentis.

180

In Theclam Virginem

LONGA victa die, cum multo pulvere rerum,
    Deterior virtus ut queat esse queror;
Quod lateat niveae cunctos ita gloria Theclae
    Et post Mariam fama secunda meam.
Ducitur antiquis Pauli praeconis ab annis,
    Ducitur Eoo carmen ab Iconio.
Bellerophontëam monstrabat fabula Tarson
    At nunc excussus non male Paulus equis.
Finitima Iconio Tarsus, Cilicemque sequuntur
    Rite suae Paulum proxima fata Theclae.
Sederat in patulis longe pulcerrima tectis
    Forte et in apricas verterat ora vias,
Virgineo insignis cultu, sed sponsa, fereque
    Jam matronalis nactaque Thecla virum.
Mollis in his aetas se temperat arte severa
    Castaque composita membra quiete tenet.

181

Milton

(translated from Dryden)

Ævo diversi tres et regione poetae
    Hellados, Ausoniae sunt Britonumque decus.
Ardor in hoc animi, majestas praestat in illo,
    Tertius ingenio junxit utrumque suo.
Scilicet inventrix cedens Natura labori
    'Quidquid erant isti' dixerat 'unus eris.'

182

Songs from Shakespeare, in Latin and Greek

(i)

'Come unto these yellow sands'

(*The Tempest*, I. ii)

Ocius O flavas, has ocius O ad arenas,
    Manusque manibus jungite;
Post *Salve* dictum, post oscula; dum neque venti
    Ferum neque obstrepit mare.
Tum pede sic agiles terram pulsabitis et sic
    Pulsabitis terram pede.
Vos, dulces nymphae, spectabitis interea; quin
    Plausu modos signabitis.
Lascivae latrare: ita plaudere. At hoc juvat: ergo
    Et Hecuba et Hecubae nos canes
Allatrent. Gallus sed enim occinit. Occinat: aequumst
    Cantare gallos temperi.

(ii)

'Full fathom five thy father lies'

(The Tempest, I. ii)

OCCIDIT, O juvenis, pater et sub syrtibus his est,
    Ossaque concretum paene coralium habet,
Quique fuere oculi vertunt in iaspidas undae:
    In rem Nereidum et Tethyos omnis abit.
Quidquid enim poterat corrumpi corpore in illo
    Malunt aequoream fata subire vicem.
Exsequias Phorcys, quod tu miraberis, illi
    Delphinis ducunt Oceanusque suis.
Fallor an ipsa vadis haec nenia redditur imis?
    Glauci mortalem flet, mihi crede, chorus.

(iii)

'While you here do snoring lie'

(The Tempest, II. i)

Vos dum stertitis ore sic supino
Grandes insidiae parantur estque
Fraus quod optat adesse nacta tempus,
Extremis digitis levis minaxque.
Qui, somnum nisi vultis hunc supremum,
Nostra voce nimis periculoso
Expergiscimini, viri, sopore.

(iv)

'Tell me where is Fancy bred'

(The Merchant of Venice, III. ii)

ROGO vos Amor unde sit, Camenae.
Quis illum genuit? quis educavit?
Qua vel parte oriundus ille nostra
Sit frontis mage pectorisne alumnus
Consultae memorabitis, sorores.
Amorem teneri creant ocelli;
Pascunt qui peperere; mox eumdem
Aversi patiuntur interire.

Nam cunas abiisse ita in feretrum!
Amorem tamen efferamus omnes,
Quem salvere jubemus et valere
Sic, O vos pueri atque vos puellae:
Eheu heu, Amor, ilicet, valeto.
Eheu heu, Amor, ilicet, valeto.

(v)

The Same

στροφή· ⎤ τίς ἔρωτος, τίς ποτ' ἄρ' ἁ πατρὶς ἦν;
χορευτὴς α'⎦ τίς δέ νιν τίκτει, τίς ἔθρεψεν, ἀνδρῶν ἢ θεῶν;
πότερ' αὐτὸν καρδίας ἢ κεφαλᾶς ἐτήτυμον εἴπω
τὸν καὶ πάλαι ὡς ἐπιστρωφῶντα μᾶλλον
τόπον; οὐ γάρ, οὐκ ἔχω πᾶ τάδε θεὶς δὴ τύχοιμ' ἄν.

ἀντιστροφή· ⎤ τὸν ἔρωτ' ἄρ' οὐχ ἑλικοβλεφάροις
χορευτὴς β'⎦ ὡς ἐν ὀφθαλμοῖσι τραφέντ' ἀκούεις παῖδα
μὲν
συνέφαβον δ' ἱμέρου καὶ χάριτος τέως νεοθαλοῦς
τηλαυγέσιν ἐν προσώπου τοῖς θεάτροις
τέλος ἐκπεσόντα φροῦδον, θανάτῳ φροῦδον ἔρρειν;

ἐπῳδός· κορυφαῖος] φροῦδος ἔρως, φροῦδος ἡμῖν.
ἡμιχόριον α'] ἀλλ' αἴλινον αἴλινον εἴπωμεν, ἄνδρες.
ἡμιχόριον β'] αἴλινον γὰρ αἴλινον εἴπωμεν.
χορός]   αἰαῖ,
φροῦδος ἔρως τὸ λοιπόν, φροῦδος ἡμῖν
ἔρως.

(vi)

'Orpheus with his lute made trees'
(King Henry VIII, iii. i)

ORPHEUS fertur et arbores canendo
Et pigros nive concitasse montes.
Si quid luserat ille, vitis uvas
Extemplo referebat, herba flores.

225

Diceres Zephyros eoque Phoebum
Conspirasse diem in sereniorem
Et ver continuare sempiternum.
Tum venti posuere, tum resedit
Omnis fluctus ab obsequente ponto.
Est hoc imperium artis atque Musae:
Importunior aegriorque nuper
Cura quae fuerat, loquente plectro
Conticescere vel mori necessest.

(vii)

The Same

στροφή]   λόγος Ὀρφέως λύραν καὶ δένδρεσιν χοραγεῖν
καὶ νιφοκτύπων ὄρεων κορυφαῖσιν θαμά, δαμείσαις πόθῳ,
κελαδοῦντι δ' εὐθὺς ἀνθῆσαι ῥόδοισίν θ' ἁλίου τε γᾶν καὶ
ψακάδος οὐρανίου βλαστήμασι καλλικάρποις

ἀντιστροφή]   χιόνος κρύος μεσούσας. πόντιον δὲ κῦμα
τῶν τ' ἐριβρόμων ἀίοντ' ἀνέμων πνεύματα γαλάνᾳ πέσεν.
κιθάρᾳ δὲ ταῖς τε Μούσαις ὡς ἔνεστ' εἰπεῖν τὸ παυσίλυπον
ἀδύνατον· κατεκοίμασ' αὐτίκα πάντα λάθα.

(viii)

Unfinished rendering of 'When icicles hang by the wall',

(Love's Labour's Lost, v. ii)

INSTITIT acris hiemps: glacies simul imbrices ad imas
    Promissa passim ut horret haec! Camillus
Pastor, primores quotiens miser afflat ore in ungues,
    Ut ore, rore, vix fovet rigentes!
Grandia ligna foco fert Marcipor uvidis struendo
    Vestigiis in atrium secutus
Aut stupet, e tepido quod presserat ubere ipse, mulctris
    Haesisse tam liquore posse nullo.

183

ROBERT BRIDGES: *In all things beautiful, I cannot see*

Incomplete Latin Version

NEMPE ea formosa est: adeo omne quod aut facit aut fit
  Cynthia continuo fomes amoris adest.
Stat, sedet, incedit: quantumst modo pulchra quod instat,
  Haec modo res! sequitur pulchrior illa tamen.
Nec mora nec modus est: nam quod mihi saepe negavi
  Suavius illam unquam posse placere placet.
Quid? Tacet. At taceat. Jam vera fatebor: ut illud,
  Ut vincit vestros, Musa, tacere choros!
Si quis in ulla volet perpellere verba silentem
  Vexet marmoreos improbus ille deos.
Hunc in Olympiaca post tot fore saecla sereno
  Intempestivum non pudet aede Jovi.

. . . .

Postremo si qua jam de re disputat, his et
  Ipsa velit Virtus dicere et ipsa Fides;
Aurea non alio sunt saecula more locuta;
  Astraeam his usam vocibus esse reor.

EDITORS' NOTES

PREFACE TO NOTES

BY W. H. GARDNER

MATTERS relating to earlier editions and to the augmented, revised, and rearranged text of this Fourth Edition have been dealt with above in the *Introduction* and more comprehensively in Professor MacKenzie's *Foreword*. Some further statement is required, however, to replace, supplement, or bring up to date the information given in the original *Preface to Notes* written by Robert Bridges for the First Edition and reproduced, with the omission of one paragraph ('Selection') in the Second and Third Editions.

1. *Certain and Possible Losses*

The poems and fragments printed in the present volume, which is the first to aim at being a complete collection, do not make up the presumed total output of Hopkins's verse, though the losses are probably confined to his early immature work.

Apart from the unknown number of early poems which by his own confession he burnt on becoming a Jesuit, it is certain that before that holocaust he had sent drafts of those and other early poems to various relations and friends. These copies might have included better drafts or finally revised versions of the verses of 1864-66 which are printed here from the early diaries C. I and C. II (described below in section 2), together with samples of certain projected works which, though mentioned in his letters, have never been traced, such as 'Grass is my Garland' and 'Judas'. Fortunately a few of the revised presentation copies have survived (viz. Nos. 4, 6, 9, 10, 21-23); many others may have been lost or destroyed by their recipients, but it is possible that in the course of time a few more may come to light. Moreover, the *Letters* mention works that were contemplated, or perhaps even begun, long after Hopkins joined the Jesuits; but not a line of the 'tragedy' on Margaret Clitheroe or of the 'odes' on Edmund Campion and the Vale of Clwyd has been found.

It is now known that when Hopkins died on 8 June 1889 his room contained a large collection of his papers. By the terms of his will (though until 1947 this seems to have been known only to the Jesuits in Dublin) the material should have been transferred to the London headquarters of the English Province of the Society of Jesus; if this had been done, and if the MSS. had been carefully preserved there intact, an edition of Hopkins's maturer poems could have been prepared by Joseph Keating, S.J., and published as early as 1909 or 1910.[1]

[1] See *The Manuscripts of Gerard Manley Hopkins*, by D. Anthony Bischoff; *Thought*, vol. XXVI, No. 103, pp. 551-7. See also J.-G. Ritz: *Robert Bridges and Gerard Hopkins: A Literary Friendship* (1960), p. 160.

In 1889 the importance of these documents was not realized. The Father Minister of the University College residence in Dublin, the Rev. Thomas Wheeler, S.J., cursorily examined the papers, destroyed some and variously disposed of others. When, some months later, Robert Bridges asked the Jesuits whether he might examine and sift Hopkins's literary remains with a view to selection or publication, Fr. Wheeler gathered the remaining papers together and on 27 October 1889 sent them to Bridges, to be used by him or Hopkins's parents 'at their discretion'.

Owing to the patient researches of the Rev. D. A. Bischoff, S.J., we can be certain that by no means all the available documents were sent to Bridges. In later years, Jesuit fathers of University College came across Hopkins's MSS. lying in odd drawers and, appreciating the original contents but not the permanent value of these papers and notebooks, either appropriated the documents or sent them to co-religionists in other houses or countries. This casual dispersal probably led to some irretrievable losses (e.g. the original MS. of 'The Wreck of the Deutschland'), but it is possible that some unrecorded later poems, or superior drafts of known ones, may yet be discovered.

2. Sources

The MSS. sent to Bridges included the two collections of poems (or poems and fragments) named by him B and H. As a guarantee of authenticity, and because of its historical interest, the passage from the original *Preface to Notes* in which Bridges gives 'some account of the authority for his text' is here reprinted verbatim:

'The sources are four, and will be distinguished as A, B, D, and H, as here described.

'A is my own collection, a MS. book made up of autographs—by which word I denote poems in the author's handwriting—pasted into it as they were received from him, and also of contemporary copies of other poems. These autographs and copies date from '67 to '89, the year of his death. Additions made by copying after that date are not reckoned or used.[1] . . .

'B is a MS. book into which, in '83, I copied from A certain poems of which the author had kept no copy. He was remiss in making fair copies of his work, and his autograph of *The Deutschland* having been (seemingly) lost, I copied that poem and others from A at his request. After that date he entered more poems in this book as he completed them, and he also made both corrections of copy and emendations of the poems which had been copied into it by me. Thus, if a poem occur in both A and B, then B is the

[1] Not true of the present edition. See note to No. 27.

232

later, and, except for overlooked errors of copyist, the better authority. The last entry written by G. M. H. into this book is of the date 1887.

'D is a collection of the author's letters to Canon Dixon, the only other friend who ever read his poems, with but few exceptions whether of persons or of poems. These letters are in my keeping;[1] they contain autographs of a few poems with late corrections.

'H is the bundle of posthumous papers that came into my hands at the author's death. These were at the time examined, sorted, and indexed; and the more important pieces—of which copies were taken—were inserted into a scrap-book. That collection is the source of a series of his most mature sonnets, and of almost all the unfinished poems and fragments.[2] Among these papers were also some early drafts.'

The MSS. named B and H are now in the Bodleian Library, Oxford; A and D are in the possession of Lord Bridges.

To these main sources must be added the two early diaries kept by Hopkins at Balliol College, Oxford, from September 1863 until early in 1866; these have been preserved at Campion Hall. They were originally catalogued by Humphry House as C. I and C. II—designations which they retain in the present volume (Editors' Notes).[3] Forty-three unrevised poems or fragments from these diaries (or later revised versions) were incorporated in *Poems*, Third Edition (1948), and a few more were added in the Fifth Impression (1956). The rest, barring certain variants, were published in *Journals and Papers* (1959), and they appear now for the first time in the collected edition of the *Poems*.

Of three poems published in magazines during the poet's lifetime or later (Nos. 26, 135, 147) neither the autographs nor authoritative MS. copies have been traced. The autographs or authentic transcripts of certain other poems are in private hands, and in each case the provenance of and justification for the accepted text is clearly stated in the note to the poem.

3. *Choice of Texts*

The most mature poems, and incidentally those on which Hopkins's fame mainly rests, are those drawn from the four MSS. called A, B, D, and H, which were first handled with skill and discernment by Robert Bridges. Having known Hopkins personally, he wisely included in his *Preface to Notes* and *Notes* information intended (in his own words) 'to satisfy inquiry con-

---

[1] Published in *Correspondence of G. M. H. and R. W. Dixon*, ed. C. C. Abbott (1935; 2nd edition, 1955).

[2] I.e. of the period 1876-89.

[3] See *Note-books and Papers of G. M. H.* (1937), p. 423, and *Journals and Papers of G. M. H.* (1959), p. 529.

cerning matters whereof the present editor has the advantage of first-hand or particular knowledge'. As far as possible his facts have been verified, and these together with all his relevant comments have been retained. Moreover we have adopted in this Fourth Edition the principle and criterion set out in the following quotation from R. B.'s *Preface* (paragraph entitled 'Method'):

'The latest autographs and autobiographic corrections have been preferred. In the few instances in which this principle was overruled, as in Nos. 1 and 27,[1] the justification will be found in the note to the poem. . . . G. M. H. dated his poems from their inception, and however much he revised a poem he would date his recast as his first draft. Thus *Handsome Heart* was written and sent to me in '79; and the recast, which I reject, was not made before '83, while the final corrections may be some years later; and yet his last autograph is dated as the first "Oxford '79".'

For an account of the rearrangement of the poems, &c., so as to give them a more correct chronological order, see above, *Foreword*, pp. xli–xlix.

As in the Third Edition, the early fragments precede the maturer ones printed by Bridges. An exception to the rule of chronological sequence is to be found in the item No. 98, '(Sundry Fragments and Images)'; here forty scattered and disconnected morsels or single lines of verse belonging to the years 1863–66 have been fancifully classified under suitable headings, the date of each being given in the relevant note. Anyone who wishes to study these and all the other early fragments in their proper chronological and 'diarized' setting is referred to the *Journals and Papers* (1959).[2]

4. *Author's Prosody*

Concerning Hopkins's preoccupation with and frequent use of Counterpoint Rhythm and Sprung Rhythm, Bridges wrote:

'His own preface together with his description of the metrical scheme of each poem—which is always, wherever it exists, transcribed in the notes—may be a sufficient guide for practical purposes. Moreover, the intention of the rhythm, in places where it might seem doubtful, has been indicated by accents printed over the determining syllables: in the later poems these accents correspond generally with the author's own marks; in the earlier poems they do not, but are trustworthy translations.'

R. B.'s 'sufficient guide for practical purposes' has now been supplemented in the manner described below (section 5). The stress-marks placed 'over determining syllables' have been carefully checked, and all now printed in the text have indisputable MS. authority. Since the freer speech-rhythms have

[1] I.e. of First Edition; in the present edition Nos. 10 and 47.
[2] See, however, Graham Storey's explanation of minor rearrangements of sequence, Preface to *Journals and Papers*, p. xxi.

invaded modern verse, Hopkins's boldly juxtaposed stressed syllables are less likely to be misread; but the regular syllabic metres of our older poetry are still viable and still condition the rhythmic sense of many readers. In some of Hopkins's greatest poems there are lines in which a vital stress might still be misplaced by those who are wholly uninformed. Although some recent editors of 'Selections' from G. M. H. have discarded stress-marks in these difficult places, there is still a need for one authoritative printed text to which reference can be made in cases of doubt.

A few scansions without direct MS. authority will be found in the *Notes*; these are clearly indicated as editorial attempts to elucidate the poet's rhythmical intentions.

5. *Special Expression Marks*

Commenting on his friend's use of other expression marks or 'notation', Bridges wrote:

> 'It was at one time the author's practice to use a very elaborate system of marks, all indicating the speech-movement: the autograph (in A) of *Harry Ploughman* carries seven different marks, each one defined at the foot.[1] When reading through his letters . . . I noted a few sentences on this sub-ject which will justify the method that I have followed in the text. In 1883 he wrote: "You were right to leave out the marks: they were not consis-tent for one thing, and are always offensive. Still there must be some. Either I must invent a notation applied throughout as in music or else I must only mark where the reader is likely to mistake, and for the present this is what I shall do." And again in '85: "This is my difficulty, what marks to use and when to use them: they are so much needed and yet so objectionable. About punctuation my mind is clear: I can give a rule for everything I write myself, and even for other people, though they might not agree with me perhaps." In this last matter the autographs are rigidly respected, the rare intentional aberration being scrupulously noted.[2] And so I have respected his indentation of the verses; but in the sonnets, while my indentation corresponds, as a rule, with some autograph, I have felt free to consider conveniences, following, however, his growing practice to eschew it altogether.'

In these and all such matters relating to the presentation of the text of the poems we have generally subscribed to the first editor's wise interpretation of Hopkins's expressed intentions and wishes. It would still be a mistake to print in the actual text all the various rhythmical and expression marks to be

[1] See the note to No. 71. For a facsimile of this MS. see *Letters to R. B.*, p. 262.
[2] The few 'aberrations' not noted by R. B. have now been indicated in the relevant notes.

found in the MSS.; yet they ought to be available to the eager student of the poet's prosodic theory and practice. In the following *Notes*, therefore, the 'outrides' and a selection of the other expression marks—those that seemed most significant—have been quoted from the MSS. The *Author's Preface*, in which G. M. H. explains his original prosody, has been placed directly in front of the sequence of poems to which it refers (though it refers to the later fragments as well), and I have sought to clarify its rather general statements by footnote illustrations which I have drawn from the poems. If the reader turns from the *Author's Preface* to the notes on individual poems he should find much prosodic help.

6. *Variants and Rejected Readings*

As the present edition is intended for the general reader as well as the student, it could not be made a complete 'variorum', giving all variants and rejected readings. The latest variants or author's corrections, as far as these are discernible, have always been adopted as the best available text, except in some of the more fragmentary early verses where the writing, still fluid, had apparently not approached the final stage; but whenever an earlier variant or rejected wording has seemed to us to clarify the poet's intention, or to contribute something of particular value to the meaning of a passage or poem as a whole, that reading has been recorded in the relevant note.[1]

7. *Content and Purpose of Notes*

Annotations taken over from the Third Edition have been thoroughly revised in the light of recent scholarship, and the many new ones cover the additional texts. In their general content the *Editors' Notes* follow the pattern set by Bridges and retained, with extensions, in the Third Edition. For the bibliographical and other information necessary for establishing the text no apology is needed. References to, or quotations from, passages in Hopkins's journal or letters in which he explains, directly or indirectly, difficult parts of his own poems can easily be justified; so also can editorial references to certain or probable sources (e.g. Biblical) of many of the poet's ideas and values.[2] But positive glosses and neat paraphrases provided by an editor, or quoted from some other commentator, may well be deprecated—on the grounds that it is wrong to suggest that there is only one correct (and limited) response to, or interpretation of, any poem or part of a poem. We recognize the danger and also the reader's right to think for himself. Never-

---

[1] See e.g. the notes to No. 28, st., 31, l. 7, and No. 67, l. 12.
[2] Cf. G. M. H. himself: '(And there it is, I understand these things so much better than you: we should explain things, plainly state them, clear them up, explain them; explanation—except personal—is always pure good; without explanation people go on misunderstanding; being once explained they thenceforward understand things; therefore always explain: but I have the passion for explanation and you have not.)' (*Letters to R. B.*, p. 275).

theless, although Hopkins's poetry admits the nuance, the connotation, and the pregnant ambiguity, his language was always directed towards some precise meaning and effect. Readers who might miss some essential core of meaning, or be put to prohibitive trouble to find it, will not mind being helped a little by a short gloss or synopsis. It is better to encumber the few with unnecessary aid than to handicap the many with too little.

Two examples of (i) precise denotation (as glossed), and (ii) significant connotation or suggestion which may or may not be perceived by the reader, will perhaps be helpful. 'Felix Randal' (No. 53) ends thus:

'When thou at the random grim forge, powerful amidst peers,
Didst fettle for the great grey drayhorse his bright and battering sandal!'

Annotations:

(i) l. 13: *random* (archit.), built with stones of irregular size and shape.

(Here, the gloss says, is the precise, technical meaning of *random* in this context; but the reader should be capable of sensing also the carefree atmosphere round the 'grim' flame-red forge in the dark smithy, and of feeling that the word *random* 'has also the significance of "thoughtless, unthinking", in contrast with the blacksmith's later mood'—James Reeves.)

(ii) l. 14: *fettle*, prepare, make ready.

(But the word suggests also that both the blacksmith and the drayhorse are 'in fine fettle'.)

Finally, my synopses or exegeses of certain complex poems and difficult passages may perhaps, despite their shortcomings, be justified by the poet's own declared intention of supplying such aids himself: '. . . one thing I am now resolved on, it is to prefix short prose *arguments* to some of my pieces'. (*Letters to R. B.*, p. 265.)

8. Appendixes

The reasons for the inclusion of Appendixes A, B, and C are given in the note to No. 10 and the texts of Nos. 81 and 120. The reprinting of the poem in Appendix D seems justified by the following extract from the letter of G. M. H. to his mother (24 December 1881):

'Father Richard Clarke, late fellow of St. John's, has now become editor of the *Month* our magazine. A learned friend of his, while routing in the British Museum, came, in a MS. of the 13th century, on a hymn to the Blessed Virgin in Latin and English, with the music, which is quite easy to read to anyone that knows a little about plainsong. He shewed it to Mr. Furnival[1] and also to Fr. Clarke, both of whom want to publish it, but

[1] Frederick James Furnivall (1825–1910), the well-known scholar.

237

Clarke will be first in the field. It is appearing in the January *Month*. . . .
He has written an article on it; . . . the Latin and English text are carefully
reproduced; and a modernisation of the latter follows, made originally
by me but altered since, perhaps not altogether for the better. The footnotes on the old english [*sic*] are mostly by me.'[1]

This hymn (MS. Arundel 248, leaf 154) was written about 1260 and was
the *Angelus ad virginem* sung by the clerk Nicholas in Chaucer's 'The Miller's
Tale'. Both the Latin and the Middle English text were first published in
The Month(January 1882, pp. 100-11); later by Furnivall, Chaucer Society,
Harleian MS. 7334 (1885), pp. 695-6. The Middle English text appears as
'Gabriel's Greeting to Our Lady' in *English Lyrics: 13th Century* (ed. Carle-
ton Brown, 1932), No. 44.

Believing that the Modern English version 'is substantially by G. M. H.',
Prof. C. C. Abbott reproduced it in Note H of *Further Letters of G. M. H.*,
adding: 'It is headed by this rubric, possibly not by G. M. H.—"We insert
for the benefit of our readers who are not skilled in the Old English forms,
a modernized version. We have kept the quaintness of the original so far as
the necessities of metre and of clearness permitted." '[2] I agree with Prof.
Abbott: there are clear signs of G. M. H.'s hand in the diction, the use
of stressmarks, and the footnotes, for which see the last of the Editors'
Notes—below, p. 341.

9. Omissions

(*a*) The 'Note on Unpublished Drafts, Fragments, &c.' written by
Humphry House for the Third Edition (pp. 275-9) has been omitted, since
all the extant verses there enumerated have been printed in the present
edition. Two pieces of verse found in the early diaries and printed in *Journals
and Papers* have been omitted from this edition because Hopkins's authorship is in doubt. One is the epitaph on Jane Green (*Journals and Papers*, p. 35),
the other is 'Latin weather-proverb' (ibid., p. 53).

(*b*) This Fourth Edition is the first to omit a part of the first editor's *Preface
to Notes*—the part for which Bridges was criticized with most cogency after
Hopkins's poems had become widely known and appreciated, namely the
short paragraph on 'Mannerism' (Third Edition, p. 204). Under the headings
Mannerism, Oddity, Obscurity, &c., Bridges warned the readers of 1918
that they would encounter in this new poet's work certain unpardonable
'faults' and 'extravagances'; but in the light of the more searching and sensi-

---

[1] *Further Letters of G. M. H.* (Second Edition, 1956), p. 161.
[2] Ibid., p. 444.

tive criticism to which Hopkins has since been subjected, the following generalizations on his 'Style' have mainly an historical interest:

'Apart, I say, from such faults of taste, which few as they numerically are yet affect my liking and more repel my sympathy than do all the rude shocks of his purely artistic wantonness—apart from these there are definite faults of style which a reader must have courage to face, and must in some measure condone before he can discover the great beauties. For these blemishes in the poet's style are of such quality and magnitude as to deny him even a hearing from those who love a continuous literary decorum and are grown to be intolerant of its absence. And it is well to be clear that there is no pretence to reverse the condemnation of those faults, for which the poet has duly suffered. The extravagances are and will remain what they were. Nor can credit be gained from pointing them out . . .' (Third Edition, p. 204).

From 1930 to 1942 the work of explaining and (to an increasing degree) of defending Hopkins was carried on by G. F. Lahey, F. R. Leavis, E. E. Phare, John Pick, and others. In 1944 the present writer examined and answered most of R. B.'s charges,[1] and the subsequent important studies by W. A. M. Peters, S.J. (1948),[2] and by the contributors to *Immortal Diamond* (ed. Weyand and Schoder, 1949) went far towards proving that the alleged 'faults of style' and 'errors of taste' were by no means as 'definite' as Bridges had believed. Under 'Mannerism' Bridges had condemned the 'occasional affectation in metaphor, as where the hills are "as a stallion stalwart, very-violet-sweet"' (No. 38, l. 10); but as early as 1927 Laura Riding and Robert Graves argued convincingly that Hopkins's bold, complex simile was poetically satisfying and original.[3] None of the many admirers of 'God's Grandeur' (No. 31) wants *now* to be told that the last two lines are a 'perversion of human feeling'. Without being prompted by Bridges, some readers may still regret 'the exaggerated Marianism of some pieces'; but the words 'exaggerated' and 'Marianism' are calculated to create a prejudice against the poet, preventing the reader from finding out how far the object of personal distaste to the first editor was, for Hopkins, a genuine article of faith felt, as an experience, on his pulses. (Would the editor of a standard edition of Marvell be justified in warning the reader against 'the exaggerated concupiscence' of *To his Coy Mistress?*) Again, Bridges was surely wrong when he

[1] *Gerard Manley Hopkins: a Study, &c.*, vol. I, pp. 57, 190, 208–10.
[2] *Gerard Manley Hopkins, a Critical Essay towards the Understanding of his Poetry.* Cf. also: *Hopkins* (the Kenyon Critics, 1944) and *Gerard Manley Hopkins, a Life* (Eleanor Ruggles, 1947).
[3] *A Survey of Modernist Poetry*, pp. 93–4.

spoke, categorically, of 'the naked encounter of sensualism and asceticism which hurts the "Golden Echo" ' (No. 59): this very 'naked encounter' (if we strip 'sensualism' of its pejorative meaning) was surely at the root of all Hopkins's deepest experience and most powerful poetic expression.

It must be admitted that Bridges sometimes saw 'confusion' and 'bad faults' for the simple reason that he had missed the point, had failed to perceive the subtle inscaping of thought, feeling, and language; on the other hand his strictures on extreme forms of grammatical licence (such as the rare omission of the *subjective* relative pronoun), on the ambiguous placing of homophones, and on some of the more ingenious rhymes, will strike many readers as being justified. As a pointer to some of the initial difficulties to be met with in Hopkins's best poetry—as seen from the angle of Victorian decorum and Georgian propriety—the last four pages of R. B.'s original *Preface* still retain their historical and critical interest: in their combination of qualified praise and modified censure they indicate the kind of critical reservation or opposition which Hopkins's poetry has succeeded, largely, in overcoming or circumventing. These pages should also keep their position here as a tribute to the poet and friend who might well be called 'the onlie begetter' of the great First Edition of 1918.

10. *Conclusion of the Original 'Preface to Notes'*

Speaking of the 'extravagances', Bridges says:

'. . . they may be called Oddity and Obscurity; and since the first may provoke laughter when a writer is serious (and this poet is always serious), while the latter must prevent him from being understood (and this poet has always something to say), it may be assumed that they were not a part of his intention. Something of what he thought on this subject may be seen in the following extracts from his letters. In Feb. 1879, he wrote: "All therefore that I think of doing is to keep my verses together in one place—at present I have not even correct copies—, that, if anyone should like, they might be published after my death. And that again is unlikely, as well as remote. . . . No doubt my poetry errs on the side of oddness. I hope in time to have a more balanced and Miltonic style. But as air, melody, is what strikes me most of all in music and design in painting, so design, pattern, or what I am in the habit of calling *inscape* is what I above all aim at in poetry. Now it is the virtue of design, pattern, or inscape to be distinctive and it is the vice of distinctiveness to become queer. This vice I cannot have escaped." And again two months later: "Moreover the oddness may make them repulsive at first and yet Lang might have liked them on a second reading. Indeed when, on somebody returning me the *Eurydice*, I opened and read some lines, as one commonly reads whether prose or verse, with the eyes, so to say, only, it struck me aghast with a kind of raw nakedness and unmitigated violence I was unprepared for: but take breath and read it with the ears, as I always wish to be read, and my verse becomes all right. . . ."

'As regards Oddity then, it is plain that the poet was himself fully alive to it, but he was not sufficiently aware of his obscurity, and
Obscu-   he could not understand why his friends found his sentences
rity   so difficult: he would never have believed that, among all
              the ellipses and liberties of his grammar, the one chief cause
is his habitual omission of the relative pronoun; and yet this is so, and the examination of a simple example or two may serve a general purpose:

'This grammatical liberty, though it is a common convenience in conversation and has therefore its proper place in good writing, is apt to
              confuse the parts of speech, and to reduce a normal sequence
Omission   of words to mere jargon. Writers who carelessly rely on their
of relative   elliptical speech-forms to govern the elaborate sentences of
pronoun   their literary composition little know what a conscious effort
              of interpretation they often impose on their readers. But it
was not carelessness in Gerard Hopkins: he had full skill and practice and scholarship in conventional forms, and it is easy to see that he banished these purely constructional syllables from his verse because they took up room which he thought he could not afford them: he needed in his scheme all his space for his poetical words, and he wished those to crowd out every merely grammatical colourless or toneless element; and so when he had got into the habit of doing without these relative pronouns—though he must, I suppose, have supplied them in his thought,—he abuses the licence beyond precedent, as when he writes (No. 41) "O hero savest!" for "O hero that savest!"

'Another example of this (from the 5th stanza of No. 48) will discover another cause of obscurity; the line
              "Squander the hell-rook ranks sally to molest him"
Identical   means "Scatter the ranks that sally to molest him": but since
forms   the words *squander* and *sally* occupy similar positions in the
              two sections of the verse, and are enforced by a similar
accentuation, the second verb deprived of its pronoun will follow the first and appear as an imperative; and there is nothing to prevent its being so taken but the contradiction that it makes in the meaning; whereas the grammar should expose and enforce the meaning, not have to be determined by the meaning. Moreover, there is no way of enunciating this line which will avoid the confusion; because if, knowing that *sally* should

not have the same intonation as *squander*, the reader mitigates the accent, and in doing so lessens or obliterates the caesural pause which exposes its accent, then *ranks* becomes a genitive and *sally* a substantive.

'Here, then, is another source of the poet's obscurity; that in aiming at condensation he neglects the need that there is for care in the placing of words that are grammatically ambiguous. English swarms with words that have one identical form for substantive, adjective, and verb; and such a word should never be so placed as to allow of any doubt as to what part of speech it is used for; because such ambiguity or momentary uncertainty destroys the force of the sentence. Now our author not only neglects this essential propriety but he would seem even to welcome and seek artistic

Homo-
phones

effect in the consequent confusion; and he will sometimes so arrange such words that a reader looking for a verb may find that he has two or three ambiguous monosyllables from which to select, and must be in doubt as to which promises best to give any meaning that he can welcome; and then, after his choice is made, he may be left with some homeless monosyllable still on his hands. Nor is our author apparently sensitive to the irrelevant suggestions that our numerous homophones cause; and he will provoke further ambiguities or obscurities by straining the meaning of these unfortunate words.

'Finally, the rhymes where they are peculiar are often repellent, and

Rhymes

so far from adding charm to the verse that they appear as obstacles. This must not blind one from recognizing that Gerard Hopkins, where he is simple and straightforward in his rhyme is a master of it—there are many instances,—but when he indulges in freaks, his childishness is incredible. His intention in such places is that the verses should be recited as running on without pause, and the rhyme occurring in their midst should be like a phonetic accident, merely satisfying the prescribed form. But his phonetic rhymes are often indefensible on his own principle. The rhyme to *communion* in "The Bugler" is hideous, and the suspicion that the poet thought it ingenious is appalling: *eternal*, in "The Eurydice", does not correspond with *burn all*, and in "Felix Randal" *and some* and *handsome* is as truly an eye-rhyme as the *love* and *prove* which he despised and abjured;—and it is more distressing, because the old-fashioned conventional eye-rhymes are accepted as such without speech-adaptation, and to many ears are a pleasant relief from the fixed jingle of the perfect rhyme; whereas his false ear-rhymes ask to have their slight but indispensable differences obliterated in the reading, and thus they expose their defect, which is of a disagreeable and vulgar or even comic quality. He did not escape full criticism and ample ridicule for such things in his lifetime; and in '83 he wrote: "Some of my rhymes I regret, but they are past changing, grubs in amber: there are only a few of these; others are unassailable; some others again there are which malignity may munch at but the Muses love."[1]

'Now these are bad faults, and, as I said, a reader, if he is to get any enjoyment from the author's genius, must be somewhat tolerant of them; and they have a real relation to the means Euphony whereby the very forcible and original effects of beauty are and em- phasis produced. There is nothing stranger in these poems than the mixture of passages of extreme delicacy and exquisite diction with passages where, in a jungle of rough root-words, emphasis seems to oust euphony; and both these qualities, emphasis and euphony, appear in their extreme forms. It was an idiosyncrasy of this student's mind to push everything to its logical extreme, and to take pleasure in a paradoxical result; as may be seen in his prosody where a simple theory seems to be used only as a basis for unexampled liberty. He was flattered when I called him περιττότατος,[2] and saw the humour of it—and one would expect to find in his work the force of emphatic condensation and the magic of melodious expression, both in their extreme forms. Now since those who study style in itself must allow a proper place to the emphatic expression, this experiment, which supplies as novel examples of success as of failure, should be full of interest; and such interest will promote tolerance.

'The fragment [On a Piece of Music, No. 148] is the draft of what appears to be an attempt to explain how an artist has not free-will in his creation. He works out his own nature instinctively as he happens to be made, and is irresponsible for the result. It is lamentable that Gerard Hopkins died when, to judge by his latest work, he was beginning to concentrate the force of all his luxuriant experiments in rhythm and diction, and castigate his art into a more reserved style. Few will read the terrible posthumous sonnets without such high admiration and respect for his poetical power as must lead them to search out the rare masterly beauties that distinguish his work.'

[1] In a yet unpublished letter to his brother Everard, of 5 November 1885, G. M. H. says: 'To touch on the *Eurydice*, &c. again, the run-over rhymes were experimental, perhaps a mistake; I do not know that I should repeat them. But rhyme, you under- stand, is like an indelible process: you cannot paint over it. Surely they *can* be recited but the effect must have been prepared, as many things must. I can only remember one, the rhyme to *electric* [ll. 23–4]: it must be read "startingly and rash". It *is* "an effect".'

[2] Superlative of Gk. περιττός, the relevant meanings being: (a) 'unusual', 'remark- able', and (b) 'abundant', 'over-subtle', 'one who overdoes things'.—[W. H. G.]

NOTES

Abbreviations used

A; B; D; H; C. I, and C. II—MSS. of the poems. See above, *Preface to Notes*, pp. 232–3.

G. M. H.	Gerard Manley Hopkins (1844–89).
R. B.	Dr. Robert Bridges (1844–1930), editor of the First Edition, 1918.
C. W.	Charles Williams (1886–1945), editor of the Second Edition, 1930.
H. H.	Humphry House (1908–55), editor of *N.* and *J.* (see below).
W. H. G.	W. H. Gardner, editor of the Third Edition (1948) and co-editor of the present edition.
N. H. M.	N. H. MacKenzie, co-editor of the present edition.
Miles	*The Poets and the Poetry of the [Nineteenth] Century: Robert Bridges and Contemporary Poets*, edited by A. H. Miles, 1893.
L. I	*Letters of G. M. H. to R. B.*, edited by C. C. Abbott, 1935; Second Edition, 1955.
L. II	*Correspondence of G. M. H. and R. W. Dixon*, edited by C. C. Abbott, 1935; Second Edition, 1955.
L. III	*Further Letters of G. M. H.*, edited by C. C. Abbott, 1938; Second Edition, 1956—to which all references are made.
N.	*Note-books and Papers of G. M. H.*, edited by Humphry House, 1937.
J.	*Journals and Papers of G. M. H.*, edited by Humphry House and Graham Storey, 1959.
S.	*Sermons and Devotional Writings of G. M. H.*, edited by Christopher Devlin, S.J. (1907-61), 1959.
Lahey	*Gerard Manley Hopkins* (biography), by G. F. Lahey, S.J., 1930.
Bodl.	Bodleian Library, Oxford.
C. H.	Campion Hall, Oxford.
Study	*Gerard Manley Hopkins: a Study of Poetic Idiosyncrasy in Relation to Poetic Tradition*, by W. H. Gardner (2 vols.), 1944-49; reprinted 1962, 1967.
I.D.	*Immortal Diamond: Studies in G. M. H.*, edited by N. Weyand, S.J. and R. V. Schoder, S.J., 1949.
Peters	*Gerard Manley Hopkins: a Critical Essay towards the Understanding of his Poetry*, by W. A. M. Peters, S.J., 1948.

EARLY POEMS (1860-75?)

1. The Escorial. Awarded Poetry Prize at Highgate School; dated 'Easter 1860'. The MS. (Bodl.) is in the hand of the father, Manley Hopkins, to disguise authorship; the ninth stanza was for some reason omitted. The notes were written by G. M. H. in an elaborately altered hand. 'Though wholly lacking the Byronic flush the poem looks as if influenced by the historical descriptions in *Childe Harold.* . . . The history seems competent and the artistic knowledge precocious.'—[R. B.] The meaning of the motto (Theocritus, Idyll VII, l. 41) is 'and I compete like a frog against the cicadas'.—[C. W.] For considerable textual changes in this edition, and previously omitted notes by G. M. H., see above, *Foreword*, pp. liv–v.

St. 2, l. 9: So in MS.; one foot missing.

St. 12: The apostrophe in *age's*, not in MS., has been added. [N. H. M.]

The following notes are all by G. M. H.:

St. 2: At the battle of St. Quentin, between the French and Spaniards, Philip II vowed the Escorial to St. Laurence, the patron saint of the day, if he gained the victory.

St. 3: St. Laurence is said to have been roasted to death on a gridiron.

St. 4: The Escorial was built in the form of a gridiron—the rectangular convent was the grate, the cloisters the bars, the towers the legs inverted, the palace the handle.

The building contained the royal Mausoleum; and a gate which was opened only to the newborn heir apparent, and to the funeral of a monarch.

St. 5: * Philip endeavoured to establish the Inquisition in the Netherlands.

St. 6: Philip did not choose the splendid luxuriance of the Spanish Gothic as the style of architecture fitted for the Escorial.

St. 7: Nor the Classic.

* The Parthenon, &c., were magnificently coloured and gilded.

† The horsemen in the Panathenaic processions.

St. 8: * The Alhambra, &c.

St. 8: The Architect was Velasquez; the style Italian Classic, partly Ionic, partly Doric. The whole is sombre in appearance, but grand, and imposing.

St. 10: The interior was decorated with all the richest productions of art and nature. Pictures, statues, marble, fountains, tapestry, &c. (*He* refers to Philip.)

* In one of Raphael's pictures the Madonna and St. Joseph play with their Child in a wide meadow; behind is a palm-tree.

† Alluding to Raphael's 'Lo Spasimo', which is, I believe, in the Escorial.

St. 11: ‡ Alluding to the dark colouring of landscapes to be seen in Rubens, Titian, &c.

¶ A beautiful youth drowned in the Nile; the statue has the position described.

‖ Hyacinthus.   § The Belvidere Apollo.

St. 12: The Escorial was adorned by succe[e]ding kings, until the Peninsular war, when the French as a piece of revenge for their defeats, sent a body of dragoons under La Houssaye, who entered the Escorial, ravaged and despoiled it of some of its greatest treasures. The monks then left the convent. Since that time it has been left desolate and uninhabited. The 12th stanza describes this.

★ Alluding to the practise [sic] of arranging swords in circles, radiating from their hilts.

St. 13: † The Escorial is often exposed to the attacks of the storms which sweep down from the mountains of Guadarrama.

St. 14: ✗ Some years ago, fearing that the Carlists would plunder the Escorial, they removed the choicest remaining treasures to Madrid.

St. 15: ★ The civil wars of late years in Spain.

† The Spaniards call it 8th wonder of the world.

2. A Vision of the Mermaids. Dated 'Christmas 1862'. The autograph (now in Bodl.) is headed by a very elaborate circular pen-and-ink drawing, 6 inches in diameter—a sunset sea-piece with rocks and formal groups of mermaidens, five or six together, singing as they stand (apparently) half-immersed in the shallows as described

'But most in a half-circle watch'd the sun,' &c.

R. B. adds: '[This poem] betrays the influence of Keats, and when I introduced the author to the public in Miles's book [*Robert Bridges and Contemporary Poets*, 1893, 2nd imp. 1906], I quoted from it, thinking it useful to show that his difficult later style was not due to inability to excel in established forms. The poem is altogether above the standard of school prizes.' R. B.'s belief that this was a school prize poem lacks foundation. The Highgate School records contain no mention of it, or of any prize for poetry awarded between 1860 (see No. 1 above) and 1865, when E. B. Birks won a prize for a Tercentenary Ode on the School. I agree with H. H. that on general grounds 'A Vision of the Mermaids' is a most unlikely subject for the Head, Dr. Dyne, to have chosen. Competition poems were not submitted in autograph; and it is practically certain that such a poem would not have been illustrated. (For these facts I am indebted to H. H.)

The poem was published in a limited facsimile edition in 1929.

Line 49: *mantle-o'er*. The uncertain hyphen seems to be an afterthought: it was accepted in the A transcript.—l. 57: MS. has a comma after *giant*.—l. 73: *hail*, previously misread as 'frail'.—[N. H. M.]

3. Winter with the Gulf Stream. Publ. in *Once a Week*, Feb. 14, 1863, and reproduced L. III, Note B, p. 437. Present text from a later version transcribed by Fr. F. E. Bacon, S.J., from the poet's revised autograph of Aug. 1871, mentioned by R. B., First Edition, p. 104, but since lost. Bacon, who initialled his transcript, 'F. E. B.', also copied a list of the rejected early readings of the printed version of 1863 which G. M. H. had added to the autograph MS. and had initialled.—[N. H. M.] R. B. says (p. 104 of First Edition): 'G. M. H. told me that he wrote it when he was at school; whence I guess that he altered it too much to allow of its early dating.' But the alterations are not so numerous as to impugn its present chronological position.

St, 4, l. 2: *clammy*, clear in MS. (not 'damming' as in Second Edition).—St. 5, l. 3: *bugle*, shaped like a buffalo horn.—St. 8, l. 2: *sets*, formerly misprinted *sits*. St. 9: *Pactolus*, the golden river which healed Midas.

4. Spring and Death. From an autograph, undated, in Bodl. This poem strongly suggests the influence of the father, Manley Hopkins, whose fanciful vein it resembles. G. M. H. copied out a number of his father's verses, but this piece is not in either of the latter's printed collections, *A Philosopher's Stone* (1843) and *Spicilegium Poeticum* (*c.* 1890): see *Study*, II, pp. 3–6.

Lines 9–11: thought and diction undoubtedly smack of G. M. H.; and with the last couplet cf. the theme of No. 55.

5. A Soliloquy of One of the Spies Left in the Wilderness. From the Oxford notebook C. I, July 1864. First printed in *The Criterion*, Oct. 1935, then in *N*. As H. H. explains, the written draft begins with the stanza now printed third; the two printed as the opening occur together lower down and are isolated. It seems likely that as with 'Pilate' (No. 80) Hopkins had begun the poem without an introduction and supplied one later. I support H. H.'s view that 'there is no other obvious beginning'. As it stands, the poem has a satisfying completeness. The Biblical sources are Exodus xii et seq. and Numbers xiii–xiv.

Variant readings in almost every stanza, the stanzas printed 2nd and 4th being written several times, each in different arrangements. For the most important variants see *J.*, pp. 28–9. For discussion of earlier variants preferred by H. H. and adopted in 3rd Edn., see above, *Foreword*, p. lvii.

6. Barnfloor and Winepress. First printed in *The Union Review*, 1865 (vol. iii, p. 579). Rough draft in *N.*, pp. 24–6; two other completed versions, both in another hand: one, dated 1865, in Bodl.; the other in A. Text adopted is the one G. M. H. printed, except in the following instances, where the reading of one or more of the MSS. seems preferable: Stanza 1, l. 3: 'first fruits'; l. 6: 'thrashing floor'; l. 7: 'this head'.

St. 2, l. 3: 'pierced' for *fenced.*—St. 4, l. 2: *Libanus*, Mt. Lebanon in Syria. With the theme of the poem cf. George Herbert's *The Bunch of Grapes:* see next note.

7. New Readings. An early draft, from C. I, July 1864, was first printed in *The Criterion*, Oct. 1935, then in *N.*, then in *J.*, p. 32. The version now given is from a presumably later copy in A; this MS. is not an autograph, but was made (as R. B. says in a note) by V. S. S. Coles. (The copyist may have inserted the unusual capitals.)—The influence of George Herbert is apparent. Of G. M. H. an Oxford friend (W. E. Addis) once said: 'George Herbert was his strongest tie to the English Church' (Lahey, p. 19).

St. 2, l. 1: the desirable comma after *sowed*, omitted in A, has been restored from the draft in C. I.

8. 'He hath abolished the old drouth.' C. I, July 1864; immediately follows, and is possibly included under title of, 'New Readings' (No. 7). The metrical form suggests a connexion with 'A Voice from the World' (No. 81). With ll. 1–9 cf. the 'new song', &c., in Rev. xiv, 3–4; with ll. 8–9 and 14–17 cf. the sestet of No. 32.

9. Heaven-Haven. Text is from A, according to R. B. the latest version. An earlier draft, under the title 'Rest', is in C. I, July 1864 (see *J.*, p. 33). Following this are the unfinished verses of No. 88—a deliberate contrast. Another version similar to that in A is in the Dolben Family Papers (Northants Record Society, Lamport Hall) and is entitled 'Fair Havens; or The Convent'. It differs only in one word ('green' for 'great' in l. 7) from the following version in Bodl., an autograph on same page as 'For a Picture of St. Dorothea' (No. 10):

Fair Havens—The Nunnery

I have desired to go
    Where springs not fail,
To fields where flies not the unbridled hail,
    And a few lilies blow.

I have desired to be
    Where havens are dumb,
Where the great water-heads may never come
    As in the unloved sea.

Title: cf. George Herbert, 'The Size' (last line): 'These seas are tears, and Heaven the haven.'

10. **For a Picture of St. Dorothea.** C. II, Nov. (?) 1864.—[W. H. G.]—
Contemporary autograph in A, and another almost identical in H, both
undated. Text from A. This poem was afterwards expanded, shedding its
relative pronouns, to 48 lines divided among three speakers, 'an Angel,
the protonotary Theophilus, (and) a Catechumen': the grace and charm of
original lost:—there is an autograph in A and other copies exist. This was
the first of the poems that I saw, and G. M. H. wrote it out for me (in 1866?).
—[R. B.] Cf. No. 25. As the dramatic version (from A) helps to elucidate
Nos. 10 and 25, it is given as Appendix A, p. 344. In the later versions there
are tentative experiments in sprung rhythm.

Two quatrains entered in C. II in March 1865 seem to be connected with
the St. Dorothea poems. See No. 98, (xix).

According to the hagiographers, St. Dorothea (martyred *c.* 303 under
Diocletian) was first tortured, then sentenced to death by Sapricius, gover-
nor of Caesarea in Cappadocia. Asked where Christ was, she replied, 'In
Paradise, where fruits, flowers, grass, and all such delights are ever fresh.'
A lawyer present, named Theophilus, jeeringly asked her to send him from
Paradise some apples and roses. Dorothea promised to do so. Just before her
execution, an angel appeared in the form of a beautiful youth and carrying
three apples and three roses. These she bade him take to Theophilus, where-
upon the lawyer acknowledged Christ and was himself martyred.—See note
to No. 25, st. 5, ll. 3-4.

11. **Easter Communion.** Lent 1865. C. II, first draft March 2–12; text
from copy entered on June 26. For the early version and variants see *J.*
p. 57.
Lines 3–4: *You striped in secret,* &c. This passage may be literal or figurative;
    it is probably both. Ascetic flagellation was not unknown among extreme
    Anglo-Catholics in the 1860's; but cf. No. 73: 'But be the war within . . .'
—l. 5: As the first draft and final version both read *Jesu's,* we have amended
the text.—[N. H. M]—l. 14: cf. Isaiah xxxv. 3.

12. **To Oxford.** Low Sunday and Monday, 1865. C. II. First printed in
The Criterion, Oct. 1935. Above the poems G. M. H. wrote: 'The two following sonnets were sent to Addis, also that on Easter Communion [No. 11],
but I have now only the rough copies of the first two, which are not quite
right.' These drafts are followed by the third (incomplete) sonnet 'To
Oxford', No. 119.—(i) l. 10: *towers musical.* Cf. No. 148, '(On a Piece of
Music)'.—(ii) l. 12: *to,* not in MS., but seems to be required by the sense of
the context.—[N. H. M.]

13. **'Where art thou friend'.** C. II, Apr. 25-7, 1865. This sonnet is probably connected with Digby Mackworth Dolben, the young religious

enthusiast and poet whom G. M. H. met for the first and only time in Feb. 1865. 'In March Hopkins had a religious crisis which led to his first confession and the beginning of the daily spiritual notes . . . the sonnet is obscure because Dolben was closely bound up with the religious crisis.' (H. H. in N., p. xxi.) Immediately before and after the sonnet there are enigmatic allusions to Dolben, which seem to support H. H.'s opinion (see J., pp. 325–6). Yet in a letter to R. B. written soon after Dolben's death (L. I, p. 16) we read: 'I looked forward to meeting Dolben and his being a Catholic more than to anything.' (Aug. 30, 1867.) It is just possible that this poem was addressed to some fascinating stranger: 'His face was fascinating me last term: I generally have one fascination or another on. Sometimes I dislike the faces wh. fascinate me but sometimes much the reverse, . . .' (ibid., p. 8). Cf. 'The Lantern out of Doors' (No. 40).

Two earlier readings are:

Line 3: 'Either unknown to me in the age that is'
Line 14: 'No, no, no, but for Christ who knew and loved thee.'

14. The Beginning of the End. Sub-title in A: 'a neglected lover's address to his mistress'. Early draft in C. II, May 6–8, 1865. After the first sonnet comes the following fragment:

'Some men may hate their rivals and desire
    Secretive moats, knives, smothering-cloths, drugs, flame;
But I am so consumèd with my shame
    I dare feel envy scarcely, never ire.
O worshipful the man that she sets higher'

Sonnets and fragment first printed in *The Criterion*, Oct. 1935, then in N. Present text of the first and third sonnets is from undated but undoubtedly later transcripts by R. B. in A: a note by R. B. says: 'These two sonnets must *never* be printed.' In the first, however, we retain from C. II the punctuation (e.g. a stop at the end of the first line, and a comma after 'fast'), the italicized '*less*' and '*more*', and *unpassion'd* in place of *impassioned* [l. 14]. In the 1st Edn. (p. 103) R. B. wrote: 'there are two sonnets in Italian form and Shakespearian mood (refused by 'Cornhill Magazine') . . .'.

15. The Alchemist in the City. C. II, May 15, 1865. As symbolism, conscious or unconscious, this poem throws light on the two sides of G. M. H.'s nature. 'This alchemist is an early projection of that personality "in hiding" which was deeply moved by the behaviour of the windhover; and all his life Hopkins was possessed by the image of the wild free bird.' (*Study*, II, pp. 87–8.) Cf. Nos. 36, 45, 51, 56, and 74.

St. 7, l. 4: *tower* replaces 'lower' of N. and 3rd Edn. Initial letter in MS. is identical with that of *tower-top* in next line.—[N. H. M.]

16. **'Myself unholy'.** C. II, June 1865. We print the latest corrections. Among earlier variants are:
Line 4: 'Or unsalt streams to teasing waters shoaly:'
Line 10: 'And partly I hate, partly condone the fall.' (Adopted in 3rd Edn.)
For a selection of cancelled variants see *J.*, p. 63.

17. **'See how Spring opens'.** From the notebook C. II, June 26, 1865. First printed in *The Criterion*, Oct. 1935. Cf. Milton's sonnet 'How soon hath Time'.
Line 14: this may refer to the diary entry of March 12: 'A day of the great mercy of God.' After his conversion in 1866 G. M. H. wrote: 'The silent conviction that I was to become a Catholic has been present to me for a year perhaps, as strongly, in spite of my resistance to it . . . as if I had already determined it' [L. III, p. 27]. See *Introduction*, p. xviii.

18. **'My prayers must meet a brazen heaven.'** From Oxford notebook C. II, Sept. 7, 1865. With this poem cf. the later, more 'terrible' desolations of Nos. 65 and 67.

19. **'Let me be to Thee'.** C. II, Oct. 22, 1865. The previous entry says: 'Note that if ever I should leave the English Church the fact of Provost Fortescue (Oct. 16 and 18, 1865) is to be got over' (*J.*, p. 71). E. B. K. Fortescue (1816–77), despite his 'Romanizing' tendencies, had remained within the Church of England and was well known as a preacher. (See *J.*, pp. 338–9; also notes to Nos. 17 and 20.)

20. **The Half-way House.** Immediately follows No. 19 in C. II, Oct. 1865.
St. 1, l. 4: a comma has been added after *Love* (cf. ll. 5 and 6).
St. 2, l. 1: *My national old Egyptian reed*, &c. This allusion to the 'bruised' or 'broken' reed of Egypt (2 Kings xviii. 21; Isaiah xxxvi. 6, &c.) seems to mean that the 'national' religion of the Established Church had failed to satisfy G. M. H. (See note to No. 17, l. 14).—l. 2: *vine*, cf. 'I am the vine', &c. in John xv. 1–5.
St. 3, l. 2: I have inserted 'see' after 'must', feeling convinced that this is what the poet intended to write.—l. 6: an expression of belief in the Real Presence.—[W. H. G.]
For the capitals in *Thee* and *Thou* inserted in this edn., see above, *Foreword*, p. lix.—[N. H. M.]

21. **The Nightingale.** From an autograph in Bodl., dated Jan. 18, 19, 1866.

22. **The Habit of Perfection.** Two autographs in A; the earlier dated Jan. 18, 19, 1866. The second, which is a good deal altered, is apparently of

same date as text of No. 9. Text follows this later version. Published in Miles.—[R. B.] The earlier autograph is sub-titled '(The Novice)'. A transcript by Fr. Bacon, S.J., undated and titled 'The Kind Betrothal', is at C. H.; considerable differences in text.

St. 3, l. 2: *uncreated light*, the *lux increata* of the Schoolmen, the creative energy of God's mind; l. 3: *ruck and reel*, variegated throng, and vortex of material interests. 'The Kind Betrothal' has: 'These pièd shows . . .'—ibid., l. 4: *Coils, keeps*, ensnares, confuses, engulfs.

St. 4, l. 1: *hutch*, place of storing.

St. 5, l. 2: *keep*, upkeep.

St. 6, l. 4: *unhouse*, &c., take the Host from the tabernacle of the altar (Cath.).

St. 7, ll. 3–4: cf. Matt. vi. 28–9.

23. Nondum. From an autograph MS. at C. H., and dated Lent, 1866. Another copy in A. Latin title means 'Not yet'.

St. 1: For the thought, cf. No. 18.

St. 6: cf. Matthew Arnold's 'The Scholar Gipsy' (1853), st. 18.

Sts. 8–9: cf. John Henry Newman's hymn, 'Lead, kindly Light',
and the strong influence of Dr. Newman generally in
the year of G. M. H.'s conversion. (See L. III, pp. 21–2, 29–30,
and *passim*.)

24. Easter. From a MS. at C. H. (Date, 1866?). Another copy, in A, which has a comma at the end of st. 4, l. 2;—ibid., l. 3: MS. 'disshevelled'.

25. Lines for a Picture of St. Dorothea. This, undated, from the Stony-hurst autograph, formerly belonging to Fr. F. Bacon, S.J., is a later version of No. 10 (but not the dramatic version to which R. B. refers in his note on that poem; see Appendix A). It embodies what appear to be the poet's first experiments in Sprung Rhythm. The following changes have been made (1970) in the text, previously printed from Fr. Bacon's transcript at C.H.: st. 3, l. 1: *South*, u.c.; l. 3: *dew-bell*, hyphenated; l. 6: *dew'*?—, dash added.

St. 5, ll. 3–4: Here, as in No. 10, it is apparently Dorothea herself, in angelic form, who appears to Theophilus; hence the latter's doubt as to whether the apparition is 'him' or 'her'.

St. 7, l. 1: *dip in blood*, &c. Her martyrdom commutes death to eternal life.— l. 6: *another Christian*, i.e. Theophilus.

The following is a specimen of the poet's signature about this date:

Gerard M. Hopkins.
July 24, 1866.

26. Ad Mariam. Printed in *The Stonyhurst Magazine*, Feb. 1894, under a letter from the correspondent signed 'O. S. J.', in which it is said to have been probably written in 1884. Of this poem R. B. wrote: 'This is . . . in direct and competent imitation of Swinburne: no autograph has been found; and, unless Fr. Hopkins's views of poetic form had been provisionally deranged or suspended, the verses can hardly be attributed to him without some impeachment of his sincerity; and that being altogether above suspicion, I would not yield to the rather strong presumption which their technical skill supplies in favour of his authorship. It is true that the "Rosa mystica" is somewhat in the same light lilting manner; but that was probably common to most of these festal verses, and "Rosa mystica" is not open to the positive objections of verbal criticism which would reject the "Ad Mariam". He never sent me any copy of either of these pieces, as he did of his severer Marian poems (Nos. 42 and 60), nor mentioned them as productions of his serious Muse' (1st Edn., p. 105).—R. B.'s opinion is supported by C. W. and Prof. Abbott; but the present editor (W. H. G.) does not subscribe to it. Both internal evidence and probability suggest that G. M. H. wrote 'Ad Mariam' as 'May Lines' during his first stay at Stonyhurst between 1870 and 1873, his intention being to please Catholics who (like many others) admired Swinburne's metres but deplored his *motifs*. 'O. S. J.' might well have mistaken the date of composition. For a fuller discussion see *Study*, II, pp. 90–4.—The *Stonyhurst Magazine* text (No. LXXII, p. 233) has no stanza divisions and prints a stop after *May* (l. 2) and *have seen* (l. 18).—[N. H. M.]

St. 3, l. 3: *much proud maiden*. With this odd use of 'much' cf. No. 40.—l. 7: 'much-thick and marsh air'.

St. 3, l. 7: *Aidenn*, Eden (Heb.).

27. Rosa Mystica. This is certainly one of the 'two or three little presentation pieces' mentioned by G. M. H. in his letter to R. W. Dixon of Oct. 5, 1878. Published in *The Irish Monthly*, May 1898, and again in Orby Shipley's *Carmina Mariana*, 2nd series, p. 183.—[R. B.] Autograph MS. at C. H. C. W.'s faulty transcription (reproduced in 3rd Edn.) has now been corrected by N. H. M. With st. 6, ll. 3–4, and st. 7, cf. No. 28, st. 22.

POEMS (1876–89)

Page 45. **Author's Preface.** This is from B, and must have been written in 1883 or not much later. The punctuation has been exactly followed, except that I have added a comma after the word *language* in the 8th line of p. 49, where the omission seemed an oversight.—[R. B.]

p. 48, l. 4: *rove over*. This expression is used here to denote the running on of the sense and sound of the end of a verse into the beginning of the next; but this meaning is not easily to be found in the word. [R. B.]

The two words *reeve* (pf. *rove*, which is also a pf. of *rive*—) and *reave* (pf. *reft*) are both used several times by G. M. H., but they are both spelt *reave*. In the present context *rove* and *reaving* occur in his letters, and the spelling *reeve* in 'The Deutschland', xii. 8 is probably due to the copyists. There is no doubt that G. M. H. had a wrong notion of the meaning of the nautical term *reeve*. No. 63, l. 10 (the third passage where *reeve*, spelt *reave* occurs, and a nautical meaning is required—see the note there—) would be satisfied by *splice* (nautical); and if this notion were influenced by *weave*, *wove*, that would describe the interweaving of the verses. In the passage referred to in 'The Deutschland' *reeve* is probably intended in its dialectal or common speech significance: see Wright's *English Dialect Dictionary*, where the first sense of the verb given is to bring together the 'gathers' of a dress: and in this sense *reeve* is in common use.—[R.B.]

28. The Wreck of the Deutschland. Text from B, title from A (see description of B on p. 232). In 'The Spirit of Man' the original first stanza is given from A, and varies; otherwise B was not much corrected. Another transcript, now at St. Aloysius' College, Glasgow, was made by the Rev. F. Bacon after A but before the correction of B. This was collated for me by the Rev. Geoffrey Bliss, S.J., and gave one true reading. Its variants are distinguished by G in the notes to the poem.—[R. B.] In 1st Edn. R. B. adopted a few A readings without noting the deviation from B: e.g. in stanzas 23, 34, 35 (q.v.). In A the poem is signed 'Brân Maenefa' (see note to No. 172, p. 326).

In a letter to R. W. Dixon, Oct. 5, 1878, G. M. H. wrote: '. . . when in the winter of '75 the *Deutschland* was wrecked in the mouth of the Thames and five Franciscan nuns, exiles from Germany by the Falck Laws, aboard of her were drowned I was affected by the account and happening to say so to my rector he said that he wished someone would write a poem on the subject. On this hint I set to work and, though my hand was out at first, produced one. I had long had haunting my ear the echo of a new rhythm which now I realized on paper . . . I do not say the idea is altogether new . . . but no one has professedly used it and made it the principle throughout, that I know of . . . However, I had to mark the stresses . . . and a great many more oddnesses could not but dismay an editor's eye, so that when I offered it to our magazine the *Month* . . . they . . . dared not print it.'

Synopsis of the Poem (by W. H. G.)

Part the First (Stanzas 1-10):

Meditation on God's infinite power and masterhood, on the direct mystical 'stress' or intuitive knowledge by which man, the dependent finite creature, apprehends the majesty and terror, the beauty and love of his Maker. Not only through beauty and joy do we know Him. Since the Incarnation and Passion, the human heart has become sensitized to the deeper mystery of suffering and loss—the paradox of God's mastery and mercy. Adoration to Him! May he subjugate and save His rebellious creature, man.

Part the Second.

(Stanzas 11-17): Sudden, unexpected disaster overtook the *Deutschland*, with her emigrants and exiles bound for America. A hurricane of wind and snow drove her on to a sandbank. For a whole night without succour, the passengers and crew of the crippled and settling ship were buffeted by the elements: many were drowned.

(Stanzas 17-31): Amid the tumult and horror, the voice of a nun was heard calling on Christ to 'come quickly'. (She was one of five Franciscan exiles: surely Five, the number of Christ's wounds, is the symbol of Sacrifice and the heavenly Reward.) But what did she mean? Her cry came from the heart of all suffering humanity. Man seeks deliverance not from danger (which is stimulating) but from the remorseless daily round of toil and disappointment. That deliverance comes only from Christ, who succeeded by failure; His Passion holds the promise of heaven in an otherwise 'unshapeable' existence (st. 29). This nun read the symbol aright: the pain and tragedy of life elucidate, and are themselves elucidated by, the Redemption. In the nun the meaning of Christ is reborn (a second Virgin Birth!). Touched by the finger of God (as the poet had been) she had created faith and hope in those around her.

(Stanzas 32-5): Return to the theme of Part the First: the poet adores the mastery, majesty, and inscrutable wisdom of God. The dead nun, prophetess of the Faith indomitable and resurgent, is asked to intercede for the conversion of 'rare-dear Britain'.

Rhythm and Scansion

Immediately before the version in A is a transcript by R. B. of what is clearly a note by G. M. H.:

'Note—Be pleased, reader, since the rhythm in which the following poem is written is new, strongly to mark the beats of the measure, according to the number belonging to each of the eight lines of the stanza,

255

as the indentation guides the eye, namely two and three and four and three and five and five and four and six; not disguising the rhythm and rhyme, as some readers do, who treat poetry as if it were prose fantastically written to rule (which they mistakenly think the perfection of reading), but laying on the beats too much stress rather than too little; nor caring whether one, two, three, or more syllables go to a beat, that is to say, whether two or more beats follow running—as there are three running in the third line of the first stanza—or with syllables between, as commonly; nor whether the line begin with a beat or not; but letting the scansion run on from one line into the next, without break to the end of the stanza: since the dividing of the lines is more to fix the places of the necessary rhymes than for any pause in the measure. Only let this be observed in the reading, that, where more than one syllable goes to a beat, then if the beating syllable is of its nature strong, the stress laid on it must be stronger the greater the number of syllables belonging to it, the voice treading and dwelling: but if on the contrary it is by nature light, then the greater the number of syllables belonging to it the less is the stress to be laid on it, the voice passing flyingly over all the syllables of the foot and in some manner distributing among them all the stress of the one beat. Which syllables however are strong and which light is better told by the ear than by any instruction that could be in short space given: but for an example, in the stanza which is fifth from the end of the poem and in the 6th line* the first two beats are very strong and the more the voice dwells on them the more it fetches out the strength of the syllables they rest upon, the next two beats are very light and escaping, and the last, as well as those which follow in the next line, are of a mean strength, such as suits narrative. And so throughout let the stress be made to fetch out both the strength of the syllables and the meaning and feeling of the words.'

* (What follows seems to fit the 6th and 7th lines of st. 31 rather than those of st. 30.—[W. H. G.])

In Part the First the distribution of the stresses in the stanza is, as G. M. H. says, 2–3–4–3–5–5–4–6; but in Part the Second the first line has *three* stresses, as the alignment in both A and B clearly shows. In L. I, p. 45, the poet warns R. B. not to look for '*hangers* or *outrides*': 'There are no outriding feet in the *Deutschland*.'

St. 1: Here, as throughout the poem, the meaning is 'fetched out' by the stressing; and the stressing is indicated partly by normal word-accent and syllabic strength, partly by contextual suggestion, and partly by alliteration and assonance. In A, all the stresses are marked in ll. 3, 5, and 8 (see below); in B, only two stresses are marked, the 2nd and 3rd ('álmost únmade') in l. 6, which is a recast of A:

'And áfter at tímes almóst unmáde me with dréad,'
Making use of the secondary stress (`) as well as the full stress (´), I
would scan:

'Thóu màstering mé
Gòd! gíver of bréath and bréad;
Wórld's stránd, swáy of the séa;
Lórd of líving and déad;
Thou has bóund bónes and véins in me, fástened me flésh,
And áfter it álmost únmade, whát with dréad,
Thỳ dóing: and dóst thou tóuch me afrésh?
Óver agáin I féel thy fínger and fínd thée.'

The cancelled version of ll. 1-2 in A and B was:

'God mastering me;
Giver of breath and bread;'

Line 8: *finger*. See note on st. 3, l. 8, and cf. st. 31, l. 6.

St. 2, l. 2: *lashed rod*. 'Why do I employ sprung rhythm at all? Because it is
the nearest to the rhythm of prose, that is the native and natural rhythm
of speech, the least forced, the most rhetorical and emphatic of all possible
rhythms, combining, as it seems to me, opposite and, one wd. have
thought, incompatible excellences, markedness of rhythm—that is
rhythm's self—and naturalness of expression—for why, if it is forcible in
prose to say "lashed ⦁ rod" [i.e. *lásh'd ród*], am I obliged to weaken this in
verse, which ought to be stronger, not weaker, into "láshed birch-ród"
or something?

'My verse is less to be read than heard, as I have told you before; it is
oratorical, that is the rhythm is so' (L. I, p. 46).—l. 5: *Thou knowest . . .
night:* probably refers to some crisis in his conversion or his initiation as a
Jesuit. 'I may add for your greater interest and edification that what refers
to myself in the poem is all strictly and literally true and did all occur;
nothing is added for poetical padding' (G. M. H. in L. I, p. 47).—*hoūr,*
so written in MS.

St. 3, l. 4: *that spell*, i.e. 'thát spèll' = 'in that brief bout', referring to st. 2.—
Cf. similar use of 'spell' in No. 23, st. 7; No. 39, l. 6; No. 153, l. 7. As
the verb in an adjectival clause qualifying *wings, spell* would have no clear
meaning (cf. Peters, p. 157); for different views, see *I.D.*, pp. 199, 335,
and *S.*, p. 305, section 195. 4.—l. 6: *dovewinged*, cf. Ps. lv. 6.—l. 7: *carrier-
witted*, with the instinct of the carrier pigeon: cf. 'homing nature' in No. 47,
ll. 5-6.—l. 8: *To flash*, &c. Cf. *S.*, p. 158: '. . . elevating [grace], which
lifts the receiver from one cleave of being to another and to a vital act

in Christ: this is truly God's finger touching the very vein of personality, which nothing else can reach and man can respond to by no play whatever, by bare acknowledgment only, the counter stress which God alone can feel ("subito probas eum"), the aspiration in answer to his inspiration. Of this I have written . . . somewhere else long ago.' As H. H. suggested, this may refer to st. 1 as well as st. 3.

St. 4, l. 7: *voel*, bare hill or mountain (Welsh); Y Voel (substantival fem. mutation of 'moel', bald, though the modern spelling would be 'Foel') is the name of a mountain near St. Beuno's College, N. Wales, where G. M. H. was then studying Theology. Pronounced 'voil' and used generically without initial capital, *voel* gives a 'local habitation' to a universal concept.—[W. H. G.] 'The meaning, obscured by *roped*, is that the well is fed by trickles of water within the flanks of the mountains.— Both A and B read *planks* for *flanks*; G gives the correction.'—[R. B.] To the present Ed., *roped* suggests the long silvery runnels down the mountain sides, a common sight in N. Wales after rain. This metaphor links the two 'metaphysical' images (hour-glass and well) to convey the idea that as the physical life disintegrates the spiritual life is built up to a serene 'poise'—by faith and grace.—l. 8: *gospel proffer*, viz., grace.

St. 5, l. 1: *I kiss my hand*, &c., cf. Job xxxi. 26–7 (kissing the hand to an object of worship is an ancient religious gesture); l. 7: *instréssed*, stressed (stress-mark from A). It must be emphasized that God's nature is a 'mystery'— it cannot be comprehended by pure reason: the antinomy of His love and stern masterhood must be borne in on the mind prepared to 'meet' Him, driven home by sensory experience and mystical illumination; it must then be dwelt on, actualized, and 'kept at stress' by the will, by faith.

St. 6, l. 1: *Not out of his bliss*, &c., elucidated by st. 7, ll. 5–6: the revelation of God in beauty and suffering dates only from Christ's Incarnation and Passion; the 'stress felt' comes from the central Christian paradox of God's final Self-revelation to man through the mystery of suffering, the 'immortal beauty' of Sacrifice.—l. 7: *rides time* . . . , a pregnant ambiguity: 'It cuts across history and the natural order, yet persists in time, is anchored in eternity.'

St. 7, ll. 7–8, and st. 8: *Though felt before*, &c. To me this passage means: 'Though the lightning-stress of mystical revelation has been felt in all ages, its main discharge into the world was from the dark cloud of Christ's Passion. It is the heart in extremity which best understands and proclaims the beauty and terror of that Sacrifice. Some are forced to cry *How bitter*! Others taste only the sweetness. But, sour or sweet, the result is overwhelming conviction.' For an indirect commentary on the image and emotion, see *J.*, p. 195, para. 2.

St. 8, l. 2: *best or worst word*, cf. st. 2, l. 1: the 'best' word is 'yes', to God's call; cf. st. 2, l. 1.—l. 5: *sour or sweet*, originally 'sour and sweet'.—l. 6: *Brim, in a flash, full*, an effective tmesis. (Cf. No. 71, l. 15).—ll. 7–8: cf. Philippians ii. 10–11.

St. 9, ll. 6–8: The paradox is central in G. M. H.'s faith. Cf. No. 34, l. 14: 'Being mighty a master, being a father and fond.'

St. 10, l. 5: *crásh Paúl* (stresses in A), i.e. the sudden conversion of Saul (St. Paul)—Acts ix.—l. 6: *Austin*, St. Augustine of Hippo (354–430), whose conversion was gradual.

St. 11, l. 5. A.: 'But wé dréam we are róoted in éarth—Dúst!'—l. 8: *cringe*, (arch.) 'bend', 'sink'; cf. Time's 'bending sickle' in Shakespeare's Sonnet cxvi. The suggested sense, 'cause to cower', seems to derive from:

> 'Whip him, fellows,
> Till, like a boy, you see him *cringe* his face
> And whine aloud for mercy.'
>
> (*A. & C.*, III, xi, 99–101.)

—*blear*, stained, grim, lustreless; or perhaps 'blurring the sight', as in Milton's

> 'Of power to cheat the eye with *blear* illusion' (*Comus*, l. 155.)

St. 12, l. 5: *under thy feathers*, cf. Matt., xxiii. 37.—l. 7: *bay*, used in architectural sense; cf. *J.*, p. 193: 'opposite bays of the sky'; l. 8: *reeve*, cf. nautical sense—'rope together', hence 'gather'. See R. B.'s note, p. 254.—l. 8: *million*. Corrupted in 2nd Edn. to 'millions'. [N. H. M.]

St. 13, l. 7: 'Wíry and white-fíery and whírlwind-swivellèd snów.' (A)

St. 14, ll. 3–4: Here occurs the first example of a rhyme which depends on running over to the next line:

> leeward/ drew her D—.

Such a rhyme is used also in st. 31, twice,

> of them/ of the M—: Providence/ of it and S—

and in 35:

> door D—/ Reward: and in other poems. Hopkins had found these 'linked rhymes' in early Welsh poetry (see *Study*, II, chap. iii). Cf. l. 14: *endured*. G. M. H. justified the rhyme in L. I, p. 180: 'You will grant that there are things in verse which may be read right or wrong, which depend for their effect on pronunciation. For instance here if I had rhymed *drew her* to *to her* I should have meant it to be read *tó her* and not *to hér* ... You will also grant that in *drew her*, rightly read, the *h* is evanescent. Good. Now then *endured* may be read with little or well marked circumflex—*endúred* something like *en-dew-ered*.'—l. 4: *Kentish Knock*, a sandbank near the mouth of the Thames.—l. 7: *whorl*, the screw-propeller,

which was lost. G. M. H. studied contemporary newspaper accounts of the shipwreck; see *I.D.*, pp. 353–74.—l. 8: *wind* (naut.) steer; '*these*. G has *there*; but the words between *shock* and *these* are probably parenthetical'. —[R. B.] As I read it, *these* includes both the high seas and the loss of propulsive and steering power.

St. 16, l. 3: 'Landsmen may not observe the wrongness: see again No. 41, st. 9, and No. 63, l. 10. I would have corrected this if the euphony had not accidentally forbidden the simplest correction.'—[R. B.] The misused idiom is a flaw; but the context elucidates the meaning.—[W. H. G.]—l. 7: *foam-fleece*, followed by full-stop in A and B, by a comma in G.—[R. B.]; *What:* lower case initial w in all MSS. and so printed in previous edns.; as the sense requires a capital, this probable error of the transcribers has now been corrected.—l. 8: *burl*, a favourite word with Hopkins, used always in the sense of 'roundness', 'fullness'; cf. *buck*, a jump with arched back.

St. 17, l. 3: Note the effect of rapidity and confusion.

St. 18, l. 5: *after*, used with verbal force, as in 'After him!' For the thought cf. Genesis viii. 21.—l. 7: *Never-eldering*, &c. Cf. Byron, *Don Juan*, IV, ii, ll. 5–6:

> 'While youth's hot wishes in our red veins revel,
> We know not this—the blood flows on too fast.'

—l. 8: *this glee, the good*, &c.: an important key to the symbolism of the poem; the poet rejoices in the fortitude and faith of the 'tall nun', her ability to read 'the unshapeable shock night' (st. 29). For the grace by which this 'prophetess towered in the tumult', see *S.*, p. 154: 'grace is any action, activity on God's part by which . . . he carries the creature to or towards the end of its being, which is its self-sacrifice to God and its salvation'.

St. 19, l. 1: *Sister*, &c. From *The Times*, Dec. 11, 1875: 'Five German nuns . . . clasped hands and were drowned together, the chief sister, a gaunt woman 6 ft. high, calling out loudly and often "O Christ, come quickly!" till the end came.'—l. 3: *hawling*, thus spelt in all three versions.—[R. B.] —l. 4: *sloggering*, delivering heavy blows.—l. 5: *that weather*, on the ana- logy of 'that day'.—l. 6: *fetch*, shift, expedient.

St. 20, l. 5: *Gertrude* (*c.* 1256–*c.* 1302), the German Catholic saint and mystic, who lived in a convent near Eisleben in Saxony, Luther's birthplace. See note to No. 140. l. 6: *beast*, cf. Psalm 80 (Cath. 79), v. 13.

St. 21, l. 2: G omits *the*.—[R. B.] l. 3: *refused them*, we have changed the traditional full stop to the comma found in A and B, restoring the im- petus of the line.—[N. H. M.]—l. 5: *Orion*, cf. the constellation named after the giant hunter (myth.); l. 6: *unchancelling*, presumably a vb. from 'chancel' (sanctuary): 'So God was, after all, the Prime Mover: he was the Hunter who beat these nuns from their monastic covert in Germany so that their faith and fortitude might be tried by ordeal and death.' (*Study*, I, p. 60.); *poising*, cf. No. 34, l. 12: 'swaying considerate scales'.

St. 22, l. 1: *finding*, device, invention (cf. Ger. *Erfindung*); the emblem by which we 'find' Christ (cf. st. 1, l. 8).—*sake*: see G. M. H.'s explanation of this word in note on No. 45, l. 10.—l. 6: *prizèd and priced*, cf. Zechariah xi. 13 and Matt. xxvii. 9.—l. 8: *rose-flake*: the red rose is the traditional Christian emblem of martyrdom; cf. No. 27, st. 6, ll. 3–4.

St. 23, l. 4: *Lovescape*, the pattern of Christ's five wounds, reproduced in the stigmata received by St. Francis. See *Little Flowers of St. Francis*, trans. T. W. Arnold, 1926, pp. 190–6.—l. 5: *his seraph-arrival*, his union with God in his vision of the Seraph (op. cit., p. 191).—l. 8: *all-fire*, no hyphen in B, but clear in A and so printed in 1st Edn.

St. 24, l. 2: *forehead*, St. Beuno's College stands on a hill in the Vale of Clwyd.—l. 6: *catches*, i.e. for breath, or for safety.—l. 8: *cross to her*, '(crucifix) held tightly to her breast', and/or 'she identifies her own suffering (*cross*) with that of Christ'—as the sequel suggests. See note on st. 19, l. 1.

St. 25, l. 2: *Breathe, arch*, &c. Cf. Gk. 'archē', first cause, and Genesis ii. 7.— l. 3: *her lover*, as a virgin the nun was the spouse of Christ.—l. 5: *the men*, &c. See Matt. viii. 25.

St. 26, ll. 5 and 6: The semicolon is autographic correction in B; the stop at *Way* is uncertain in A and B, is a comma in G.—[R. B.]—l. 8: *The treasure*, &c. Cf. 1 Corinthians ii. 9.

St. 27, l. 6: The nun's plight was not conducive to earnest meditation.— l. 8: *burly*, bluster (from 'hurly-burly').

St. 28, ll. 1–4: The bold aposiopesis merges 'the frantic efforts of the drowning to save themselves and the poet's attempt to evoke and express the vision of the nun'. (*Study*, I, p. 62.) The effect of hysteria is probably deliberate.—l. 5: *Ipse* (Lat. emphatic pronoun), 'His very self'.

St. 29, l. 2: *single eye*, clear and fixed on God; cf. Luke xi. 34.—l. 3: *night* [*sic*]—[R. B.] I see no reason for the *sic*: for the use of 'shock' as an epithet, cf. No. 98 (xiii), l. 2, and note; also 'shock tactics'. Line 3 is the key to the symbolism of the whole poem. See Synopsis, p. 255.—ll. 7–8: *The Simon Peter . . . light*. The images 'describe the combination of steadfastness, fear, and high example in the tall nun'. (*Study*, I, p. 185.) Cf. J. E. Keating: 'The nun has repeated the "confession of Peter", on which, in the Catholic view, the authority and ministry of the Church . . . are established.' (*The Wreck of the Deutschland*, 1963, p. 96.) Many commentators ignore the adversative effect of '*but a blown* beacon', which suggests a very human reaction to the winds of adversity.—l. 8: 'Tárpéian-fást, but a blówn beácon of líght.' (A)

St. 30, l. 5: Feast of the Immaculate Conception of the Blessed Virgin Mary, Dec. 8.—l. 6: *so to conceive thee*, i.e. the nun, also a virgin, had re-conceived and re-delivered Christ. Cf. st. 34, and for a similar concept see No. 60, ll. 55–64.—l. 8:*Word*, possibly vocative, in apposition to *Jesu* (l. 1); *heard and kept thee*, cf. Luke ii. 19 and 51, and xi. 27–8.

St. 31, l. 6:
'Fínger of a ténder of, O of a féathery délicacy, the bréast of the'
All five stresses are in A and B. See 'Note' by G. M. H., above, p. 256.—
l. 7: Cancelled A version is: 'Maiden could swing with, be musical of it and'—l. 8: 'Stártle the poor shéep back! is the shípwreck . . .'; *gráin for thee*, cf. No. 32, ll. 12–13 and note 2(b) on p. 47.

St. 32, l. 2: *Yore-flood*, the old, i.e. Noachian deluge; or perhaps an allusion to Genesis i. 2.—ll. 3–4: *The recurb*, &c., the stemming and restemming of wave and tide; cf. Job xxxviii. 8–11.—l. 5: *stanching, quenching*, &c. For *stanch* in the sense of 'stop the flow', 'make firm', see No. 72, l. 7 ('stanches, starches'); and the general idea that God, 'master of the tides', checks and represses the 'ocean'—the 'motionable', fluctuating, restless mind of humanity—is strengthened by 'quenching' and by the rest of the stanza ('wharf', 'Ground', 'granite'). Cf. the use of 'motionable' in No. 143, l. 1.—l. 8: *Death*, the braggart of st. 11, ll. 1–4; *bodes but abides*, 'knows what will happen but does not therefore forestall the free acts of men'. (Robert Boyle, S.J.) J. E. Keating interprets: 'even when [God] threatens, he remains the creature's hope'.

St. 33: This stanza deals with the 'Salvific Will of God'—His desire that all sinners should be saved, through grace and the Church.—l. 3: *love glides* = 'love (that) glides'.—l. 4: *lower than death*, cf. the Creed: 'was crucified . . . He descended into Hell . . . '; also suggests the saving grace extended to souls in Purgatory.—l. 5: *pent in prison*, cf. 1 Peter iii. 19.—l. 8: *fetched*, 'reached': the subject of this verb is *giant* (l. 7), its object is the rel. pron. omitted after *mark* (l. 6); the words between *risen* and *fetched* are parenthetical. In oceanology, the 'fetch' is the distance waves run under the drive of a constant unimpeded wind; cf. 'the storm of his strides'. Some critics read ll. 6–8 differently, making *uttermost* the subject of *mark* (vb.), and *fetched* a past participle. (See E. W. Schneider in *PMLA*, March 1966, p. 119; and, in support of my reading, J. E. Keating, *The Wreck of the Deutschland*, pp. 105–6.)—[W. H. G.]

St. 34, l. 2: We have preferred the MS. 'A' reading, *Double-natured* to the B reading, formerly printed, 'Doubled-naturèd', but we have retained the metrically familiar *-èd*.—[N. H. M.]—l. 5: *he*, so in B; 'He' in A and

262

1st Edn.—l. 8: *shire*. G has 'shore'; but *shire* is doubtless right: it is the special favoured landscape visited by the shower.—[R. B.] Stress-marks in A indicate: 'A relèased shówer let flash . . . ' though the slur is not in MS.—*fire hard-hurled*, cf. Luke ix. 54–6.

St. 35, l. 3: G. M. H. wrote to R. B.: 'But the long, e.g. seven-syllabled, feet of the *Deutschland*, are strictly metrical.' (L. I, p. 45). I can find no seven-syllabled foot except, possibly, here:

x: / x x x x / x / x xx x x x /
'Remember us in the roads, the heaven-haven of the reward:' though A gives '. . . heaven-háven . . .'; *reward*, so in B; 'Reward' in A and 1st Edn.—ll. 4–8: These lines, heavily loaded with strong syllables, produce the effect of symphonic climax and finale.

29. **The Silver Jubilee:** 'in honour of the Most Reverend James first Bishop of Shrewsbury.' A. St. Beuno's, Vale of Clwyd. Summer 1876.— Text, title, and date from autograph in B. 'It was published with a sermon by Father John Morris, S.J., on the same occasion. Another copy in H.'—[R. B.] See also Nos. 172 and 173, and L. III, pp. 139–40.

30. **Penmaen Pool.** Early copy in A. Text, title, and punctuation from autograph in B, dated 'Barmouth, Merionethshire. Aug. 1876'. But that autograph writes *leisure* for *pleasure* in first line; *skulls* in st. 2; and in st. 8, *month* has a capital initial. Several copies exist, and vary.—[R. B.]

St. 3, l. 2: *Cadair Idris* is written as a note to *Giant's stool*.—[R. B.]; *Giant's Stool*, in the autograph the S, being twice the size of the 'o's' and, e.g., the 's' of 'staff' above it, must be intended as a capital letter, and is now so printed.—[N. H. M.]

St. 8, l. 4: Several variants. Two good copies read *darksome danksome*; but the early copy in A has *darksome darksome*, which B returns to.—[R. B.]

St. 9, l. 3: A has *But praise it*, and two good copies *But honour it*.—[R. B.]

31. **God's Grandeur.** 'Standard rhythm counterpointed.' Two autographs, Feb. 23, 1877; and March 1877; in A.—Text is from corrections in B. The second version in A has *lightning* for *shining* in l. 2, explained in a letter of Jan. 4, 1883. B returns to original word.—[R. B.] In B, l. 1 is counterpointed: 'The world is charged with the grandeur of God.' The first word in l. 5 is written 'Generations'. A note by G. M. H. in the 'A' MS. refers to Nos. 31 and 32: 'To be read, both of them, slowly, strongly marking the rhythms and fetching out the syllables.'

Line 1: cf. 'All things therefore are charged with love, are charged with God and if we know how to touch them give off sparks and take fire, yield drops and flow, ring and tell of him.' (*S.*, p. 195.)—l. 2: *shook foil*.

In the letter mentioned above, G. M. H. writes: 'I mean foil in its sense of leaf or tinsel. . . . Shaken goldfoil gives off broad glares like sheet lightning and also, and this is true of nothing else, owing to its zigzag dints and creasings and network of small many cornered facets, a sort of fork lightning too.' (L. I, p. 169.)—l. 3; *ooze of oil*, e.g. from the crushing of olives; cf. No. 5, ll. 52–3.—l. 13: *Holy Ghost*, cf. Genesis, i. 2 and Milton, *P.L.*, i. 19–22.

32. The Starlight Night. Feb. 24, 1877. Autograph in A.—'Standard rhythm opened and counterpointed. March, 1877.' ['opened' means that both octave and sestet are opened with a 'sprung' line.] A.—Later corrected version 'St. Beuno's, Feb. 1877' in B.—Text follows B. The second version in A was published in Miles's book *Poets and Poetry of the Century*. For the thought in l. 8, cf. George Herbert:

> 'Take stars for money; stars not to be told
> By any art, but to be purchasèd.'
> (*The Church Porch*, st. 29.)—[R. B.]

Line 1: cf. the 'sprung leadings' of No. 33.—l. 4: *delves*, pl. of obs. 'delf', mine, pit; earlier version has 'diamond wells'.—l. 6: *whitebeam . . . abeles*, the leaves of these trees have whitish undersides, which are swung uppermost by a wind.—l. 9: *What?*, i.e. 'You ask, *What price shall I offer?*' In a version in H we find 'patience'; and the second half of this line is marked '*rallentando*'. (Cf. notes to Nos. 33, 34, 38.)—l. 12: *barn*, cf. Matt. xiii. 30.—l. 13: *shocks*, stooks; *piece-bright paling*, cf. the 'hurdles' in the isolated stanza printed here as No. 98 (xxix). For the thought cf. No. 8, st. 2.—l. 14: *hallows*, saints.

33. Spring. '(Standard rhythm, opening with sprung leadings), May 1877.' Autograph in A.—Text from corrections in B, but punctuation from A. Was published in Miles's book from incomplete correction of A.—[R. B.] Another autograph, owned by Lady Pooley, is almost identical with A, bears the same date, but is described as follows: '(unfolding rhythm, with sprung leadings: no counterpoint)'. In both versions the initial capital of *Spring* (l. 1) is clear. The 'sprung leadings' are marked by large colons indicating a strong stress on the opening syllable, viz.—Line 1: ' ⁚ Nothing is so . . .'; l. 3: ' ⁚ Thrush's eggs . . .'; l. 5: ⁚ ' The ear . . .'; l. 9: ' ⁚ What is . . .'; l. 13: ' ⁚ Innocent-minded Mayday . . .'. Line 2 reads: 'When weeds, in wheels, shoot up long, lovely, and lush;' In Lady Pooley's MS., ll. 1–9 are tied in the left margin by a curved stroke, along which is written 'staccato'. Just before ll. 10 and 14 is written 'Rall.' (= Rallentando]. See above *Foreword* p. xliv.

34. In the Valley of the Elwy. '(Standard rhythm, sprung and counter-pointed.)' Autograph in A. Text is from corrected B, which dates as contemporary with No. 39, adding 'for the companion to this see No. 58'. —[R. B.] Another autograph, owned by Lady Pooley, is almost identical with A and is dated 'May 23 1877'. See above, Foreword, p. xliv. In the left margin of this MS. 'Rall.' is written before ll. 9 and 14, and 'Sf.' (i.e. Sforzando) before l. 10 (see note to No. 33).

Line 1. In B marked thus: 'I remember a house. . . .' So also l. 9: '. . . waters, meadows, . . .'—ll. 3 and 7 may be scanned: '. . . bréathed at very entering'; 'Will, or mild nights the new morsels . . .'

Line 8:—A: 'Why, it seemed of course; ⁚ seemed of right it should.'
B: 'Why, it séemed of coúrse; séemed of ríght it shóuld.'

Line 11:—A: ' ⁚ Only the inmate . . .'

Pooley MS.: ' ⁚ Only, the inmate . . .'

G. M. H. called this imposing of sprung and counterpointed rhythms upon standard rhythm 'the most delicate and difficult business of all'.

Of the thought in the octave G. M. H. says: 'The kind people of the sonnet were the Watsons of Shooter's Hill, nothing to do with the Elwy. . . . The frame of the sonnet is a rule of three sum *wrong*, thus: As the sweet smell to those kind people so the Welsh landscape is NOT to the Welsh; and then the author and principle of all four terms is asked to bring the sum right' (L. I, pp. 76–7).

35. The Sea and the Skylark. Originally 'Walking by the Sea'. 'Standard rhythm, in parts sprung and in others counterpointed, Rhyl, May 1877.' A. This version deleted in B, and the revision given in text written in with new title.—G. M. H. was not pleased with this sonnet [i.e. the *first* version— W. H. G.], and wrote the following explanation of it in a letter 1882 (L. I, pp. 163–4): 'It was written in my Welsh days . . . when I was fascinated with *cynghanedd* or consonant-chime. . . . *Rash fresh more* (it is dreadful to explain these things in cold blood) means a headlong and exciting new snatch of singing, resumption by the lark of his song, which by turns he gives over and takes up again all day long, and this goes on, the sonnet says, through all time, without ever losing its first freshness, being a thing both new and old. *Repair* means the same thing, *renewal*, resumption. The *skein* and *coil* are the lark's song, which from his height gives the impression . . . of something falling to the earth and not vertically quite but tricklingly or wavingly, something as a skein of silk ribbed by having been tightly wound on a narrow card or a notched holder or as twine or fishing-tackle unwinding from a *reel* or *winch* or as pearls strung on a horsehair: the laps or folds are the notes or short measures and bars of them. The same is called a *score* in the musical sense of score and this score is "writ upon a liquid sky trembling to welcome it", only not horizontally. The lark in wild glee *races the reel round*, paying or dealing out and down the turns of the skein or *coil* right to the earth *floor*, the ground, where it lies in a heap, as it were, or rather is all wound off on to another winch, reel, bobbin or spool in Fancy's eye by the moment the bird touches earth and so is ready for a fresh unwinding at the next flight. . . . *Crisp* means almost *crisped*, namely with notes.'—[R. B.] Hopkins had no cause to be displeased with the revised version.

Lines 4–8: The earlier A version marks a very crisp *staccato:*

    'Left hand, off land, I hear the lark ascend

    With rash-fresh more, repair of skein and score,

    Race wild reel round, crisp coil deal down to floor,

    And spill music till there's none left to spend.'

36. The Windhover.

'(Falling paeonic rhythm, sprung and outriding.)' Two contemporary autographs in A.—Text and dedication from corrected B, dated St. Beuno's, May 30, 1877.—In a letter June 22, 1879: 'I shall shortly send you an amended copy of The Windhover: the amendment only touches a single line, I think, but as that is the best thing I ever wrote I should like you to have it in its best form.'—[R. B.] For G. M. H.'s distinction between paeons and outriding feet see note to No. 38. In the present poem the heavily stressed outriding feet are distinguished from the smoother paeons by the looped outrides (from A and B). The rest of the metrical marks, however, are mine.—[W. H. G.]:

    'I caught this morning morning's minion, king-

      dom of daylight's dauphin, dapple-dawn-drawn Falcon,

        in his riding

    Of the rolling level underneath him steady air, and

        striding

    High there, how he rung upon the rein of a wimpling wing . . .'

Other outrides are: l. 6, 'skate's heel'; l. 8, 'achieve of'; l. 11, 'lovelier, more dangerous', l. 12; 'wonder of it'. In l. 9, the comma after *plume* is clearly marked in both autographs in A, and its omission from R. B.'s transcript in B was obviously an oversight (corrected in 1st Edn.). Wrongly taken out in the 5th impr. of 3rd. Edn., this comma has now been restored to the text.—*oh, air*, so in B.—In l. 10, A has 'And'; the intended expressional rhythm seems to be:

'Búckle! AND the fíre that bréaks from thée then, a bíllion

where 'AND' takes an extra-metrical emphasis. See note to No. 71, last para., sign (3).

Line 2: For the image, cf. the Dauphin's praise of his horse in *Hen. V*, III. vii. 11: '*le cheval volant*, the Pegasus, *qui a les narines de feu*! When I bestride him I soar, I am a *hawk*: he trots the air.'—l. 4: *rung upon the rein*, &c. (earlier A version—'rung the rein'), seems to combine the sense of beating wings, as the bird hovered, with the suggestion of pivoting on the tip of a tensed wing as he banked or spiralled. To 'ring on the rein' is a term of the riding-school (p.t. 'rung . . .')—said of a horse that circles at the end of a long rein held by its trainer.—*Wimpling*, 'beautifully pleated, curved, and rippling'.—Cf. also 'to ring' (falconry), to rise in spirals.— l. 7: *My heart in hiding*, variously explained as 'timid', 'shrinking from noble enterprise or danger'; or 'hiding' in the sense expressed by St. Paul: 'Set your affections . . . not on things on the earth. For ye are dead, and your life is hidden with Christ in God;' and by G. M. H. himself: '*Erat subditus illis*: the hidden life at Nazareth is the great help to faith for us who must live more or less an obscure, constrained, and unsuccessful life.' (*S.*, p. 176).—ll. 9–14: This pregnant sestet derives much of its power and fame from its controlled (or at least 'significant') ambiguity. Key words, such as 'here Buckle!' (ll. 9–10) and 'O my chevalier' (l. 11) have been variously interpreted; but on the following core of meaning there has been general agreement among informed critics: 'I *inscape* this wind-hover as the symbol or analogue of Christ, Son of God, the supreme Chevalier. May the human equivalents of this bird's heroic graces and perfectly disciplined *physical* activity be combined and brought to a much higher *spiritual* activity in my own being, just as these attributes were once and for all so transmuted in Christ. It is the law of things that characteristic natural action or 'selving', however humble it may be, frequently gives off flashes of heart-stirring beauty; how much more then should characteristically Christ-like action (including conscientious toil and willing self-sacrifice) give glory and be pleasing to Christ our Lord!' [For G. M. H. on 'selving' see Nos. 45 and 57.]

Line 9: *here*, here in my heart, in me (or 'in this bird'?).—l. 10: *Buckle!* This presumably imperative (but possibly indicative) vb. is the main crux of the poem. Which of three possible meanings did the poet intend? Each one has been regarded, by *some* commentators, as exclusively or primarily apposite: (1) the arch. 'prepare for action', 'come to grips', 'engage the enemy'; (2) 'clasp, enclose, fasten together' as under one discipline; (3) the more common meanings, 'bend, crumple up, collapse' under weight or strain. Meaning (2) is clearly implied in ll. 1–8—the bird's controlled flight; (1) makes the militant kestrel-hawk the symbol of the Christian knight valiantly warring against evil, and is supported by the chivalric imagery—'dauphin', 'riding', 'rein'; (3) suggests the abnegation of 'mortal beauty' (cf. No. 62) and the readiness to suffer and be immolated. In its complex 'discipline—fight—fall' meanings and connotations, *Buckle!* links the joyful panache and mastery of the octave to the poignant yet triumphant resignation of 'Fáll, gáll themselves, &c.' of l. 14. As a Jesuit, G. M. H. meditated regularly on the Kingship and soldiership of Christ (see the *Spiritual Exercises* of St. Ignatius Loyola, and poems Nos. 63 and 73) and on His Crucifixion; he was also deeply concerned with his own personal and vocational 'imitation of Christ'.—*AND*, 'and as an assured result'; *from thée then*, the stress on 'thee' seems essential if the pron. means 'Christ our Lord' (to whom the poem is dedicated) or 'my heart in hiding' (l. 7); but if 'thee' is the bird the stress might fall on 'then'. The dedication was added by G. M. H. only at the last revision; nevertheless it is highly probable that his motive in introducing Christ *by name* was in part, at least, to clarify the deeper symbolic implications of the sestet.—ll. 12–13: *shéer plód makes plough . . . shine*, cf. Virgil's *sulco attritus splendescere vomer* [Georg. I. 46]; also cf. Luke ix. 62 and L. II, p. 88: 'The question is . . . whether I am not to undergo a severe judgment from God . . . for the reserves I may have in my heart made, for the backward glances I have given with my hand upon the plough'; cf. also, as a link between *Buckle!* (3) and ll. 13–14: (i) 'Poor was his station, laborious his life, bitter his ending: through poverty, through labour, through crucifixion his majesty of nature more shines.' (S., p. 37); (ii) 'Christ Jesus . . . annihilated himself, taking the form of servant.' (L. I, p. 175).—*sillion*, strip of arable, furrow.—ll. 13–14. With this image and *Buckle!* cf. (i) 'Christ our Lord . . . was doomed to succeed by failure; his plans were baffled, his hopes dashed, and his work was done by being broken off undone.' (L. II, p. 137); (ii) 'In his Passion all this strength was spent, this lissomness crippled, this beauty wrecked, this majesty beaten down. . . . Glory to Christ's body in its weariness . . . in its Passion, death and burial.' (S., pp. 36 and 38).—l. 13: *ah my dear*, cf. George Herbert, 'Love', st. 2:

'I the unkinde, ungratefull? Ah my deare,
I cannot look on thee.'

37. Pied Beauty. 'Curtal Sonnet: sprung paeonic rhythm. St. Beuno's, Tremeirchion. Summer 1877.' Autograph in A.—B agrees.— [R. B.]
Line 2: *brinded*, early form of 'brindled', streaked.—l. 4: *Fresh-firecoal*, &c., cf. 'Chestnuts as bright as coals or spots of vermilion'.(*J.*, p. 189.)

38. Hurrahing in Harvest: 'Sonnet (sprung and outriding rhythm. Take notice that the outriding feet are not to be confused with dactyls or paeons, though sometimes the line might be scanned either way. The strong syllable in an outriding foot has always a great stress and after the outrider follows a short pause. The paeon is easier and more flowing). Vale of Clwyd, Sept. 1, 1877.' Autograph in A. Text is from corrected B, punctuation of original A. In a letter of 1878 he wrote: 'The Hurrahing sonnet was the outcome of half an hour of extreme enthusiasm as I walked home alone one day from fishing in the Elwy.' A also notes 'no counterpoint'.—[R. B.] Early draft in Bodl. is titled 'Heart's Hurrahing in Harvest'. Later G. M. H. wrote: 'An outriding foot is, by a sort of contradiction, a recognized extra-metrical effect; it is and it is not part of the metre; not part of it, not being counted, but part of it by producing a calculated effect which tells in the general success.' (L. I, p. 45.) The 'outriding' effect is common before the caesural pause in Shakespeare's later blank verse, e.g.:

'For goodness dares not check thee; wear thou thy wrongs'
(*Macb.*, IV. iii. 33).

The outrides marked in the MSS. are as follows: l. 1, 'ends now', 'barbarous'; l. 2, 'wind-walks'; l. 8, 'Rapturous . . . greeting'; l. 9, 'azurous'; l. 10, 'Majestic . . . stalwart'; l. 14, 'hurls for him . . . earth for him'. (See 'Author's Preface', p. 48, and *Study*, I, chap. iii.)
'arise'.—[N. H. M.]—l. 4. In A the last three words are marked '*rall*' (i.e. *rallentando*).—ll. 12 and 13: The scansion in A is:

'Wánting; whích two whén they ónce méet,
The héart réars wíngs bóld and bolder . . .'

39. The Caged Skylark. '(Falling paeonic rhythm, sprung and outriding.)' Autograph in A. Text from corrected B which is dated 'St. Beuno's, 1877'. In line 13 B writes *uncúmberèd*.—[R. B.] [Now printed as four syllables (N. H. M.).] Five outrides are marked in B: l. 4, 'drudgery'; l. 8, 'barriers'; l. 10, 'babble and'; l. 13, 'uncumberèd'; l. 14, 'footing it'.

Line 2: *bone-house*, the body; cf. O.E. *bān-hūs* (*Beowulf*, l. 2508).—l. 5: *aloft on turf*. The cage is hung aloft, and it has long been customary to place inside the cage of a skylark 'a turf full of clover' (cf. Webster's *Duchess of Malfi*, IV. ii: 'Didst thou ever see a lark in a cage? &c.', which probably supplied G. M. H. with his original *motif*, though the comparison of the soul to a caged bird is traditional).—l. 7: *deadly*, death-like.—l. 11: 'But his ówn nést, wíld nést . . .' [A]. *Note*: As No. 39 had been given to Bridges before Aug. 8, 1877 (see L. I, p, 42), it should precede No. 38.

40. The Lantern out of Doors. '(Standard rhythm, with one sprung leading and one line counterpointed.)' Autograph in A.—Text, title, and accents in ll. 13 and 14, from corrections in B, where it is called 'companion to No. 13 (= 46), St. Beuno's 1877'.—[R. B.] Line 1: *night*. See p. lxvii. —l. 4: *wading*, cf. O.E. *wadan*, walk, and also Spenser's 'Vertue gives her selfe light, through darknesse for to wade.' (*F.Q.*, I. i. 12.)—l. 5: We assume counterpointing thus: 'Men go by me whom . . .'—ll. 9 and 10: The verb is 'wind eye after', and Hopkins says: 'I mean that the eye winds / only in the sense that its focus or point of sight winds and that coincides with a point of the object and winds with that. For the object, a lantern passing further and further away and bearing now east, now west of one right line, is truly and properly described as winding' (L. I, p. 66).

41. The Loss of the Eurydice. A contemporary copy in A has this note: 'Written in sprung rhythm, the third line has 3 beats, the rest 4. The scanning runs on without break to the end of the stanza, so that each stanza is rather one long line rhymed in passage than 4 lines with rhymes at the ends.'—B has an autograph of the poem as it came to be corrected (1883 or after), without the above note and dated 'Mount St. Mary's, Derbyshire, April 1878.'—Text follows B.—The injurious rhymes are partly explained in the old note.—[R. B.] For a different opinion on the rhymes see *Study*, I, pp. 147-9, and the note on ll. 23-24 below. See G. M. H.'s own very sensible comments on his less conventional rhymes—in. L. I, p. 180, and above in 'Preface to Notes', p. 243; see note to No. 28, st. 14.

For the first version of ll. 73-84, see L. I, p. 48. As Prof. Abbott points out, the later version, 'illustrates the poet's care in correction'.

Contemporary newspaper accounts of the foundering of the *Eurydice* are given in *I.D.*, pp. 375-92.

Lines 3-4: *un-*/*warned*. MS. has '-/Warned', and a capital follows the hyphen in all other instances of synapheia except one—the poet's late correction, 'king-/ dom', in ll. 1-2 of No. 36. We retain R. B.'s rationalized spelling here and in Nos. 61, 62, 65, 66, and 72.—l. 6: *furled:* 'How are hearts of oak furled? Well, in sand and sea water. . . . You are to suppose a stroke or blast in a forest of "hearts of oak" . . . which at one blow both lays them low and buries them in broken earth. *Furling* (*ferrule* is a blunder for *furl*, I think) is *proper* when said of sticks and staves.' (G. M. H. in L. I, p. 52.)—

l. 8: *forefalls*, the forward (i.e. seaward) slope of a hill; or cliffs dropping
to the 'foreshore'.—l. 22: *Bright sun*, &c., 'that is/a bright sun was darting
fire from the bay of heaven, but that was of no avail, for did not a fatal
north wind . . .'. (G. M. H. in L. II, p. 33.)—ll. 23-4: The linked rhyme
should be read fairly quickly but without distortion of the sounds; then
'electric' gathers up and *electrifies* the more slowly pronounced corres-
pondences in 'wrecked her? he/ C—'. The device is nearer to Welsh
cynghanedd than to conventional English rhyme. See above, 'Preface to
Notes', p. 243n.—[W. H. G.]—l. 35: *shorten sail*. The seamanship at fault:
but this expression may be glossed by supposing the boatswain to have
sounded that call on his whistle. [R. B.]—l. 37: scanned, L. I, p. 52: 'Thís
was thát féll capsíze.' We have restored the auto. stop after *capsize*, helpful
to the sense, where previous edns. had a comma.—[N. H. M.]—l. 47:
Cheer's death, i.e. despair. [R. B.] l. 50: *Right, rude of feature*, seems to be a
personification, obscured by inversion: 'he thought he heard Right, rude
of feature, say . . .'. Read aloud, the passage would be ambiguous.
[W. H. G.]—l. 53: *It is even seen*. In a letter of May 30, 1878, he explains:
'You mistake the sense of this as I feared it would be mistaken. I believed
Hare to be a brave and conscientious man: what I say is that *even* those
who seem unconscientious will act the right part at a great push . . .'.
[R. B.]—l. 55: *No or Yes?*, capital Y now introduced from autograph in
B.—[N. H. M.]—l. 68: *rivelling*, literally, 'causing to wrinkle'. I quote
Study I, p. 131: 'The wide invisible air is shrunken into a visible corruga-
tion, puckered by the driving wind into successive gusts of thick snow-
flakes which at the same time force the shipwrecked Sydney Fletcher to
screw up his face in a painful effort to see.'—l. 85: in the auto. ends with a
stop, which we restore as helping the syntax.—[N. H. M.]—l. 89: *bygones*,
i.e. the Reformation and the confiscation of Roman Catholic churches and
cathedrals by the Protestants; hence 'Robbery's hand' in l. 91. The poet
complains that shrines once revered are now neglected; and the 'curse' of
this is brought out by the present disaster—so many fine men cut off without absolution. [W. H. G.]—l. 101: *A starlight wender*, i.e. the island was
so Marian that the folk supposed the Milky Way was a fingerpost to guide
pilgrims to the shrine of the Virgin at Walsingham. *And one*, that is Duns
Scotus, the champion of the Immaculate Conception. See L. I, p. 77 and
Sonnet No. 44. [R. B.]—l. 105: *Well wept*. Grammar is as in 'Well hit!
well run!' &c. The meaning 'You do well to weep'. [R. B.]—l. 112:
O Hero savest. Omission of relative pronoun at its worst. = O Hero *that
savest*. [R. B.] G. M. H. explains in L. I, p. 78: 'The words are put into the
mouth of a mother, wife, or sweetheart who has lost a son, husband, or
lover respectively by the disaster and who prays Christ, whom she

addresses "Hero savest", that is, "Hero that savest", that is, Hero of a
Saviour to save (that is, have saved) her hero, that is, her son, husband,
or lover: "Hero of a Saviour" (the line means) "be the saviour of my
hero".'—ll. 114-15: *Have . . . heard*, see note to No. 45, l. 1.

42. The May Magnificat. '(Sprung rhythm, four stresses in each line of the
first couplet, three in each of the second. Stonyhurst, May 1878.)' Autograph
in A.—Text from later autograph in B. He wrote to me: 'A Maypiece
meant for the "Month of Mary", . . . in which I see little good but the freedom
of the rhythm.' (L. I, p. 65). In penult. stanza *cuckoo-call* has its hyphen
deleted in B, leaving the words separate.—[R. B.]
St. 6, l. 1: *bugle blue*, i.e. blue like the flower of the plant called 'bugle'
(*Ajuga reptans*), which blossoms in May.
St. 11, l. 1: *greybell*, i.e. the bluebell opening.

43. Binsey Poplars, 'felled 1879. Oxford, March 13, 1879. Autograph in
A. Text from B, which alters four places. l. 8, *weed-winding*: an early draft
has *weed-wounden*.—[R. B.] The number of stresses to the line (varying from
6 down to 2) is clearly indicated by the indentation: e.g. l. 3—'Áll félled,
félled, are áll félled' (so scanned in B); and ll. 16–18:

> 'Whére we, éven whére we méan
> To ménd her we énd her,
> Whén we héw or délve:' (My scansion—W. H. G.)

In B, l. 8 reads:
> 'On meadow and river and wind-wandering weed-winding bank'.

44. Duns Scotus's Oxford. 'Oxford, March 1879'. Autograph in A. Copy
in B agrees but dates 1878.—[R. B.] The rhythm is sprung and outriding.
Outrides: l. 2, 'echoing . . . swarmèd, . . . charmèd'; l. 3, 'below thee'; l. 4,
'encounter in'; l. 8, 'keeping'; l. 10, 'lived on . . . waters'; l. 11, 'haunted'. . .
'all men'; l. 12, 'rarest-veinèd'; l. 13, 'insight'.

Johannes Duns Scotus (1266 or 1274–1308), the important Scholastic
philosopher rightly called the Subtle Doctor, is supposed to have studied and
lectured at Oxford about 1301. In Aug. 1872 Hopkins first came upon
Scotus's two commentaries on the *Sentences* of Lombard (the *Opus Oxoni-
ense*) and was immediately 'flush with a new stroke of enthusiasm. It may
come to nothing or it may be a mercy from God. But just then when I took
in any inscape of the sky or sea I thought of Scotus.' (*J.*, p. 221.) For the influence upon G. M. H. of the Scotist theory of knowledge see above,
Introduction, pp. xx–xxii; also *Study*, I, pp. 21–31, and Peters, op. cit.

Line 4: *coped*, &c., set off one against the other and well matched.—l. 12: *realty*. Thus in MS.; Scotus was a subtle expounder of the 'real', in the philosophical sense.—l. 14: see note to No. 41, l. 101.

45. Henry Purcell. '(A! `xandrine: six stresses to the line. Oxford, April 1879.)' Autograph in A with argument as printed. Copy in B is uncorrected except that it adds the word *fresh* in the last line.—[R. B.] For a reproduction of the A version see *Study*, I, p. 101.—[W. H. G.] The rhythm is sprung and outriding. Outrides, &c. (from A and B MSS.): l. 1, 'fair fallen, ... have fallen'; l. 2, 'To me'; l. 4, 'sentence ... listed'; l. 5, 'meaning'; l. 6, 'all that'; l. 8, 'sélf there ... thrusts on'; l. 9, 'angels ... lay me'; l. 10, 'sakes of him ... moonmarks'; l. 11, 'stormfowl'; l. 13, 'wuthering of his palmy snow-pinions'; l. 14, 'Off him ... motion'.

Lines 1–2 are marked in B:

'Have fáir fállen, O fáir, fáir have fállen, so déar
To me, ...'

Line 1: ' " Have fair fallen." ... *Have* is the sing. imperative (or optative if you like) of the past, a thing possible and actual both in logic and grammar, but naturally a rare one. As in the 2nd pers. we say "Have done" or in making appointments "Have had your dinner beforehand", so one can say in the 3rd pers. not only "Fair fall" of what is present or future but also "Have fair fallen" of what is past. The same thought (which plays a great part in my own mind and action) is more clearly expressed in the last stanza but one of the *Eurydice*, where you remarked it.' Letter to R. B., Feb. 3, 1883.—L. I, p. 174. Cf. p. 171: 'I *meant* "fair fall" to mean *fair (fortune be)fall*'. Cf. *King John*, I. i. 78: 'Fair fall the bones that took the pains for me.' In *ibid.*, p. 170, G. M. H. says: 'The sonnet on Purcell means this: 1–4. I hope Purcell is not damned for being a Protestant, because I love his genius. 5–8. And that not so much for gifts he shares, even though it shd. be in higher measure, with other musicians as for his own individuality. 9–14. So that while he is aiming only at impressing me his hearer with the meaning in hand I am looking out meanwhile for his specific, his individual markings and mottlings, "the sakes of him". It is as when a bird thinking only of soaring spreads its wings: a beholder may happen then to have his attention drawn by the act to the plumage displayed.'

Line 2: For the Scotist significance of 'especial', both here and in No. 43, l. 22, see *Introduction*, pp. xx–xxiii and *Study*, I, pp. 22–8.—l. 3: *with the reversal*, &c., 'May Purcell have died a good death ... so that the heavy condemnation under which he outwardly or nominally lay for being out

273

of the true Church may in consequence of his good intentions have been reversed'. . . . "Low lays him" is merely "lays him low", that is/strikes him heavily, weighs upon him. . . . "Listed", by the by, is "enlisted".' [L. I, p. 171.]—l. 6: *nursle*, foster (from Spenser).—[W. H. G.]—ll. 9–14: 'The sestet of the Purcell sonnet is not so clearly worked out as I could wish. The thought is that as the seabird opening his wings with a whiff of wind in your face means the whirr of the motion, but also unaware gives you a whiff of knowledge about his plumage, the marking of which stamps his species, that he does not mean, so Purcell, seemingly intent only on the thought or feeling he is to express or call out, incidentally lets you remark the individualising marks of his own genius.

'*Sake* is a word I find it convenient to use: . . . It is the *sake* of "for the sake of", *forsake, namesake, keepsake*. I mean by it the being a thing has outside itself, as a voice by its echo, a face by its reflection, a body by its shadow, a man by his name, fame, or memory, *and also* that in the thing by virtue of which especially it has this being abroad, and that is something distinctive, marked, specifically or individually speaking, as for a voice and echo clearness; for a reflected image light, brightness; for a shadow-casting body bulk; for a man genius, great achievements, amiability, and so on. In this case it is, as the sonnet says, distinctive quality in genius. . . . By *moonmarks* I mean crescent shaped markings on the quill-feathers, either in the colouring of the feather or made by the overlapping of one on another.' L. I, p. 83.—[R. B.] In ibid., p. 84, G. M. H. adds: 'My sonnet means "Purcell's music is none of your d—d subjective rot" (so to speak).' —l. 11: *so some great stormfowl* . . . A time-clause and a conditional clause separate this subject from the continuation of the main clause in l. 14; '. . . but meaning motion fans fresh our wits with wonder'. (*but* = 'only', 'simply').—l. 13: *wuthering*, 'a Northcountry word for the noise and rush of wind'. (L. I, p. 83.)

46. The Candle Indoors. '(Common rhythm, counterpointed.) Oxford, 1879.' A. Text takes corrections of B, which adds, 'companion to No. 6' (= 40). A has in l. 2 *With a yellowy*, and 5 *At that*.—[R. B.] Cf. letter of June 22, 1879, L. I, p. 84: 'A companion to the Lantern, not at first meant to be though, but it fell in.' In all MSS. (l. 5) 'window' and (l. 6) 'wondering'. Line 4: *to-fro tender trambeams*, &c., the delicate lines of light (caused by the eyelashes) which radiate from the candle-flame and, like 'tender' antennae, are subservient to the least motion of the eyelid; silk threads used for the weft of the best silk goods are called 'trams', 'tram-silk'; moreover, in 1879 'tram' could mean a continuous metal rail; *truckle at*, 'cf. "wince *at* a blow", "quail *at* the sight" ' (cf. R. V. Schoder, S.J., in *I.D.*, p. 206).—

274

l. 8: *There/* . This oblique stroke, often used by G. M. H. in his prose, indicates here a very slight pause in recitation to confirm *There* as the adv., not the poss. adj. (their), and to throw the first main stress on to *God.*— ll. 9–14: cf. Matt. v. 13–16.

47. The Handsome Heart (Common rhythm counterpointed.) 'Oxford, 1879'. [Sent to R. B. with No. 46 on June 22, 1879; see L. I, p. 84.—(W. H. G.)] A_1.—In Aug. of the same year he wrote that he was surprised at my liking it, and in deference to my criticism sent a revise, A_2.—Subsequently he recast the sonnet mostly in the longer 6-stress lines, and wrote that into B.— In that final version the charm and freshness have disappeared: and his emendation in evading the clash of *ply* and *reply* is awkward; also the fourteen lines now contain seven *whats*. I have therefore taken A_1 for the text, and have ventured, in l. 8, to restore *how to*, in the place of *what*, from the original version which exists in H. In 'The Spirit of Man' I gave a mixture of A_1 and A_2. In l. 5 the word *soul* is in H and A_1: but A_2 and B have *heart*. *Father* in the second line was the Rev. Father Gerard himself. He tells the whole story in a letter to me (L. I, p. 86).—[R. B.] While applauding R. B.'s discrimination and taste in selecting A_1 as the most acceptable text, I find the word-play of *plied* and *reply* significant: 'it heightens the effect of a swing back to the first spontaneous equilibrium of the boy's moral nature ...' (see ll. 3–4 and *Study*, II, pp. 293–4).—[W. H. G.] Line 1: *your choice*, &c. G. M. H. called this sonnet 'autobiographical ...'. 'Last Lent ... two boys of our congregation gave me much help in the sacristy in Holy Week. I offered them money for their services, which the elder refused, but being pressed consented to take it laid out in a book. The younger followed suit; then when some days after I asked him what I shd. buy answered as in the sonnet.' (L. I, pp. 84, 86.)—l. 6: *Doff darkness*, i.e. in its literal application to the soul, 'remove the stain of Original Sin'. —l. 7: *wild and self-instressed*, moved by its own natural impulse, i.e. towards the Good. The uncorrupted will, when once it knows the Good, is prone to pursue it. Following Duns Scotus, G. M. H. stressed not only the *freedom* of the will but also its primacy over the intellect. For 'wild' in the sense of 'free, natural' cf. Nos. 60 (l. 1) and 148 (st. 7).—l. 12: *buy*, i.e. by prayer (cf. No. 32, l. 9).—l. 13: The aposiopesis expresses the poet-priest's sudden anxiety lest the boy should not train his will to resist evil.

48. The Bugler's First Communion. '(Sprung rhythm, overrove; an outride between the 3rd and 4th foot of the 4th line in each stanza.) Oxford, July 27, (?) 1879'. A. My copy of this in B shows three emendations. First draft exists in H. Text is A with the corrections from B. At nine lines from end, *Though this*, A has *Now this*, and *Now* is deliberately preferred in H.—

B has some uncorrected miscopyings of A. *O for, now, charms* of A (st. 9) is already a correction in H. I should like a comma at end of first line of 5th stanza and an interjection-mark at end of that stanza.—[R. B.]

Most of the outrides in the last lines of all the twelve stanzas will be detected without trouble: each occurs in the third foot, e.g. (outrides from MS. but my stressmarks—[W. H. G.]:

St. 1: 'Sháres their bést gifts súrely, fall hów things wíll),'

St. 2: 'Cáme, I sáy, this dáy to it—to a Fírst Commúnion.'

St. 3, l. 4: *housel*, the consecrated elements of the Eucharist (here = the wafer). Outride = 'housel his . . .'

St. 4, l. 1: *sendings*, i.e. of grace.

St. 5, l. 2: *Squander*, cause to scatter, i.e. to disperse. For the omission of the rel. pron. after *ranks*, see Preface to Notes, p. 241.

St. 6, l. 4: 'Híes héadstrong to its wéllbeing of a self-wíse self-wíll.'

(My stress-marks.—W. H. G.)

St. 9, ll. 2–3: Cancelled lines in H may help to elucidate:

'But O O O! this stands unsealed. For the ointment
Now, Church-arms and charms ban fast off bad
And lock love ever in a lad!'

St. 10, l. 1: *me quickenings lift*, a 'classical' transposition = *least quickenings lift me*; or *me quickenings* may be a substantival compound.

St. 12, l. 2: *brandle*, obs. for 'shake'; *ride and jar*, shock and clash (as of a cavalry charge)—note the many military images in this poem.—l. 4: *Forward-like*, &c. 'Presumptuous of me, and perhaps my fears are premature; but however, that is just how I feel about this lad. And belike (or 'like enough') heaven turned a favourable ear to my pleas' (*Study*, I, p. 133). Outride = 'however and'.

49. Morning, Midday, and Evening Sacrifice. 'Oxford, Aug. 1879'. Autograph in A. Copied by me into B, where it received correction. Text follows B except in ll. 19 and 20, where the correction reads *What death half lifts the latch of, What hell hopes soon the snatch of.* And punctuation is not all followed: original has comma after the second *this* in ll. 5 and 6. On June 30, 1886, G. M. H. wrote to Canon Dixon, who wished to print the first stanza alone in some anthology, and made *ad hoc* alterations which I do not follow. The original seventeenth line was *Silk-ashed but core not cooling*, and was altered because of its obscurity. 'I meant (he wrote) to compare grey hairs to the flakes of silky ash which may be seen round wood embers . . . and covering a "core of heat" . . . *Your offering, with despatch, of* is said like

276

"your ticket", "your reasons", "your money or your life . . .". It is: "Come, your offer of all this (the matured mind), and without delay either!" '—[R. B.] See L. I, p. 98. R. B.'s 'which I do not follow' is not quite accurate. See L. II, p. 132, note 5. We have restored G. M. H.'s revisions: '*the* wimpled lip'; 'What death half lifts the latch of,/ What hell hopes soon the snatch of,'—[N. H. M.]

Line 2: *wimpled lip*, the 'Cupid's bow', beautifully 'rippled' in the middle of the upper lip.—l. 4: *all . . . fellowship*: cf. *Rom. & Jul.*, I. iii. 83: 'every married lineament'.—l. 6: *fuming*, passing away like smoke (cf. Spenser, *F.Q.*, II. iv. 26).

50. Andromeda. 'Oxford, Aug. 12, 1879'. A—which B corrects in two places only. Text rejects the first, in l. 4 *dragon* for *dragon's*: but follows B in l. 10, where A had *Air, pillowy air*. There is no comma at *barebill* in any MS., but a gap and sort of caesural mark in A. In a letter Aug. 14, 1879, G. M. H. writes, 'I enclose a sonnet on which I invite minute criticism. I endeavoured in it at a more Miltonic plainness and severity than I have anywhere else. I cannot say it has turned out severe, still less plain, but it seems almost free from quaintness and in aiming at one excellence I may have hit another.'—[R. B.] We have restored the 'sort of caesural mark' in A and have accepted G. M. H.'s revision, *dragon food*.

The symbolism of this sonnet, clearly suggested in the first line, is tentatively elucidated in the following notes (cf. *Study*, I, pp. 185-6, and see A. Heuser, *The Shaping Spirit of G. M. H.*, pp. 77 and 114, and J.-G. Ritz, *Le Poète G. M. H.*, p. 218).

Line 1: *Time's Andromeda*, the Church of Christ; *rock rude*, England (Ritz) or St. Peter (cf. Matt. xvi. 18: 'Thou art Peter, and upon this rock I will build my Church. . . .' Cf. also No. 28, st. 29, ll. 7-8.)—l. 4: *dragon food*, Devil's prey.—l. 7: *wilder beast from West*, the new powers of Antichrist, which for G. M. H. would include rationalism, Darwinism, industrialism, the new paganism of Swinburne and Whitman, possibly Nietzsche.—l. 9: *Her Perseus*, Christ (see l. 13). Mr. A. Heuser, citing *S.*, pp. 198-9, and Revelation xii, argues that Perseus stands for St. Michael, or Christ 'steaded' in Michael; or alternatively he is St. George of England.—l. 13: *Then to alight disarming*, &c, i.e. presumably, at the second Advent— or at the conversion wished for in No. 28, st. 35, l. 4; with 'no one dreams' cf. 2 Peter iii. 10: 'But the day of the Lord will come as a thief in the night.' As R. B.'s note on the odd (and now restored) punctuation of the last line would suggest, *disarming* probably governs *thongs and fangs*; and for me the whole passage means that Christ, having conquered Sin and Death ('With Gorgon's gear') will come unexpectedly ('no one dreams') and with retributory sword ('barebill') to redeem His Church—to sever her bonds ('thongs') and destroy her enemies ('fangs'). As the text stands, the ambiguity of *disarming* is significant: 'the Redeemer's coming will allay fears, deprive Evil of its power, and bring final peace' (*Study*, loc. cit.).—l. 14: The comma after *barebill*, substituted by R. B. for the oblique stroke in A (cf. No. 46, l. 8) and kept in the 2nd and 3rd Edns., has now been replaced by the original mark; this indicates the intended hyperbaton better than a comma, which, by putting *thongs* and *fangs* in apposition to *barebill*, confuses the thought. The 'sort of caesural mark' was copied by R. B. in B. In the early H draft there is no mark at all.

51. Peace: 'Oxford, 1879'. Autograph in B, where a comma after *daunting* is due to following a deletion. An early draft [in H] dated Oct. 2, 1879, has *taking* for *reaving*.—[R. B.] A Curtal Sonnet in 'standard' Alexandrines (see 'Author's Preface').—Line 4, *own my heart*, 'is merely "my own heart", transposed for rhythm's sake and then *tamquam exquisitius*, as Hermann would say. *Reave* (l. 7) is for rob, plunder, carry off.' (L. I, p. 196.)—l. 8: *só he dóes leave*, i.e. 'and so he *does*, he leaves Patience'.—l. 9: *plumes*, &c., grows feathers, becomes the fully fledged dove of Peace.

52. At the Wedding March. '(Sprung rhythm.) Bedford, Lancashire, Oct. 21, 1879.' A. Autograph uncorrected in B, but title changed from 'At a Wedding' to that in text.—[R. B.]—B is R. B.'s transcript from the autograph A, but G. M. H. later added to it in his own hand the date we quote, also lengthening the title to emphasize the March itself. On copying the poem, R. B. had inadvertently changed 'Then let the March' (St. 3, l. 1) to '. . . march.' When he printed the poem, he restored the capital M, but the correction was lost with the 2nd Edn.—[N. H. M.]

53. Felix Randal. '(Sonnet: sprung and outriding rhythm; six-foot lines.) Liverpool, April 28, 1880'. A. Text from A with the two corrections of B. The comma in l. 5 after *impatient* is omitted in copy in B.—[R. B.] This comma is now restored. In l. 1, the 'he is' of earlier edns. is now corrected to 'is he' (all MSS.). The stresses, elision-loops, and outrides marked in A and B (most of which are necessary guides to the rhythm) are as follows:

Line 1 (A): 'Félix Rándal the fárrier, O is he déad then? my dúty all énded,

     (B): 'Félix Rándal the fárrier, O is he déad then? my dúty all énded,'

l. 3 (A): 'Pining, pining, ...rambled in it . . .'

  (B): 'Pining, pining,...............rambled in it . . .'

278

l. 5 (A and B): 'broke him. Impatient,' (no comma in B)

l. 7 (A): 'Mónths ⁚ sóoner, since Í had our swéet repríeve and ránsom'
(see l. 13).

(B): 'Mónths eárlier, . . .'

l. 8 (A): 'Téndered to him. Áh well, God rést him áll road éver he offénded !'

(B): 'Téndered to him. &c.'

l. 9 (A): 'This ~~often~~ seeing the sick endéars them, me tóo it endears.'

(B): 'This seéing the síck endéars them tó us, us tóo it endéars.'

l. 11 (A): 'my heart, child, Felix,'

(B): 'my heart, child, Felix,'

l. 12 (A and B): 'forethought of,'

l. 13 (A): 'When thou at the random grim forge, ⁚ powerful amidst ⁚ peers,'

[The large colon, ⁚ , indicates that the syllable on each side of it is
stressed; cf. l. 7.]

l. 14 (A and B): 'drayhorse'

Line 7: *sweet reprieve*, &c. Holy Communion preceded by confession and
absolution (Cath.)—l. 8: *all road ever* (dial.), in whatever way [he] may
have.—l. 13: *random* (archit.), built with stones of irregular size and shape.
—l. 14: *fettle*, prepare, make ready. See above, 'Preface to Notes', p. 237.

54. Brothers. '(Sprung rhythm; three feet to the line; lines free-ended and
not overrove; and reversed or counterpointed rhythm allowed in the first
foot.) Hampstead, Aug. 1880.' Five various drafts exist. A₁ and A₂ both of
Aug. 1880. B was copied by me from A₁, and author's emendations of it
overlook those in A₂. Text therefore is from A₂ except that the first seven
lines, being rewritten in margin [of B] afresh (and confirmed in letter of
Apr. 1881 to Canon Dixon), as also corrections in ll. 15–18, these are taken.
But the B corrections of ll. 22, 23, almost certainly imply forgetfulness of
A₂. In last line B has correction *Dearly thou canst be kind;* but the intention of
I'll cry was original, and has four MSS. in its favour.—[R. B.] 'Thou
dearly canst be kind.' was the earliest reading of the last line in H. We restore *Dearly* and other presumably later corrections in B (see ll. 10, 21–23,
33–34). Cf. the repetition at the end of 'Binsey Poplars' (No. 43). The fifth
version was sent to Dixon, Jan. 1881—L. II, pp. 42, 49, 174. The rewritten
early lines are only partially confirmed in L. II, p. 49, despite R. B.'s parenthesis above.—[N. H. M.]

In Aug. 1879, G. M. H. wrote: 'I find within my professional experience now a good deal of matter to write on. I hope to enclose a little scene that touched me at Mount St. Mary's' [College, Chesterfield]. (L. I, p. 86.)

55. Spring and Fall. '(Sprung rhythm.) Lydiate, Lancashire, Sept. 7, 1880.' A. Text and title from B, which corrects four lines, and misdates 1881. There is also a copy in D, Jan. 1881, and see again Apr. 6, 1881. In l. 2 the last word is *unleafing* in most of the MSS. An attempt to amend the second rhyme was unsuccessful.—[R. B.] For this entirely unnecessary 'attempt' see L. I, p. 119. D version is in L. II, p. 174.

Line 2: *unleaving*, a clear correction in A, copied by R. B. in B.—l. 8: *worlds of wanwood leafmeal lie*, for rejected: 'Though forests low and leafmeal lie'; *wanwood* seems to be a noun, governed by 'of' (the meaning of *wan-*, 'bloodless', being combined with the older meaning 'dark', 'gloomy'—O.E. *wann*). *Leafmeal* I take for an adverb, made by substitution' from *piecemeal* on the analogy of Shakespeare's *inch-meal* and *limb-meal*: hence it suggests the leaves falling one by one, then rotting to form pale, mealy fragments.—l. 9: *will*, we have restored the italics indicated in the autograph (A) by underlining, for which R. B. substituted a stress mark.—[N. H. M.].—l. 11: *are the same*, i.e. are *all* the same, all sorrows have one main source (ll. 14–15).—l. 13: *ghost*, spirit (of the living), with a proleptic suggestion of 'phantom'—the living spirit foreknowing, through sensory experience, its own state after death. Lines 8 and 14 connect the Fall of the Leaf with the Fall of Man: 'and unto dust shalt thou return' (Genesis iii. 18).

56. Inversnaid. 'Sept. 28, 1881'. Autograph in H. I have found no other trace of this poem.—[R. B.] But see L. I, pp. 73–4. [W. H. G.]

Line 3: *coop*, a hollow or enclosed place; *comb*, crest; or water pouring, 'combing', over and through obstacles (see G. M. H.'s sketch 'At the Baths of Rosenlaui' in *J.*, plate 28, and cf. ibid. p. 67: 'Brush and comb (how vastly absurd it is!) both apply to . . . of water ribs.'—l. 6: *twindles*, seems to be a portmanteau coinage inscaping 'twists', 'twitches', and 'dwindles'; cf. *J.*, p. 223: 'the foam dwindling and twitched into long chains of suds . . .'; but possibly verbal use of obs. 'twindle' (twin) is intended, to suggest the splitting of a whirlpool into two.—l. 9: *degged* (Lancs. dial.), sprinkled. —l. 11: *heathpacks*, heather; *flitches*, ragged, russet flakes, tufts or clumps (cf. *Study*, I, p. 117).

57. 'As kingfishers'. Text from undated autograph in H, a draft with corrections and variants. In ll. 3 and 4 *hung* and *to fling out broad* are corrections in same later pencilling as l. 5, which occurs only thus with them. In sestet the first three lines have alternatives of regular rhythm, thus:

'Then I say more: the just man justices;
Keeps grace and that keeps all his goings graces;
In God's eye acts &c.'

Of these lines, in 9 and 10 the version given in text is later than the regular lines just quoted, and probably preferred: in l. 11 the alternatives apparently of same date.—[R. B.] On the stresses previously printed see above, *Foreword*, p. xl. In 1.7 MS reads 'goes its self'.

In this 'Scotist' sonnet G. M. H. deals with the ontological significance of natural, individual, and characteristic activity.

Line 3: *tucked*, (obs.) plucked.—l. 7: *Selves*, a verb meaning 'fulfils its own individuality'.—l. 9: *justices* (vb.), 'acts in a godly manner, lives fully energized by grace, justness, sanctity'. (R. V. Schoder, S.J., in *I.D.*, p. 210.)

—l. 11: '*⁚* Acts in God's eye what in God's eye he is—' (MS.)—l. 12: *for Christ plays*, &c., cf. *S.*, p. 154: '. . . Christ in his member on the one side, his member in Christ on the other. It is as if a man said: That is Christ playing at me and me playing at Christ, only it is no play but truth; That is Christ *being me* and me being Christ.' With the theme of this sonnet cf. *S.*, p. 195: 'All things . . . are charged with God . . . give off sparks and take fire, yield drops and flow, ring and tell of him.' As I have said in *Study*, I, p. 27: 'God the Son assumes *all* Nature; hence the individual, intrinsic degree of Christ sums up the degrees of all men. The whole sonnet is a poetic statement of the Scotist concept that individual substances, according to the metaphysical richness of their being, make up one vast hierarchy with God as their summit.'

On the same sheet and immediately above the draft of No. 57 the poet wrote the following apparently unrelated fragment:

{ The dark-out Lucifer detesting this
{ Dark-out-for-ever Lucifer hates this,
{ Entrellises the touch-tree in live green twines
{ Self-trellises the touch-tree in live green twines
And loops the fruity boughs with beauty-bines

58. Ribblesdale. 'Stonyhurst, 1882'. Autograph in A. Text from later autograph in B, which adds 'companion to No. 10' (= 34). There is a third autograph in D, June 1883, with different punctuation which gives the comma between *to* and *with* in l. 3. The dash after *man* is from A and D, both of which quote 'Nam expectatio creaturae', &c., from Romans viii. 19–20: 'For the earnest expectation of the creation waiteth for the revealing of the

281

sons of God. For the creation was subjected to vanity, not of its own will, but by reason of him who subjected it.' (R. V.)

Line 1: *throng*, 'I mean "throng" for an adjective as we use it here in Lancashire' (L. II, p. 109); the sense is 'dense', 'thick'.—l. 2: *louchèd*, 'a coinage of mine and is to mean much the same as *slouched, slouching*' (ibid.). As R. B. noted, the word is found in the *Eng. Dialect Dict.*—ll. 6–7: *deal . . . down*. I take *down* to be an adverb, modifying *deal*—a fusion of 'deal out' and 'lay down'; cf. G. M. H.'s note on No. 35: 'paying or dealing out and down . . .'; *reel*, (vb.) roll briskly, with lively dance and stagger of wavelets.—l. 10: *heir*, cf. Romans viii. 17.—l. 11: *selfbent*, self-interest, obstinate individualism.—l. 12: *reave*, taken with 'bare' = strip, despoil. —ll. 13–14: Cf. Byron, *Don Juan*, VI, vi, ll. 5–8:

> 'God is love, they say,
> And Love's a god, or was before the brow
> Of earth was wrinkled by the sins and tears
> Of—but Chronology best knows the years.'

59. The Leaden Echo and the Golden Echo. 'Stonyhurst, Oct. 13, 1882'. Autograph in A. Copy of this with autograph corrections dated Hampstead 1881 [*sic*] in B.—Text takes all B's corrections, but respects punctuation of A, except that I have added the comma after *God* in l. 19 of 'The Golden Echo'. For the drama of Winefred, see among posthumous fragments, No. 152. In Nov. 1882 he wrote to me: 'I am somewhat dismayed about that piece and have laid it aside for a while. I cannot satisfy myself about the first line. You must know that words like *charm* and *enchantment* will not do: the thought is of beauty as of something that can be physically kept and lost and by physical things only, like keys; then the things must come from the *mundus muliebris*; and thirdly they must not be markedly oldfashioned. You will see that this limits the choice of words very much indeed. However I shall make some changes. *Back* is not pretty, but it gives that feeling of physical constraint which I want.' (L. I, p. 161.) And in Oct. 1886 to R. W. D., 'I never did anything more musical.' (L. II, p. 149.)—[R. B.] Also L. I, p. 106: ' . . . it is dramatic and meant to be popular'.

Under text in A is a note by G. M. H.: 'I have marked the stronger stresses, but with the degree of stress so perpetually varying no marking is satisfactory. Do you think all had best be left to the reader?'

'The Leaden Echo.' l. 1: *keep . . . lace*, thus in MS.—l. 4: *Dówn*, follows *frówning* in previous line.—l. 9: *Be beginning*; with the suggestion of a bell-like echo here and in last four lines cf. the repetition of *yonder* in 'The Golden Echo'.

'The Golden Echo.' l. 1: *Spare!* = Forbear!—l. 2: (*Hush there!*), someone is weeping.—l. 5: *Tall*, combines the sense 'high' with the older sense 'comely', 'handsome'.—l. 10: *wimpled-*, see note No. 49, l. 2.—l. 11: *fleece of beauty*. G. M. H.'s gloss on 'fleecèd bloom' in No. 152 (p. 190) would seem to apply here too: 'I mean the velvetiness of roseleaves, flesh, and other things, *duvet*' (L. I, p. 215).—l. 13: *own best being*, the resurrected body will reassume its most comely form.—l. 14: *maidengear*, one word in B, hyphenated in A, probably because the poet reached the edge of his paper with 'maiden'.—[N. H. M.]—l. 17: "*soaring sighs*", thus in A, from which we restore the comma after it.—l. 20: *every hair*, &c. Cf. Matt. x. 30.—ll. 22–3: *Nay, what we had*, &c. Explained by G. M. H.: 'Nay more: the seed that we so carelessly and freely flung into the dull furrow, and then forgot it, will have come to ear meantime' etc. (L. I, p. 159).—l. 26: *fashed*, (Scot.) troubled, vexed, *cogged*, deceived, cheated.

60. The Blessed Virgin compared to the Air we Breathe. Original title: **Mary Mother of Divine Grace Compared to the Air we Breathe.** 'Stonyhurst, May 1883'. Autograph in A.—Text and title from later autograph in B. Taken by Dean Beeching into 'A Book of Christmas Verse' 1895 and thence, incorrectly, by Orby Shipley in 'Carmina Mariana'. Stated in a letter to R. W. D. June 25, 1883, to have been written to 'hang up [among the] verse-compositions "in the tongues" . . . I did a piece in the same metre as *Blue in the mists all day*.' Note Chaucer's account of the physical properties of the air, 'House of Fame', ii, 256, seq.—[R. B.] Cf. also L. I, p. 179: 'We hang up polyglot poems in honour of the Blessed Virgin this month. I am on one in English in three-foot couplets. . . . It is partly a compromise with popular taste, and it is too true that the highest subjects are not those on which it is easy to reach one's highest.'

In this poem G. M. H. says that just as the atmosphere sustains the life of man and tempers the power of the sun's radiation, so the immaculate nature of Mary is the softening, humanizing medium of God's glory, justice, and grace. Through her the ineffable Godhead becomes comprehensible—sweetly attuneable to the limited human heart; through her God's glory, as 'the life of God', becomes actualized in Man.

Line 5: *-flixed*, *-furred* (*flix* = fur on breast of rabbit or beaver).—l. 40: *has let dispense*, &c., i.e. God dispenses His providence in accordance with her intercessory prayers.—l. 53: *Yet no part*, &c. 'The grace all comes from Christ, not intrinsically from Mary herself.' Cf. ll. 30–33. In criticizing the 3rd Edn. gloss, to which 'intrinsically' has now been added, Fr. R. Boyle, S.J., concedes our main point but demands a nicer theological adjustment: 'If one were speaking of the absolute source of grace, Gardner's statement is true. But . . . relative to us and dependent on Christ, the grace we receive does come from Mary herself, and it is this extraordinary and mysterious fact which Hopkins is imaging.' (*Metaphor in Hopkins*, p. 210.) —ll. 68–72; Cf. No. 57, ll. 12–14.—ll. 94–109: 'Such "bare glory" was the wrath, vengeance and destruction attributed to "god of old". It was the advent of Christ and the Holy Family that made meekness and love the prime aspirations of the religious in the Western world' (*Study*, I, p. 188). See also R. Boyle, op. cit., chap. 3.

61. Spelt from Sibyl's Leaves. '(Sonnet: sprung rhythm: a rest of one stress in the first line.)' Eight stresses to the line: called by G. M. H. 'the longest sonnet ever made'. Cf. L. I, pp. 245–6: 'Of this long sonnet above all remember what applies to all my verse, that it is, as living art should be, made for performance and that its performance is not reading with the eye but loud, leisurely, poetical (not rhetorical) recitation, with long rests, long dwells on the rhyme and other marked syllables, and so on. This sonnet shd. be almost sung: it is most carefully timed in *tempo rubato*.'—[W. H. G.] Autograph in A—another later in B, which is taken for text. Date unrecorded.—[R. B.] But as H. H. says in *N.*, p. 425, early drafts of this poem appear in the 'Dublin Note-Book' and belong to the end of 1884 or beginning of 1885; they are contemporary with first drafts of Caradoc's soliloquy (see No. 152). Hence the earliest possible date is 1885.—[W. H. G.] See above, *Foreword*, p. xlii. The stress-marks in this poem are a selection from A and B.

With the title and theme cf. the Latin hymn *Dies irae*: 'As David and the Sibyl testify . . . what terror shall affright the soul when the Judge comes . . .' Cf. also the *Aeneid*, Bk. vi, ll. 11–12, 268–72, 539–43.

Line 1: *attuneable*, susceptible (and conducive) to harmony.—l. 3: *hornlight*, cf. 'In the sunset . . . cloud holding the yellow-rose light like a lamp . . .' (*J.*, p. 201). Cf. also the *horn* sides of the old type of 'lanthorn' (lantern).— l. 4: *earlstars*, one word in MS.—[N. H. M.]—ll. 5 and 6: *astray* thus divided to show the rhyme. [R. B.]—l. 6: *throughther*, an adj., now confined to dialect. It is the speech form of *through-other*, in which shape it eludes pursuit in the Oxford Dictionary. Dr. Murray compares Ger. *durcheinander*. Mr. Craigie tells me that the classical quotation for it is from Burns's 'Halloween', st. 5, *They roar an' cry a' throughther*.—[R. B.]; *pashed*, beaten.—l. 7: *Disremembering* (Irish), forgetting; *round*, (obs.) whisper to. [W. H. G.]—l. 8: *With*, i.e. I suppose, *with your warning that*, &c.; the heart is speaking.—[R. B.]—l. 9: *beakleaved*, hyphenated in A, but virtually one word in the later auto. B, exactly like *selfwrung*, *self-strung* [l. 13].—[N. H. M.]—l. 9: *dragonish*, for G. M. H. on dragon-Devil symbolism, see *S.*, pp. 198–9 and 243; *damask*, (vb.) damascene, ornament with patterns, like those on a sword-blade.—l. 10: *oracle*. This

284

word, which reverts to the title, suggests the Cumaean Sibyl who conducted Aeneas into the underworld (*Aeneid*, vi). [W. H. G.]—l. 11: *part, pen, pack*, imperatives of the verbs, in the sense of sorting 'the sheep from the goats', [R. B.] Cf. Matt. 25. 31-33.—l. 12: A has *wrong right*, but the correction to *right wrong* in B is intentional. [R. B.]—l. 13 *ware*, i.e. be aware and beware.—l. 14: *sheathe-*in both MSS., but I can only make sense of *sheath-*, i.e. 'sheathless and shelterless'.—[R. B.] G. M. H. usually preferred the verb to the noun; hence *sheathe-* and *shelter-* can be verbal elements in the compound epithet made with *-less*, on the analogy of 'tireless'; cf. 'partless air' in No. 25, st. 5, l. 6.—*thoughts against thoughts*, &c. Cf. *S.*, p. 243: 'the worm of conscience, which is the mind gnawing and feeding on its own most miserable self' (*Meditation on Hell*), and No. 69, ll. 3-4. The stress on *against* emphasizes the painful friction and renders necessary the unusual stress on *in.*—[W. H. G.] The following is G. M. H.'s signature at this date:—[R. B.]

your affectionate friend
Gerard M. Hopkins S.J.
May 29 1885.

62. To what serves Mortal Beauty? '(Common rhythm highly stressed: sonnet.) Aug. 23, 1885.' Autograph in A.—Another autograph in B with a few variants from which A was chosen, the deletion of alternatives incomplete. Thirdly a copy sent to R. W. D., apparently later than A, but with errors of copy. The text given is guided by this version in D, and *needs* in l. 9 is substituted there for the *once* in A and B, probably because of *once* in l. 6.— Original draft exists in H, on same page with 39 and 40 (= 63 and 64 in this edition).—[R. B.] The first drafts are on the back of the draft of No. 155.

In D (L. II, p. 129) the poet writes: '(sonnet: alexandrines: the mark ⌐—⌐ over two neighbouring syllables means that, though one has and the other has not the metrical stress, in the recitation-stress they are to be about equal)'.

Examples are: l. 1, 'To what serves mortal beauty'—l. 3, 'See: it does this: keeps warm'—l. 6, 'windfalls of war's storm,'—ll. 10-11, 'love's worthiest, were all known;/ World's loveliest—men's selves.' This explains the term 'highly stressed' in A.

Line 1: *mortal beauty . . . dangerous*, cf. L. 1, p. 95 : 'I think then no one can admire beauty of the body more than I do . . . But this kind of beauty is dangerous,' et seq.—l. 2: *the O-seal-that-so feature*. The cancelled 'face feature-perfect' of H shows the intention; the compound epithet in text suggests an invitation to painter or photographer, and seems to derive from *Hamlet*, III. iv. 60–2:

> 'A combination and a form indeed,
> Where every god did seem to set his seal,
> To give the world assurance of a man.'

—l. 7: *Gregory*, i.e. Pope Gregory I, 'the Great' (*c.* 590–604), who, on seeing the blue-eyed, fair-haired slaves for sale in the Roman Forum, said *Non Angli sed angeli* ('Not Angles but angels'), and sent Augustine to Christianize Britain.—l. 11: *selves*. *Self . . .* The Scotist *haecceitas* again; see *Introduction*, p. xxi, and cf. No. 57 and note (p. 281).—l. 12: *own* (vb.), governs *gift* in l. 13.—[W. H. G.]

63. (The Soldier.) 'Clongowes, Aug. 1885.' Autograph in H, with a few corrections which I have taken for lines 6 and 7, of which the first draft runs:

> 'It fancies; it deems; dears the artist after his art;
> So feigns it finds as &c.'

The MS. marks the caesural place in ten of the lines: l. 2, after *Both*; l. 3, at the full stop; l. 11, after *man*.—l. 6, *fancies*, *feigns*, *deems*, take three stresses. —[R. B.] In l. 6, which was written beneath the poem in H and followed by a question mark, there are actually seven stresses.—[W. H. G.] In l. 7 I have added a comma at *smart*. In l. 10 I have substituted *handle* for *reave* of MS.; see note on *reave*, p. 254; and in l. 13, have hyphened *God made flesh*. No title in MS.—[R. B.] For obvious nautical reasons, and with ample support from critics, the ed. of 3rd Edn. restored *reeve* (thus corrected in spelling) to l. 10. (See *Concise Oxford Dictionary*.)

Line 6: *dears the artist after his art*, i.e. holds the artist dear for the sake of his art.—l. 8: In MS.:

> 'And scarlet wear the spirit of war there express.'

—l. 9: *Mark Christ our King*, &c. The sestet was 'inspired by the Ignatian analogy between a great temporal king and the spiritual King, Christ'. (*Study*, I, p. 18.) Cf. *The Spiritual Exercises*, Second Week: 'My will is to conquer the whole land of the infidels: therefore whoever shall wish to come with me must be content to eat as I do, and so to drink and dress, etc., as I do. In like manner he must labour as I do by day, and watch at night, etc., so that in like manner afterwards he may share with me in the victory . . .' So Christ says to every man: 'My will is to conquer the whole

world and all mine enemies, and so to enter into the glory of my Father
...' Cf. 2 Timothy ii. 3: 'Thou therefore endure hardships, as a good
soldier of Jesus Christ.'

64. (Carrion Comfort.) Autograph in H, in three versions: 1st, deleted
draft; 2nd, a complete version, both on same page with 62 and 63; 3rd, with
65 on another sheet, final (?) revision carried only to end of l. 12 (two
detached lines on reverse). Text is this last with last two lines from the 2nd
version. Date must be 1885, and this is probably the sonnet 'written in
blood', of which he wrote in May of that year.—I have added the title and
the hyphen in *heaven-handling.*—[R. B.] I now demur at the opinion that
this was the sonnet 'written in blood' (L. I, p. 219); as l. 9 shows, this poem
is not 'terrible' as Nos. 65 and 67 are. [W. H. G.]

Rhythm: sprung and outriding; six stresses to the line. These outrides, &c.,
elucidate the rhythm: l. 1, 'comfort'; l. 5, 'terrible'; l. 8, 'tempest, me
heaped there; me frantic ...'; l. 11, 'Hand rather, my heart, lo! ... stole
joy,'; l. 12, 'héaven-handling'; l. 13, 'mé that fóught him? O whích one?
is it each one?'; l. 14, 'I wretch'. In l. 10 I would scan: 'Nay in áll ...'

Line 5: *rude*, used with adv. force: 'in an uncouth, violent manner'.—l. 6:
rock (vb.), 'wouldst rock' governs 'foot'. Early draft has: 'Yet why, thou
terrible, wouldst thou rock rude on me/ Thy wring-earth tread ...'

65. 'No worst'. Autograph in H, on same page as third draft of 64. One
undated draft with corrections embodied in the text here.—l. 5, at end are
some marks which look like a hyphen and a comma: no title.—[R. B.] The
'comma' is in fact a stress-mark upon *sing* in the line below.—[N. H. M.]

Rhythm: five stresses to the line; standard, but freely sprung in parts.
Line 6 is marked thus:

'Woe, wórld-sorrow; on an áge-old ánvil wínce and síng—'.

Line 8 has 'fell'.

This sonnet is the first to sound the uttermost depths of what St. Ignatius
calls 'desolation'; this is 'a darkening of the soul, trouble of mind, movement
to base and earthly things, restlessness of various agitations and temptations,
moving to distrust, loss of hope, loss of love; when the soul feels herself
thoroughly apathetic, sad, and as it were separated from her Creator and
Lord' (*Spiritual Exercises*, First Week, 'Discernment of Spirits'). Cf. sonnets
Nos. 66–69 and 74–76. For the Shakespearian 'underthought' of Nos. 65,
67, and 69 see *Study*, I, p. 175 et seq.

Line 3: *Comforter*, the Paraclete (Holy Spirit)—l. 4: *your relief*. For G. M. H.

on 'the Blessed Virgin's protection' see L. III, pp. 147–8.—l. 5: *herds-long*, i.e. troubles 'come not single spies, but in battalions'.—The hyphen after *chief* in MS. is here restored.—[N. M. H.]—l. 6: *world-sorrow*, cf. Ger. *Weltschmerz* and also No. 28, st. 27, ll. 2–4 and Synopsis.—l. 8: *force*, perforce; cf. Shakespeare's 'force perforce', 'of force'.—l. 10: *Frightful*, &c. First draft in H has: 'Frightful, sheer down, not fathomed.'

Note on Nos. 66, 67, 68, 69. These four sonnets (together with No. 149) are all written undated in a small hand on the two sides of a half-sheet of common sermon-paper, in the order in which they are here printed. They probably date back as early as 1885, and may be all, or some of them, those referred to in a letter of Sept. 1, 1885: 'I shall shortly have some sonnets to send you, five or more. Four of these came like inspirations unbidden and against my will. And in the life I lead now, which is one of a continually jaded and harassed mind, if in any leisure I try to do anything I make no way—nor with my work, alas! but so it must be.' I have no certain nor single identification of date.—[R. B.] In spite of the above evidence for the date 1885 (see L. I, pp. 219 and 221, and the note to No. 64), R. B. placed these poems, in the 1st Edn., *after* the two poems of Sept. 1887 (Nos. 70 and 71). His reason for doing so is explained in a note by him recorded in *J.*, p. xiii: the small handwriting of the 'doubtfully dated sonnet MS.' resembles that of some Retreat notes of 1889. In the 3rd Edn. R. B.'s placing was kept; but in the present edn. these poems are given what is, in all probability, their correct chronological position. It is true that the first draft of 'Tom's Garland' (No. 70) appears on the same sheet as the only (auto.) draft of 'No worst' (No. 65); but it is almost certain that the five H sonnets (65–69) are earlier than the completed 'Tom's Garland' and 'Harry Ploughman'. See above *Foreword*, p. xlvii.

66. 'To seem the stranger'. H, with corrections which my text embodies. No title.—[R. B.]

Line 3: *in Christ not near*, i.e. they were not Roman Catholics; his parents had been 'shocked' by his conversion. See L. III, pp. 29 and 91.—l. 4: *my peace / my parting*. So in MS. The faint oblique stroke indicates a slight pause to 'fetch out' the painful paradox of *peace* and *parting*. Cf. Matt. x. 34–8.—l. 5: *whose honour*, cf. No. 156.—l. 8: *wars are rife*, i.e. the Irish struggle for political freedom. Though opposed to Gladstone's policy, G. M. H. was sympathetic towards Irish grievances.—l. 9: MS. has: 'now I am at a third'—l. 11: *Only what word*, &c. Cf. L. III, p. 170: ' . . . the grief of mind I go through over politics, over what I read and hear and see in Ireland about Ireland and about England, is such that I can neither express it nor bear to speak of it'. (March 2, 1885.)—[W. H. G.]—l. 14:

288

began. I have no other explanation than to suppose an omitted relative pronoun. like *Hero savest* in No. 41. The sentence would then stand for 'leaves me a lonely (one who only) began'.—[R. B.] My suggestion (*Study*, I, p. 141) that 'began' is a noun-equivalent, on the analogy of the qualified preterite in the 'turf' expression, 'an also-ran', was supported on other grounds by W. A. M. Peters, S.J.: '*Began* is a noun . . . the poet calls himself a "began", not a beginner.' (*Peters*, p. 131.)

67. 'I wake and feel'. H, with corrections, which text embodies: no title. —[R. B.]

Line 2: *hours,* thus in MS. (= dissyllable).—l. 4: *And more must,* &c., a typically bold ellipsis: 'more [sights] must [see, more (such) ways must go . . .]'. For other examples see No. 69, l. 7 and Peters, pp. 91–93.— ll. 9–14: cf. G. M. H.'s Ignatian *Meditation on Hell* (*S.*, p. 243): '*they,* their sins are the bitterness, tasted sweet once, now taste most bitter; no worm but themselves gnaws them . . .'.—l. 9: *most deep decree.* This was the earliest draft; in transcribing it the poet substituted *most just decree,* only to change back to the original word.—[N. H. M.] Peters says: 'But he could not understand how it was *just;* its justice was beyond his grasp, and so he wrote "God's most *deep* decree".' (op. cit., p. 51). Cf. No. 66 l. 12 and No. 74.—l. 12: *Selfyeast, &c. . . . sours.* Ambiguous: is 'Self-yeast' or 'dough' the subj. of *sours*? First draft variants suggest the former:

> 'Flesh fills, blood feeds / this curse
> Of my self stuff, by self yeast soured. I see
> The lost are like this, with their loss / to be
> Their sweating selves, as I am mine, but worse.'

> 'this curse—
> Self stuff, and by selfyeast so soured
> by yeasty self so soured'

'Selfyeast of spirit my selfstuff sours.'

—l. 14: *but worse.* The lost souls in Hell are in a worse plight; though at times (as the 'afterthought' syntax suggests) G. M. H. could hardly believe it.

68. Patience. MS. as for No. 67. No title.

Line 2: *Patience is.* The initial capital is mine, and the comma after *ivy* in line 6.—[R. B.]—l. 8: *eyes,* the ivy-berries.—l. 10: *dearer,* used in the Shakespearian sense—'more seriously'.—ll. 12–14: Peters (pp. 84–5) points out the transitional nuance—'patient' (suffering) and 'Patience' (sympathizing).—l. 14: *combs,* honeycombs. Cf. No. 51, ll. 7–9.

69. 'My own heart'. MS. as for No. 67. No title.

Line 6: I have added the comma after *comfortless*; that word has the same grammatical value as *dark* in the following line. 'I cast for comfort, (which) I can no more find in my comfortless (world) than a blind man in his dark world. . . .' [R. B.]—l. 9: *Jackself*, i.e. G. M. H.'s everyday, hard-working self. [W. H. G.]—l. 10: MS. accents *let*. [R. B.]—l. 11: *let joy size*, &c. I quote *Study*, I, pp. 116, n. 3: 'The meaning is: (*a*) "Be a little more casual, relax for health's sake"; and (*b*) "Be reconciled to having your pleasure whenever and however God wills it".' [W. H. G.]—ll. 13 and 14: the text here from a good correction separately written (as far as *mountains*) on the top margin of No. 149. There are therefore two writings of *betweenpie*, a strange word, in which *pie* apparently makes a compound verb with *between*, meaning, 'as the sky seen between dark mountains is brightly dappled', the grammar such as *intervariegates* would make. This word might have delighted William Barnes, if the verb 'to pie' existed. It seems not to exist, and to be forbidden by homophonic absurdities. [R. B.]— But for G. M. H. the verb 'to pie' *did* exist—as a 'back-formation' from 'magpie' or 'pied': in *J.*, p. 232, he speaks of 'white pieings' on the 'dull thunder-colour' of pigeons (cf. No. 45, l. 12).

70. Tom's Garland. 'Sonnet: common rhythm, but with hurried feet: two codas. Dromore, September, 1887.' With full title, A.—Another autograph in B is identical. In l. 9 there is a strong accent on *I*.—l. 10, the capital initial of *country* is doubtful.—Rhythmical marks omitted.—[R. B.] G. M. H.'s model for this sonnet with two codas was Milton's satirical 'caudated' sonnet, 'On the New Forcers of Conscience'. Cf. L. I, p. 266: 'I wanted the coda for a sonnet in some sort "nello stilo satirico o bernesco". It has a kind of rollic at all events. The coda is an immense resource to have.' In A the poet notes: 'Heavy stresses marked double, thus // and stresses of sense, independent of the natural stress of the verse, thus \\.' The 'hurried feet' and some of the stress-marks in A are:

l. 3: 'By him and rips . . .'

l. 5: 'Low be it: lustily he his low lot (feel'

l. 7: 'Seldomer heartsore;'

l. 9: 'Little I reck ho!'

l. 10: 'Country is honour enough in all us—'

l. 15: 'Undenizened, beyond bound'
[W. H. G.]

The author's own explanation of this poem may be read in a letter written to me from 'Dublin, Feb. 10, 1888: . . . I laughed outright and often, but very sardonically, to think you and the Canon could not construe my last sonnet; that he had to write to you for a crib. It is plain I must go no farther on this road: if you and he cannot understand me who will? Yet, declaimed, the strange constructions would be dramatic and effective. Must I interpret it? It means then that, as St. Paul and Plato and Hobbes and everybody says, the commonwealth or well ordered human society is like one man; a body with many members and each its function; some higher, some lower, but all honourable, from the honour which belongs to the whole. The head is the sovereign, who has no superior but God and from heaven receives his or her authority: we must then imagine this head as bare (see St. Paul much on this) and covered, so to say, only with the sun and stars, of which the crown is a symbol, which is an ornament but not a covering; it has an enormous hat or skull cap, the vault of heaven. The foot is the day-labourer, and this is armed with hobnail boots, because it has to wear and be worn by the ground; which again is symbolical; for it is navvies or day-labourers who, on the great scale or in gangs and millions, mainly trench, tunnel, blast, and in other ways disfigure, "mammock" the earth and, on a small scale, singly, and superficially stamp it with their footprints. And the "garlands" of nails they wear are therefore the visible badge of the place they fill, the lowest in the commonwealth. But this place still shares the common honour, and if it wants one advantage, glory or public fame, makes up for it by another, ease of mind, absence of care; and these things are symbolised by the gold and iron garlands. (O, once explained, how clear it all is!) Therefore the scene of the poem is laid at evening, when they are giving over work and one after another pile their picks, with which they earn their living, and swing off home, knocking sparks out of mother earth not now by labour and of choice but by the mere footing, being strongshod and making no hardship of hardness, taking all easy. And so to supper and bed. Here comes a violent but effective hyperbaton or suspension, in which the action of the mind mimics that of the labourer—surveys his lot, low but free from care; then by a sudden strong act throws it over the shoulder or tosses it away as a light matter. The witnessing of which lightheartedness makes me indignant with the fools of Radical Levellers. But presently I remember that this is all very well for those who are in, however low in, the Commonwealth and share in any way the Common weal; but that the curse of our times is that many do not share it, that they are outcasts from it and have neither security nor splendour; that they share care with the high and obscurity with the low, but wealth or comfort with neither. And this state of things, I say, is the origin of Loafers, Tramps, Cornerboys, Roughs,

Socialists and other pests of society. And I think that it is a very pregnant sonnet and in point of execution very highly wrought. Too much so, I am afraid. . . . G. M. H.' (L. I, pp. 272-4.)—[R. B.]

Line 2: *fallowbootfellow*, i.e. Tom's fellow navvy, now stamping off duty with him with his similar reddish-yellow, clay-caked heavy boots. (Cf. 'fallow' = idle, resting.) *Note*: As No. 71 was completed before No. 70 (see L. I, pp. 262-6, quoted above and below), their order might well be reversed.

71. Harry Ploughman. 'Dromore, Sept. 1887'. Autograph in A.—Autograph in B has several emendations written over without deletion of original. Text is B with these corrections, which are all good.—[R. B.] The indentation of the shorter 'burden lines' is now a compromise between the inconsistent readings of the two autographs (and nearer to B), to indicate more clearly the number of stresses in each line.

Line 3: *knee-nave*, variant is 'knee-bank', i.e. -boss, -knob = knee-cap.— l. 6: *barrowy brawn, his*, variant is 'barrowy-brawnèd'.—l. 7: *curded*, 'formed lumps', bunched, became knotted. [W. H. G.]—l. 10: *features* is the verb.—[R. B.]—l. 13: *'S is his*. We restore the stop at *plough*, where R. B. had put a colon 'for the convenience of the reader'.—l. 14: *-bridle* suggests 'twist' and 'rise'; variant is 'windloft or windlaced'. [W. H. G.]—l. 15: the tmesis = *his lily-locks windlaced*. Cf. 'Saxo cerecomminuit -brum' of Ennius. [R. B.]—l. 16: *churlsgrace*, from 'churl' (arch.) peasant. [W. H. G.]—l. 17: *frowning*, i.e. the 'frowning wrinkles' in Harry's boots.—l. 18: *cold furls*, earlier variant 'flame-furls'.—l. 19: other earlier variants are:

'With-a-wét-sheen-shot furls.'
'With-a-wét-fire-flushed furls.'

—[W. H. G.]—ll. 17-19: In the last three lines the grammar intends: 'How his churl's grace governs the movement of his booted (in bluff hide) feet, as they are matched in a race with the wet shining furrow overturned by the share'. G. M. H. thought well of this sonnet and wrote on Sept. 28, 1887: 'I have been touching up some old sonnets you have never seen and have within a few days done the whole of one, I hope, very good one and most of another; the one finished is a direct picture of a ploughman, without afterthought. But when you read it let me know if there is anything like it in Walt Whitman, as perhaps there may be, and I should be sorry for that.' And again on Oct. 11, 1887: 'I will enclose the sonnet on Harry Ploughman, in which burden-lines (they might be recited by a chorus) are freely used: there is in this very heavily loaded sprung rhythm a call for their employment. The rhythm of this sonnet, which is altogether for recital, not for perusal (as by nature verse should be), is very highly studied. From much considering it I can no longer gather any impression of it: perhaps it will strike you as intolerably violent and artificial.' And again on Nov. 6, 1887: 'I want Harry Ploughman to be a vivid figure before the mind's eye; if he is not that the sonnet fails. The difficulties are of syntax no doubt. Dividing a compound word by a clause sandwiched into it was a desperate deed, I feel, and I do not feel that it was an unquestionable success.'—[R. B.] (The 'compound' is, presumably, 'windlaced' in l. 15, and the meaning: 'see his locks, which are fair as lilies, laced, plaited, by the wind'.)

The A version is reproduced in facsimile in L. I, p. 262. The 'highly studied' rhythm is brought out by seven reading-marks analogous to musical notation, including the hurried feet and outrides seen in earlier poems: there are (1) ╱ = 'metrical stress'; (2) ∧ = 'strong stress; which does not differ much from (3) ⌒ = pause or dwell on a syllable, which need not, however, have the metrical stress'; (4) ~ = 'quiver or circumflexion, making one syllable nearly two ...'; and (5) ⌢ = 'slur', tying two syllables into the time of one; (6) ⌢ 'over three or more syllables gives them the time of one half foot'; (7) ‿ = 'the outride; under one or more syllables makes them extrametrical: a slight pause follows as if the voice were silently making its way back to the highroad of the verse'. The following lines illustrate their use:

Line 1: 'Hard as hurdle arms, with a broth of goldish flue'

l. 4: 'Head and foot, shoulder and shank—' (B has 'shoulder')

l. 6: 'Stand at stress ...'

l. 8: 'Soared or sank—' (B has 'or')

ll. 9–10: 'Though as a beechbole firm, finds his, as at a rollcall, rank

And features in flesh what deed he each must do—'

l. 12: 'He leans to it, Harry bends, look ..... waist

In him, all quail to the wallowing o' the plough ...'

l. 16: 'Churlsgrace, too, child of Amansstrength ...'

l. 17: 'Them—broad in bluff hide ...'

72. Heraclitean Fire. '(Sprung rhythm, with many outrides and hurried feet: sonnet with two [sic] codas.) July 26, 1888. Co. Dublin. The last sonnet [this] provisional only.' Autograph in A.—I have found no other copy or trace of draft. The title is from A.—[R. B.]

The stresses, ties, and outrides marked in the MS. are as follows:

Line 1, 'púffball . . . pillows'; l. 2, 'thoroughfare . . . roysterers . . . gay-gangs . . . marches'; l. 3, 'roughcast . . . whitewash'; l. 4, 'Shivelights . . . ín long ⌐ lashes'; l. 5, 'boisterous'; l. 6, 'creases'; l. 7, 'crúst . . . stánches, stárches'; l. 9, 'Fóotfretted in it. Million-fuelèd . . . bonfire'; 'dearest ⌐ to her, her'; l. 11, 'Mán, how fást his fíredint'; l. 12, 'Bóth are in an ⁿ unfáthomable, áll is in an enórmous dárk'; l. 15, 'Is ány of him at áll so stárk'; l. 17, 'A héart's-clarion. Awáy grief's gásping'; l. 20, 'Fáll to the resíduary worm'; l. 23, 'Thís Jack, jóke, poor pótsherd'.

Title: according to Heraclitus (c. 535–c. 475 B.C.) all things are in a state of flux, being differentiations produced by strife (πόλεμος) of a single mobile principle—fire.—l. 1: *chevy*, scamper, chase.—l. 4: *Shivelights*, strips of light (cf. *Tit. And.*, II. i. 87). [W. H. G.]—l. 6: construction obscure: *rutpeel* may be a compound word, MS. uncertain. [R. B.] Comparing *yestertempest's, shadowtackle, footfretted* and *matchwood*, we are compelled to take *rutpeel* as a compound also.—[N. H. M.]—ll. 5–9: mean that the wet mud, squeezed into road-ruts and footprints, is dried, pummelled, and dust-blown by the boisterous wind, so that the marks of man are obliterated. [W. H. G.]—l. 8: ? omitted relative pronoun. If so = 'the manmarks that treadmire toil foot-fretted in it'. MS. does not hyphen or quite joint up *foot* with *fretted.*—l. 12: MS. has no caesural mark.—[R. B.] —l. 14: *disseveral*, another deft coinage (= separate and aloof).—l. 18: *foundering deck*, cf. the symbolism of the 'Deutschland', No. 28, st. 29.— l. 23: *Jack*, a common fellow; *patch*, a paltry fellow, fool; also a detached piece, makeshift fragment—cf. *potsherd* and Job. ii. 8. The conclusion in text is the poet's correction of '. . . patch, matchwood, is immortal diamond,/Diamond.' [W. H. G.]—On Aug. 18, 1888, G. M. H. wrote: 'I will now go to bed, the more so as I am going to preach tomorrow and put plainly to a Highland congregation of MacDonalds, MacIntoshes, MacKillops, and the rest what I am putting not at all so plainly to the rest of the world, or rather to you and Canon Dixon, in a sonnet in sprung rhythm with two codas.' And again on Sept. 25, 1888: 'Lately I sent you a sonnet, on the Heraclitean Fire, in which a great deal of early Greek philosophical thought was distilled; but the liquor of the distillation did not taste very Greek, did it? The effect of studying masterpieces is to make me admire and do otherwise. So it must be on every original artist to some degree, on me to a marked degree. Perhaps then more reading would only *refine my singularity*, which is not what you want.' Note that the sonnet has three codas, not two.—[R. B.] The 'early Greek philosophical thought ... distilled' here, besides that of Heraclitus, seems to be that of (i) the hylozoists who postulated a basic substance: Thales (water), Anaximenes (air); (ii) of Empedocles (who for a *single* principal substituted earth, water, air, and fire); together with (iii) that of Parmenides, whose 'great text ... is that Being is and Not-being is not—' (See *J*, pp. 127–30). For an exegesis of this poem see *Study*, I, pp. 161–4.

73. St. Alphonsus Rodriguez. Text from autograph with title and 'upon the first falling of his feast after his canonisation' in B. An autograph in A. sent Oct. 3 [1888] from Dublin asking for immediate criticism, because the sonnet had to go to Majorca: 'I ask your opinion of a sonnet written to order on the occasion of the first feast since his canonisation proper of St. Alphonsus Rodriguez, a laybrother of our Order, who for 40 years acted as hall-porter to the College of Palma in Majorca: he was, it is believed, much favoured by God with heavenly lights and much persecuted by evil spirits. The sonnet (I say it snorting) aims at being intelligible.' And on Oct. 19, 1888, 'I am obliged for your criticisms, "contents of which noted", indeed acted on. I have improved the sestet. . . . [He defends 'hew'] ... at any rate whatever is markedly featured in stone or what is like stone is most naturally said to be hewn, and to *shape*, itself, means in old English to hew and the Hebrew *bara* / to create, even, properly means to hew. But life and living things are not naturally said to be hewn: they grow, and their growth is by trickling increment. . . . The [first] line now stands "Glory is a flame off exploit, so we say".'—[R. B.]

The rhythm is 'standard', with 'heavy stressing' (as in l. 2, which I would scan: 'gashed flesh', 'galled shield') and frequent Miltonic elision ('by of world', 'Majorca Alfonso'—ll. 13–14). For the thought, cf. the sestet of *The Windhover* (No. 36).

74. 'Thou art indeed just'. Quotation from Jer. xii. 1 for epigraph ('Lord, I know well that right is on thy side, if I plead against thee, yet remonstrate with thee I must; why is it that the affairs of the wicked prosper; ...' —Knox.) 'March 17, 1889'. Autograph in A.—Similar autograph in B, which reads l. 9, *Sir, life on thy great cause.* Text from A, which seems the later, being written in the peculiar faint ink of the corrections in B, and embodying them.—Early drafts in H.—[R. B.] In a letter to R. B. [March 24, 1889] G. M. H. says: 'Observe, it must be read *adagio molto* and with great stress.' Counterpoint rhythm occurs in l. 3, 'Why do sinners', and l. 4,

'Disappointment', l. 11, *fretty chervil*, cow-parsley (*Anthriscus sylvestris* or *Chaerophylum sylvestre*), which has richly serrated, lacy leaves.—l. 13: *eunuch*. See Matt. xix. 12, and L. I, p. 270: 'Nothing comes: I am a eunuch—but it is for the kingdom of heaven's sake'.

75. 'The shepherd's brow'. In H. Various consecutive full drafts on the same sheet as No. [76], and date April 3, 1889. The text is what seems to be the latest draft: it has no corrections. Thus its date is between [74] and [76]. It might be argued that this sonnet has the same right to be recognized as a finished poem with the sonnets [66–69], but those had several years' recognition whereas this must have been thrown off one day in a cynical mood, which he could not have wished permanently to intrude among his last serious poems.—[R. B.] This sonnet is the last of five full drafts, so it is obvious that G. M. H. took it seriously. The fourth part of *Gulliver* is not placed among Swift's fragments, and this poem is important as expressing a mood the obverse of which is the highest Christian idealism. Yet R. B. was surely acting with discretion when he refused this poem a place in the 1st Edn. between (the present) Nos. 74 and 76: there, and in the year 1918, it would have struck a jarring note and would have been widely misunderstood (cf. G. M. H. in L. I, p. 148: 'A cynical vein much indulged coarsens everything in us.') In the 3rd Edn. I followed R. B. and kept this sonnet as the last fragment of the period 1876–89; but its place here among the finished poems is justified by R. Boyle, S.J.: 'The poem is not cynical at all. It states a truth, however, that the conventional . . . Bridges was not likely to want to face. Hopkins faced it fully . . . ' (*Metaphor in Hopkins*, p. 133). Cf. *Study*, I, p. 156: 'This is not the smiling, aloof cynicism of La Rochefoucauld but the bitter self-implicated cynicism of Hamlet—the cry of the disappointed idealist.' G. M. H. is stressing man's essential limitations. Cf. Nos. 34, 35, and 58.

Line 8: *viol*, cf. Isaiah xiv. 11: 'Thy pomp is brought down to the grave, and the noise of thy viols'; and 12: 'How art thou fallen from heaven, O Lucifer . . .'.—ll. 9–11: *He! Hand to mouth*, &c. Fr. R. Boyle's comment is apt: 'Let the man's name be blazoned in brilliant neons, yet he, not ashamed of spiritual crime, locks the bathroom door when he must act as a mere animal.' (op. cit., p. 132.)—*Jack*, cf. 'every man jack' and the Shakespearian term of reproach (1 *Hen. IV*, iii, 3, l. 98).—l. 12: *And I*, &c., cf. No. 74, ll. 7–9.—ll. 13–14: The aposiopesis is obviously deliberate and seems to mark the culmination of disgust: 'And I that . . . but why mention my own earnestness? Life is a grotesque masquerade of inverted or distorted images, and my own trials and tantrums are equally unheroic.' The first draft has, as one reading:

'In spoons have seen my masque played and how tame
My tempest and my spitfire freaks how fussy.'

Cf. George Eliot: 'even Milton, looking for his portrait in a spoon, must sub-
mit to have the facial angle of a bumpkin.' (*Middlemarch*, Book I, chap. x.)

76. To R. B. April 22, 1889. Autograph in A. This, the last poem sent to
me, came on April 29.—No other copy, but the working drafts in H.—
In l. 6 the word *moulds* was substituted by me for *combs* of original, when the
sonnet was published by Miles; and I leave it, having no doubt that G. M. H.
would have made some such alteration.—[R. B.] In the 3rd Edn. I restored
the original word, which G. M. H. might have used in the double sense of
(1) unravel; put in order, as by combing, and (2) store, mature—as in a
honeycomb; cf. No. 68: 'Patience fills/ His crisp combs . . .'—[W. H. G.]
See also above, *Foreword*, pp. lii–iii.

'Hurried feet' in A, marked by 'slurs', are: l. 4, mother of; l. 7, 'widow of';
l. 10, 'rapture of'. Hence I scan: 'I wánt the óne rápture . . .'

UNFINISHED POEMS, &c.

A. Poems written 1862–68

77, 78, 79. These three pieces appeared in a letter of G. M. H. to E. H.
Coleridge dated 'Sept. 3rd 1862' and were first published in *The Times Lit.
Supplmt.*, Sept. 25, 1948. See L. III, pp. 5–14.

77. Il Mystico. In a letter to E. H. Coleridge, G. M. H. says: 'The best thing
I have done lately is *Il Mystico* in imitation of *Il Penseroso*, of which I send
you some extracts. It is not finished yet; write back whether you approve.
. . . The description at the beginning is founded on Milton's "The cherub
Contemplation".' At the end of the printed text the poet wrote 'etc., etc.'
Line 1: The asceticism shows the influence of Tennyson's 'St. Simeon
Stylites' (see L. III, p. 8).—l. 13: *heavenly*, the 3rd Edn. reading, 'pointed',
was due to dittography. [N. H. M.]—ll. 75–6: 'In *Il Mystico* I had formerly
instead of the lines resembling them which I have put in the enclosed copy,
"And when the silent heights were won, Alone in air to face the sun." Now
is that or is it not a plagiarism from Tennyson's *Eagle*, "Close to the sun in
lonely lands," (see the poem)? I am in that state that I want an unpre-
judiced decision.' (loc. cit.)—l. 141: *ecstacy*, G. M. H.'s normal spelling
of the word, and one of the nine variant forms noted in the O. E. D.

80. Fragments of 'Pilate'. From Oxford notebook C. I. Text as printed
by H. H. in *N.*, pp. 12–15, now corrected from the MS. by N. H. M.

Drafts of all the fragments now printed were made in June 1864, though, as H. H. says, 'the printed text of the last two and a half stanzas is from a fair copy made in October and therefore represents the poem in a more finished form. The order of the parts is uncertain: stanzas 2–7 run continuously and numbers are given from the MS. There is no stanza numbered 1: it is only conjectured that "The pang of Tartarus . . ." was meant to begin the poem; and it is impossible to say how much is missing' (op. cit., p. xviii). In C. II, the last incomplete stanza, as printed on p. 119, is immediately followed by a half-stanza which, for reasons given in J., p. 319 (section 49.2) was not available when H. H. prepared his text for N. and (later) for Poems, 3rd Edn. Since, however, these four lines (a) do not fit the metrical pattern required for continuity, (b) seem to begin a new stanza and a tentatively new line of thought, and (c) spoil the climax of the poem as hitherto printed, we prefer to add them here (from J., p. 49):

> 'But if this overlast the day
> Undone, and I must wait the year,
> Yet no delay can serve to grate away
> A purpose desperately dear'

—[W. H. G.]—The punctuation of the MS. has been restored. For improvements in the deciphering of the MS., see above, Foreword, pp. lviii–ix, and lxiv. The original drafts show no indenting. This has been added by H. H. and modified by us, to mark the intermingling of four-stress with five-stress lines.—[N. H. M.]

St. 2, ll. 1–4: a revised version is found in the MS. seven pages below, following st. 7. It will be seen that four of the five rhyme words have been kept, but the changes in syntax and sense would have entailed modification of the rest of the stanza, as well as st. 3:

> 'Betwixt the morsels of the snow,
> Under the mastering blue black heat,
> When the winds blow, when strong rains twist and flow
> Along my face and hands and feet.

[N. H. M.]

81. A Voice from the World. C. I and C. II, June 1864–Jan. 1865. At least five sections of the poem are missing. In N. (p. xix) H. H. says: 'There is no clue to the ultimate arrangement of the parts.' The poem Beyond the Cloister, mentioned in Jan. 1867 (L. III, p. 36), is almost certainly a later title of A Voice from the World, as Hopkins says in the same letter that part of it was written in the summer of 1864 and that he 'did send this piece first to Macmillan's which is always having things of Miss Rossetti'. Immediately

following the drafts of the last two sections comes the beginning of a scheme
of arrangement for all the sections of the poem. No. (i) is the first section
as printed; the other five are the missing sections, viz.—

(ii) *I, looking earthward, what see I?*
(iii) Alas! and many times alas!
(iv) I do not say you nothing need.
(v) You have the woman's purity.
(vi) So far when mad afflictive tears.

This scheme is deleted; new numbers (i)–(xiii) are written in the margin,
but not used. (*J.*, p. 52.)—See also No. 118 and note. See also above, *Foreword*, p. lxiv, for changes made in 4th Edn. text of this poem.

82. 'She schools the flighty pupils.' C. I, June 1864. *J.*, p. 26.

83. The Lover's Stars. C. I, July 17 (?) 1864. Described by G. M. H. as 'a
trifle in something like Coventry Patmore's style'. (L. III, p. 213.) 'The three
fragments seem to represent a confusion of two alternative plans for the
poem.'(*J.*, p. 314, n. 29.2) Our own presentation of the three main fragments
differs from that given in *J.*, pp. 29–30. The seven stanzas are now printed
in an order which seems slightly more logical and closer to the poet's intention, though certain alternatives have been omitted and there are still some
obvious anacolutha. A fourth and later fragment is a revision of st. 2 (as
now printed):

> The other leaves the West behind
> Or it may be the prodigal South,
> Passes the seas and comes to find
> Acceptance round his mistress' mouth.

As N. H. M. says: 'This last version will not fit either the syntax of the
first stanza or the poem's antithesis between the "destined lover" and the
luckless "other" man. It probably foreshadows a revision which G. M. H.
never carried out.'
St. 4, l. 1: *keeps*, later variant of 'holds'.
St. 5, l. 4: *haven*, later variant of 'roads'.

84. 'During the eastering'. From C. I, between July 19 and 22, 1864.
Printed *J.*, p. 30.
Line 1: with this use of 'easter' as vb. cf. No. 28, st. 35, l. 5.

85. '— Hill,/ Heaven.' Follows No. 84 in C. I, July 1864. *J.*, p. 31.

299

86. The Peacock's Eye. From C. I, between July 22 and 24, 1864. It is *preceded* by a shorter version:

> 'The peacock's eye
> Winks away its azure sheen
> Barter'd for a ring of green.
> The bean-shaped pupil of moist jet
> Is the silkiest violet.' (*J.*, p. 31.)

The longer version in the text is *followed* by the words:

> 'Overloaded, apparently'.

87. Love preparing to fly. From C. I, between July 22 and 25, 1864. Printed *J.*, p. 31.

88. 'I must hunt down the prize'. From Oxford notebook C. I, July 1864. Printed *N.*, p. 27. See note to No. 9. Apropos of the first draft of 'Heaven-Haven' and its sequel (the present poem), Prof. R. G. Howarth, of Cape Town, quotes the last lines of Sir Thomas More's address to Fortune:

> Trust shall I God, to enter in a while,
> His haven of heaven sure and uniforme.
> Ever after thy calm, looke I for a storme.

89. 'Why should their foolish bands'. Same source, August 1864. Printed *N.*, pp. 27-8.

A well-aimed thrust against lugubrious, un-Christian funerals.
Line 7: *fray*, frighten.

90. 'Why if it be so'. Immediately follows No. 89, and may be a development of the same theme. Both were written in Wales. Printed *N.*, p. 28.

91. 'It was a hard thing'. From C. I, same date as No. 89. Printed *N.*, p. 28.

92. 'Glimmer'd along'. From C. I, Aug. 1864. Printed *J.*, p. 35.
Line 4: *The lawless honey*, &c. As the editors of *J.* note (p. 316, n. 35.1.), this is possibly a reference to 1 Sam. xiv, 24 ff. Cf. 'the men . . . Which once were disobedient' of fragment No. 93.—ll. 12-13: cf. No. 36, ll. 13-14.

93. 'Late I fell'. From C. I, after No. 92. Printed *J.*, p. 35. These two stanzas are separated from the adjacent entries by horizontal lines and seem unconnected. See note on No. 92.

94. 'Miss Story's character!' From C. I, August-September, 1864. Probably begun at Maentwrog, Merionethshire, where G. M. H. stayed at a

boarding house with his friends, E. Bond and A. E. Hardy. In a letter to
A. W. M. Baillie of Aug. 14, 1864, he wrote: 'We have four Miss Storys
staying in the house, girls from Reading. This is a great advantage—but not
to reading.' Text is second of two drafts; written below is a variant of
ll. 19–20:

> 'Has wit enough, if she would make it known,
> And charms—but they shd. be more freely shewn.'

Line 12: *inly*, corrected from 'only' of 3rd Edn.—[N. H. M.]

95. 'Did Helen steal'. From C. I, Aug. 1864. Printed *J*., p. 36.

96. Seven Epigrams. Six from C. I: (i) written 'In the van between
Ffestiniog and Bala' in Aug. 1864; l. 2, *see*, formerly printed as 'seen'.
(ii)–(vi) of same date; (v) l. 1, *Herclots's*, so in MS.—[N. H. M.]—(vii)
brought back from C. II, Dec. 1864 or Jan. 1865. The last one, in quotation
marks, might have been intended as a speech in one of the longer poems.
One remaining epigram (Aug. 1864) is given here:

> '*On a dunce who had not a word to say for himself.*
> He's all that's bad, I know; a knave, a flat,
> But his effrontery's not come to that.'

See *N*., pp. 28–9, 39, and *J*., p. 37.

97. By Mrs. Hopley. From C. I, Aug. 1864. (*J*., p. 37.) Thomas Hopley,
who ran a school in Eastbourne, had served four years' penal servitude for
causing a pupil's death through physical punishment. Though his family
had seemed to admire him fondly, Mrs. Hopley sued him for divorce in
July 1864 after his release. (See Mrs. E. E. Duncan-Jones, *TLS*, 10 Oct.
1968, p. 1159.) See above, *Foreword*, p. lix.
'Variation of ll. 3–5:

> 'And did he on the children of his brains
> Bestow but half the . . . . . . pains
> The children of his loins receive instead'.

As in this piece and No. 94, there is a critical acerbity in the following
lampoon from C. I, Nov. (?) 1864 (*J*., pp. 50, 319):

> 'Proved Etherege prudish, selfish, hypocrite, heartless,
> No scholar, a would be critic, a *dillettante*,
> Cream-laid, a surface, who could quote, to startle us,
> *The Anatomy*, Politian, a little Dante,—
> And so forth. Then for his looks—like pinkish paper:
> Features? A watermark; other claims as scanty.
>   In such wise did the gentle . . . vapour'.

The tone and ingenious rhymes suggest that G. M. H. had read Byron's *Don
Juan*, and this is supported by other evidence (see notes to No. 28, st. 18,

301

l. 7 and No. 58, ll. 13–14). We annotate as follows: l. 1: *Etherege*. Not identified; could hardly be Sir ('Gentle') George Etherege, the dramatist (?1634–92); l. 2: *dillentante*, thus in MS.; l. 4: *The Anatomy*, presumably Rich. Burton's *Anatomy of Melancholy; Politian*, Angelo Poliziano (1454–94), Italian poet.

98. (Sundry Fragments and Images).

(a) All from C. I; first printed in J. (i) 1863. Cancelled in pencil, probably by G. M. H. himself. (J., p. 9); (ii) and (iii) Aug. 1864 (J., 34, 36); (iv)–(vi) Sept. 1864 (J., 39).

(b) All from C. I or II; first printed in J. (vii) Apr. 1864 (J., 22); (viii) July 1864 (J., 31); (ix) and (x) Aug. 1864 (J., 36); (xi) and (xii) Sept. 1864 (J., 38, 43); (xiii) Sept. 12–14, 1864 (J., 46): l. 2, *shock* (adj.), shaggy—cf. 'shock night' in No. 28, st. 29, l. 3, and note.—(xiv)–(xvi) Oct. 1864 (J., 48–9); (xv) possibly intended as part of *Richard*, No. 107.—(xvii) Dec. (?) 1864 (J., 52); (xviii) March 1865 (J., 57); (xix) March 1865 (J., 58): seems related to *For a Picture of St. Dorothea*, entered Nov. (?) 1864 (see No. 10 and note). As the Eds. of J. suggest, these stanzas 'may be a first, abandoned attempt at the later dramatic version of *St. Dorothea*' (see Appendix A).

(c) All from C. II, except (xx), which is from C. I (J., 39). (xxi)–(xxvi) Sept. 1864 (J., 43–7); (xxvii) Oct.–Nov. 1864 (J., 50). Cf. No. 61, l. 4.— (xxviii) Oct.–Nov. 1864 (J., 50); (xxix) Jan. 22, 1866 (J., 72): in 1868 this quatrain, slightly altered, was incorporated in *The Elopement* (No. 135, st. 4);—l. 3, *hurdles bright*, cf. the 'piece-bright paling' of No. 32, l. 13.

(d) (xxx) and (xxxi) both from C. II, Jan. 1865 (J., 55).

(e) First two from C. I; last two from C. II. (xxxii) Jan.–March 1864 (J., 18): occurs in a prose synopsis of (presumably) a projected work on Ajax.— (xxxiii) March 1864 (J., 20): concludes a prose note describing a heron (?) chased away from elm-trees by two rooks.—(xxxiv) March 1865 (J., 58).

(f) All from C. II, except the last. (xxxv) Oct.–Nov. 1864 (J., 48); (xxxvi) Dec. 1864–Jan. 1865 (J., 52); (xxxvii) Apr. 1865 (J., 59); (xxxviii) July (?) 1865 (J., 65); (xxxix) July 1865 (J., 67). This line is preceded by: 'Water rushing over a sunken stone and hollowing itself to rise again seems to be devoured by the wave before which it forces up,

Reverted, with thrown-back and tossing cape.'

(xl) Journal, June 19, 1866 (J., 141).

99. Io. From C. I, Sept. 1864 and later. '[Besides work on a dramatic version of *Floris in Italy*] I have done very little since I wrote last, except three verses, a fragment, being a description of Io (transformed into a heifer). It sounds odd.' (Letter to Baillie, Sept. 10, 1864; L. III, p. 221.)

Title: Zeus fell in love with Io and changed her into a heifer to conceal her from the jealousy of Hera. The latter obtained the heifer from Zeus and set the herdsman Argos, who had eyes all over his body, to guard her. Argos ('her jailor') was killed by Hermes.—l. 9: *dew-lap*, formerly printed as 'dew-laps'.—[N. H. M.]—There are several variants:

l. 6: 'She rests half-meshing from the too-bright sky.'

ll. 11–12 (*J.*, p. 48):

'Her hue's a honied brown and creamy lakes,
{ Like a cupp'd chestnut damaskèd with breaks
{ As a cupp'd chestnut's damaskèd in breaks.'

l. 14: 'The feathery knot of locks . . .'

ll. 17–18: the last of three variants, the others being:

(i) 'Day brings not back his basilisking stare,
Nor night beholds a single flame-ring flare.'
(ii) 'Night is not blown with flame-rings everywhere,
Nor day new-basilisks his tireless stare.'

Other fragments in C. I, which may be connected with 'Io' are:

'in her cheeks that dwell
Centred like meteors, bright like pimpernel.' (*J.*, p. 39.)

'Although she be more white,
More white,
Than a skeinèd, than a skeinèd waterfall,
And better veinèd than pea blossoms all
And though she be so light
As thin-spun whirling bat's wings in the air etc.' (*J.*, p. 50.)

'Her looks more moving than the peacock's eyes.' (*J.*, p. 50.)

Also No. 98, (xiv). With the 'skeinèd' and 'veinèd' above, cf. No. 61, l. 11.

100. The rainbow. [*sic*] C. I, Sept. 1864 (*J.*, p. 39).—l. 2, *his*. MS. 'its'; after changing 'It' to 'He', G. M. H. failed to change the possessive adj.

101. '—Yes for a time.' C. I, Sept. 7, 1864 (*J.*, pp. 39–40).

102. Fragments of 'Floris in Italy'. Begun in C. I, Aug. 1864 (or perhaps, as a poem, in July—see L. III, p. 213), this play occupied G. M. H. sporadically till Sept. 1865, or possibly later. The original narrative version may have been on 22 pages (109–22, and 125–32) torn out of C. I (June 1864). The arrangement of separated fragments to form section (i) follows that in *J.*, pp. 40–2, explained in op. cit., Preface, p. xviii. Between (i) and (ii) there are two roughly-sketched fragments in prose—a comic scene and a storm scene 'with a half-mad man outside the cave of a dead hermit'.— (ii) C. I, Sept. 1864 (*J.*, p. 45).—(iii) C. II, *c.* Sept. 9, 1865 (*N.*, p. 50). (iii) ll. 9–12. Early variants entered July or Aug., 1865 (see *J.*, p. 65) are:

> 'Or try with eyesight to divide
> One star out from the daylight air,
> And find it will not be descried
> Because its place is charted there.

or

> But only try with eyesight to divide
> One star by daylight from the strong blue air,'

—the rest as printed. Immediately before (iii) comes the entry:

'After "Because its place is known and charted there."

> My love in lists of loves I would not find,
> Much less all love in one conscribèd spot.
> Tho' true love is by narrowest bands confined,
> New love is free love, or true love 'tis not.'

(See *J.*, p. 70.)

103. 'I am like a slip of comet.' From C. II, Sept. 13–14, 1864. Printed *N.*, p. 30. This is possibly part of a speech for the projected play *Floris in Italy* (cf. No. 102). First printed in *The Criterion*, Oct. 1935.
Line 14: *Amidst*, later alternative to 'Between'.—l. 16: *And then goes out*, corrected reading, omitting 'she'.—[N. H. M.]

104. 'No, they are come'. Same source, Sept. 1864. Printed *N.*, p. 31. The sentence beginning in l. 9 is the last of three variants (see *J.*, p. 46), the original being:

> 'You see the unsteady flush
> Heave through their flaring columns.'

In l. 11, *capes* is a variant of 'mantles'.

105. 'Now I am minded'. From notebook C. II, same date as No. 104. Printed *N.*, p. 31.—ll. 7, 8: *grey*, MS. reads 'grey' in l. 7, 'gray' in l. 8. —l. 16: see above, *Foreword*, p. lxiv, for hiatus formerly printed.— [N. H. M.]

106. 'The cold whip-adder'. Same source, Oct. (?) 1864. First printed in *The Criterion*, Oct. 1935, then *N.*, p. 32.

107. Fragments of 'Richard'. From C. II. Numbering of fragments is mine: (i) entered Oct. or Nov. (?) 1864; (ii) follows it. Last two belong to July 16–24, 1865.—(i), l. 16, *Haemony* from Lat. Haemonia = Thessaly.—

(ii), l. 6, *and*, MS. 'of'; l. 8, *much*, so in MS.—(iv), l. 9, *Great butter-burr leaves*, &c. The flowers of the common butter-bur (*Petasites vulgaris*) 'appear in early spring, and are succeeded by downy, kidney-shaped leaves, 1–5 feet in diameter, which, by shading the ground, check the growth of all other plants'. Johns.—[H. H.]

The earliest 14-line draft of this modern pastoral poem (from C. I, May–June 1864) is in stanzas:

> 'He was a shepherd of the Arcadian mood,
> That not Arcadia knew nor Haemony.
> Affinèd to the earnest solitude,
> ⎰ The listening downs and breezes seemèd he.
> ⎱ The winds and listening downs he seem'd to be.
>
> He went with listless strides, disorderedly.
> And answer'd the dry tinkles of his sheep
> With piping unexpected melody.
> With absent looks inspired as one drunk deep
> In nectar filter'd thro' the thymy leaves of sleep.
>
> He rested on the ⎰ frontal ⎱ of the down
>   ⎱ forehead ⎰
> Shaping his outlines on a field of cloud.
> His sheep seem'd to step from it, past the crown
> Of the hill grazing:' (See *J.,* p. 27.)

Cf. also No. 98 (xv).

108. 'All as the moth'. From C. II, Nov.–Dec. 1864. (J., p. 51.)
Line 3, *-plighted*, woven, braided.

109. The Queen's Crowning. From C. II, Dec. 1864. Printed *N.*, p. 34.
In *N.* (p. 358) H. H. says: 'The ending of this ballad has an obvious likeness to "Sweet William's Ghost" (Child, No. 77); the lily and rose are common to several ballads; in "The Gipsy Laddie" (Child, No. 200) the second and fourth lines of all stanzas but one rhyme on "e", "y" sounds. See Andrew Lang's "Recipe to forge a Border Ballad". Farrer, *Literary Forgeries*, xxvi.'
St. 13, l. 4 and st. 14, l. 4: *to*, in both cases the MS. has a theta, G. M. H.'s 'shorthand' sign for 'the', clearly a slip of the pen for 'to'.—[N. H. M.]
St. 14, l. 1: comma added by Ed.—l. 2: rejected alternative is 'They bow'd him on his knee'.

110. 'Tomorrow meet you?' Immediately follows No. 109 in C. II.

111. Fragment of 'Stephen and Barberie'. From C. II, Jan. (?) 1865. Printed *J.*, p. 52. The only identified fragment of a projected narrative poem.

112. 'I hear a noise'. C. II, Feb. 1865 (*J.*, p. 54.) Four entries later appears:

> 'and then as thick as fast
> The crystal-ended hyacinths blow.'

followed by:

> 'The dented primrose and bead-budded may.' (*J.*, p. 55.)

113. 'When eyes that cast'. From C. II, Feb. 1865. (*J.*, p. 56.)

114. The Summer Malison. From C. II, Feb. or March 1865. See *N.*, p. 41; *J.*, p. 56.
St. 1, l. 6: *lodged*, beaten down, laid flat.

115. 'O Death, Death'. From C. II, between March 2 and 12, 1865. (*J.*, p. 58.) Cf. the Creed: 'He descended into Hell . . .' and also Psalm ix. 17 and Psalm xxiv. 9.

116. 'Bellisle! that is a fabling name'. From C. II, Apr.–May 1865. (*J.*, p. 60.) Line 1: *Bellisle* [*sic*]; cf. 'To Oxford' (No. 119, l. 6—'Belleisle'), for which this fragment is probably a first draft.

117. 'Confirmed beauty'. Follows No. 116 in C. II. (*J.*, pp. 60–1.)
Line 4: Last word badly smudged; I accept Fr. A. Bischoff's reading, and N. H. M. agrees.—ll. 6–7: In MS. l. 6 follows l. 7, but G. M. H. has indicated the transposition.—*Pharaoh's ears*, &c., cf. Genesis xli. 6.

118. 'But what indeed'. From C. II, May–June (?) 1865. (*J.*, p. 62.) Probably intended as part of 'A Voice from the World' (No. 81).

119. To Oxford. From C. II, June 1865. (*J.*, p. 63.) See note to No. 12.
Line 6: *Belleisle*, presumably a 'fabling name' (see No. 116) for the 'river-rounded' Oxford (see No. 44).—l. 9: '*As when . . . . blest*', first line of penultimate stanza of Tennyson's 'A Dream of Fair Women'; cf. Dante, *Inf.* v, 121–3.
After l. 12 G. M. H. has written: 'The last two lines I have forgotten and must get.'

120. Continuation of R. Garnet's [*sic*] 'Nix'. From C. II, June–July 1865. (*J.*, p. 64.)
The Nix, by Richard Garnett, first appeared in *Primula. A Book of Lyrics* (Anon.), 1858. G. M. H. read the version with slight variations of text printed by Coventry Patmore in *The Children's Garland from the Best Poets*, 1862,

p. 196. G. M. H. quoted Patmore's text, with further slight variations, in his Platonic dialogue 'On the Origin of Beauty'. (*J.*, p. 111.) Patmore's text is printed below, Appendix C, p. 351.

121. 'A noise of falls'. From C. II, Aug. 1865. (*J.*, p. 66.)

122. 'O what a silence'. Follows No. 121 in C. II. (*J.*, p. 66.)
Lines 3–8: cf. the lark and its 'music' in No. 35, ll. 5–8.—ll. 13–19: transposed from four entries later, as obviously belonging here.

123. 'Mothers are doubtless'. From C. II, Aug. 1865. (*J.*, p. 67.)
Line 4: *who* . . . Next word illegible; one word written over another. The original phrase appears to have been 'born in', over which is written what may be 'hold of'.—[N. H. M.]

124. 'Daphne'. From C. II, Sept. 1, 1865. (*J.*, p. 68.) 'Daphne' was a character in the projected play *Castara Victrix*. See *J.*, pp. 65, 68, and the next fragment, No. 125.

125. Fragments of 'Castara Victrix'. From C. II, Sept. 1865. (*J.*,pp. 68–9.)
An entry in C. II dated Aug. 4 (?) runs: '*Castara Victrix* or *Castara Felix*. Silvian, the king, and his two sons Arcas and Valerian. Carindel. The fool. Carabella. Pirellia. Piers Sweetgale. Daphnis. Daphne.
    The melancholy Daphne doats on him.' (*J.*, p. 65.)
Line 4: see above, *Foreword*, p. lxiv.

126. Shakspere. From C. II, Sept. 13, 1865.

127. 'Trees by their yield'. Same source, Sept. 28, 1865. (*N.*, p. 51.)
G. M. H. wrote above the text: 'A verse or more has to be prefixed.' With ll. 1–4 cf. Matt. xii. 33 and No. 74.

128. A Complaint. Two autographs: one formerly in the possession of the family (now in the Bodl.); the other in A, on paper embossed *Oxford Union Society* and watermarked '1865'. This enables us to date the second MS. within narrow limits (1865 to June 1867). The forgotten birthday may have been as early as Oct. 1863 (see L. III, p. 84), but the evidence of the watermark suggests that it might well be placed with the poems of the late autumn, 1865.—[N. H. M.] G. M. H.'s eldest sister, Milicent, was born on Oct. 17, 1849. H. H. says: 'There is no reason to believe that Milicent between the age of 14 and 18 was given to writing occasional verse or was capable of conceits of this kind.' I agree with H. H.'s assumption that these verses were Gerard's engaging, indirect way of saying he was sorry.

129. 'Moonless darkness stands between'. From C. II, Dec. 25, 1865.
Line 2: see above *Foreword*, p. lxv. In last line MS. has 'Xmas'.

130. 'The earth and heaven, so little known'. From C. II, Jan. 5, 1866.
There is no external clue to the poet's final intention, but cf. No. 15. In st. 3,
'favourite of the gale,' has been cancelled in MS. but not replaced.—
[N. H. M.]

131. 'As it fell upon a day'. (*J.*, p. 71.) Just above this first line, in C. II,
is written: 'Katie, age 9. (Jan. 8, 1866.)' G. M. H.'s second sister, Kate (b.
Mar. 7, 1856, d. 1933), was 'a sort of humourist' (L. III, p. 240).

132. 'In the staring darkness'. Follows No. 131 in C. II. (*J.*, p. 72.) Under
it is written: 'Grace (8). (same day.)'. G. M. H.'s youngest sister, Grace
(1857–1945), specialized in music.

133. Summa. From A.—This poem had, I believe, the ambitious design
which its title suggests. What was done of it was destroyed, with other
things, when G. M. H. joined the Jesuits. My copy is a contemporary autograph of sixteen lines written when he was still an undergraduate; I give the
first four.—[R. B.] The remaining twelve lines have now been added. Cf.
L. I, p. 24: I cannot send my *Summa* for it is burnt with my other verses:
I saw they would interfere with my state and vocation.' (To R. B., Aug. 7,
1868.)

With the thought, basic to G. M. H.'s faith, cf. L. III, pp. 19–20 and L. I,
pp. 27–8.

134. 'Not kind! to freeze me'. Written in pencil on one of the seven
sheets of the only extant draft of No. 166 (q.v.; see also *J.*, p. 534). On same
sheet, the beginning of a letter to Aunt Laura Hodges (with whom G. M. H.
stayed in Jan. 1868) suggests that this quatrain, with No. 166, was written
while the poet was teaching at the Oratory School, Edgbaston, Birmingham
—Sept. 1867 to Easter 1868—and probably in his last term there, the first
in 1868. I agree with Eds. of *J.* (p. 326) that these lines may be an 'intimate
comment' on the premature death (by drowning) of Digby Mackworth
Dolben (1848–June 28, 1867), the young poet and religious enthusiast whose
'Catholic' fervour profoundly impressed G. M. H. (see L. I, pp. 16–17; *J.*,
pp. 60, 71, 236, 325), and who, himself deeply influenced by G. M. H.'s
conversion, was at the time of his death about to be received into the Roman
Catholic Church by Dr. J. H. Newman. The quatrain could have been conceived (if not written down) in Aug. 1867 (L. I, p. 16).

Line 1: *forecast*. That G. M. H. thought of Dolben as in Heaven (saved) is indicated by a note in *J.*, p. 236: 'I received as I think a great mercy about Dolben.' See also L. III, pp. 147–8, and No. 13.

135. The Elopement. I am indebted to the Rev. D. A. Bischoff, S.J., for the following: 'Early in 1868, two of the fifth form of the Oratory School, Edgbaston, Birmingham, joined with one of the junior masters, J. Scott Stokes, in editing a weekly journal called *The Early Bird or The Tuesday Tomtit*. Each issue was limited to three handwritten copies, the first appearing on Feb. 18, 1868. It suffered an early death. One of the issues, however, carried these verses by G. M. H., then a junior master at Dr. J. H. Newman's school; they were followed by a parody, "The Robbery", written by R Bellasis and W. Sparrow. The original handwritten copies have disappeared. The only record of these verses is found in an anonymous essay, "Early Magazines", *The Oratory School Magazine*, No. 13, Nov. 1895, pp. 5–8.'

St. 1, l. 1: *rud red*, i.e. colour of red ochre (rud, ruddle).

St. 4, l. 2: *press*: 1895 text has 'guess'; but in the Oxford notebook C. II under 'Jan. 22, 1866' is the isolated stanza printed in the present edn. as No. 98 (xxix), which has:

'They seem to press and stare'.

Hence 'guess' was probably due to a misreading of G. M. H.'s handwriting. With st. 4, ll. 1–4, cf. No. 32, l. 13.—[W. H. G.]—*The Oratory School Magazine* omits the hyphens in *linen-winded* (st. 3, l. 6) and *to-night* (st. 4, l. 1); it inserts a stop in mid-sentence at the end of st. 5.—[N. H. M.]

136. St. Thecla. G. M. H.'s autograph of this and No. 180 (the Latin version facing the English text) was found in 1952 by Fr. R. Burke Savage, S.J., among the papers of the late Fr. Connolly, S.J., editor of *Studies*. The MS. is now in the archives of the Jesuit community at 35, Lower Leeson Street, Dublin.

Title: Thecla lived at Iconium, Asia Minor. When St. Paul was preaching on the beauty of chastity she listened to him from a window (or roof), and later, leaving her mother and her bridegroom, decided to follow the apostle of Christ. Although the *Acta Pauli et Theclae* (c. A.D. 180) have been declared apocryphal, she is considered a martyr by the R.C. Church; for according to old traditions she 'suffered the torments of flames and wild beasts, confessing her faith in Christ, and escaped death only by the miraculous intervention of God'. (R. C. Breviary.)

Lines 8–10: Bellerophon attempted to fly to Heaven on Pegasus, the winged horse; but Zeus by means of a gadfly caused the horse to throw its rider.—l. 9: *these were none*, i.e. merely mythological.—l. 10: cf. Acts xxi. 39 and xxii. 3–10.

UNFINISHED POEMS

B. Poems written 1876–89

137. Moonrise. June 19, 1876. H. Note at foot shows intention to rewrite ·
with one stress more in the second half of each line, and the first is thus
rewritten 'in the white of the dusk, in the walk of the morning'.—[R. B.]
Line 1: *not-to-call night*, hyphens in MS. now inserted. [N. H. M.]—l. 5:
cusp, sharp point (of the moon); *fanged*, gripped, held (dial.).

138. The Woodlark. Draft on one sheet of small notepaper in H. Fragments in some disorder. Dating of July 5, 1876.—[R. B.] The new arrangement in the text is that given by the Rev. Geoffrey Bliss, S.J., in *The Month*,
June 1936. Fr. Bliss says: 'It will be seen that for the three missing lines (I do
not know what will be thought of me!) I have supplied lines of my own,
enclosing them in rather unnecessary square brackets. The excuse for this
impiety is a pious one: I would have the effect of a lovely piece of verse to
be, at least for a moment, not interrupted by gaps in its strain.' Where most
would fail, Fr. Bliss has, I think, succeeded. But see the notes below (on
ll. 19, 25) which establish better readings.—[W. H. G.]
Line 19: In 1st Edn., R. B. preferred the deleted line, 'And the braided ear
breaks out of the sheaf,' noting however: 'The word *sheath* is printed for
sheaf of MS., and *sheaf* recurs in corrections.' R. B.'s reading was retained
in the 2nd and 3rd Edns., but I agree with N. H. M. that the MS. offers
more authority for the line now restored.—l. 23: *rudred*, rosy-cheeked.—
l. 25: *Tatter-tangled*. MS. reads: 'Tassel-tangled', 'Tatter-)' being written
just before it in the margin. The initial capital of 'Tassel-' is not made l.c.,
and the bracket after 'Tatter-' seems to preclude the triple compound
'Tatter-tassel-tangled', as formerly printed. We now accept 'Tatter-
tangled and dingle-a-danglèd' as the poet's latest intention: the line occurs
in seven forms, all with this basic rhythm.—[N. H. M.]

139. On St. Winefred. Autograph, undated, in H, together with the Latin
version, No. 175 (see note on it below). Above the English and the Latin,
which are on separate sheets, is the heading 'A. M. D. G.', and underneath
the subscription 'L. D. S.' [Laus Deo Semper]. G. M. H. was preoccupied
with St. Winefred in the period 1874–77 and frequently visited her Well
at Holywell, N. Wales: 'Barraud and I walked over to Holywell and
bathed at the well and returned very joyously. The sight of the water in
the well as clear as glass . . . trembling at the surface with the force of the
springs, and shaping out the five foils of the well quite drew and held my
eyes to it. . . . The strong unfailing flow of the water and the chain of
cures from year to year all these centuries took hold of my mind with

wonder at the bounty of God in one of his saints, the sensible thing so naturally and gracefully uttering the spiritual reason of its being (which is all in true keeping with the story of St. Winefred's death and recovery). . .: even now the stress and buoyancy and abundance of the water is before my eyes.' (*J.*, p. 261—Oct. 8, 1874.)—[W. H. G.] No. 139 is written on poor quality unwatermarked paper, apparently to be put on a statue. The writing matches very closely with that of his St. Beuno's poems. See above, *Foreword*, pp. xlv–vii, for arguments in favour of dating it *c.* 1877. — [N. H. M.] Cf. Nos. 152 and 175.

140. 'To him who'. Text is an underlined version among working drafts in H. Probable date, 1877. See *Foreword*, pp. xlv–xlvi.

As S. Mary Jeremy points out (*TLS.*, 14 Nov. 1952), these lines are evidently a paraphrase of the following passage in *The Life and Revelations of St. Gertrude* (1865):

'When I [Christ] behold anyone in his agony who has thought of Me with pleasure, or who has performed any works deserving of reward, I appear to him at the moment of death with a countenance so full of love and mercy, that he repents from his inmost heart for having ever offended Me, and he is saved by this repentance.' (Reprint of 1949, Newman's Press, Maryland; p. 201.)

For St. Gertrude see No. 28, st. 20, l. 5, and note.

Line 6: *freed* = got rid of, banished. This sense of the word is obsolete; it occurs twice in Shakespeare, cf. *Cymb.* III. vi. 79, 'He wrings at some distress . . . would I could free't!'.—[R. B.] The first version read: 'Will grieve his ever sinning and be freed.'—[N. H. M.]

141. 'What being'. Two scraps in H. I take the apparently later one, and have inserted the comma in l. 3.—[R. B.]

142. Cheery Beggar. Undated draft with much correction in H. Text is the outcome.—[R. B.] The probable date is 1879.

Line 4: *fineflour*, thus (twice) in MS., both in discarded draft and its revision. The 'fineflower' misprinted in all earlier edns. was from R. B.'s wife's transcript, in A. The allusion is to the pollen washed down from the stamens ('goldnails') by the rain. Cf. No. 32, l. 11.—[N. H. M.]

143 and 144. These are my interpretation of the intention of some unfinished disordered verses on a sheet of paper in H.—[R. B.] On the back is a draft of 'Binsey Poplars' (1879).—[W. H. G.]

144. l. 1: *furl* is I think unmistakable: an apparently rejected earlier version had *Soft childhood's carmine dew-drift down.*—[R. B.]—l. 3: *swarthed*, darkened (from 'swarthy').—l. 11: *windlong*, cf. 'groundlong babyhood' in No. 75.

145. (Margaret Clitheroe). Auto. draft in H, undated and without title. For rearrangement of stanzas in this Edn., see above, *Foreword*, p. lxv.— [N. H. M.]

'On trial at York in 1586 for sheltering Catholic priests, [Margaret Clitheroe,] in order to save the jury from convicting her against their consciences . . . refused to plead and was therefore pressed to death with heavy weights, the penalty for remaining mute. She was declared a martyr ['Blessed'] by Pope Pius XI in 1929.' (C. Devlin, S.J., *S.*, p. 279.)

Line 2: *in the chief of bliss.* First version was, 'out of sight with bliss'.—l. 18: *clinching-blind.* The judge who sentenced her was named Clinch. —l. 27: *But no*, no comma in MS.; but we keep the comma supplied by C. W., being convinced that the poet did not mean to say that 'no Christ' lived in the martyr.—[W. H. G.]—l. 31: *The Utterer*, &c., the Holy Trinity.—l. 42: *Thecla*, i.e. St. Thecla. See note to No. 136.

146. 'Repeat that'. From a scrap in H without date or title.—[R. B.]

147. 'The Child is Father'. From a newspaper cutting with another very poor comic triolet sent me by G. M. H. They are signed BRAN. His comic attempts were not generally so successful as this is.—[R. B.] In A, R. B. notes that the verses were 'for some private magazine'.

This is the third of 'A Trio of Triolets' by G. M. H. which was published in *The Stonyhurst Magazine* (Stonyhurst College, Whalley, Lancashire), Vol. 1, No. IX, March 1883, p. 162. As an example of the way he could sometimes

<blockquote>'call off thoughts awhile
Elsewhere; leave comfort root-room;' (No. 69.)</blockquote>

I give the other two triolets:

<blockquote>'No. 1—Λέγεταί τι καινόν;

"No news in the *Times* to-day,"
Each man tells his next-door neighbour.
He, to see if what they say,
"No news in the *Times* to-day,"
Is correct, must plough his way
Through that: after three hours' labour,
"No news in the *Times* to-day,"
Each man tells his next-door neighbour.'</blockquote>

Of this and No. 3 ('The Child is Father to the Man') G. M. H. wrote: 'These two under correction I like' (L. I, pp. 190, 317–18); No. 2, which 'was

not good, and they spoilt what point it had by changing the title', is as
follows:

'No. 2—*Cockle's Antibilious Pills*
"When you ask for Cockle's Pills,
Beware of spurious imitations."
Yes, when you ask for every ill's
Cure, when you ask for Cockle's Pills,
Some hollow counterfeit that kills
Would fain mock that which heals the nations.
Oh, when you ask for Cockle's Pills
Beware of heartless imitations.'

148. (On a Piece of Music). Autograph in H, undated. The present text is
a new interpretation of the dubious two-column arrangement of the stanzas
in the MS.; it is, indeed, a compromise between C. W.'s version and that
given by Father Geoffrey Bliss, S.J., in *The Month*, Feb. 1936. The stanza
printed last was probably intended, originally, to begin the poem: St. 3, in
brackets, was a later variant of it and could be omitted. The subject of the
poem, as R. B. said (1st Edn., p. 101; this edn., p. 243), is that the artistic
individuality is something beyond the artist's control; but the second half
of the poem develops the counter-*motif* of st. 2:—though pure art may be
'good' and morally neutral, the man underlying the artist has moral obli-
gations; and moral beauty (the 'right') is the higher perfection. (Cf. *Study*, I,
pp. 28–31.]—[W. H. G.]—We now enclose the title in brackets, thus drawing attention to the absence of MS. authority for it. It was supplied by R. B.
—[N. H. M.]

149. (Ashboughs) (my title). In H in two versions; first as a curtal sonnet
(like 37 and 51) on same sheet with the four sonnets 66–69, and preceding
them: second, an apparently later version in the same metre on a page by
itself; with expanded variation from seventh line, making thirteen lines for
eleven. I print the whole of this second MS., and have put brackets to show
what I think would make the best version of the poem: for if the bracketed
words were omitted the original curtal sonnet form would be preserved and
carry the good corrections.—The uncomfortable *eye* in the added portion
was perhaps to be worked as a vocative referring to the first line (?).—[R. B.]
Title and l. 4: *Ashboughs*. We have omitted the hyphen formerly inserted.
Probable date, 1885.

Rhythm: sprung, five-stress lines; rhythm-marks extend to l. 5 only and
appear to be experimental:

'Not of all my eyes see, wandering on the world,

Is anything a milk to the mind so, so sighs deep

Poetry to it, as a tree whose boughs break in the sky.

Say it is ashboughs: whether on a December day and furled

Fast or they in clammyish lashtender combs creep . . .'

(a), l. 5: *lashtender*, cf. No. 107 (iv), ll. 5–6.—l. 9, *Mells*, mixes; *snowwhite* now restored as a single word.—[N. H. M.].—**(b)**, l. 7: MS. reads: 'Heaven with it whom she childs things by.'

150. 'The times are nightfall'. Revised and corrected draft in H. The first two lines are corrected from the original opening in old syllabic verse:

> 'The times are nightfall and the light grows less;
> The times are winter and a world undone:'

—[R. B.] The fragment seems to be a first sketch for No. 61.

151. 'Hope holds to Christ'. In H, a torn undated scrap which carries a vivid splotch of local colour.—[R. B.] See above, *Foreword*, p. xlix.
Line 4: R. B. printed 'An ever brighter burnish than before', and noted the later alternative, now restored, as a variant.—[N. H. M.]—l. 9: *darkles*, remains in darkness.

152. St. Winefred's Well. G. M. H. began a tragedy on St. Winefred, Oct. 1879, for which he subsequently wrote the chorus, No. 59 above. He was at it again in 1881, and had mentioned the play in his letters, and when, some years later, I determined to write my *Feast of Bacchus* in six-stressed verse, I sent him a sample of it, and asked him to let me see what he had made of the measure. The MS. which he sent me, Apr. 1, 1885, was copied, and that copy is the text in this book, from A, the original not being discoverable. It may therefore contain copyist's errors. [For earlier variants see *J.*, p. 531, G. I*a*.—W. H. G.].
Twenty years later, when I was writing my *Demeter* for the lady-students of Somerville College, I remembered the first line of Caradoc's soliloquy, and made some use of it. On the other hand, the broken line *I have read her eyes* in my 1st part of *Nero* is proved by date to be a coincidence, and not a reminiscence.—Caradoc was to 'die impenitent, struck by the finger of God'.—[R. B.] The transcript in A is in the beautiful hand of Mrs. Robert Bridges. The one in H, formerly thought to be by G. M. H.'s father, I have identified by comparison with letters as by his mother. It has no independent authority, since it was made from the copy in A. The autograph drafts in the Dublin Note-book cover only Act II, ll. 1–30. Changes in this 4th Edn. include: Act

II, l. 7: In all previous edns. *knew* was followed by a stop, but the MSS. and the original drafts in *Dublin Notebook* have none, nor does the sense require it; l. 12: *seems*, comma supplied from A and drafts; l. 24: *foamfalling*, now one word; l. 40: caesura after 'his' (A) instead of before it (H). In l. 70 both transcripts read 'mobs'. In section *C*, l. 8: *womb-not-bearing* was three separate words in A, and so printed 1st. Edn.: the hyphens were added (by R. B.?), possibly from the original. For the changed position of this poem in this Edn. see above, *Foreword*, pp. xlviii–ix.—[N. H. M.]

Winefred (*c.* A.D. 650) was the daughter of Teuyth (Teryth) and niece of St. Beuno, who instructed her in Christian piety. According to the legend, the chieftain Caradoc severed her head from her body as she was fleeing, in defence of her chastity, to Beuno's chapel. The saint restored her to life, and the famous spring gushed from the spot where her head fell. Later she became an abbess, and died fifteen years after her miraculous resuscitation (see Butler's *Lives of the Saints*, vol. ii, Nov. 3). See note on No. 139 for G. M. H. on the Well.

Of the rhythm G. M. H. says: 'It is in an alexandrine verse, which I sometimes expand to 7 or 8 feet, very hard to manage but very effective when well used' (L. II, p. 143). Again, ' . . . I hold that each half line is by nature a dimeter, two bars or four feet, of which commonly one foot is silent or lost at the pause. You will find it sometimes employed in full . . . . as the feeling rises the rhythm becomes freer and more sprung' (L. I, p. 212). In both A and H the caesural pauses are clearly indicated in all but a few lines; in H nearly half the total number of A's alexandrines are each written as *two* lines, the second starting with a capital. Caesural marks added to printed text follow A. A normal 'alexandrine' (my scansion—W. H. G.) is:

'What is it, Gwen, my girl? ⌒ l why do you hover and haunt me? ⌒' (p. 187, l. 1).

One line is marked thus in A:

'I can scour thee, fresh burnish thee, l sheathe thee in thy dark lair; these drops' (p. 189, l. 15).

No lines are clearly marked with 7 or 8 stresses, but the following (stresses from A) seem to be expanded to 7 and 8 feet respectively:

'Or they go rich as roseleaves l hence that loathsome came hither!' (p. 192, l. 24);

'Deed-bound I am; one deed treads all down here l cramps all doing. What do? Not yield,' (p. 191, l. 66).

315

153. To his Watch. H. On a sheet by itself; apparently a fair copy with corrections embodied in this text, except that the original eighth line, which is not deleted, is preferred to the alternative suggestion, *Is sweetest comfort's carol or worst woe's smart.*—[R. B.]

Line 7, *One spell*, &c., 'We have only one spell on earth and must use that one well'.

154. 'Strike, churl'. H, on the same page with a draft of part of No. 67.

Line 4: *Have at* is a correction for *aim at.*—This scrap is some evidence for the earlier dating of the four sonnets.—[R. B.] See note to Nos. 66–9.

155. 'Thee, God, I come from'. Unfinished draft in H. Undated, probably 1885, on same sheet with first draft of No. 62.

Line 2: *day long.* MS. as two words with accent on *day.*—[R. B.]—ll. 6–7: *thy stress*, &c., cf. the 'Deutschland', stanzas 1 and 5–8.—[W. H. G.]— l. 14: *reconciled.* The necessary stop, found in the MS. and in 1st and 2nd Edns., has now been restored.—[N. H. M.]—l. 17: above the words *before me* the words *left with me* are written as alternative, but text is not deleted. [Later alternative now restored.—N. H. M.] All the rest of this hymn is without question. In l. 19 *Yea* is right. After the verses printed in text there is some versified *credo* intended to form part of the complete poem; thus:

> 'Jesus Christ sacrificed
> On the Cross. . . .
>
> Moulded, he, in maiden's womb,
> Lived and died and from the tomb
> Rose in power and is our
> Judge that comes to deal our doom.'—[R. B.]

156. 'What shall I do'. Sent me in a letter with his own melody and a note on the poem. [See L. I, pp. 283–4, 290, 292, 301.] 'This is not final of course. Perhaps the name of England is too exclusive.' Date Clongowes, Aug. 1885 .—[R. B.] Described by its author-composer as 'a patriotic song for soldiers', it exists complete with tune by G. M. H. and accompaniment by W. S. Rockstro in a vol. of MS. airs by G. M. H. in Bodl. Text from MS. Letters to R. B., Vol. II. Cf. L. I, p. 292 and *J.*, pp. 491–2. For correction to the text see above, *Foreword*, p. lii. *Note*: R. B.'s date may be right for st. 1, but the song was not finished till Sept. 1888 (L. I, p. 283).

157. On the Portrait, &c. 'Monasterevan,Co. Kildare, Christmas, 1886.' Autograph with full title, no corrections, in A. Early drafts in H.—[R. B.]

St. 2, l. 4: *heft*, from 'heave'; suggests 'aspiration', 'ambition' (cf. *King Lear*, II. iv. 167: 'thy tender-*hefted* nature').

St. 3, l. 4: *burling*, cf. dial. 'burl', to pour; also purling, swirling.

St. 6, ll. 3–4: *a warning*, &c. The reference here to the young man who 'had great possessions' (Matt. xix. 22) is made clear by the end of l. 4 in H: 'When Christ weighed', and the following from a discarded stanza:

> 'yet rise he could not; fell
> Rather: he wore that millstone you wear, wealth.'

St. 7, l. 1: *list*, in obs. sense of 'pleasure', 'desire', as well as modern sense of 'tilt', 'leaning'.—ll. 3–4: Like Scotus, G. M. H. is trying to reconcile freedom and necessity (see *Study*, I, pp. 31–2).

St. 8, ll. 1–3: *Your feast of*, &c. The ellipses are explained by one of the versions in H.:

> feast of
> 'Your ~~lovely~~ youth and . . . .'
> 'Worst ~~will~~ batten on best: . . .'

In H there is an additional discarded stanza:

> 'Ah, life, what's like it?—Booth at Fairlop Fair;
>
> Men boys brought in to͡ have each our shy there, one
> Shot, mark or miss, no more. I miss; and 'There!—
> Another time I . . .' 'Time' says Death 'is done'.

158. 'The sea took pity'. Undated pencil scrap in H.—[R. B.]

159. Epithalamion. Four sides of pencilled rough sketches, and five sides of quarto first draft, on 'Royal University of Ireland' candidates' paper, as if G. M. H. had written it while supervising an examination. Fragments in disorder with erasures and corrections; undated. H.—The text, which omits only two disconnected lines, is my arrangement of the fragments, and embodies the latest corrections. It was to have been an Ode on the occasion of his brother [Everard's] marriage, which fixes the date as 1888. It is mentioned in a letter of May 25, whence the title comes.—I have printed *dene* for *dean* (in two places). In l. 9 of poem *cover* = *covert*.—[R. B.] *Dean* now restored.—[N. H. M.] See L. I, p. 277.

Line 4: *dean*, dene, dell, valley; *clough*, ravine (rhymes with 'rough'); *cleave*, a cleft (O.E. *cleofa*).—l. 11: *of* may be *at*, MS. uncertain. [R. B.]—l. 19: *gambol*, not 'gambols', as formerly printed.—[N. H. M.]—l. 36: *coffer*, box-like basin (cf. 'coffer-dam').—l. 37: *selfquainèd*, for G. M. H.'s use of 'quain' (dial. for 'quoin' 'coign', ext. angle of a wall) see *J.*, p. 205: 'a square scaping . . . in big pack-clouds . . . a strong large quaining and squaring in them which makes each pack impressive and whole'. See also *Introduction*, p. xxix, for 'quain' suggesting a back-formation from 'quaint', (singular, fanciful; cf. Chaucer's 'queynt', curiously contrived, ornamented); cf. the 'quaining' and 'peaked quains' in the 'new world of inscape' in ash-tree tufts (End of Mar. 1871—*J.*, pp. 205–6).—l. 38: *shivès:* obs. 'shive' = splinter, slice, sliver (cf. *Tit And.*, II. i. 87: 'easy it is/ Of a cut loaf to steal a shive'); cf. *shivelights* in No. 72, l. 4. For some words hitherto omitted from the text, see above, *Foreword*, pp. li–ii.—[W. H. G.]

TRANSLATIONS, LATIN AND WELSH POEMS, &c.

160. Prometheus Desmotes. Autograph from the school and Oxford notebook B. II; undated, but ll. 20–36 were sent to E. H. Coleridge in the letter of Sept. 3, 1862, quoted in note to No. 77. (See L. III, p. 6.) For 'B. II' see *J.*, p. 529.

Line 5. Comma after *you* not in MS. Added by H. H. in *N.*, p. 4.—l. 18: *burthen*, so in MS., not 'burden' as formerly printed.—l. 23: *Or*, formerly printed 'of'.—[N. H. M.]

161. From the Greek. C. II, March 1865. The original is:

$$E\ddot{\iota}\ \mu\epsilon\ \phi\iota\lambda o\hat{\upsilon}\nu\tau a\ \phi\iota\lambda\epsilon\hat{\iota}s,\ \delta\iota\sigma\sigma\dot{\eta}\ \chi\acute{a}\rho\iota s\cdot\ \epsilon\dot{\iota}\ \delta\acute{\epsilon}\ \mu\epsilon\ \mu\iota\sigma\epsilon\hat{\iota}s,$$
$$\tau\acute{o}\sigma\sigma o\nu\ \mu\dot{\eta}\ \mu\iota\sigma\hat{\eta}s,\ \ddot{o}\sigma\sigma o\nu\ \dot{\epsilon}\gamma\acute{\omega}\ \sigma\epsilon\ \phi\iota\lambda\hat{\omega}.$$—Anonymous.

Note on Nos. 162–6. The autographs of these poems were discovered with the Journal A. III in Feb. 1947 by the Rev. D. A. Bischoff, S.J., in the Jesuit house at Farm Street, London. Besides the fair copies (162, 164, 165) I now print all the rough drafts which yield coherent texts. The poems in Latin were almost certainly written in the period 1864–7, while G. M. H. was still at Balliol; the English verses were probably written between Sept. 1867 and April 4, 1868, when the poet was teaching at the Oratory School, Edgbaston, Birmingham. All these manuscripts are now lodged at C. H.

162. Inundatio Oxoniana. At top left of *recto* 'Mr. Hopkins' is written in another hand; pencilled subscription 'G. M. Hopkins'. Undated; but there was a flood in Oxford in 1865, and the river rose to unusual heights; yet it gained only a passing mention in Jackson's Oxford Journal for that year, and is not mentioned at all under 'Inundations' in Haydn's *Dictionary of Dates*.

At the end of l. 19 I have changed the comma into a stop, and at the end of l. 20 I have added a comma.—[W. H. G.]

Translation:

Oxford Floods

'For long have the spring pastures felt the onslaught of fierce clouds with their unceasing showers, and the abundance of the sopping sky comes down upon us and, carried by the winds, and tearing away the threshold of the spurned river-bank, becomes a sea over the wide-spreading fields. Here and there a marooned patch of grass rises all the gayer amid the gleaming flood, a plot which, uplifted in a gentle slope, flourishes green (*viret*): but already the waste of wetness has hidden all else. Scarcely does the Isis bring down its waters undivided from the rest, and in its own channel; unbridled blasts assail the watery expanses, and men enjoy scudding over new shoals with a following souther. Some sail over the pathless tracts of the woods and glide in among the shadowy willows; among the tree-tops of a wood that has been pieced and scattered, the submerged poplar gives passage to unfamiliar boats.

'But if at last the sun has ridden in circuit five times through a clear sky; if the ether kindles a fiery smile for as many days, the waters will recede and depart. Then often a sea-smell is borne across the open country and nimbly seizes upon the damp air,—such a smell as stealthily penetrates to the centre of the city, and passes through the inmost parts of houses; nor anywhere do you escape the baneful scummy flotsam (lit. 'seaweed'). How many a virulent sickness springs from this! How often will men lament that they went near it. You come to our houses and you find them exposed to the fever next door! But it is possible to go away for a change and to have left the place, and to flee at once from the sickening heats: *we* do not dwell permanently among these cares. Those who are bound to the soil, the native population accustomed to the danger, will be safer staying in the homes of their forefathers: assuredly the pestilence has been driven away from them by a benign power, for though the west-wind may renew its warm showers on our ploughlands all through the night, it vexes the recumbent acres without doing damage, and a harmless sheet of water is drawn over the fields. Nay, scarcely could as many lilies, their own children, blush in *dry* meadows as you may see tossing their heads near familiar streams, had not the destined water sported a little in abundant flood as it came, had not the choppy waves been able to spread themselves first and to have left in their wake deposits of mud. Thus too, after the floods, the riverside tree puts forth its pleasant twigs with more vigour; thus too the willows grow; while the horseman, too, looks the more eagerly for the untrodden plains and rides into the lush grass.'

Classicists whom I have consulted are not unanimous about this poem; but the majority think that the style, in parts involved and obscure, is not due to metrical difficulties: 'it seems deliberate, and is therefore of interest in any study of the writer's development'.
Line 4: *ferentibus*. So in MS.; 3rd Edn. 'furentibus' now corrected.—
[N. H. M.]—I am indebted to Prof. B. H. P. Farrer for the following notes.
—l. 20: *adiisse*: the 'subject' of this infinitive is not expressed; is it *se*

(preferably) or *algam* or *vim morbi?*—l. 21: *petis*, a somewhat abrupt Juvenalian touch, cf. *averteris* (l. 19); *nostri*, probably governed by *vicinam*, 'next door to us', but also suggesting a possessive adjective for *tecta*; *obnoxia* appears to govern *vicinam febrem* directly, i.e. to stand for *obnoxia ad* or *in*, by a licence for which there may be classical parallels, as G. M. H. is careful in this way.—l. 34: *limos . . . sequaces*, pencilled correction of 'limum . . . sequacem'. This unusual use of the plural of *limus* seems hardly an improvement, unless the poet wished to emphasize the idea of mud deposits 'in a succession of streaks and patches'. See above, *Foreword*, p. lxi.

163. Elegiacs: *'Tristi tu, memini'*. Autograph MS., C. H.: rough drafts with many variants. See *J.*, p. 534. Undated, but written over pencilled draft of first few lines of a letter to R. B. of 30 Aug. 1867 (L. I, p. 16) and on a sheet containing very rough drafts of No. 164. Variant of first couplet has a colon after *fuisti* (l. 1) and 'Non illo' for *Illo nec* (l. 2). On another sheet is what appears to be a condensed variant of the whole:

> Tristis eras dum me venturum, Cythna, putares.
> Et veni et redeo: jam quoque tristis eris.
> Adsum gratus ego necopini apparitor ignis,
> Inter ego gelidas stella serena nives.

Translation:

'I remember, girl, when your lot (plight?) was a sad one, nor at that time had my early love (for you) ceased. And now I am going away: again you are being left alone: so this occasion is a sadder one; yet that other was sad too. I am here welcome as one who lights and tends an unexpected fire, I am a tranquil star amid a waste of snows.'

Line 4: *aetas*, for 'day', 'occasion', is unusual; but cf. Statius, *Theb.* 3. 562, *crastina . . . aetas*, 'the morrow'; l.5: *apparitor*, lit. 'the attendant of'. The condensed variant quoted above may help to clarify the meaning:

'You were sad, Cythna, as long as you thought that I was only likely to come. I have come and I am going back: now, too, you will be sad. I am here welcome as one who lights and tends an unexpected fire, I am a serene star amid frozen snows.'

On the same sheet as the drafts of No. 163, and resembling it in theme and metre, is the following autograph distich (second of two versions), which was first printed in *Study*, II, p. 86 (punctuation, *sic*):

> Quo rubeant dulcesve rosae vel pomifer aestas
> Est rubor in teneris virginis ille genis.

'Why need the lovely roses or the fruitful summer show their red (bloom)? That red is in the soft cheeks of a maiden.'

164. Elegiacs: After *The Convent Threshold*. Autograph MS., C. H.

Undated; no title. See Appendix B for Christina Rossetti's poem (Sections 1 and 9), and cf. No. 81, 'A Voice from the World'.

Line 10: *Purpurei infecta*, so in MS., not 'Purpurea infecti' as previously printed.—ll. 17 and 41: the commas inserted in the 3rd Edn., for the reader's convenience, after *pectus* and *palmas*, have now been removed. —[N. H. M.]

Translation:

'The stream of a brother's blood flows between us, Aulus, and the fresh blood of our slain father is fixed between us. O you who have ever been the best and dearest man in the world to me, that blood now keeps me far sundered from you. There is a road which leads aloft through the stars, and a golden staircase which replaces day by day and night by night: setting foot on this road I shall mount up to the farthest heights of heaven and up to the glassy halls and to the glassy sea. The feet which you say surpass the white lilies in beauty are deeply crimson with a blot of sin. My feet have a crimson stain, and with its sombre gouts I stand for all to see (*exsto*) as a token of my own guilt—the joys that were mine, and the tears after the joys, and the love that fell to the ground and was not raised up again. And yet they (my feet) have not so much blood on them, nor is it so ingrained in them but that doubtless it can be washed away if water be brought: yet—if only I could open the unseen depths of my heart!— in the unseen depths of my heart this guilt lies hidden. But the sea that glows red with mingled flame and glass [Revelation xv. 2]—that (sea the prophet saw) was molten glass and clear fire—ah, I pray that it may supply healing balms for my maimed feet, antidotes for my marks of shame and for the snare set for me. And since heaven has been shown to us with the pathway built up to it, O set foot with me on the road that leads up to the stars.'

.   .   .   .

'I will tell you of the dreams I dreamed last night (and) in a twilight when it was doubtful whether it was night or day. At that time my plenteous hair was wet with cold dew: the dew had gathered distilled from the cold ground. You came there and you asked whether I had been touched by a vision of you, whether that sleep of mine, too, was still mindful of you. The heart that once used to leap at that likeness of you lay now a mass of inert dust at your importunate words. Yet I understood your questions, nor was I unable to reply, and I said these few words in a heavy stupor: "Sad is our bridal bed, its valance is filled with woe; it rests on cold unyielding stones. Seek for yourself a pleasant bed, a new marriage; place your soft limbs, I give you leave, on an attractive couch. You have a second spouse who will cherish you better than I, you have a love that is sweeter than mine." On hearing this you beat your hands together in wild excitement and your limbs seemed all of a sudden to give way and shake. These were the last things I saw; at the same time I rolled headlong into the inmost parts and empty coffers of the solid earth. But I did not think it was in applause, as at a holiday dance, that you beat your hands together, or that your limbs were trembling from too much wine.'

165. Horace: 'Persicos odi'. Autograph at C. H., undated, on four pages of notepaper. On one sheet (with a corner cut out) is part of a letter which mentions the visits of Fr. Ignatius Ryder to the Oratory, Edgbaston, and concludes: 'I do not expect to be long here: if I get a vocation to the priesthood . . .' (see L. III, p. 52; also *J.*, p. 534). Probable date, between Nov. 1867 and Easter 1868.

Line 1: *Persian-perfect art*, a comparison of contemporary autographs makes it clear that G. M. H. intended, not a dash (as formerly printed), but a hyphen, producing a compound adjective to translate Horace's 'Persicos apparatus'.—[N. H. M.]

166. Horace: 'Odi profanum volgus'. Autograph MS., C. H. Pencilled on seven sides, with many corrections and variants. The first stanza is preceded by the unrelated quatrain here printed as No. 134 ('Not kind! to freeze me with forecast,' etc.). If, as my note on p. 308 suggests, this quatrain contains an allusion to Dolben, and consequently to G. M. H.'s impending vocation to the priesthood, there may be a subliminal connexion with Nos. 165 and 166, both of which commend the simple life. Probable date, between Sept. 1867 and Easter 1868.

Text now embodies some of the latest variants, earlier ones including:
St. 1, l. 2: 'Grace guard your tongues!——'
St. 3, ll. 1–2: cancelled version ran:
'Say man than man may more enclose
In rankèd vineyards;'
St. 6, l. 1: was rewritten: 'Sleep that comes light and not afraid' but the linkage of this line with st. 5 seems to us too elliptical for adoption in the text.
In st. 12, after the initial 'Why', the first half of the stanza is left blank.

167. 'Jesu Dulcis Memoria'. Autograph MS., C. H. Undated; no title. Written in ink and pencil on three sides, with many variants. The stanzas here translated, drawn from two different versions of this Latin hymn, have been arranged by me as one poem. Stanzas 5 and 6, found on a separate sheet and in reverse order, have been combined with the others to form what seems to me a satisfactory climax. Some earlier variants are as follows:

St. 1 (concluding lines):

> 'Not honey and honeycomb come near
> The sweetness though when He is here.'

St. 2:   (i) 'There's no such touching music heard,
> There's never spoke so glad a word,
> So sweet a thought there is not one . . .'

(ii) 'No music so can touch the ear,
> No news is heard of such sweet cheer,
> So dear a thought there is not one . . .'

St. 3:   'Thou art the hope, Jesu my sweet,
> The soul has in its sighing-fit;
> The loving tears on Thee are spent,
> The inner cry for Thee is meant.'

St. 5:   (i) 'Who taste of Thee will hunger more,
> Who drink be thirsty as before:
> What else to ask they never know
> But Jesus' self, they love Him so.'

(ii) 'Jesu, like dainties to the heart
> Daylight and running brooks Thou art, . . .'

Written probably at the same time (1867–68?) and in the same mood as No. 167 is the following translation of the first four lines of another Latin hymn:

> *Ecquis binas*
> O for a pair like turtles wear,
> O wings my spirit could put on!
> And where I see the sweet cross-tree
> I in an instant would be gone.

Cf. No. 28, st. 3, ll. 4–8.—[W. H. G.] St. 5, l. 4: for change in text see above, *Foreword*, p. lxv.—[N. H. M.]

168. S. Thomae Aquinatis Rhythmus. Autograph in H, undated. There are three versions, (1) which seems to be an early draft, (2) a draft partially

323

deleted, but not much unlike the present text, (3) the text given here. In this there are two undeleted alternatives: (1) St. vi, l. 1, has as a note '*or* Like what tender tales tell of the Pelican;' (2) St. vii, l. 1, brackets 'shrouded' with 'veilèd' as of equal possibility. [C. W.]

St. vi, l. 1: the legendary 'pious' Pelican suckled its young on blood from its own breast.—l. 3: *worth*, misprinted 'world' through dittography in 2nd and 3rd Edns.—[N. H. M.]

169. Oratio Patris Condren. Autograph in H, undated. This version is written on the back of a page containing part of a deleted draft of No. 168. There are two other drafts, one in ink on a sheet containing the Latin original; the other in pencil on a separate leaf. The title is given in the first as '*To Jesus living in Mary*: a prayer of Fr. Condren of the French Oratory of St. Philip Neri'. There is also an autograph in B, both of English and Latin, which substitutes for ll. 5–6 one of the H variants, i.e.:

'In those most perfect ways Thou wendest,
In the virtues of that life Thou spendest,'—[C. W.]

170. O Deus, ego amo te. Autograph in H, undated. There are two versions, one with several variations, the other unaltered on the same sheet as and at the conclusion of No. 168. In this original, l. 7 reads 'sufferedst lance and lance'; 'nails and lance' has been substituted here from the other versions.—[C. W.] These other versions are headed: A.M.D.G. *St. Francis Xavier's Hymn.* See next note.

171. The Same (Welsh Version). The unique draft, in H, is in an unknown hand; it is undated and without alterations. The ascription to G. M. H. is based upon internal evidence of style. Welsh title means, 'The Sigh of St. Francis Xavier, Apostle of the Indians'. (The original, attributed to this saint, is in any good collection of Latin hymns.) On seeing a copy of the Welsh poem, Sir Idris Bell wrote: 'The Welsh is certainly better than in the *cywydd*, No. 172, and as the metre is of the English type there are no metrical errors.' In a letter to Sir Idris, Dr. T. Parry writes: 'I should say that it is Hopkins's own work, or at least that it can hardly be a product of the fifteenth or sixteenth century, because the metre is much more regular than what is found in the older period. . . . The syntactical structure of lines 1 and 2 in verse iii strike me as being characteristic of Hopkins. You will notice that they contain a "sangiad". The normal order of words would be "Aneirif ddolur a phoen chwŷs darfu it eu dwyn". Hopkins, as you know, was very fond of this device. . . . The language is considerably less faulty for the obvious reason that the author was not compelled to wrestle with *cynghanedd*. The way he has gone astray in the last verse is sufficient proof, I think, that the author was not a Welshman.'

The following errors have been pointed out by the above-named scholars:

St. 1, l. 4: *Y berni* should be *A ferni*; *am fyth* should be *am byth* (the usual soft mutation after *am* does not affect *byth*, which is a borrowing from Irish: 'G. M. H. probably realised that "am byth" was irregular, and "corrected" it to "am fyth".'—[T. P.]).

St. 2, l. 1: The reflexive verb is wrongly used in *hymgofleidiaist*. The use of *oll*, here and especially in st. 3, is unidiomatic. In l. 3, MS. has no commas round *hoelion*; they are obviously necessary.

St. 3: At end of l. 1, MS. has a semi-colon; the sense demands a comma. 'Darfu . . . dwyn' form a compound verb, and should normally go closely together.—[T. P.]

St. 5: *Ond megis*, &c. 'A natural Welshman could not possibly avoid bringing in the conjunctive pronoun here—"Megis y ceraist ti fi y caraf . . . etc." I find that a taste for the conjunctive pronouns is always a good test of a writer's mastery of Welsh.'—[T. P.] Line 2 seems to mean: 'I shall love thee, I love thee', which is less natural than l. 19 of No. 170. Moreover, the construction should be 'dy garu'r wyf'.

Dr. Parry concludes: 'Everything considered, I think the poem betrays very definite signs of being the work of a person who has learnt the language but is not sufficiently acquainted with all the details.' See next note (No. 172).

Translation.

The Sigh of St. Francis Xavier Apostle of the Indians

1. Not because Thou hast redeemed me do I love Thee, Lord, in truth, nor because of those who do not love Thee and are condemned to eternal fire.

2. Thou, thou, who didst embrace me (all of me), my Jesus, on the Cross; from lance, nails, and slanderous tongues didst suffer great agony:

3. Infinite grief hast Thou endured, and pain and sweat on my behalf, sinner that I am—even unto death for my sake.

4. Therefore, most loving Jesus, why should I not love Thee steadfastly? Not so as to receive heaven at Thy hands, or any reward; nor lest I receive torment for ever;

5. But just as Thou didst love me, so shall I love Thee and *do* love Thee, only because Thou art God and art to me a Ruler.[1]

172. Cywydd. Autograph (with many corrections) in H. An emended version of the text, with annotations, was first published by W. H. G. in *Transactions* (1940) of the Cymmrodorion Society. The present text is

[1] *Ruler*: MS. 'Rhwyf'. This noun, which means 'oar' in modern Welsh, bears also the obsolete meanings 'ruler' and 'need'.—[W.H.G.]

author's original, with its nineteenth-century orthography unchanged (e.g. 'cyrhaedd' for 'cyrraedd', 'bummed' for 'bumed', and the now discarded circumflex on 'fod', 'hen', 'dyn', &c.).

G. M. H. learnt Welsh while a 'theologian' at St. Beuno's College, N. Wales, between 1874 and 1877. His authorship here is proved by internal evidence and the bardic signature 'Brân Maenefa' (see notes to Nos. 28, end of para. 1, and 147, and cf. 'Maenefa' in No. 137); also by the letter to his father of Aug. 6, 1876 (L. III, p. 140): '. . . we presented him with an album containing . . . compositions, chiefly verse, in many languages. . . . For the Welsh they had to come to me, for, sad to say, no one else in the house knows anything about it; I also wrote in Latin and English . . .' (see Nos. 29 and 173). A *cywydd* is a peculiarly Welsh poem with no English equivalent. It has seven-syllabled lines all of which include *cynghanedd*, the strict system of rules governing stress, alliteration, internal rhyme, and end-rhyme. In G. M. H.'s poem the *cynghanedd* is incorrect in all lines save 7 and 10. Thanks to information supplied by Dr. T. Parry of University College, Bangor, I was later able to correct a number of errors which had crept into the text and notes as published in the *Transactions*.—[W. H. G.]

Author's prefatory note: l. 1: *pharcedig*, mod. 'pharchedig'; *Dr. Th. Brown*. G. M. H. must have intended to dedicate his *cywydd* to James, Bishop of Shrewsbury, whose diocese included the six counties of North Wales, and whose silver jubilee he celebrated in No. 29. In writing 'Dr. Th. Brown' he must have confused the Christian name of the Bishop of Shrewsbury with that of Dr. Thomas Brown, Bishop of Newport and Menevia, who was first consecrated bishop as early as 1840, and whose jubilee, even after his translation to Newport and Menevia, could not have fallen in 1876. (See *J.*, pp. 259 and 440.)—l. 2: *cyrhaedd*; 'am gyrhaedd' is deleted.—l. 3: *Jubil*, i.e. 'Jiwbil'; *daiar*, mod. 'daear'.—l. 4: *fwy*, after 'mwy' deleted.—l. 5: *mai gobeithia*, incorrect for 'y gobeithia' or 'ei fod yn gobeithio'; in MS., after *hefyd*, 'ei fod yn' is deleted. In same line he intends 'hynny i gael ei gyfnewid'; and *o waith* should be 'trwy waith' = 'through the work'.

In a letter of 1877 (L. III, p. 241) G. M. H. speaks of having 'none but a small and bad (Welsh) dictionary at command'. The St. Beuno's College library (later transferred to Heythrop Coll., Oxon.) contained two small dictionaries (Thos. Richards's *Thesaurus*, 1753, and W. Spurrell's *Eng.-Welsh Dict.*, 1848), together with the two vols. of W. Owen Pughe's once-authoritative *Welsh-Eng. Dict.* (3rd edn., 1866–73) and the two vols. of the *Eng.-Welsh Dict.* of D. Silvan Evans (1852–8). Dr. T. Parry tells me that almost every Welsh dictionary compiled and published in the nineteenth century drew upon the work of Pughe (first edition 1793-1803); and most of G. M. H.'s peculiar spellings are given as first preferences only in Silvan Evans. The poet's 'small and bad dictionary' might have been Spurrell's or one of the many editions of a work by Wm. Richards, LL.D.; all of these give unusual words and definitions derived from Pughe.

Line 1: *llewyn*. Dr. Parry writes: 'It is worth noting the meaning given to it by Pughe (1st Edn.)—"A point to which anything verges; a radiating point." (Wm. Richards also gives "a radiating point".) This was undoubtedly the meaning which Hopkins attached to the word; St. Beuno's was the focal point, the centre from which the true faith would radiate throughout Wales.'—l. 2: *ffrydan*, not found in Mod. Welsh; but both Spurrell and Pughe give 'ffrydan—a streamlet', and Silvan Evans, s.v. 'a small stream', gives 'ffrydan'. 'It is', says Dr. Parry, 'a perfectly natural formation from *ffrwd*—stream, and the diminutive ending -*an*.' —l. 3: *gadwyd*, for 'a gadwyd'; omission of the relative, and similar contractions, are common with nineteenth-century writers.—l. 7: Under 'a ddwg', &c. is a deleted variant—'gwan yw, nid gan ddŷn'.—l. 10: *drag'wyddawl*, contraction of 'dragywyddawl'; Mod. Welsh 'dragwyddol'—l. 11: *ddyniol*, Pughe gives the correct form, 'dyn*ol*'.—l. 13: *ela*, a spurious form of the 3rd pers. sing. future of 'myned' —to go, as given (Dr. Parry tells me) on p. 88 of W. Owen Pughe's fantastic grammar of the Welsh language (1803).—l. 14: *Tardd*, so in MS., formerly misread as 'Fardd'; 'llîf' is deleted. For the meaning, see translation of the whole text given below. Dr. Parry writes: 'This use of "llîf" is not very common, but a parallel example is the scriptural "gwlad yn llifeirio o laeth a mêl",—"flowing with . . . ". And anyhow, Hopkins was not the man to use words in their common connections only.'—l. 16: *feddygiaeth*, i.e. 'feddyginiaeth'. The form Hopkins uses is given by Pughe and Silvan Evans.—l. 17: *gwela*, form of the 3rd pers. sing. future of 'gweled', as given by Pughe (*Grammar*, p. 109). 'Hopkins obviously seeks a decidedly future meaning; hence the use of the termination -*a*. Cf. "ela" above.'—[T. Parry.]—l. 18: *glân îr gwyryfon*. In the *Transactions*, îr was wrongly changed to i'r. Pughe gives the adj. 'ir' a substantival meaning—'what is pure, what is fresh'; similarly, *gwyryfon* can be either noun (plural genitive—'of [the] virgins') or adjective (plural). Dr. Parry prefers the reading given in translation below, and as a parallel 'stringing of adjectives' without commas cites 'skeined stained veined variety' (*Spelt from Sibyl's Leaves*).—l. 19: *Brân*, probably taken from the character in the second branch of the Mabinogi, *Bendigaid Fran*, Brân the Blessed.—[T. P.] But there is, perhaps, a puckish humour in the fact that in Welsh *brân* = crow, rook (cf. the motto to No. 1—'a *frog* against the cicadas').

By collating the various suggestions proffered by Sir Idris Bell, Dr. T. Parry, and Mr. M. Harris (of Dynevor School, Swansea) I arrive at the following translation:

'Address to the Very Rev. Dr. Th. Brown, Bishop of Shrewsbury, on his reaching his five and twentieth year, which is known as the Jubilee; and the poet complains that earth and sea give greater testimony to the old religion of North-West Wales than man; and he says also that he hopes that this will be changed through the work of the bishop.

'Our focal point here is bright and glad with the streamlet of many a fountain, a holy remnant kept for us by Beuno and Winefred. Under rain or dew, you will hardly find a country beneath heaven which is so luxuriant. Weak water[1] brings faithful testimony to our vale, but man bears no such witness. The old earth, in its appearance, shows an eternal share of virtue; it is only the human element that is faulty; it is man alone that is backward. Father, from thy hand[2] will issue a spring from which will flow the beautiful prime good. Thou bringest by faith a sweet healing, the nourishment of religion; and Wales even now will see true saints—pure, holy, virgin.[3]

Brân Maenefa sang this
April the twenty-fourth 1876.'

173. Ad Episcopum Salopiensem. Autograph in H. Above the poem is written 'A.M.D.G.' (Ad Majorem Dei Gloriam) and below it 'L.D.S.' (Laus Deo Semper). Deleted under the title are the words 'annum agentem et sui praesulatus et restituti apud Anglos episcoporum ordinis vicesimum quintum, qui jubilaeus dicitur' (In the twenty-fifth year both of his prelacy and of the restoration of the episcopal hierarchy in England, which year is called the Jubilee). An earlier and longer autograph version with variants (also in H) is followed by an autograph note dated 'April 1876': 'They said the beginning was unintelligible and struck out the first nine couplets, so that I had to make the address begin—Quod festas luces juvat instaurare Beatis . . .'. The discarded couplets are printed and translated below the present note.

The Catholic hierarchy was restored in 1850, and the Silver Jubilee of James Brown, Bishop of Shrewsbury, fell in 1876. See Nos. 29, 172, and notes.

[1] Cf. the 'frail water' in No. 152, p. 192, l. 15.
[2] For the thought—a fount issuing from a hand—cf. No. 155, ll. 2–3:
'All day long I like fountain flow
From thy hand out, . . .'
[3] The possible alternative reading, 'the holy purity of the virgins', might be an allusion to the eleven thousand virgins of St. Ursula; for these are mentioned by Tudur Aled, the Welsh poet (d. 1520), in his 'Cywydd i Wenfrewi Santes' (Ode to St. Winefred), a copy of which I saw, in 1936, among G. M. H.'s papers at Amen House (O.U.P.). It was a cutting from the *Montgomery Mercury* of July 8 (?) 1875, and included a translation and commentary signed 'H. W. L.'. For St. Beuno and St. Winefred see note to No. 152.—[W. H. G.]

Line 8: *lamina*, (hitherto printed as 'laurea'—see above, *Foreword*, pp. lx—lxi) lit. 'thin metal plate', used here by synecdoche for the bishop's mitre. The obvious source is Exodus xxviii. 36-8, the Vulgate version of the instructions given to Moses concerning Aaron, the High Priest:

> Facies et *laminam* de auro purissimo: in qua sculpes opere caelatoris, Sanctum Domino. Ligabisque eam vitta hyacinthina, et erit super tiaram imminens fronti pontificis. Portabitque Aaron iniquitates eorum, quae obtulerunt et sanctificaverunt filii Israel, in cunctis muneribus et donariis suis. Erit autem *lamina* semper in fronte eius, ut placatus sit eis Dominus.

Monsignor Knox translates:

> 'And thou shalt make a plate of pure gold, inscribed with all the engraver's skill, with the words, Set apart for the Lord. This is to be bound with a blue cord on to the mitre, and will hang over the priest's forehead. Whatever fault is found in offering and gift, by Israel's sons dedicated and hallowed, Aaron must charge himself with it; and the Lord will overlook it, so long as the plate hangs ever on Aaron's forehead.'

By the thirteenth century the mitre had received the significance relating it to Aaron's head-dress. Cf. *Ceremonialis Episcoporum* Liber I, cap. 17; quoted du Cange, Glossarium Mediae et Infimae Latinitatis, s.v. *mitra*:

> Mitrae usus antiquissimus est, et eius triplex est species: una quae pretiosa dicitur, quia gemmis et lapidibus pretiosis, vel laminis aureis vel argenteis contexta esse solet: . . .

The Precious Mitre, still used on feast-days, is no longer 'composed . . . of gold or silver plates'.—[W. H. G.]—ll. 9-10: *Ut reor*, &c. There seem to be two lines of thought here, one mathematical, the other topical. Mathematically, 25 years may be said to 'square' or complete a century by adding the last quarter (cf. Horace, *Epist.* I, vi. 35: *quae pars quadrat acervum*, 'the part that squares the heap', the last quarter). Similarly, the bishop will 'halve' a century (*dimidiare*) if he reaches his Golden Jubilee. Topically, he may be said to have added the third quarter to the nineteenth century, while if he reaches his Golden Jubilee he may be said to 'cleave the centuries', because it will occur at the turn of the century.— l. 11 seems to require a comma at the end.

Discarded opening of the address:

> Vertitur in gyrum toto pulcherrima gyro,
> Attamen est quo sit pulchrior urna loco.
> Scilicet hic { hominis vultus habet: ecce recurrunt:
> { faciem spectas: modo verte, recurret:

$$\text{Non}\begin{cases}\text{alium spectas qui venit}\\\text{aliam cernis quae placet}\end{cases}\text{ore novo.}$$

Miramur rediisse quod ipse redire coegit   5
    Orbis et in modulum testa rotata suum.
Sic iterat caelum spatiis sua tempora certis
    Quaeque nitere vides astra videbis ait;
Quod si Cassiope magis hac tibi parte venustast
    Hac te Cassiope parte venusta manet.   10
Indidit hoc nobis varium qui temperat annum,
    Sol ubi prae cunctis igneus unus inest;
Et per versa vices series succedat ut arvis
    Et media his aestas ut sit aprica magis.
At si quid rerum minus ipse notaverat ordo   15
    Addita non illud signa latere sinunt.
Obscuras olim tulit ambitus ille calendas
    Nostra sed insignes esse rubrica facit.

Notes on the orginal opening.

Line 2: *urna.* G. M. H. probably had in mind one of the Roman clay face-pots manufactured in Essex in the second and third centuries A.D.—l. 11: A second thought, 'vario . . . anno', is cancelled.—l. 13: *per versa vices*: the normal order, 'versa per vices', is boldly altered for metrical reasons.— l. 18: *rubrica*: there is a play on two meanings of this word, (i) red chalk, (ii) the title, rubric, of a law, &c., because written in red.

Translations:

'*To the Bishop of Shrewsbury*'

(a) *Discarded opening* (see above).

'Most beautiful is an urn ('face-pot') when it is turning round in a full circle, yet there is a certain position in which it is still more beautiful. This is because that position presents the features of a man: see, they recur: you do not see another man who comes with a new face. [*Original version*: This is because in that position you see a face; just turn the urn, it will come back again: you do not see another face which pleases with new features.] We are surprised that that has returned which the circular movement itself, and the urn revolving according to its own symmetry, has compelled to return. Just so the sky repeats its rhythms in fixed regions, and "the stars you see shining there you will see again", it says. "But if Cassiope (a constellation) is more lovely to you in a certain quarter, it is in this quarter that the lovely Cassiope awaits you". He who rules the changing year, in which there is one sun which burns more fiercely than all others, has caused this to be so for us, and (has ordained) that in turns a changed lot should come upon the fields, and that midsummer should bring them more sun. But in case the very order of the universe had failed to indicate clearly something within itself, additional signs do not allow that thing to escape our notice. That old circling year of ours brought us a first day that was undistinguished, but the title of my poem has turned it into a red-letter day.'

(b) *The approved text* (No. 173).

'Because it pleases us to celebrate anew, in their honour, the festivals of the Saints, and it is our wont to heap up their birthdays with the roses due to them, we, Father, your dutiful flock, rejoicing in these tokens and in this custom, honour you on this memorable day; and the paying of those respects which would have been fitting at any other time of your life has now, on this late occasion, come round to us. For, still in your prime, you have reached the twenty-fifth year since the time when the sacred mitre crowned your head. As I believe, that number adds a quarter to the mortal centuries: you add a quarter to the centuries; may you in the same manner be able to halve them. If the famous Pius [Pope Pius IX, 1846–78] attains to the years of Peter, and more, then surely there is one [i.e. you] whose years will be those of the long-lived John. But I am not a soothsayer turning my mind to that time: I only conjecture that the day which is here now is auspicious; may it be—but assuredly it *is* a happy one for your country and for you: that you should be what you are, she, your country, regards as her concern too. With you as a shepherd, as seemed good to God, we English began, as an integrated flock, to form part of the sacred flock (of our Church). Indeed, gracious England even communes thus with herself at your jubilee: "All may see that it is from that time (1850?) that I have been accounted holy. With these men to aid, after such great disasters, after generations so inhuman,— with their aid, you, O ancient Faith, have been revived for me. Therefore, Heaven keep you, forerunners of events so desired, you the vanguard of my good fortunes. From this time I now number my days; I am now as one clad in white in your calendar, I who through you have been able to please God as His bride." '

174. Ad Reverendum Patrem Fratrem Thomam Burke O.P., &c.
'Apr. 23, 1877.' Autograph in H; no corrections. Text has the heading 'A.M.D.G.' and the subscription 'L.D.S.'. This 'presentation piece' may have been called for by G. M. H.'s Rector. Thomas Nicholas Burke (b. 1830), Order of Preachers, was the celebrated Dominican orator who had lectured and preached with great success in America from 1870 to 1873. He returned broken in health, but continued his mission throughout Great Britain until

his death at Tallaght, Ireland, in 1882. He visited St. Beuno's in G. M. H.'s last year at the college.

Line 16: *pater . . . stelliger*, i.e. St. Dominic (1170–1221): it is said that at the baptismal font a bright star illuminated the infant Dominic's forehead, symbolizing the future greatness of his intellect.—ll. 19–20: The Latinized names are of eminent Dominican theologians, all commentators on Aquinas: *Gudinus* (Antoine Goudin), 1639–95; *Godatus*, MS. 'Gobatus'; the poet must have meant Godatus (Pedro de Godoy), the Spanish bishop, died 1677, who was often linked in writing as in life with the French *Gonetus* (Jean Baptiste Gonet), *c.* 1616–81; *Cajetanus* (Tommaso di Vio), 1468–1534, cardinal, professor, voluminous thomist exegete and defender of the *Summa Theologica* against the attacks of Scotus.—ll. 23–4: Burke was at one time novice-master at Woodchester.—ll. 33–4: in 1872 Burke had published four lectures, 'The Case of Ireland Stated', in refutation of the English historian, J. A. Froude.—l. 35: *Guenefrida*, for St. Winefred and the healing properties of her Well see Nos. 139, 152, 172, 175.

Translation:

'To the Reverend Father, Brother Thomas Burke, O.P.
on his visit to St. Beuno's College.

'Seeing an unknown man walking about in our garden, relaxing at our tables, and performing unfamiliar religious offices, I wondered who he could be. In the whiteness of his clothing he was nearer than we are to the guileless doves, and by his dress was such as might call to mind a sheep. Later when I enquired: "What is the name and order of this monk who is thus disposed to be singular in the midst of our community, whose tonsured head is covered by a cowl of pure wool and whose plain white gown descends to the middle of his foot, a strange double robe falling from back and breast, while a large rosary rubs his left side?"—they replied: "This is the voice of one crying throughout the world and preparing a way for the Lord through the hearts of men; to this man the Ocean (Atlantic) did service with subdued waves; it has heard him on its western seaboard and on its eastern. But 'monk' is not correct: he is one of a Brotherhood, one whom the famous Father who wore the star acknowledges as his; one skilled at interpreting the oracular words of Thomas Aquinas, if indeed there is still anything obscure in the utterance of him whom Gudinus, Godatus, Gonetus and Cajetanus strive to make so clear, who has already long endured countless interpreters, and whom each man twists, without hesitation, to suit his own conceptions. Moreover this man (Fr. Burke) was once the guide of tender novices and their shining example on their unaccustomed path. But the whole man is not engrossed in these matters, or, if you like, he is completely engrossed in them, but in such a way that he can be light-hearted amid serious affairs, for he mingles jests with his sacred duties, so that neither his voice nor his facial expression remains always the same."—These and other things they told me, and added his name, but this latter my Muse (metre?) did not allow me to use, or would have allowed it only with difficulty. Such a man I should now warmly greet; but one doubt keeps me hesitant, namely, whether he would wish to be praised by me, an Englishman*—he who (in controversy) lays my countrymen low throughout the world. But whatever happens, my St. Winefred gives me healing from all ills: may she give it to him, and soften his hostile breast with love. And whatever else may be of benefit to a faithful people (the Irish), may he owe that also, by way of gift, to our soil.'

175. In S. Winefridam. A free translation of No. 139. Autograph from H (MS. now in Fourier Library, College of Notre Dame of Maryland, Baltimore, Maryland); undated, with many corrections. 'A.M.D.G.' above, 'L.D.S.' below the text; version here printed is clearly final.
Translation:

> '*To St Winefred who, in addition
> to the favour of her miracles,
> bestows care on a bath and a mill.*

Graciously her summer hand tempers her bath for tired limbs, and graciously her winter hand tempers it for stiff ones. Why, having deemed our toils worthy of her right hand (aid), she is even of service to the ever-turning mill, and is not ashamed to be so. Evidently, though she is high in Heaven she does not despise honest squalor, although she enjoins maidenly grace as well.'

The original version is not unattractive:

> Apparat aestiva fessis sua balnea membris,
>   Apparat hiberna balnea rite manu;
> Quin etiam nostri partem dignata laboris
>   Utilis assiduae, nec pudet esse, molaest;
> Ut quae expers maculae sordes non temnat honestas
>   Et quae virgineum suadeat ipsa decus.

Among some fragments of Latin verse in H are the following unfinished elegiacs, which seem to be an elaboration of the thoughts on St. Winefred's Well expressed in the *Journal* entry of Oct. 8, 1874 (quoted in the note to No. 139); but cf. also *J.*, p. 258 (Sept. 10).

* It is noteworthy that the poem is dated April 23—St. George's Day.

333

Iam si rite sequor prisci vestigia facti
Haec sunt egregie numine plena sacro.[1]

Quin etiam nostros non aspernata labores
Utilis assiduaest, nec pudet esse, molae,
Scilicet et sordes ut quae patiatur honestas
Et quae virgineum suadeat ipsa decus.

. . . .

Atque tribus primum quod flumen fontibus exit
Haec est tergemini credita forma Dei,
Qui quod sincero juncti simul aequore crescunt
En tibi simplicitas quam colis, alma fides.[2]
Quid quod ab occulta submissus origine sese
Inque hominum adspectus fons agit inque diem?

. . . .

Quod puteal cernis distinctum cardine quino[3]
    Qua   inclusas   fronte coronet aquas[4]
Hoc est quod species, quae fiunt nuntia rerum,
Quinque subit mentem, qua $\left\{ \begin{array}{l} \text{datur} \\ \text{patet} \end{array} \right.$ ire, viis.

Translations: (the reference numbers refer back to the notes on the Latin texts):

'Now if I duly follow the traces of the ancient deed, these are outstandingly full of holy power.[1]

'Why, not having disdained our labours, she is even of use to the busy mill, nor does it shame her so to be, as is natural for one who both endures honourable squalor and yet in herself encourages maidenly modesty.

. . . .

'And first (take) the fact that the river issues from three springs: this is the nature, as we believe, of our threefold God; and take the fact that

---

[1] Cf. *J.*, p. 261: '. . . the sensible thing so naturally and gracefully uttering the spiritual reason of its being (which is all in true keeping with the story of St. Winefred's death and recovery) and the spring in place leading back the thoughts by its spring in time to its spring in eternity:' (Oct. 8, 1874).

[2] For the thought, cf. No. 28, st. 4, ll. 5–8.

[3] With our translation of the dubious *cardine quino*, cf. G. M. H., loc. cit.: 'the water . . . trembling at the surface with the force of the springs, and shaping out the five foils of the well quite drew and held my eyes to it'. Of the similar five-pointed well at Ffynnon-y-capel or Ffynnon-Fair the poet wrote: 'the five points are perhaps to recall the five porches of Bethesda and their symbolism'.(*J.*, p. 258.)

[4] Lacuna after *Qua*; another between *inclusas* and *fronte*, marked by a bold caret and a gap.—[W. H. G.]

these springs join together and increase with a clear level surface: there you have the singleness of heart which you nourish, gracious faith.[2] What of the fact that the spring, rising from a hidden source, makes its way into the sunlight and into the sight of men?

[Space left, presumably for the moral of this.—(W. H. G.)]

. . . .

'The stone edging of the well which you see distinctly shaped in five foils[3] (in order that) with this kerb it may engarland its enclosed water[4]— this is because the outward form (appearance), which announces all things which are created, enters the mind by the five ways by which it is free to enter.'

176. 'Haec te jubent salvere'. Autograph in H, undated, with corrections and variants; seems to be a 'presentation piece' addressed to a new Jesuit Provincial.

Lines 5–7: earlier variant reads:

'Sed candidatus ille quem cernis chorus
Ipso colore prospera
Et auguratur et tibi ore optat meo . . .'

Translation:

'These regions give you greeting, as far as they can, drenched as they are with too much rain, (and) the mower, abandoning the soaked meadows, gives you much greeting. But our band (choir?) clad in white, which you see, appears, by its very colour, to predict happy things and by my mouth wishes for you both kindnesses and joys. I therefore pray that this your unshorn flock, with its shepherds, may turn out well, as also may the province which is being committed to your right hand as a new spiritual charge.'

177. 'Miror surgentem'. Autograph in H, undated and with many corrections.

Lines 9–10: earlier variant:

'Quosque agitare putes septena cacumina ventos,
Septem agitantur enim.'

Translation:

'I wonder at Orion rising through the clear night, even though the bright moon is close at hand and presses more heavily on the small stars nor allows them to shine with her. Yet I marvel how this Orion grows up the sky and how it gleams with its own fire, which a force that is not its own makes bright in the heavens, while (lit. 'and') its soft lustre comes and goes: why, you would think that some winds had the power to whirl its seven star-points round and round. I marvel too that the breezes and the tepid South wind are wafted so pleasantly, and that winter and the first Kalends which the new year keeps are so warm, for from that day which has just set, the fairest in the year, we say the days (of the year) take their start. O heavenly Jesus, you who gather up in your hand us men and these lofty stars, all things come from you: I pray that the year too may take its beginning from you; it will (then) be a good year. All things are in you: may our race (also) live in you because we are your limbs: all the breezes that we enjoy and the sky to which we look up have, I assert, been granted to us (for use), but many, indeed, have no gratitude; yet even if gratitude is lacking, gracious nature, bountiful nature is also at hand to help all men; nature, to whom that provident hand of yours is stretched out everywhere.'

Also in H, in the same style of handwriting and written apparently at the same time as No. 177, are the following incomplete lines, in the same metre, which may have been intended as a more personal development of the same theme:

> 'Quique haec membra malis vis esse obnoxia multis
>   Ne nimium esse velis,
> Non ego namque mea haec haerentia sorte repugno
>   Aut memorem esse piget,
> Intersit mediae tantum indulgentia poenae
>   Quamque subire jubes
> Sit tua crux: tecum, quod sum torquendus, et oro
>   Torquear arte tua.
> Sed miserere tuis tam multis millibus Indis,
>   Iam miserere tuis,
> { Quamque rogare alium peccat gens credula vitam
> { Quamque rogare alium properant peccantque salutem
>   Da Deus interea.'

Translation:

' . . . And you who wish these limbs to be a prey to many evils, do not wish them to be too much so, for I do not contend against these woes that cleave to my lot, nor am I ashamed to be mindful of them; only let clemency attend my moderate punishment and let the cross which you bid me carry be yours: because I am to be tortured, I pray that it may be with you, and that I may be tortured according to your skill. But have pity on your so many thousands of Indians—have pity now on your folk; and that a stranger may pray for the life wherein a superstitious race sins [*Variant*: 'and that a stranger may ask for that welfare wherein they prosper and sin'], grant this, God, in the meantime.'

Line 3: *mea*. The deleted 'meae' suggests that at first the normal dative construction with *repugno* was intended. Prof. Farrer adds: 'As the line stands, the poet seems to have intended *repugno* to govern *haec haerentia* (sc. 'esse') as an object clause: "I do not oppose the fact that there are these evils, attached to my lot." '

178. Ad Matrem Virginem. Autograph, undated, now at C. H. Either Stonyhurst 'May Lines' (like Nos. 26, 42, and 60), or (possibly) composed at Christmas, 1881, during G. M. H.'s Tertianship. During this 'Third Year Novitiate', Jesuits were expected to write verses 'in the tongues', to keep their hand in at such composition. (See L. II, pp. 75 and 108).

Translation:

'To the Greater Glory of God,
A Hymn of Thanksgiving to the Virgin Mother
at the Feast of the Nativity.

'Mother of my Jesus, Mother of mighty God, teach me about Him, the small sweet God.

'How much did you love Him whom you conceived, who did not have to be conceived as a fearful Lord, but as the Word made flesh brought into smaller compass in you? And He too does not despise even my heart: my heart, though so unworthy to receive so great a sign, oh unworthy to carry Him who was with me this morning, he enters, O Mary, in the Eucharist. He himself wishes to enter: I do not wish to withhold myself. Shining example, teach me to love.

'Tell me—so that He may be loved the more—what manner of being He seemed when He lay hidden in your womb and had not yet appeared to sight, when your voice made Elizabeth happy, a mother made happy through a mother, a boy cousin made happy through a boy cousin.* Teach me to rejoice, O rose, in your spring, O branch, in your flower, O fleece, in your dew, O ark, in your law, O throne, in your king, O army, in your commander, O moon, in your light, O star, in your rays, O mother, in your child. For I am still puffed up and rank with the foul world; I have saddened the Holy Spirit and caused grief to my Guardian when to my God I showed Jesus wounded and battered in my flesh.

'Just how did you feel when you saw at long last, in full view, the Lord himself as a little baby on the hay, beheld Him trembling who fixes firmly the universe, and rolled in swaddling clothes Him who, when not yet born of you, unrolled in serenity the everlasting years? What did you say then, and what did you hear? Although He could not speak, He yet

* See Luke i. 44.

337

spoke. Allow me to embrace Him, grant me a little of the love given to you, and kisses meant for your mouth. He who wants to give himself for me, to speak to me although He cannot yet use words, to dwell with me, —O grant that I may gaze upon Him, O Mother of mighty God, Mother of my Jesus.

'Glory to God for ever.'

179. (May Lines). Autograph in H, undated. Text has the heading 'A.M.D.G. et B.M.V.' (Ad Majorem Dei Gloriam et Beatae Mariae Virginis), and the subscription 'L.D.S.'. The epigraph ('*Ab initio*, &c.') is from Ecclesiasticus xxiv. 14. Fr. Vincent Turner, S.J. supports my opinion that these verses are Stonyhurst 'May Lines' (cf. Nos. 26 and 42); he would assign the poem to the period 1882–84, 'when Hopkins was a priest and had read his theology'. As regards diction and subject-matter, Fr. Turner tells me that *post praevisa merita* and *demerita* are stock technical phrases in the theology of predestination, and in this hymn, G. M. H. is playing with them and around them. There is subtlety in the poem, and a good deal of theology in the background; 'but immediately it's a song'.

Line 7: *Iterum*, for 'Alterum' deleted.

Translation:

'*I was created from the beginning and*
before the ages, and I shall not cease
even unto the age that is to be.

O doubly predestined, you who from all eternity have been the Mother of Christ, (predestined) after the foreseeing of the merits of the Innocent One, a second time after the sins of our race,—though the former privilege is the purer crown, yet it is the latter which the more readily brings home to the heart the gifts of God. Assuredly I should marvel at you simply as God's mother (*deiparam*), but then I should not take such delight in the sustenance you provide; I should confess you a virgin made mother, but not as the one who is, among all mankind, for ever unsullied. But, as your two-fold glory, there will always be those things which stand fast and those which have fallen away—both the redeemed sins of mankind and the foreseen merits of the Innocent One.'

The last six lines contain a chiasmus. Fr. Turner adds: 'In this hymn Hopkins does, I think, presuppose the well known Scotist theory that the Word would have become Incarnate (though *in carne impassibili*, i.e. "incapable of suffering") even if there had been no Fall and therefore independently of redemption. For otherwise there would hardly be any sense in the *Iterum* in l. 7.'

Line 2, *Quae*, see above *Foreword*, p. lxv.

338

180. In Theclam Virginem. See note to No. 136.

181. Latin Version of Dryden's Epigram on Milton. From *The Stony-hurst Magazine*, Vol. I, No. II, July 1881. The original text (quoted from the O.E.T. edn of Dryden's works, ed. Kinsey, vol. II, p. 540) is as follows:

> 'Three *Poets*, in three distant *Ages* born,
> *Greece, Italy* and *England* did adorn.
> The *First* in loftiness of thought Surpass'd;
> The *Next* in Majesty; in both the *Last*.
> The force of *Nature* cou'd no farther goe:
> To make a *Third* she joynd the former two.'

182. Songs from Shakespeare, in Latin and Greek. Autographs in A. In a letter to R. B. of Oct. 13, 1886, G. M. H. says: 'Fr. Mat Russell of ours ... who edits a little half-religious publication the *Irish Monthly*, wrote to me lately for an opinion of some Latin verses furnished him; and this led to ... my suddenly turning a lot of Shakspere's songs into elegiacs and hendecasyllables (my Latin muse having been wholly mum for years) and sending him one copy (and the rest I believe I can and shall get published in the Trinity *Hermathena* by means of Mr. Tyrrell). ...' Again, on Oct. 21, 1886: 'You will have seen that in one of the pieces were some phrases borrowed from Horace and Virgil. In original composition this is most objectionable, but in translation it is lawful, I think, and may be happy, since there it is question of matching the best of one language with the best, not the newest, of another. These verses cannot appear in *Hermathena*, which admits no translations. Mr. Tyrrell said he liked them much, but he did not himself approve of my Catullian rhythms. I employ them of choice, taking Catullus for my warrant only, not my standard, for metrically Catullus was very unsure.'

(i) Text is that printed in the *Irish Monthly*, vol. xv, 1887 (p. 92); it differs slightly from the version in A, completed by Oct. 21, 1886 (see L. I, p. 232). Lines 9–12: A reads (with one correction from L, loc. cit.):

> 'Lascivae latrare; ita plaudere. At hoc juvat: ergo
> Nos Hecuba et Hecubae nos canes
> Adlatrent. Gallus sed enim occinit, occinat: aequumst
> Cantare gallos temperi.'

(ii) Text as in A and *Irish Monthly*, vol. xiv, 1886 (p. 628), except for l. 7, where 'Phorcys' came at the end of the line, making it metrically indefensible.

339

(iii) Line 5; *Qui*, see above, *Foreword*, p. lxvi.

(iv) A letter from Prof. A. E. Housman to R. B., of June 29, 1921, comments on this version rather adversely, but on (vi) favourably. (See L. I, p. 320.)—l. 9, *cunas*, see above, *Foreword*, p. lxvi.

(v) Text is from a copy pasted into A, following an earlier version, which is shorter by one line (the 4th) in each strophe. Beneath title of first version is written: '(Greek: Dorian rhythm, freely syncopated, as in drama).' For G. M. H.'s 'great discovery' about the nature of Dorian rhythm see L. I, pp. 233-4, and below, note to (vii). There he says: 'I added two metrical schemes to my Greek verses for you. They are inconsistent; that is to say, one is fuller than the other.' The scheme for (v) fits only the shorter version; the 'fuller' scheme is that given below in note to (vii).—l. 3, καρδίας and l. 9, προσώπου, see above, *Foreword*, p. lxi.

(vi) See note to (iv).

(vii) 'Dorian rhythm, syncopated, and with triplets in resolution.' The metrical scheme is as follows:

σχῆμα

In the Greek autograph the marks ⌐ and ⌐ (which indicate a long syllable equal to − ∪ and − − respectively) are placed over the syllables which *precede* the vertical lines affected, thus: δένδρεσιν (l. 1), οὐρανίου (l. 4); − ∪ is (presumably) a trochee equal to −; ⋏ stands for a pause equal to −. These metrical signs derive from the prosodic system of J. H. H. Schmidt's *Griechische Metrik* (1872), though G. M. H. does not follow that system closely. In the letter already quoted he says: 'The Dorian rhythm . . . arises from the Dorian measure or bar. The Dorian bar is originally *a march step in three-time executed in four steps to the bar*. Out of this simple combination of numbers, three and four, simple to state but a good deal more complicated than any rhythm we have, arose the structure of most of

Pindar's odes and most of the choral odes in the drama. In strict rhythm every bar must have four steps. Now since four were to be taken to three-time, say three crotchets, (1) one crotchet had to be resolved, (2) only one at a time, and that (3) never the last. Hence the two legitimate figures of the Dorian bar were these: ∪ ∪ − − (the rising Ionic) and − ∪ ∪ − (the choriambus).' He admits certain irregularities: ∪ ∪ − ∪ (third paeon); − ∪ − − (second epitrite); resolution of the first long into three shorts instead of two, 'exactly as we employ triplets in music'; −∪ − ∪̆ (double trochee). 'When the measure is more loosely used two new licences appear—syncopation, by which syllables are lengthened so that three fill a bar and so that the last of one bar becomes the first of the next; and triple resolution, so that a bar can have five syllables. By means of syncopation the measure can be made dactylic and practically brought into common time. The strict Dorian can only be found in odes meant to be marched to.' Of his peculiar stressing he says: 'Naturally the strongest place in the Dorian bar is the second crotchet, not the first, and I have so marked it in the schemes I sent, but perhaps it would be best to mark the first as strongest. . . .' Students of prosody will note the influence of these Greek rhythms upon G. M. H.'s own Sprung and Outriding Rhythms. (See *Study*, vol. ii, chap. ii.)—l. 2, νιφοκτύπων, see above, *Foreword*, pp. lxi-ii.

(viii) Line 5, *Marcipor*, see above, *Foreword*, p. lxvi.

183. Incomplete Latin Version of R. B.'s *In all things beautiful*. From letter to R. B. of Oct. 31, 1886 (L. I, p. 242). Headed '(first draught)'. In gap after l. 12 are the words: 'Here follow the first three lines of the sextet, which I do not correctly remember: please send me them.' Immediately below the lines is the sentence: 'They are not satisfactory, I feel.' On Nov. 26 G. M. H. wrote: 'I have improved the Latin of "In all things beautiful". I asked you to send me three missing lines and you have not done so.' Text used for the translation probably that in *Growth of Love*, Daniel Press edn. (1889), p. 32 (final form, *Poetical Works of R. B.* (O.U.P.), 'Growth of Love', Sonnet 31).
Line 7: *fatebor*, MS. 'fabebor'.

Appendix D: Modern English Version of Angelus ad virginem. See above, *Preface to Notes*, p. 238. The footnotes on the Middle English version, 'mostly by me' [G. M. H.], seem to begin on p. 103 of the article. Footnote 4 first analyses the metre of the Latin hymn, and then refers to the Mid. Eng. version, using literal translations into Mod. Eng. to explain the metrical subtleties:

'The English metre reproduces the Latin exactly, as will be found when allowance has been made for the *e* of inflection, which is sounded or dropped freely. In the English, however, there is this curious addition. The 8th and 10th lines of each stanza have in the Latin a peculiar grace of cadence, due to the way in which, though consisting properly of three (accentual) iambic feet of two syllables, they naturally fall into two feet of three syllables (mostly dactylic feet), and so give rise to a counterpoint rhythm. It was not possible to reproduce this grace in the English, owing to the shortness of the words, which are much more often monosyllables than in Latin. In compensation the translator has aimed at another effect: in each 8th and 9th line he seems to have supplied mid-line rhymes, at the 3rd syllable of the line, and by this means also of necessity changed the rhythm, breaking the line up into two shorter lines of three syllables each, and giving at the break or place of meeting the kind of rhythmic effect called *antispastic* or reversing. This may have been suggested to him by the phrasing of the music at this place. Thus he has:

Flésh of *thée*, | máiden bríght, ‖ mánkind *frée* | fór to máke—
Áll mankín' | wórth ybóught ‖ Thórough *thi*[*ne*] | swéet childíng—
Thát I *síth* | hís will is ‖ Maíden *wíth* | óuten láw—
Whére through *ús* | cáme God wón ‖ Hé bought *ús* | óut of pain—
Ús give *fór* | thínë sáke ‖ Hím so *hére* | fór to sérven.'[1]

The footnotes on the Mid. Eng. text which (at my guess) were written by G. M. H. are:

St. 1, l. 3: The accentuation *blissfúl tidíng* is no licence. All compound words, even words compounded with suffixes like *ly* or *ness*, have in verse a variable accent in old English. The accent is also often found on the last syllable of words ending in *ing* or *er* (p. 105).

St. 2, l. 8 [al manken wrth ibout]: This seems to be *All mankind worth ybought*, All mankind becomes bought, comes to be redeemed.

St. 3, l. 9 [maiden withhuten lawe]: *Withouten law*, contrary to the general law of humanity. The Blessed Virgin was not at this time without law in the sense of being free of a husband, for her so-called espousals were in fact marriage (p. 107).

St. 4, l. 8 [war þurw us kam god won]: *Where through us came God won*. Perhaps: Through whom God came to be won over, reconciled, to us,— or, came to be one with us.

St. 5, l. 1 [Maiden moder makeles]: Although there is a German word *makel*,

[1] Note that the metrical pattern of the fully modernized text (see Appendix D), which G. M. H. said had been 'altered since, perhaps not altogether for the better', differs from that indicated here. (See above *Preface to Notes*, p. 238.)

a spot, and its derivative *makellos*, immaculate, yet *makeles* would seem to be nothing but *matchless*, from *make* the older form of *mate*.[1]

[1] The etymology for *make*, *match-* (from O.E. *gemaecca*) is correct, but *mate* is apparently from M. L. G. or M. Du. 'mate'. This whole note, so uninformed as regards Middle English that the attribution to G. M. H. is more than doubtful, strikes us nevertheless as typically Hopkinsian. As N. H. M. says: 'Though the derivation from the German is dismissed, yet the writer glances at it lovingly, and rejects it with seeming reluctance. He would have liked to keep all three meanings: *spotless*, *mate-less*, and *match-less*. Ogilvie's *Imperial Dictionary* (e.g. 1859 edn.—see L. III, p. 284) gives *makeless* as "matchless; without a mate", but though it explains *make* as "mate", it does not derive the second from the first.'

SOME CORRECTIONS TO THE TEXT
OF THE SECOND IMPRESSION

3. Winter with the Gulf Stream. St. 8, l. 2: *sets* (formerly misprinted *sits*).

15. The Alchemist in the City. St. 9, l. 4: *wilderness*, (comma replaces full stop).

24. Easter. St. 4, l. 2: *woe*, (comma replaces full stop). St. 5, l. 3: *prayer*, (comma added).

39. The Caged Skylark. l. 3: *fells*, (comma replaces semi-colon).

40. The Lantern out of Doors. St. 1, l. 1: *night*. (full stop replaces comma).

46. The Candle Indoors. l. 13: *Are you that liar* (capital letter).

47. The Handsome Heart. l. 13: *granted?* (query instead of exclamation mark).

48. The Bugler's First Communion. l. 30: *freshyouth* (now one word.)

60. The Blessed Virgin . . . l. 124: *worldmothering* (now one word).

61. Spelt from Sibyl's Leave. l. 5: *her dapple is at end* (MS. B, cited as text, replaces MS. A reading).

80. Pilate. St. 5, l. 4: *O fretful fire* (O replaces *The*).

153. To his Watch. l. 3: *force* (comma now omitted).

APPENDIX A

St. Dorothea

(Lines for a Picture)

The Angel

I BEAR a basket lined with grass.
I am só light and fair
Men must start to see me pass
And the básket I bear,
Which in newly-drawn green litter
Carries treats of sweet for bitter.

See my lilies: lilies none,
None in Caesar's gardens blow—
Quinces, loók, whén not one
Is set in any orchard, no;
Not set because their buds not spring;
Spring not, 'cause world is wintering.

The Protonotary Theophilus

Bút they cáme fróm the south,
Where winter's out and all forgot.

The Angel

The bell-drops in my mallow's mouth
Hów are théy quenchèd not?—
These drops in starry shire they drew:
Whích are théy? stars or dew?

A Catechumen

That a quince we pore upon?
O no, it is the sizing moon.
Now her mallow-row is gone
In floats of evening sky.—So soon?
Sphered so fast, sweet soul?—We see
Nor fruit nor flowers nor Dorothy.

344

Theophilus

How to name it, blessed it,
Suiting its grace by *him* and *her*?
Dorothea—or was your writ
Servèd by sweet seconder? —
Your parley was not done and there!
You fell into the partless air.

You waned into the world of light,
Yet made your market here as well:
My eyes hold yet the rinds and bright
Remainder of a miracle.
O this is bringing! Tears may swarm
While such a wonder's wet and warm!

Ah myrtle-bend never sit,
Sit no more these bookish brows!
I want, I want, if I were fit,
Whát the cóld mónth allows—
Nothing green or growing but
A pale and perished palmtree-cut.

Dip in blood the palmtree-pen
And wordy warrants are flawed through;
And more shall wear this wand and then
The warpèd world it will undo.—
Próconsul,— cáll him near—
I find another Christian here.

345

APPENDIX B

The Convent Threshold[1]

By CHRISTINA ROSSETTI

THERE's blood between us, love, my love,
There 's father's blood, there 's brother's blood;
And blood's a bar I cannot pass:
I choose the stairs that mount above,
Stair after golden skyward stair,
To city and to sea of glass.
My lily feet are soiled with mud,
With scarlet mud which tells a tale
Of hope that was, of guilt that was,
Of love that shall not yet avail;
Alas, my heart, if I could bare
My heart, this selfsame stain is there:
I seek the sea of glass and fire
To wash the spot, to burn the snare;
Lo, stairs are meant to lift us higher:
Mount with me, mount the kindled stair.

Your eyes look earthward, mine look up.
I see the far-off city grand,
Beyond the hills a watered land,
Beyond the gulf a gleaming strand
Of mansions where the righteous sup;
Who sleep at ease among their trees,
Or wake to sing a cadenced hymn
With Cherubim and Seraphim;
They bore the Cross, they drained the cup,
Racked, roasted, crushed, wrenched limb from limb,
They the offscouring of the world:
The heaven of starry heavens unfurled,
The sun before their face is dim.

[1] The text is that of the first edition, published in *Goblin Market and other Poems*, 1862.

You looking earthward, what see you?
Milk-white, wine-flushed among the vines,
Up and down leaping, to and fro,
Most glad, most full, made strong with wines,
Blooming as peaches pearled with dew,
Their golden windy hair afloat,
Love-music warbling in their throat,
Young men and women come and go.

You linger, yet the time is short:
Flee for your life, gird up your strength
To flee; the shadows stretched at length
Show that day wanes, that night draws nigh;
Flee to the mountain, tarry not.
Is this a time for smile and sigh,
For songs among the secret trees
Where sudden blue birds nest and sport?
The time is short and yet you stay:
To-day, while it is called to-day
Kneel, wrestle, knock, do violence, pray;
To-day is short, to-morrow nigh:
Why will you die? why will you die?

You sinned with me a pleasant sin:
Repent with me, for I repent.
Woe's me the lore I must unlearn!
Woe's me that easy way we went,
So rugged when I would return!
How long until my sleep begin,
How long shall stretch these nights and days?
Surely, clean Angels cry, she prays;
She laves her soul with tedious tears:
How long must stretch these years and years?

I turn from you my cheeks and eyes,
My hair which you shall see no more—
Alas for joy that went before,
For joy that dies, for love that dies.

347

Only my lips still turn to you,
My livid lips that cry, Repent.
Oh weary life, Oh weary Lent,
Oh weary time whose stars are few.

How should I rest in Paradise,
Or sit on steps of heaven alone?
If Saints and Angels spoke of love,
Should I not answer from my throne:
Have pity upon me, ye my friends,
For I have heard the sound thereof:
Should I not turn with yearning eyes,
Turn earthwards with a pitiful pang?
Oh save me from a pang in heaven.
By all the gifts we took and gave,
Repent, repent, and be forgiven:
This life is long, but yet it ends;
Repent and purge your soul and save:
No gladder song the morning stars
Upon their birthday morning sang
Than Angels sing when one repents.

I tell you what I dreamed last night:
A spirit with transfigured face
Fire-footed clomb an infinite space.
I heard his hundred pinions clang,
Heaven-bells rejoicing rang and rang,
Heaven-air was thrilled with subtle scents,
Worlds spun upon their rushing cars:
He mounted shrieking: 'Give me light.'
Still light was pour'd on him, more light;
Angels, Archangels he outstripped
Exultant in exceeding might,
And trod the skirts of Cherubim.
Still 'Give me light,' he shrieked; and dipped
His thirsty face, and drank a sea,

Athirst with thirst it could not slake.
I saw him, drunk with knowledge, take
From aching brows the aureole crown—
His locks writhed like a cloven snake—
He left his throne to grovel down
And lick the dust of Seraphs' feet:
For what is knowledge duly weighed?
Knowledge is strong, but love is sweet;
Yea all the progress he had made
Was but to learn that all is small
Save love, for love is all in all.

I tell you what I dreamed last night:
It was not dark, it was not light,
Cold dews had drenched my plenteous hair
Through clay; you came to seek me there.
And 'Do you dream of me?' you said.
My heart was dust that used to leap
To you; I answered half asleep:
'My pillow is damp, my sheets are red,
There's a leaden tester to my bed:
Find you a warmer playfellow,
A warmer pillow for your head,
A kinder love to love than mine.'
You wrung your hands; while I like lead
Crushed downwards through the sodden earth:
You smote your hands but not in mirth,
And reeled but were not drunk with wine.

For all night long I dreamed of you:
I woke and prayed against my will,
Then slept to dream of you again.
At length I rose and knelt and prayed:
I cannot write the words I said,
My words were slow, my tears were few;
But through the dark my silence spoke
Like thunder. When this morning broke,

My face was pinched, my hair was grey,
And frozen blood was on the sill
Where stifling in my struggle I lay.

  If now you saw me you would say:
Where is the face I used to love?
And I would answer: Gone before;
It tarries veiled in Paradise.
When once the morning star shall rise,
When earth with shadow flees away
And we stand safe within the door,
Then you shall lift the veil thereof.
Look up, rise up: for far above
Our palms are grown, our place is set;
There we shall meet as once we met
And love with old familiar love.

APPENDIX C

The Nix

By RICHARD GARNETT

THE crafty Nix, more false than fair,
Whose haunt in arrowy Iser lies,
She envied me my golden hair,
She envied me my azure eyes.

The moon with silvery cyphers traced
The leaves, and on the waters play'd;
She rose, she caught me round the waist
She said, Come down with me, fair maid.

She led me to her crystal grot,
She set me in her coral chair,
She waved her hand, and I had not
Or azure eyes, or golden hair.

Her locks of jet, her eyes of flame
Were mine, and hers my semblance fair;
'O make me, Nix, again the same,
O give me back my golden hair!'

She smiles in scorn, she disappears,
And here I sit and see no sun,
My eyes of fire are quenched in tears,
And all my darksome locks undone.

APPENDIX D

Angelus ad virginem

GABRIEL, from heaven's king
Sent to the maiden sweet,
Brought to her blissful tidíng
And fair 'gan her to greet.
'Hail be thou, full of grace aright!
For so God's Son, the heaven's light,
Loves man, that He | a man will be | and take
Flesh óf thee, maiden bright,
Mankind free for to make
Of sin and devil's might.'

Gently tó him gave answér
The gentle maiden then:
'And in what wise should I bear
Child, that know not man?'
The angel said: 'O dread thee nought.
'Tis through the Holy Ghost that wrought
Shall be this thing | whereof tidíng | I bring:
Lost mánkind shall be bought
By thy sweet childbearíng,
And back from sorrow brought.'

When the maiden understood
And the angel's words had heard,
Mildly, of her own mild mood,
The angel she answéred:
'Our Lord His handmaiden, I wis,
I am, that here above us is:
As touching me | fulfillèd be | thy saw;
That I, since His will is,
Be, out of nature's law
A maid with mother's bliss.'

352

The angel went away thereon
And parted from her sight
And straightway she conceived a Son
Through th' Holy Ghost His might.
In her was Christ contained anon,
True God, true man, in flesh and bone;
Born óf her too | when time was due; | who then
Redeemed us for His own,
And bought us out of pain,
And died for us t'atone.

Fillèd full of charity,
Thou matchless maiden-mother,
Pray for us to him that He
For thý love above other,
Away our sin and guilt should take,
And clean of every stain us make
And heaven's bliss, | when our time is | to die,
Would give us for thy sake;
With grace to serve him by
Till He us to him take.   Amen.

INDEX OF TITLES, &c.

(Page numbers given)

355

356

INDEX OF FIRST LINES

358